CASTE

SURAJ MILIND YENGDE

Caste

A Global Story

HURST & COMPANY, LONDON

First published in the United Kingdom in 2025 by
C. Hurst & Co. (Publishers) Ltd.,
New Wing, Somerset House, Strand, London, WC2R 1LA
Copyright © Suraj Milind Yengde, 2025
All rights reserved.

The right of Suraj Milind Yengde to be identified
as the author of this publication is asserted by him in accordance
with the Copyright, Designs and Patents Act, 1988.

A Cataloguing-in-Publication data record for this book
is available from the British Library.

ISBN: 9781805262893

Printed and bound in Great Britain by Bell & Bain Ltd, Glasgow

www.hurstpublishers.com

Yengdes, and my mentors, whose legacy I inherit

CONTENTS

Foreword by Amartya Sen	ix
Introduction	1
1. Colonial Dalitality: The Occidental and Oriental Treatment of Caste	23
2. Affairs of Letters: Dalit Responses to Black Literature	47
3. Race and Caste: In the Age of Dalit–Black Lives Matter	89
4. The Dalit Republic of Diaspora: A Case Study of Trinidad	139
5. Cosmopolitan Dalit Universalism: Dalit Activism and the Promise of a Casteless World	197
6. Conclusion: Biography of Dalit Agonism—Field Notes from the Diary of an Archivist	257
Acknowledgements	273
Appendix: List of Dalit Organizations	285
List of Illustrations	299
Notes	301
Bibliography	335
Index	357

FOREWORD BY AMARTYA SEN

I am delighted to play a role in the publication of this outstanding book on the practice of caste across the world. Suraj Milind Yengde powerfully recognizes that even though the extreme inequities of the Indian caste system give the country a distinction—a shameful uniqueness—that is hard to match, nevertheless inequalities based on caste-like divisions can also be found in many other countries across the world.

The "global story" of caste that Yengde presents in this hugely informed and enlightening book has clearly been strengthened by his own experience of coming from an "untouchable" background, and his political experience in pro-equity movements in India.

However, the book is also based on Yengde's well-researched knowledge of caste practices around the world, as well as his direct observations in many of the affected countries. Each country can learn from one another's experience in the manifestation and attempted remediation of caste-based discrimination. Yengde's investigation of "the missing links of untouchability" is particularly educational.

Caste: A Global Story is a remarkably helpful contribution to understanding and confronting the challenges of hardened inequalities worldwide. We have reason to be grateful to Suraj Milind Yengde for this distinguished work.

INTRODUCTION
THE OCCIDENTAL AND ORIENTAL TREATMENT OF CASTE

There are ample histories of caste. There are even more theories about caste. Some theories are invested in explaining the origins of caste;[1] some address the issue of caste through the perspective of social institutions, providing a sociological perspective;[2] some look at the pervasiveness of caste in everyday life;[3] some explain caste as a notional hierarchical institution;[4] while some delineate caste as an economic enterprise. And yet almost no theory succeeds in providing a concrete picture of caste as an organization of systems. At times, caste is seen as a relic of the past, while at other times it is regarded as a building block of modern society. Various ideologies have attempted to decipher the strange institution of caste. Some have looked at it as a race theory,[5] others have described it as a theological problem,[6] while a few others have come to see it as a colonial problem.[7] The predominant proposition today is colonial intervention in the caste problem. The colonial government's interest in the caste issue was a function of the imperial desire to strengthen control over the vast, complex subcontinent of India.

However, we are left with the unresolved problem of how to deal with the immensity of caste as an institution and a practice and its centrality in society. It is a penal institution that enforces a strict code of conduct, whose violation doesn't only impose penalties on individuals but authorizes further sanctions on the entire community. However, to theorize caste we need an adequate understanding and analysis of its forms and practices. To make sense of caste in its totality, a definitive study has to be undertaken, drawing from textual, hermeneutical, comparative and empirical knowledges of untouchability.

When was untouchability created?

One theory about the origin of untouchability that is now widely recognized was developed by Dr B.R. Ambedkar (1891–1956), a leading scholar of caste and social stratification, and a leader of the untouchables, who not only undertook an interdisciplinary investigation but also complemented it with anthropological and historical perspectives wherever inconsistencies appeared. He relied on the Hindu-Aryan hermeneutics to make his case. In *The Untouchables: Who Were They and Why They Became Untouchables* (1948), Ambedkar put forward a pioneering theory of caste and untouchability. This treatise not only offers an introduction to the origins of untouchability but also deals with its biopolitics and ontology.[8] It remains among the foremost authoritative texts on untouchability. Given the near absence of textual evidence for the origin of untouchability, Ambedkar deployed "imagination and hypothesis" as a tool for discovering the missing links of untouchability.[9] He textually interpreted the Vedas, the oldest scriptures of Hinduism, through an analysis of social life, highlighting how untouchables were over time placed on the outskirts of villages. This segregation was tied to their faith in Buddhism and the practice of eating beef. Ambedkar

INTRODUCTION

refuted the logic of racial difference promoted by the advocates of racialist science. He did not find any racial difference between caste Hindus and untouchables. This was corroborated by Rigvedic evidence as well. Ambedkar theorized that untouchables were "Broken Men" (the literal meaning of Dalits), who became untouchables as the wandering tribes gradually settled.[10]

The concept of impurity was only later attached to untouchability to further restrict the freedom of specific tribes. Consequently, the definition of untouchables became increasingly associated with pollution, contamination and impurity. This idea was reinforced by the Manusmriti (or the Laws of Manu), a text of the second or third century CE that defined various actions and behaviours as untouchability. However, impurity was attributed not only to the untouchables' bodies but also to women and other twice-born castes, known as the dominant-caste *savarnas*, who were higher up in the caste hierarchy. Untouchability intensified when it became politically advantageous to have a surplus labour force that was condemned to subordinated labour from birth. For this reason, Ambedkar noted that "untouchability among Hindus is in a class by itself ... it has no parallel in the history of the world".[11] Ambedkar referred to the histories of outcastes and impure categories of people segregated for their sinful nature worldwide. However, he incorrectly found no kinds of untouchability based on hereditary status in any other part of the world that were similar to those in India.[12]

Through outcasting, an individual was punished by being shunned and avoided, depriving them of access to the basic needs required for survival. However, in the case of Hindu untouchability, it was not only individuals but entire groups that were subjected to ostracism and "territorial segregation" rather than social isolation.[13] This had the result of creating Hindu ghettos or *cordons sanitaires*.[14] The untouchables were in effect victims of the transition from a primitive to a modern society.

After the nomadic tribes were defeated, they became a resourceless minority, vulnerable to attacks. They needed the patronage of the settled tribes, who formed the dominant touchable castes. The defeated tribes took on roles as mercenaries, offering protection against assaults from other warring tribes. A degree of mutual cooperation emerged, and an occupational hierarchy developed. Eventually, spatial segregation also became a feature of untouchability. What distinguished untouchables and touchables was thus their different tribal associations.[15]

A glance at antiquity

There are many theories that have attempted to trace the history of untouchability. Textual and archaeological evidence, supported by genetic studies, offer different timelines for the origins of untouchability and caste. Depending upon the criteria used, discipline-specific methodologies have offered various ways of identifying untouchability alongside the caste system. As regards textual evidence, the hermeneutical reading of ancient texts is considered one of the best and most acceptable forms of identifying caste and untouchability, especially as the texts—such as the Rig Veda, one of the four ancient canonical Hindu texts—are still regarded as sacred and authoritative and their message eternal and unchangeable. This attitude has legitimized untouchability and the concept of caste in both historical and present-day Indian contexts. Meanwhile, advances in genetic studies have provided strong evidence for the theory of the Steppe people's invasion of the Harappan lands, ruled by the First Indians (the "Out of Africa" migrants in India).[16] When the Steppe dwellers arrived in India, they brought a distinct culture that left its mark and spread more widely through Indo-European languages, religion and culture. According to genetic studies, these Steppe dwellers were brahmans who developed their cultural practices in the newly occupied land.[17] Over several centuries, they elaborated their beliefs and proposed a new societal organization structured according to caste, which acted as a regulatory social mechanism. By the time of the composition of the Manusmriti in the second or third century CE, the caste structure was firmly established.

The existence of untouchability in Indian social life was attested by the Chinese Buddhist monk and traveller Fa-Hein (or Faxian). When he arrived in Mathura in central India in 404 CE, after three years of journeying from China, he recorded his observations of daily life in the prosperous and thriving cityscapes.[18] Here, residents did not have to register their households or attend to any magistrates or their rules. The only blemish on this utopia was the presence of the Chandals, who were known as "wicked men" who "lived apart from others".[19] "When they enter the gate of a city or a market-place, they strike a piece of wood to make themselves known, so that men know and avoid them, and do not come into contact with them." Historically, Chandals were an aboriginal tribe dwelling in the regions of Bihar before being driven to the present Bengal region. Chandals performed menial jobs and were relegated to the lowest, untouchable caste. Today, they are known as Namasudra. They are also considered the precursors of those who identify as Bengalis in present-day Bengal.[20]

Another text written shortly after Fa-Hien's travelogue provides further evidence of the existence of castes in historical Indian society. The Greek historian and diplomat Megasthenes was sent in the early fourth century CE by the Greek king Seleucus I Nicator to the court of Chandragupta Maurya, often considered the first emperor of India. In the book he subsequently wrote entitled *Indica*, Megasthenes presented an intimate snapshot of the societal arrangements in India at the time.[21] He recorded the existence of seven castes in the social hierarchy and named them according to their rank. The first was made up of philosophers, "which in point of number is inferior to other classes, but in point of dignity pre-eminent over all ... They are believed to be the most dear to the gods."[22] This group was followed by husbandmen, who were by far the largest in number; cowherds and shepherds; artisans, involved in making tools and equipment for the husbandmen and for military purposes; military personnel, who were maintained at the king's expense; overseers and superintendents acting on behalf of the king; and, lastly, counsellors and assessors, the smallest group in number but the most respected of the castes in the kingdom, being advisers, treasurers, generals and chief magistrates.

Upon closer examination, it is apparent that these castes are essentially professional groups; Megasthenes recorded occupational groups that acted as castes. It can be surmised that castes at the time existed alongside professions, with professionals given social standing according to their background—their caste. Another interpretation suggests that Megasthenes was inspired by Herodotus, who had observed seven castes in Egypt, and may have drawn an immediate analogy with Egypt. Since the time of Alexander, Egypt and India had been seen as interchangeable exemplars of civilization.[23] This attribution was so profound that, as H.G. Rawlinson argued, the Greeks "frequently confused" the two. Furthermore, subcaste categorization might have appeared perplexing to a foreigner unaccustomed to the Indian social system.[24]

Rawlinson goes on to explain that Megasthenes might have confused the existing divisions of brahmanical castes, the four *varnas* of Hindu society, with those of the official bodies created by Chandragupta. In the brahmanical Hindu caste system, Megasthenes's philosophers or counsellors and assessors could be brahmans. This class had a monopoly over state posts "such as judge, governor, deputy governor, ruler of a province, quaestor, superintendent of agriculture, admiral or general", according

INTRODUCTION

to the second-century Greek historian Arrian, as reported in *Indica*.[25] Megasthenes's soldiers might have been the kshatriyas, although it is unclear if their identity was fixed by caste or whether it was still evolving.[26] The artisans in Megasthenes's table could be the vaishyas, the providers of services, although it is unclear if they were yet independent of other caste professions. They could easily be placed in the ranks of assessors looking after the treasury, though the assessors could also belong to the brahman castes. They were the elite civil servants who could traverse the expanse of the empire. Husbandmen, artisans, shepherds and cowherds made up the shudras, who formed the majority of the people.

In this scheme there is no reference to Chandals or untouchable caste groups. It might be that the untouchable castes were not yet strictly demarcated. They could have belonged to the larger shudra fold, falling within some of the professions mentioned above, or perhaps Megasthenes wasn't able to discover a tribe of outcastes from the vantage point of the town culture in which he stayed. Megasthenes could also not find any existence of slavery, which was widespread in the Graeco-Roman world. Rawlinson argues that had Megasthenes seen the situation of Chandals or pariahs, as observed by the Chinese Buddhist scholar and traveller Xuanzang in the seventh century CE, he "might have modified his opinions".[27] "Under the caste-system," Rawlinson observed, "the status of Pariah ... fared far worse than the Greek or Roman slave."[28]

Commentators have noted that the nature of caste as it existed at the time of Megasthenes's travels in India was probably different from his understanding of Indian society.[29] Other Greek commentators such as the geographer Strabo already started to question Megasthenes's account just a few centuries later, even to the extent of calling him, and other Greeks, such as Onesikritos and Nearchos, who wrote on India, a "set of liars" and saying that "no faith whatever" could be placed in their writings.[30] However, a number of scholars have spoken up for Megasthenes and his account of Indian society. They remind us that he looked at India from a Greek point of view, which was already encumbered with fables and stories from India. Nevertheless, Megasthenes's *Indica* remained a guiding document for other great commentaries and accounts (by Aristoboulos and Onesikritos, among others) that were later built on it. Although his text is now lost, extracts from it appear in Strabo's writings, which is where we can now read what remains of his travelogue. That is why, despite its limitations, Megasthenes's account remains a much closer link to parts of our knowledge of India than others we have.

Al-Bīrūnī's India

Perhaps the most influential account of India from the Middle Ages was written by al-Bīrūnī, a polymath Uzbek scholar and traveller who was the author of *Kitab-ul-Hind* (History of India).[31] This book surveyed Indian life as observed in the eleventh century CE by al-Bīrūnī, who visited the country at the time it was ruled by the Afghan sultan Mahmud Ghazni.

Al-Bīrūnī revelled in the riches of Indian philosophy and science—Vedic philosophy, astrology, astronomy and laws.[32] Though his patron Mahmud Ghazni thought his Hindu subjects were heathen infidels, al-Bīrūnī discovered in Indic civilization great philosophers, astronomers, mathematicians and grammarians. While he showered praise on whatever he found valuable and exciting in Indian science and practical life, al-Bīrūnī didn't hold back in expressing reservations about what he saw as wrong or ignorant. He thought Islam was superior to Brahmanism, which he found fault with for its tolerance of inequality in relation to caste, the undemocratic character of its faith and practice, and the rituals pertaining to cleanliness and impurity.³³ As for caste (*tabaqat* or *jataka*), al-Bīrūnī noted, "We Muslims, of course, stand entirely on the other side of the question, considering all men as equal," and this, he continued, is "the greatest obstacle which prevents any approach or understanding between Hindus and Muslims".³⁴ Al-Bīrūnī found the differences between these two faiths hinged on the question of equality, which was an alien concept to Hindus.

Al-Bīrūnī thought the corpus of Sanskrit writings of great value. However, he was dismissive of the esotericism that "kept people in the dark" by "throwing an air of mystery about the subject."³⁵ He was probably the first Muslim scholar to study the Puranas, a vast genre of Hindu literature. His exegesis of the Indic philosophy was extraordinary in its range and depth. The scriptural sources he studied included books on the brahmanic faith, Sankhya philosophy, the Vishnu Purana, the Vishnu Dharma, the Matsya Purana, the Aditya Purana³⁶ and a large body of non-Puranic literature that encompassed studies of geography, astronomy, chronology and astrology. Some of these he translated into Arabic, such as Kapila's writings on Sankhya philosophy and Patanjali's *Yogasutra*. By the end of his life al-Bīrūnī had authored 146 books, including about twenty on India, only a few of which survive today.

In *Kitab-ul-Hind*, al-Bīrūnī dedicated an entire chapter to castes in India. The title of the chapter was "On the Castes, called 'Colours' (*Varna*), and on the Classes below Them". According to al-Bīrūnī, the Hindu sources that he consulted declared that the brahmans, being the highest caste, were created from the head of the Brahman; the kshatriya from the shoulders and hands; the vaishya from the thigh; and the shudras from the feet. The shudras were followed by a caste called Antyaja—literally, untouchable, outside the caste.³⁷ The Antyajas were a whole community apart from the brahmanic order, who rendered all kinds of services to the rest. These were unrecognized caste groups, meaning that they had no caste identity as such. The Antyajas consisted of eight caste groups: fullers, shoemakers, jugglers, basket-makers, sailors, fishermen, hunters of wild animals and birds, and weavers. They intermarried freely with each other, with the exception of fullers, shoemakers and weavers. They lived outside the villages. In addition, there were other groups who were also not part of the caste system. They were even lower in the hierarchy in terms of their jobs. Hadi, Dom, Chandal and Badhatua were employed in cleaning and in dirty work. According to general beliefs, these castes originated from an intermixture of brahman women and shudra men. The Dom and Badhatua were considered the lowest in the descending order of purity.[38]

Al-Bīrūnī quotes from the Bhagavad Gita, where Krishna offered justification for the existence of the caste system. He also spoke against the intermixing of vocations. If castes were to change their duties, Krishna said, then it would be a sin because carrying out one's task is a divine injunction. As al-Bīrūnī recorded from the Puranic texts he drew on, Krishna was a shudra.

Al-Bīrūnī's primary sources were brahmanical. He did not come across non-brahmanic texts because he travelled primarily in northern India. In his sojourns, al-Bīrūnī was baffled by the monopoly brahmans held over all matters related to religion and society. Yet he found them ignorant. He noticed brahmans reciting the Vedas as a sacred activity among themselves, though none knew the actual meaning of the texts. The brahmans, who were his primary interlocutors as they were the custodians of the scriptures, continued to exclude *mlecchas* (foreigners) from their intimate circles. Al-Bīrūnī was also perturbed by the strict social hierarchies that he observed. Caste, he believed, was the major difference between Islam and brahmanical Hinduism with its belief in purity and segregation.

The brahmans strictly regulated the access of non-brahmans to the canonical sources of brahmanical thought. This applied

INTRODUCTION

rigidly and absolutely to the untouchables. The kshatriyas, vaishyas and shudras were given some degree of access, depending on their rank in the hierarchy, but for an outcaste to perform any sacred activity or spiritual work meant that his tongue would be cut off, as prescribed by the Laws of Manu. The social arrangements of the time were extremely rigid.

One chapter in the second volume of the *Kitab-ul-Hind* dealt exclusively with the rights and duties of each caste or *varna*. Those of the kshatriyas were identified as ruling and defending the people. The vaishyas were responsible for cultivating the land and tending cattle. A shudra, al-Bīrūnī noted, is "like a servant to the Brahman, taking care of his affairs and serving him".[39] The status of the shudras and vaishyas vis-à-vis the brahmans appears similar. If one of them recited the Veda, their tongue would be chopped off. However, the practices of almsgiving and meditation were not forbidden to them.[40]

The Chandals were a people who had sinned. They were "not Hindu", noted al-Bīrūnī, but unclean *mlecchas* who "kill men and slaughter animals and eat the flesh of cows".[41] To remove the curse that had befallen a brahman, King Rama was instructed to find out why this had happened. Rama discovered that a Chandal had been performing worship. Then the king, duty-bound, "shot at him, and pierced his bowels". This particular incident is referred to in the Valmiki Ramayana as the murder of Shambuka, a shudra who was killed for pursuing *dharma* and practising penance. In al-Bīrūnī's account of the practice of differences between groups, one can discern that by the eleventh century, when he wrote his account, castes were already the norm.

* * *

The authors I have cited in this section were all non-Indians who commented on a wide spectrum of social features of historical India, and in each of them, we see a recognizable mention of castes. All their observations have both merits and flaws. They include intelligent commentaries that reveal the power and durability of the original texts. At the same time, one wonders whether the non-native authors were attracted to a particular version of India's story or whether they were trying to draw from existing sources of knowledge. Both the merits and flaws of their observations will become more apparent as we look at the perspectives of the Dalit worlds—a phenomenon not bounded by geography and certainly not limited by the pervasiveness of caste corporality.

Pre-modern Dalit modernity

Over time, Brahmanism and Buddhism engaged in cultural wars popularly known as revolution and counter-revolution. Alongside these two historical poles, there were spiritual seekers who supported Indian materialism.[42] The Lokayats, or Charvakas, were among the first proponents of anti-brahmanic values.[43] They rejected the Rig Veda and its authority, denied the existence of the soul, karma and liberation, and opposed almsgiving and sacrifices, which led them to be labelled as devils (*asuras* or *rakshas*) or non-believers (*nastiks*).[44]

The Lokayats emphasized perception (*anubhava*) as the only means of knowledge, approved of sensuous pleasures, and saw consciousness as a product of matter.[45] Their stance made them untouchables in society, or, rather, they were part of the scientific tradition of indigenous India that resisted integration with Aryan Vedic life. Given their native identity and strong opposition to Vedic practices, it can be inferred that they may have belonged to tribes opposed to Vedic culture. They were later termed untouchables, or Chandals—the outcastes.

The diverse and opposing traditions of the Indic past were invested in different pursuits of spirituality, which resulted in

INTRODUCTION

unique ways of living their lives. They developed distinct cultures and forms of resistance against each other within the political context of inter-tribal warfare. Caste was a defining feature of these tribal associations, though it was not the main reason for the existence of closed-group formations. However, within the caste superstructure, outcastes were consigned to work unrecompensed on menial tasks that were given humiliating designations.

Later, during the Mughal and post-Mughal periods, caste was refined to make it more workable and stringent. After many interactions with outsiders, caste society, comprising native groups, became more prominent and mainstream as the political economy of the new states began to take shape. As caste practices became a regular part of society, castes themselves became more identifiable and acquired thinner definition. By the time British rule arrived in India, caste was already part of Indian governance. The British government identified the independent bureaucracies that existed as caste spheres in public conduct and took them over, using them to implement an administrative solution to their governance problems in the complex geography of the subcontinent.

During various stages of imperial and native rule, the lives of Dalits were not consigned helplessly to their fate. There were innovations and stories of valour in which they cooperated with existing regimes, providing support and knowledge as native-class Moolnivasis—the natives of the land. The Moolnivasi expertise in craft, warfare and geographical knowledge proved crucial in the conquering missions of many rulers. The strict caste modernities we witness today had not yet emerged, which is why the history and recorded past of the outcaste groups did not feature prominently in the predominant discourse. The questions of who was Dalit and who not, and, in particular, what was Dalit and what not, were seldom addressed.

Dalit universality, a primary concern of this book, was expressed as a kind of enterprising tutelage of rulers and administrators. As a result, many Dalit contributions to the understanding of creation, to modernization, grammar and logic were assimilated into the hegemonic discourse as the knowledge of the community or the king. For example, their work was attributed to whoever was king or was seen as a product of Hindu, Muslim or Buddhist civilizations. Dalit modernity became a feature of the caste system but was not recognized as Dalit universalism. The system simply marginalized Dalits as a body and as a value, diminishing the claims of status and dignity to which they aspired. Dalits always upheld the principles of righteousness and truth, constant appealing to their conscience, and their identity being informed with a sense of spirit and respect.

An understanding of history is relevant to our study of examining castes in modern times. It is crucial for caste scholarship to engage with earlier works that have addressed caste concerns. Each author, employing their own descriptive and analytical skills, has proposed various interpretations of caste for reasons specific to their context. When Megasthenes wrote about India and the prevailing hierarchical system, for instance, his intentions can be inferred from the audience he wrote for—mostly educated aristocratic elites, as well as regular gentry across the Hellenic world who had access to his writings.

Subjectivity of caste scholarship

In caste scholarship, the subjectivity of the author is crucial for assessing the merit of the project. In ancient times, authors examining society did not begin by outlining concepts or developing theories. They instead reported their observations of society, drawing on a mix of knowledge from native informants and their own analytical positions. What they revealed was a certain perceived reality. Today, when we talk about caste, there are extreme positions defending its rationale, and others that offer justification under the moral code of ancestral inheritance. This range of perspectives has informed modern caste scholarship.

In the past, those who saw the practice of caste as abhorrent or absurd said so. But their accounts of the conditions in which the caste-oppressed lived were not informed by the victims' voices. The victims were merely bystanders. It was not until the dawn of modernity that a strong, autonomous written Dalit perspective would emerge to provide a concrete rebuttal of the caste system.

Until recently, the response to the caste system was conducted within the domain of spirituality. Its existence was often justified by ascribing it sacrosanct status as enjoined by religion. Moreover, the Dalit position against caste was recorded or interpreted predominantly by non-Dalits like the mystics Raidas, Kabir and Chokamela. Raidas identified his position as a *chamar* (tanner), ending his famous couplets with "so says Ravidas, chamaran", while Chokamela identified with his Mahar caste. These caste positions favouring the voices of Dalits were meant as a challenge to the prevailing state-Brahmanism.

It took several hundred more years for the Dalit viewpoint to emerge prophetically. In the nineteenth century, the caste perspective began to evolve by incorporating the voices of Dalits, spoken and written by themselves. The early Dalit position followed a trajectory of assimilation, eventually breaking away from the tradition and ethics of caste logic and the religious social order. Their project was not one of complete eradication, which may have seemed sensible given the unfavourable attitude of the state. However, the British colonial apparatus inadvertently provided space for this evolution. Under the Raj, the communities dispersed into various caste units found and then exploited an opportunity to negotiate their needs and claims with those in power.

It is against the backdrop of these debates and movements that we examine the nature of caste and its impact on the groups of people classified as lower in the caste hierarchy. The global story of caste that I seek to explore begins with my own story.

Nanded to global—a caste shibboleth

I

Nanded, my hometown in Marathwada, has been home to one of the most radical forms of Dalit politics for over a hundred years. The Arya Samaj, the Hindu reform movement, established one of its earliest centres in Marathwada.[46] Fearing Muslim influence on the subaltern castes, the Arya Samaj started to reconvert the latter by offering *janeu*, the sacred thread. However, this was not looked upon favourably by non-Dalit villagers, who by way of punishment forcibly tattooed Dalit converts with hot iron rods. Marathwada has also seen a significant presence of Sikhs, Nanded being an important holy place for the Sikh religion. The radical message of mystics and spiritual teachers like Kabir, Raidas, Nanak and Gobind was carried by practitioners of the Sikh faith.[47] In particular, the vision of society that Kabir and Raidas preached found especial resonance among the Dalits of Marathwada.

Following in this tradition, Marathwada Dalits carved out for themselves a political space, whose potential for mobilization and receptivity to radical ideas were noticed by B.R. Ambedkar. Issues around land, education and sovereignty were all highly politicized in Marathwada. Those who rejected their oppression as lower castes looked for ways of fighting back. To them, Ambedkar-led politics seemed like a promising avenue. In particular, Mahars (a caste of Dalits) in my region gave their allegiance to Ambedkar. Though Ambedkar was yet to visit them, they had heard about him and his voluminous writings. He came from their caste-community and had a national as well as international appeal. Dalit leaders from the wider Telugu-, Marathi- and Kannada-speaking regions, such as Bhagya Reddy Varma, B.S. Venkat Rao and B. Shyam Sundar, eventually joined Ambedkar and worked under his leadership.

My district and region were one of many centres of radical politics. Nanded's representative to India's independent parliament in 1957 belonged to a crop of radical Dalit politicians: Harihar Rao Sonule was our statement of our collective belief in constitutional promise. He was one of the early batch of Dalit MPs from the All India Scheduled Caste Federation who were intent on gaining rights for Dalits in the newly independent country.

II

In our house in Janta Colony, Ambedkar Nagar, Nanded, my father listened to the morning Marathi news on DD Sahyadri—a government-owned satellite TV station. We had a black-and-white 14-inch television set made by a Videocon company. Each morning the same ritual was followed as I prepared for school. One day in 1997 my father held me and made me watch the TV: Kofi Annan was being elected as the secretary general of the United Nations Organization. My father called it Oono—UNO. He wanted me to register that a Black man had ascended to the topmost position of an inter-governmental body, never mind that Annan originally came from the crop of Ghanaian elites. My father perhaps wanted me to see that the UN and other international bodies could not only be accessible to native elites the world over, but could be a space even of Dalit politics. When the Taliban blew up statues of the Buddha, he and his associates protested by petitioning the UN—in a letter written in Marathi. Years later, when I was an intern at the UN's human rights office in Geneva, I was dismayed by its sheer inability to provide non-political solutions to issues of the day.

The UN has the capacity to hold states accountable, though this is less true in the case of states like India, which worked to undermine the cause of Dalits. The usual accusation the Indian government makes is that the Dalits' cause at the UN level is promoted by Christian-sponsored NGOs and that they do not have a legitimate interest in the issue. We saw this played out at the UN World Conference against Racism held in Durban in 2001. When I was at the UN, an Indian NGO activist befriended me and asked me to be wary of such NGOs. I was innocent then and didn't understand this man was an Indian government spy.

The NGOs that I was alerted against told me much later that, in their understanding, the government was not much concerned with caste. Its attention was focused rather on the secessionist movements. What happened to the advocacy of caste justice internationally? It seems the advocacy has taken a form that doesn't threaten the sovereignty of the Indian state and its prerogative to determine its own internal affairs. Both parties—advocates and government—seem to have agreed that there needs to be a new discourse around caste.

In the United States, the Dalit cause was taken up by the coordinated efforts of professional class Dalits who had settled there. Their activism began with protests against atrocities within India and led to attempts to hold the Indian state accountable by placing the issue of caste on the agendas of US political and policy circles. Later, activists like Laxmi Berwa and Yogesh Varhade took the UN route that their predecessors like B.R. Ambedkar, P.N. Rajbhoj and Bhagwan Das had followed.

Solidarity represents one way of connecting the Dalit movement with a larger cause. But the desire for international solidarity did not significantly influence the activities of Dalits in India. Their work evolved in response to the radical shifts of

INTRODUCTION

Cold War-era politics. The movement was split between left and right. Some aligned with a nativist theory of liberation, while others drew on the left's internationalism.

One faction was led by Namdeo Dhasal, the well-known leftist Panther. Left-wing *savarna* scholars wrote extensively about Dhasal and promoted his image. Raja Dhale, on the other hand, who led the other faction, was primarily known to circles of academics and writers because of his distance from leftist politics. Later he became so disillusioned with the Panthers' leadership that he left and pursued a career in a political party run by Ambedkar's grandson, only to end up dismayed by it.

A vast number of Dalit Mahars who identified with Ambedkar and Buddhism embraced Dhale. My father was an associate of his in Nanded and was particularly interested in Dhale's literary activities. They remained friends. My name, Surudhay—kindhearted—was given me by Dhale. However, because it was often mispronounced, I shortened the name to Suraj. When I was a student leader in Nanded, I invited Dhale to visit the university and deliver a lecture. He came and the old cadres packed the hall. He spoke but it wasn't an impressive speech. When my father passed away, Dhale paid a visit to my home. I was in South Africa; I rang him to thank him for the visit. In his usual way, Dhale said that he had not done anything extraordinary. "Milind was my associate, and I paid a visit" was his response.

Dhale was known to call a spade a spade. He restricted himself to the activism of literature. He read many books. Whenever my father visited Mumbai, he would seek an audience with Dhale. I recall once we spent an entire day in Vikhroli, the area where Dhale lived. Years later when I was studying to become a scholar, I sought an audience with Dhale. He refused. He said that, like me, he had little time available; it was better that we should not impose ourselves on each other's time. His response made me feel he had become rude and bitter as an old man. A few years later when I spent about eight months in India, I realized why he had spoken in this way. In India, a meeting can easily last several hours. Dhale was also in a hurry to finish what he was writing—as he indicated to me.

Over the years, as my name became known in academic and literary circles, reports about me must come to the attention of Dhale, for he commented to my cousin Nitin that "Suraj has now become an important person". When Dhale died, the national media reached out to me to write an obituary. I was on the way to deliver a series of talks in Kolhapur. But I asked people to send me some books on Dhale and some of his original writings. I wrote the article on my journey from Aurangabad to Kolhapur, two sites driven by Ambedkar's politics. Dhale was immensely widely read. He was among the first Dalits in the movement to actively pursue Black literature. In his young days, he dabbled in translating Black poets into Marathi. There are many such anecdotes about my father who was my primary interlocutor to this history, and Dhale him that touch my thinking and practice.

The global story of caste or the story of global castes thus begins with my experience of growing up as a Dalit. It's also a story of Marathwada, India, which had the audacity to connect with the larger world. That is why the Dalit–Black nexus, which started as an investigation of literature and experience in Marathwada, became a precursor to the formation of an active political solidarity.

One of the projects I hope to develop after this book is to examine castes around the world. There is plenty of literature on the status of castes in various societies. I have started working on this theme simultaneously. The potential is immense, as our discussions have been limited so far to ideology and politics. Caste has typically been approached and studied as an external institution, but rarely from the perspective of those deeply affected by social inequality and economic disadvantage imposed

INTRODUCTION

by the system. The external interpretation and perception of caste have often hindered understanding of the lived experience. This external perspective has been the modus operandi of scholars not personally affected by caste. A noted scholar from Punjab once told me that he could write about caste dispassionately because he did not carry the burden of personal experience. In this book, we will examine the analyses and observations of Indian caste society by those subjected to it as well as by foreigners. This will serve as a prelude to a detailed study of castes globally. Our story is thus centred on India's caste hierarchy and the various forms it takes worldwide.

1

COLONIAL DALITALITY
CENSUS CASTES

During the British colonial era, Dalitality was given recognition as one of the foundations of Indian history. During this period, the diverse and heterogenous caste groups among the untouchables were identified and organized over time by recognizing their subjection, occupations,[1] and socio-spiritual separateness. One of the early ways this was done was through the census and colonial officials' reports at district and village levels. Census collection and official reportage effectively identified Dalit subjectivity within the framework of bio-politics.

This chapter, like the rest of the book, positions Dalits as active agents in the caste system. It argues that Dalits were often seen as passive subjects in the elites' interpretational battles over the meaning and concept of caste. However, Dalits also played a key role in understanding and conveying their own experiences and the theoretical origins of caste.[2] They were autonomous individuals who did not conform to the categories proposed by colonial officials. Some groups, however, did identify with the colonial labels imposed on them.[3] This identification was reinforced by religious Hindu reformist organizations like Arya Samaj, which invented a history of caste groups to subsume Dalits within the Hindu Aryan interpretation.[4]

Colonial officials found the idea of Dalit autonomy and independence from Hindu and Muslim faiths unimaginable. In Punjab, census collectors overlooked Dalit religious practices that didn't subscribe to Hindu gods. The Chuhras of North India worshipped local deities, their clan gods, animals and *pirs* (saints), and did not worship the pantheons of Hinduism or aspire to the dominant Muslim, Christian or Sikh identities. They were considered untouchables in all these practices. They were known as Chuhras in the Hindu context, as Mussalis in the Muslim context, as Mazhabis in that of the Sikhs, and Indian Christians in that of Christians.[5] Dalits believed their faith, rooted in brotherhood and spiritual honour, was superior to that of Hindus and Muslims. They did not follow rigid, conservative faith conventions and selected elements from each tradition that preached liberation. Their gods and saints represented freedom, which is why they had figures like "Nanak, Dadu, Mardana, Kabir, Loi, Brahman, Ram, Allah, Pandvas, Krishna, Pir Khwaja, Joseph, Moses, Ranjana, Manjun and Jastri", among many others.[6] In other regions, Buddha and the Buddhist heritage were significant.

Colonial officials were aware of these distinctions and the independent existence of the Dalit faith. Earlier ethnographic works had recorded this.[7] However, there were still attempts to associate Dalits with the Hindu fold, with the sentiment that, if not immediately, they would gradually become Hindus. This was because the concept of Hinduism wasn't fixed, making it hard for the British to define who was a Hindu. Even the 1911 census noted, "It is extremely difficult to say at what stage a man should be regarded as having become a Hindu."[8] The British Raj officials were eager to find similar practices or traces of Dalit faith within the brahmanic Hindu religion. But Dalit practices were often anti-brahmanical, if not entirely separate from Brahmanism.

However, a delegation of Muslims, who had received recognition as a "special interest" group, appealed to the Viceroy in 1906 to enumerate untouchables separately. The Muslim constituency fought hard not to be treated as a minority group. They wanted to be represented as the equals of Hindus. Accordingly, the Muslim delegation asked for the creation of a separate untouchable category, apart from the Hindus but at the same time on a par with them. The Census Commissioner, Edward A. Gait, took up the suggestion and sent a memo to the provinces, which was leaked to the press. The proposal was later abandoned, and the lower-caste interest groups of North India, especially the untouchable castes, were officially subsumed within the "inclusive" Hindu category.[9] This inclusivity was partly the result of the confusion and fog clouding the minds of the civil administration. With limited tools at their hand, the easy solution was to hegemonize Hindus by homogenizing castes.

Census officials made it their task to develop a methodology that would make Chuhras easily identifiable with the Hindus. One outcome was the Brahmanization of the Dalits. What this amounted to is unclear. Did it mean having a priesthood within the Dalits? Was it a belief in the supernatural among a free order of worshippers? On this principle of vagueness, bureaucrats created a list of beliefs and of Dalit deities that existed in the Hindu faith or else resembled them. Consequently, colonial officials could state that the Chuhras worshipped "Valmiki without their conscious knowledge" and in this way they unknowingly became the creators and originators of Hindu mythology.[10] This smacks of British Orientalism in respect of caste subjects. As a result, independent viewpoints and religious traditions were conceived and elaborated in the language and culture of Brahmanism. This was partly due to the knowledge then available about

Brahmanism, which made it easy for ill-informed white officials to draw unfounded comparisons. Colonial ethnographers refused to take on board the autochthonous, freedom-seeking, anti-brahmanical, non-Hindu, non-Muslim and non-Christian histories of Dalits, who had always been independent of these fixed, rigid categories and who had never identified themselves as Hindus.

By defining caste groups according to purity, profession and their relations to other castes, the colonial authorities were able to construct the caste order. Central to this process of definition was the census, which sought to map out India's immense diversity for the purposes of regulation and legislation. Postcolonial scholars have seen it as a form of colonization, in which a Judaeo-Christian understanding was applied to Indian society. As a result, the census grossly miscalculated the location of castes in society. Already in 1881 the census established a new "Hindu" identity otherwise unknown to vast stretches of the hinterland, so as to make sense of Indian diversity. At the same time, the brahman-run Arya Samaj (founded in the 1870s) and other liberals from the dominant-caste groups actively pursued a Hindu identity agenda as a way of developing a unified front against the British Empire. The Arya Samaj's initial aim was not to ally itself with the lower castes but to consolidate unity among the divergent Hindu elites. However, as debates around the census arose, the twice-born, *savarna*-caste Hindu elites realized the need to assimilate the Dalits into their fold. Consequently, various incentives such as subsidized education were offered to Dalits to convert to a Hindu identity.[11]

Thus, the 1881 census came, as it were, to the rescue of the nationalists, for non-Christians—Muslims, Jews and Parsees— were all made to fit in opposition to the new invented category of Hinduism. A country of reputedly 33 million gods and various religions, each different in their practices but united in their worship and pantheistic culture, was forced into a Hindu identity. This posed a problem in categorizing caste within the newly created Hindu canon, as opposed to the traditional Manu-inspired Vedic caste system.

The British official E.A.H. Blunt studied the caste system in North India at the start of the twentieth century, basing his analysis on census directives that identified castes, primarily focusing on untouchability, in respect of their relations with other castes.[12] Modernists argue that the current caste system is a nineteenth-century construct by the British administration.[13] To help manage the vast diversity of a large country with many regional differences, caste was studied to understand Indians better for the sake of effective governance. The strict hierarchies and divisions gave colonial authorities more reason to deepen and extend their colonization efforts. This is why data collection began even before the census, with district gazetteers being published from 1850 onwards.[14] For the British, this was another step in understanding the Indian condition. In 1901, the imperial administration identified 1,641 castes and subcastes. By 1931, further anthropological studies identified an additional 4,147 castes and subcastes.[15] These numbers kept increasing as more caste associations and their organizations sought recognition. This had mixed results. The British made errors, misidentifying caste groups and further stereotyping certain castes by their occupations—like martial castes, potters and washermen—and labelling some as "criminal castes".

Despite these discrepancies, the census gave India's disparate castes a sense of political unity within the emerging nation-state. As the Indian nation evolved, diverse caste groups organized to demand more rights, resources and a share in development. This is why the Government of India Act of 1935, a precursor to the 1950s Indian Constitution, provided stability by allowing for an early form of political caste councils. Unintentionally, social movements led by untouchables established a solid platform on which to appeal for their rights. Under leaders like B.R. Ambedkar, Rettamalai Srinivasan, N. Sivaraj, Bhagya Reddy Varma,[16] B. Shyam Sunder in Deccan, and Swami Achutanand[17] and Mangoo Ram Mugowalia[18] in North and Central India, a united Dalit movement emerged. Representatives of Dalits (officially known as Scheduled Castes) introduced a rights-based approach in parliament and provincial assemblies, demanding government accountability towards outcastes and lower-caste shudra groups.

Colonial anthropology of caste

In the colonial era, caste was primarily studied as a theological curiosity. Then the discoveries of new artefacts from archaeological studies alongside the growing field of anthropology encouraged colonial officials to take a particular interest in Indian society. As a result the new discipline of anthropology gained more traction among the colonial government and scholars of the era. Pioneering work in this field was carried out by Sir Herbert Risley (1851–1911), whose extensive data gathering in the Chhota Nagpur area and Bengal produced a magnum opus, *The Tribes and Castes of Bengal*.[19] Although the work was later to receive criticism from many quarters, including structuralists and modernists, Ambedkar included, it nevertheless found a sympathetic audience in the colonial administration.

Risley built upon the findings and authority of the French physical anthropologist Paul Topinard, whose experiments in cranial anthropometry measured and described the differences among human beings in terms of physical traits—particularly the nasal and cephalic index. This was used to argue for the racial origins of castes and tribes of Chhota Nagpur (in Jharkhand in particular, where Risley conducted his field study). Originally developed in response to Darwin's theory of the survival of the fittest, this hypothesis was elaborated by the technologists of empire. Risley was one of the important architects of the 1901 census of India. In 1908 he published a book entitled *The People of India* which presented his contribution to the census.[20]

In America, similar anthropometric studies were carried out on non-white groups by comparing arbitrary bodily features. Throughout the colonial world, according to what was then regarded as the most advanced form of scientific inquiry, the dark-skinned, non-white races were judged by the physical and cultural standards of the superior "white" European Caucasian race. Caste, in turn, was the object of a similar inquiry and was overwhelmingly analysed as a racial category based on biological traits.

Ambedkar would later refute the biological claims of superiority. "In my opinion there have been several mistakes committed by the students of Caste, which have misled them in their investigations. European students of Caste have unduly emphasized the role of color in the Caste system. Themselves impregnated by color prejudices, they very readily imagined it to be the chief factor in the Caste problem. But nothing can be farther from the truth," Ambedkar submitted.[21] However, he agreed with scholars who saw caste in terms of a religious order. Ambedkar was critical of those who regarded caste as a natural order of things. He referred to these scholars as "orthodox apologists", who argued that caste was a source of structural disintegration as part of the evolutionary process.[22] This was in tune with the social Darwinism of the time. In response, Ambedkar went on to argue that the principle of imitation, a theory developed by Gabriel Tarde, played an important role in turning classes into strong units of castes. In his view, cultural unity did exist among the Indian population, despite caste or perhaps because of it.

In addition to the anthropological scholarship of the colonial period, there was increasing interest in Indic studies, especially in the field of religion. A range of scholars undertook a theological or religious approach to caste. F. Max Müller (1823–1900), a prominent nineteenth-century German-British Sanskrit scholar, translated several sacred Indian texts—mostly Hindu writings like the Rig Veda. It was in the course of these translations that Müller developed his theories of caste. B.G. Tilak (1856–1920), a Marathi brahman writer and nationalist, located the origin of the brahmans in the Arctic region, which he described as an Aryan homeland, having inferred this from Vedic textual evidence.[23]

Many readings of caste

After briefly reviewing the history of caste in colonial times, it is difficult to pinpoint a single defining aspect of caste. Recently, interest in the study of caste has increased, especially in view of its neglect by postcolonial scholarship. In the 1970s, there was in-depth social science analysis of the caste system. Anthropological and historical work tried to understand caste from a comparative perspective. Responses in that era and the following decades varied, but they agreed on one thing: the changing nature of the caste system.

What does the changing nature of the caste system mean? Susan Bayly has summarized diverse perspectives.[24] According to her, caste should be examined through the values it promotes. Caste can be seen both as a colonial creation and as a historical fact from pre-colonial times. However, this does not diminish its important role in society. Bayly argues that caste was a "real and active part of Indian life" for many centuries before the colonial Raj, especially during the Mughal era and earlier, and "not just a self-serving orientalist fiction".[25] She makes this point to counter scholars who see caste as a purely colonial concept.

No single perspective can fully explain caste. The challenge with studying caste, a complex and elusive structure, is its undefined and non-geographical nature. One of the main difficulties is distinguishing between caste, caste and society, and caste within society. How should we prioritize society? Is it a single unit or a collection of independent political and cultural organizations? Commentators believe there is no uniformity and no comprehensive theory of caste. Is it an ideology, a conceptual category, a theory or a social rule? Given this lack of consensus among scholars, various schools of thought have examined caste through its specifics.

For many, it is a colonial invention, a "fabrication" by colonial administrators and their Indian aides, especially brahman administrators and informants.[26] Nicolas Dirks argues that the colonial census was based on several "assumptions" about the social order of caste, focusing on "hierarchy and precedence".[27] Dirks suggests that treating caste anthropologically entrenches social structures in caste bodies rather than nation-states, an idea—of caste versus nation—he advanced early on. His critique was directed at the French sociologist Louis Dumont and his "orientalist" perspective.

Dumont studied caste as a legacy of purity, seeing it as central to Indian society. He argued that status in the Hindu order stems from the purity of castes, which are fixed in hierarchical gradations. This, he believed, forms the basis of Hindu thought, with the existence of "impure", "unclean", untouchable castes. Dumont particularly focused on the centrality of the brahmans, viewing caste purely as a vertical hierarchy. He saw caste as providing a snapshot of the Hindu past and present,[28] a view that received mixed reactions from various disciplines.[29] However, Dumont wasn't the first to connect caste with purity and pollution within the brahmanical hierarchy. Emelié Senart was most likely one of the first to highlight pollution as a key feature of caste.

S.V. Ketkar also recognized pollution as a defining feature of caste. However, in his work *History of Caste in India* (1909), he argued that endogamy, or marrying within one's own group, was a significant aspect of caste.[30] In his view, "classes become castes by becoming endogamous", meaning the desire to maintain a pure bloodline led to people not marrying outside their caste.[31] This thesis was supported by Ambedkar seven years later in his essay "Castes in India",[32] in which he described endogamy as a feature tied to the subordination and control of women. Ambedkar stated, "Endogamy is the only characteristic that is peculiar to caste,"[33] and through this, he believed, one can understand the origin and development of caste.

Caste has evolved from the "abstract stereotypes"[34] of upper and lower classes during Mughal times to becoming a central part of contemporary practice. Bayly distinguishes between the rise of caste into *jatis* and *varnas* during the Mughal and pre-Mughal times.[35] In pre-Mughal times, with the transfer of kingship to warrior clans and ruling elites, they used the "symbols and languages of caste" as part of their statecraft.[36] This meant new titles and statuses were created to fit the ever-evolving definition of caste. By contrast, the "Brahman-centred" caste values of *jati* and *varna* were rigidly conceived, relying strictly on notions of ritual purity. Neo-kshatriya clans seeking higher status imitated brahman practices by wearing sacred threads and acknowledging the "indispensability of Brahmans to human and cosmic order".[37] The Brahmanization of politics and social status began by forcibly isolating lower, impure castes, and reached its peak during colonial times with a focus on untouchability–touchability, as Bayly, Dirks and others have noted.

The brahman became a value symbol, tied to Hindu identity in the cosmology of various kings, aristocrats and landed gentry. The Rajputs, Jats, Nayaks and others in northern India were appointed as guardians of the land, eventually becoming revenue-collecting administrators. On the other hand, the tillers of the land were assimilated into the caste hierarchy, solidifying into a caste. For instance, Jats in Rajasthan, Haryana and Uttar Pradesh have different histories but share a common caste name, being non-elite Rajputs.[38] These titles were part of caste formation, with identities revolving around relations to the land within the same *gotras* (lineages). In agrarian economic relations, the system of tilling the land and sharing profits formed the basis for the development of *khaps* (community organizations). Though non-elites, Jats were also non-servile, thereby acquiring a middle-caste pastoralist position. Along with them were arms-bearing Shudra-positioned groups who, like the Jats, gained new wealth and power through their military skills. The dependence on them of the Rajputs paved the way for this new status, identifying them as self-made dynasts or non-brahman shudra rulers.

Self-made rulers from the Kurmi, Koli, Ahir, Marava, Gujar and Maratha groups did not adopt brahmanical formalities. However, they aimed to achieve a status similar to the kshatriya, whose attempt to maintain "dharmic correctness" was appealing to new lords and self-made rulers.[39] This approach made it easy for them to adopt caste concepts and terms, as these were now commonly used in the practice of Hindu values. The self-made rulers in the South, North and Deccan regions were keen to be recognized as rulers, as equals in superiority. Their ambition to join the ranks of Rajputs or Rajput-like figures was driven by a desire to lead opulent lives and adhere to moral codes. They still felt the need to demonstrate their ability to maintain pure bloodlines and reject any "impure" relations outside endogamy.[40] Bayly argues that to become kshatriyas, these new self-made rulers had to rely on caste codes and rank their subjects in caste-like terms. The shudra rulers were unconcerned with ideals of purity or brahman-centred universality. These new rulers—the Jats, Ahirs, Marathas and Kolis—underwent a process of forming modern castes.⁴¹ They challenged brahman values while simultaneously upholding brahmanical dictates to gain recognition and acceptance beyond their territories.

The new lords had humble origins, which did not conform to the dharmic ideal of kshatriya lordship. To gain legitimacy, they had to adapt the caste system to suit their ideals and beliefs, while also downplaying purity and other everyday caste boundaries. This was also a strategic decision, as many self-made rulers were supported by diverse tribes and groups not included in the brahmanic caste system. Without the support of armed hillmen, forest-dwelling tribes and pastoralists, these rulers would not have survived. Therefore, adhering strictly to the Vedic caste system was not feasible as it would have led to rebellion in their fragile new kingdoms. By modifying castes and forming new modern-day castes, self-made rulers created a hybrid form of strategic caste identities. Did they contribute to creating a caste system or a caste superstructure? Besides naming and ranking the various classes of their subjects into castes, they were probably not responsible for the development of the caste system, which materialized in the late eighteenth century and beyond.⁴²

Bayly argues that the process of landed relations gaining ritual status began during the Mughal rule.⁴³ This made revenue collection easier. With the expansion of Mughal rule, particularly in the sixteenth and seventeenth centuries, a class of brahman lords emerged, acquiring the status of revenue collectors and protectors of "Brahmans and Brahmanical caste codes".⁴⁴ This elevated their status not only as holders of economic power but also as ritual leaders. Brahmans adopted *jati* titles with lordly designations like Maithili and Bhumihar in Bihar, and Saraswat and Chitpavan in the Deccan, to claim supreme status among brahmans and non-brahman elite castes. These newly formed brahman elite caste groups solidified their base by controlling large areas of land and establishing their authority as patrons of kings—as counsellors—and also of the masses. During the British colonial period, the traditional caste ideology became widespread, emphasizing purity and pollution, superior and inferior identities, and meritorious and unmeritorious birth.[45]

* * *

The development of the caste system, which originated in medieval history, was the work of the modern era. It was often difficult to categorize people or groups into *varna* castes if they were unconcerned with these labels and statuses. The various caste names and associated designations did not come into use until the early eighteenth century, when "a whole range of standardised social classifications had become central to the language of officials, scholars, and military men".[46] This system was essentially inherited from the pre-Mughal governance structures used by the Rajputs and other regional powers, which adopted it officially. Scribes (Kayastha and brahmans) began using epithets for various groups, creating caste identities that were "rapidly assimilated into vernacular languages" through their use in the Mughal courts and among the military.[47]

Western and Indian scholars have been hesitant to link caste society today with that of the medieval era because of its changing nature. They have often refused to equate the "caste-like observances" of the past with those of today's society.[48] Many have attempted to develop new theories of caste, rooted in theology, anthropology, sociology, ethnic studies and other fields.[49] However, they have largely missed the significance of untouchability and the condition of those "othered" and ethnicized as "untouchables". Failing to consider this theoretical perspective, theories of the caste system have often privileged the changing nature of higher communities, such as brahmans and kshatriyas,[50] or the consolidation of the *savarnas* as clean castes by the brahmans.[51]

Caste understood in terms of Dalit subjectivity

To better understand caste and subcastes, I propose viewing caste through the lens of Dalit subjectivity. The Dalit perspective must be highlighted and integrated into discussions of caste as a central thesis. To fully comprehend the Dalit ontology, we need to explain the Dalit experience. Without this viewpoint, one cannot define caste as a concept or institution. The Dalit's experience in this system, as both a subject and an object of refusal or acceptance, is essential to a theory of caste. Dalits have diverse lives and varying objectives, and they navigate their roles pragmatically.

There is no single Dalit experience, nor are their responses to caste identical. Dalits' reactions vary depending on their experiences, which combine class, education and spatial context. Their engagement with caste, whether as upholders or as rebels, is shaped by their investment in the future. Many Dalits who live in subjection have made a reluctant peace with their condition. They find ways to protest their deplorable conditions when atrocities are committed against them. They direct their anger towards the government for failing to protect them from attacks by both state and non-state actors. Among the various caste categories, some Dalits benefit from the system as employees or shareholders, and these individuals find reasons not to rebel, instead giving the overall structure the benefit of the doubt. This reflects a pragmatic investment in the system of values and in the future.

For all categories of Dalit, the aspiration not to commit violence is common. Dalits are unable to lead a violent revolution against the state because they are unarmed and resourceless. Doing so might also negatively affect their well-being. However, this has not stopped them from protesting or fighting back with vehemence against injustices.

Dalit personal life is complicated. Though it is difficult to generalize, Dalits have tried to find ways to work through the system. Many have given up their last names, indicating their caste, to achieve what I call "disguised promotion". Disguised promotion is an effective way for Dalits to remain anonymous and pretend to assimilate without being intimidated. To do so, they need to learn new lifestyles and the patterns of the foreign, non-Dalit society, by adopting new accents, pursuing unfamiliar pastimes, and participating in non-Dalit religio-social life. Dalits in this category do achieve relative success. However, they are not entirely immune from caste penetrating their lives.[52]

Many Dalits take dominant-caste names for their protection. They do not rebel or make much of the non-Dalit public sphere. They recognize that Dalits in this phase are trying their best to thrive. Much of this disguised promotion happens in a supposedly caste-neutral place—secular workspaces or neighbourhoods. Neighbourhood here refers to the ecosphere in which everyone shares, such as the air one breathes or the landscape one has access to. Many Dalits outside Dalit neighbourhoods can very effectively mask their Dalit identity and invent a new life for themselves where the everyday acknowledgement of Dalit identity is not required. Such Dalits create non-caste histories of their past by not mentioning their caste or lineage but by talking about the hardships they have to undergo only in economic terms. They also, at times, speak of social hardships, not as they are experienced by a caste group but as a barrier to acquiring social capital.

The reason for adopting a disguise is to secure and justify advancement and promotion that is deserving and meritorious.[53] Often, Dalits are not fairly compensated for their labour. This creates psychological trauma for failing to receive what is their due. Thus, so as to claim what legitimately belongs to them, "disguised promotion" becomes an effective strategy to overcome caste barriers. This disguise is certainly not a hundred per cent caste-proof, and often caste comes back to haunt people, such as during marriages, in the villages, in subcaste networks, or in religious caste practices. In addition, disguised Dalits are also the object of occasional scorn and derision and are mocked by other Dalits. Having few alternatives, Dalits in disguise usually respond with non-violent acceptance.

This explanation can help us to place Dalit identity in the context of the caste system. Dalit identity has to demonstrate its existence either through fight or defeat. However, many have chosen a compromising middle path. This approach is valued in the Dalit community, especially among the upwardly mobile middle class. Caste violation is a form of caste protection. Here, the disguised Dalit is violating their caste loyalty, while in a parallel universe they are compensated with job protection, promotion and personal development. This experience can perhaps help us realize the liabilities of caste in various contexts throughout the world, be they closeted sexual identities, racial identities, or Dalit groupings. In all of these contexts, biological traits are of no import, and social characteristics take precedence.

Dalit separatism

From early on, Dr Ambedkar advocated for a separate identity for Dalits. For this, Ambedkar was labelled anti-national. During the Round Table Conference negotiations in the 1930s, Ambedkar philosophically established the separateness of untouchables from the majority Hindu community. When he was defeated on this score by Gandhi's violent tactics, Ambedkar felt betrayed and was left to fight off attacks from the Brahmanical Congress. Sixteen years after that experience, Ambedkar responded with an indictment of the Hindus and their desperate attempt to bring the untouchables into their fold. In his *What Congress and Gandhi Have Done to the Untouchables* (1946), Ambedkar stated that Dalits "are separate from the Hindus ... [They] constitute a separate and a distinct element in the national life of India." He convinced the Viceroy, Lord Linlithgow, of this position.

Hitting back at the arguments that envisaged Dalits as Hindus, Ambedkar counterposed two questions:

> In what sense are they Hindus? In the first place, the word "Hindu" is used in various senses and one must know in what sense it is used before one can give a proper answer to the question. It is used in a territorial sense. Everyone who is an inhabitant of Hindustan is a Hindu. In that sense it can certainly be claimed that the Untouchables are Hindus. But so are the Muslims, Christians, Sikhs, Jews, Parsis, etc."

The second question was about the difference between the dogmas of Hinduism and the cults of Hinduism. The dogmas of Hinduism were "caste and untouchability". According to the dogmas, there was nothing that tied the untouchables to the Hindus, Ambedkar argued. Similarly, one can ask what binds the autonomous people of India's various tribal (Adivasi) groups to the Hindus. Their names, gods, rituals, traditions and festivals are all very different and have at times been diametrically opposed to those of self-identified Hindus. For argument's sake, let's agree for a moment that Adivasis and Dalits are Hindus. Then why, one may ask, were fellow Hindus designing policies that worked against the former's development? We can also highlight an absence of Hindu solidarity with Tribal or Dalit Hindus when it comes to inter-caste violence and riots as well as support of laws that are detrimental to the progress of Tribals and Dalits. Following this logic, we can explain the gulf between the dominant castes and outcastes: the religious identity of the latter as Hindu was based on political expediency.

Dalit politics and organizing

To further our understanding of caste coloniality, we need to look at how it has reappeared on the national scene in the post-colonial era as a marker of pride and a challenge against oppression. The way caste has been theorized for some time by both natives and foreigners has not encouraged the development of new forms of cultural arrangements. By this, I mean newer forms of subcaste identities existing independently instead of being subsumed within broader bureaucratic frameworks. These subcaste identities exist in the English-language categories of caste classification—Scheduled Caste, Scheduled Tribes, Other Backward Classes, Backward Class, Economically Backward Castes, Most Backward Class, etc. However, these bureaucratic groups only exist within the marginalized and oppressed sphere.

Those with resources and wealth have managed to present a powerful unified image of themselves. Despite brahmans having over 1,880 subcastes across India, their myth of a common brahman identity persists, regardless of the significant differences in class, caste, region and profession. By creating an "otherized" identity within the Hindu theological sphere, brahmans and allied castes have aligned themselves with the ideology of hegemonic control. This allows them to perpetuate a system of macro-casteism in the public sphere by laying claim to their generic caste status without necessarily upholding their primary, subcaste-based identity. Over the past 400 years, *jati* formations have evolved into solid institutions consisting of hierarchical ranks within networks of similar lineage or descent groups. Hence, marriage within these subgroups became a means for the higher elites in the caste system to find suitable partners within endogamous groups. Such practices were centred around the belief in "ritualized hierarchy", which became the core of what Bayly calls the "Indian moral order".[54]

In response, the anti-caste sphere adopted macro-caste identities and countered the dominant sphere's macro-castes. Unintentionally, this census-derived categorization became the norm. Paradoxically, those now challenging the Dalit position have focused on the limitations of the British census. By rejecting the British-based categorizations, they attempt to justify the existence of caste without acknowledging the oppression of Dalits. This sanitized reinterpretation of history has attacked Western scholars' examination of Indian society and has tried to turn a misnomer of caste into a total experience. This has been achieved by portraying the Portuguese term *castas* as a colonial, European invention imposed on native or indigenous societies. The grammar of caste, or the iteration of caste, continues to shape public discussion and political discourse. Within this framework, new forms of anti-caste Dalit organization emerged, drawing inspiration from the strategies of Jyotirao Phule and Dr Ambedkar.

Conclusion: social organization of castes against caste

Large-scale political organization in the post-independent era led to the formation of BAMCEF (Backward and Minorities Central Employees Federation), which was started by a central government Dalit employee, Kanshi Ram, and D.K. Khaparde in 1973. BAMCEF's aim was to organize the disparate Backward castes, which included Dalits, Adivasis, minorities converted to non-Hindu religions, and Backward classes. This group, by virtue of the new policy of reservation, held jobs in the government sector and thus had a steady income. Because most people from this category were poor and depended heavily on their caste oppressors for employment, Kanshi Ram started raising consciousness among them. This work of organization relied on education, awareness, and the reinterpretation of history through an anti-caste lens. It was very much in line with Ambedkar's historical methodology. Through BAMCEF, the caste-oppressed employees contributed to a monthly fund, which helped mobilize poor people by organizing training sessions, cadre camps, and conferences at district, regional, state and national levels. As things improved, Kanshi Ram started a militant organization to respond to atrocities and violence in 1981. It was called DS-4 (Dalit Shoshit Samaj Sangharsh Samiti) and was made up of ten wings comprising students and women, among others. Following this social organizing, in 1984 Kanshi Ram launched the first pan-Indian anti-caste political party with wide reach in the country called the Bahujan Samaj Party (BSP).

BSP was the first autonomous political body organized and led by subalterns in post-independent India. It continues to be among the most influential political parties in the country. BSP disrupted the hegemony of the dominant castes and gave power and strength to those who had always been patronized and mistreated by dominant-caste leaders. Kanshi Ram called the two largest political parties—Congress and the Bharatiya Janata Party (BJP)—two snakes with similar qualities.[55] Alongside BSP, various factions of the Republican Party of India, started by Ambedkar, continue to operate in India. However, they have not been able to create an impact and show of strength like BSP. Much of the Republican leadership succumbed to the hegemony of Congress and BJP.

Like other national-level parties, BSP suffered from divisions and fallout. Much of the blame for this was placed on BSP's national leader, Mayawati, who was a chief minister of India's largest state, Uttar Pradesh, four times between 1995 and 2012. It is alleged that after Kanshi Ram's death, Mayawati did not encourage the leadership of BAMCEF and all other social groups established by Kanshi Ram, which provided a base and financial support for the activities of BSP. As a result of the sidelining of veterans by the BSP leadership, many disgruntled leaders withdrew from active organizing. This led to the formation of other organizations and political parties by veteran leaders in their respective states. One such group is the Bhim Army, which started in Uttar Pradesh; another is the Bahujan Mukti Party in North India, Bahujan Republican Socialist Party in Maharashtra.

Those Dalit and Backward-caste youth who did not find a place in BSP went on to launch new social organizations. They worked in the education sector to deal with the problem of atrocities. Simultaneously, they created cultural awareness, building on Kanshi Ram's work and replicating his activities and style. Bhim Army was founded by Vinay Ratan and Chandrashekhar Azad. After four years of organizing, Bhim Army leaders launched the Azad Samaj Party (ASP) in the middle of the Covid pandemic on 15 March 2020, the birth date of Kanshi Ram, to assert their political rights. Chandrashekhar Azad became its national president and a member of parliament in 2024.

ASP's politics are currently viewed with suspicion by older people, because of the repeated betrayals by Dalit leaders, while the party finds acceptance among the youth owing to the flamboyant style of Azad and its determination to fight back against atrocities. In a telephone conversation, Azad told me that "ASP will take time to be accepted because we are going to those people who have been misused and betrayed. We have to keep working until we gain trust." The Dalit community's hesitation in falling behind ASP comes from the suspicion that Azad was set up by media in opposition to Mayawati. The resistance is plainly visible on social media and on the ground; however, it has not yet taken a violent turn. Mayawati's refusal to engage with the Indian media because of the way it manipulates her views has given space to Azad, who is often seen on television debates.

There has been a huge increase in access to technology and media throughout the country. The availability of cheap data has given rise to a nationwide reliance on social media. ASP's social media strategy is rooted in community organizing. *Time* magazine, which included Azad in its 2021 TIME100 Next list of emerging world leaders, the only Indian to be enlisted, mentioned ASP's creative use of social media. Other Dalit political parties are often not techno-savvy, allowing parties like ASP to flourish. Will their social media and print media presence convert into votes at the ballot box? It remains to be seen.

The modalities of Dalit resistance have been formed through collective struggle and organizational engagement. Although BAMCEF, founded by Kanshi Ram, did not continue as the parent body of BSP, it persisted as an organization with multiple splinter groups. One faction is led by the influential speaker and powerful leader Waman Meshram. Another BAMCEF faction operates as Mulnivasi Sangh (Indigenous Group), headed by B.D. Borkar. There are also two other factions active in Punjab and Uttar Pradesh. Like the spirit of the Dalit Panthers, BAMCEF remains alive today, though by contrast with the former it is more organized and ideologically firm in its political stance. The Buddhist Society of India and the Samata Sainik Dal, organizations created by Dr Amedkar, have a non-political presence in select circles.

There is great diversity in Dalit organization. But a common position has been that of reinterpreting history and bringing it to the service of the Bahujans (subaltern majority). This can be seen in the historical project of practising a form of ethical politics, which will be explored in the next chapter. How did the dawn of politics in the second half of the twentieth century occur? What were the precursors? How did radical anti-caste organization take shape in the light of the international solidarities expressed in the 1970s? The next chapter will examine these questions, arguing that Dalit politics were internationalist in nature and concerned with humanity worldwide. In all this, literature played a central role in pivoting the dialogue of caste and technologies of oppression.

2

AFFAIRS OF LETTERS
DALIT RESPONSES TO BLACK LITERATURE

The anti-caste Dalit movement in India was envisaged by and expressed through a literary culture. From the nineteenth century onwards, Dalit literati advocated for social change through the print media, pamphleteering and books. The record of literary texts and various literary initiatives spanning a hundred years makes clear that literary engagements preceded social movements. They provided a theoretical base for analysing society so as to work out a durable anti-caste praxis. Many anti-caste activists started engaging with the most easily accessible print medium, newspapers, to voice their concerns and develop a nuanced reading of social conditions. The earliest phase of Dalit literary culture thus emerged in the print media sphere. In this chapter we will briefly consider the genealogy of print culture among Dalits and then examine how over time the Dalit movement developed a universalist vision in its politics by incorporating a stance of solidarity with Black people in America.

This chapter looks critically at the emergence of a literary response to caste and its institutions. Simultaneously, it analyses the growing divergence between the Dalit and the Black literary and activist worlds. Their sense of connection and agreement was less real than symbolic. Limited resources prevented them from designing projects and courses of action in unison. At the same time, the Dalit movement continued to articulate and develop an authentic and original body of Indic thought, beyond traditional brahmanical preoccupations, exploring its hermeneutical dimensions and developing innovative approaches to its interpretation. This became one of the most prominent concerns of the writers and poets who were at the forefront of the post-Ambedkar Dalit movement in India.

This chapter also widens the scope of our inquiry by highlighting the global story of caste. The most effective way for activists to empower their narratives was by developing a shared literary imagination, enabling people from different social groups and different parts of the world to envisage an ideal future. This was developed textually through such themes as oppression, state violence, exploitation of labour and other interest groups, the diaspora, migration, and new forms of world-making. These formed the basis for theorizing Dalit subjectivity as a form of kinship that could be related to other subjectivities oppressed by social castes elsewhere in the world.

A brief history of modern Dalit writing

The first known Dalit newspaper was published in the Tamil language. Called *Sooryodhayam*, it was started around 1872 by Pandit Thiruvenkatasamy, who identified himself as Adi Dravida. However, no records of this newspaper exist besides copies in the colonial archives and references to it by another leading social reformer from Tamil Nadu, Pandit Iyothee Thass.[1] Thass also started two prominent Tamil-language journals; the first, *Dravida Pandian*, in 1876 with the Rev. John Rathinam;[2] the second,

Oru Paisa Tamizhan (later renamed *Tamilan*), in 1907; the latter ran till his death in 1914. Likewise, Rettamalai Srinivasan, a contemporary and collaborator of Thass, and a celebrated Dalit rights activist and leader of the Tamilians, edited a widely circulated and internationally read newspaper, *Parayan*, which started life in 1893. Like *Parayan* and other Tamil periodicals of the time, *Adi-Dravidan*, a monthly journal begun in 1919, was widely read internationally, especially by the Tamil-speaking diaspora of the British colonies who took out subscriptions to it. This international readership for Indian newspapers was not uncommon: plantation workers and indentured labourers in the British colonies of Burma, South Africa, Ceylon (Sri Lanka), Fiji, Mauritius, Singapore, Malaya and Tanganyika all had access to the vibrant Dalit print media.[3]

In the same era, Gopal Baba Walangkar, the grandfather of modern Dalit activism, wrote with subtle fervour for newspapers like *Dinmitra* and *Sudharak*. His monthly journal *Vital Vidhwansak* (begun in 1888) attacked the caste Hindu supremacy of brahmans. His forthright writing against caste and untouchability helped establish the Dalit movement in the Marathwada region.

The credit for starting the Dalit community's first Marathi-language magazine goes to Shivram Janba Kamble, who began the publication of *Somvanshiya Mitra* in 1908.[4] This called on Dalits to organize and protest against caste atrocities and appeal for their rights. Fagoji Bansode, a Dalit labour leader from the Nagpur region, started the Marathi newspapers *Maratha Deenbandhu* in 1901, *Antanjay Vilaap* in 1906 and *Maharancha Sudharak* in 1907.[5] To support his publishing activities, Bansode also set up a printing press, which published *Nirashrit Hindu Nagarik* (1910). Along with the Dalit activist Kalicharan Nandagawali, Bansode edited *Vital Vidhwansak* (1913). Following this, he started another newspaper, *Chokhamela* (1916), named after a famous Mahar saint, whose biography he also wrote. *Majoor Patrika* (1918–22), a newsletter for labourers, was also published by Bansode's press. Besides inserting the issue of Dalit rights within the framework of labour, he also articulated the Dalit position as that of a native oppressed community existing under Hindu laws. He used this twin approach to fight against caste and empire.

A similar approach was followed by Dr B.R. Ambedkar, who started four periodicals to support his movement. The first was *Mooknayak* (Leader of the Voiceless), which began on 31 January 1920. This periodical, which ran for three years and had to close down owing to financial constraints in 1923, helped Dalits make sense of their situation in British India under a brahmanical Hindu regime.

As Ambedkar became active in full-time politics, he relied on a new periodical, *Bahishkrit Bharat* (Outcaste India), first issued in 1927. After publishing forty-three issues, the periodical closed on 15 November 1929. Then came *Samata* (Equality) in 1928, followed by *Janata* (The People) in 1930. This was the longest-running periodical of the Dalit community, being in print for a quarter of a century. Eventually, in 1956, *Janata* was renamed *Prabuddha Bharat* (Enlightened India).

Meanwhile, other Dalits who came under Ambedkar's influence also started publishing newspapers. Prominent among them was Dadasaheb Shirke's *Garud* (1926).[6] The Buddhist activist and lieutenant of Ambedkar, P.N. Rajbhoj, started *Dalit Bandhu* in 1928; Keshav Narayan Dev (Patitpaavandas) began *Patitpaavan* in 1932; L.N. Hardas edited two periodicals, *Maharattha* (1933) and *Dalit Ninad* (1947); and V.N. Barwe issued *Dalit Sevak* to propagate Gandhian views on caste.

The Dalit print media were not solely focused on finding immediate solutions to particular problems or incidents, but sought to develop an overall response to the system of oppression. This was achieved through the performance of gestural anecdotes and personalized narratives. The emergence of the Dalit literary canon was a creative response to the Dalits' own situation. Through expression in the literary sphere, the movement sought to validate its ideas and actions.[7] Dalit writers practised eloquence as their elite art, subverting the standards of other groups and asserting their claims on diction and expression. This way of standardizing the discourse of Dalit groups helped to highlight and, at the same time, radicalize two key elements: first, memorializing their past, and, second, directing the Dalit community towards a politics of resistance.

After the death of Dr Ambedkar in 1956,[8] there was a decades-long struggle within the Dalit movement, which was both political and cultural in nature. But out of this emerged a new response to old problems, which was refreshing for people from all backgrounds. The Dalit community embraced the new expressions and filled the halls to listen to speeches, poems, stories and lectures. Meanwhile, the guardians of the brahmanical canon proceeded with caution, often finding Dalit articulations caustic and thus profane. In their writings Dalits turned public life into social metaphors and eventually inserted it into the dialectics of caste.

The more opposition the Dalit literary sphere received, the more enthusiastically it embarked on creating a counter-culture through periodicals, small magazines and publishing houses. Like the nineteenth-century Dalit literature, the post-Ambedkar canon was internationalist in nature. The obvious source it drew upon and analogous model it viewed with interest was Black American literature. The leading voice of the Dalit literary tradition in Marathi, Raja Dhale, invested in translating Black American poets and took keen notice of their activities. The literary revival that took place was young, energetic and sophisticated.

This aspect is an important part of the history of Dalit literary culture and protest politics. Post-Ambedkar, there was a watershed moment in which the younger generation found themselves without leaders to supervise them or provide guidance. They were, in some ways, starting afresh, drawing inspiration from their heroes like Ambedkar who were now dead. An examination of the post-Ambedkar Dalit movement is thus essential in comprehending the multidimensional aspects of Indian democracy—in particular the position of Dalits as urban ghettoized poor or rural outcastes. To do so this, we need to investigate the traditions and events that gave rise to their situation.

Rise of the Dalit sahitya

How do we assess the social history of a community that was trying to re-establish its importance as a central actor in India's story? At the same time, it wanted to challenge the post-colonial state's victimization of Dalits because the structures of caste, both urban and rural, were still in place. The Dalits' condition was exacerbated by the helplessness of the Dalit leadership, which couldn't succeed in filling Ambedkar's shoes. This deficiency was noticed by the urban class of Dalits, who challenged this worrying situation through literature and public protest by blending the two and making of literature a protest movement. As it was viewed as the work of the Dalit movement, many non-Dalits refrained from contributing to the literary journals run by Dalit literary figures.[9]

This chapter is not a literary analysis nor an exercise in comparative literature. Its primary purpose is to map the history of the one-sided love affair of the Dalit community with Black American literature. It does not cover African literature, where new writers were theorizing at an impressive pace, but instead focuses on the disconnected relations between the Dalit and Black American literary worlds. This story of admiration from a distance, expressed in non-English, remained uncommunicated to the other side. There are ample reasons for the lack of reciprocation and recognition from the American side. The primary issue was one of language, as Dalits mainly wrote in their mother tongues, which were mostly regional, being attentive to the needs of their own readers. This was also the case with cultural exchange, social solidarity and, more importantly, political revolt.

Dalit literature and the origin of its politics

Dalit literature was Socratic in that it critically examined external and internal conflicts. This ability to self-critique is what differentiated these writers from the self-professed righteousness of others. Gangadhar Pantawane observed two types of self-critique. The first was to overcome the inferiority complex imposed by the caste system. Self-critique was meant to empower Dalits "to break down the slave-psychology" imposed on them by the casteist Hindu social order.[10] The second was a critique directed against elite Dalits for their arrogance and sense of superiority by which they set themselves apart from the lower-class Dalit population and in this way isolated themselves from the majority of the community.[11]

After Ambedkar's death in 1956, the Dalit leadership suddenly found itself rudderless. Many of Ambedkar's lieutenants attempted to develop a credible space for carrying out the politics inherited from Ambedkar's time as leader. The following decades were marked by turmoil for Dalits. There was a spike in incidents of caste atrocities. Complete dependence on the state for their survival made Dalits vulnerable. As a result, given the frustrations arising from the inability of Dalit leaders to galvanize a broader coalition (as imagined by Ambedkar in his Republican Party), many of these leaders were coopted by the ruling Congress party.

One of the major struggles initiated by Dalits after Ambedkar's death was a land rights satyagraha. Under Ambedkar's leadership, the Scheduled Caste Federation (SCF) announced a land rights movement in the Marathwada region, centred on the city of Aurangabad, in 1953.[12] Ambedkar advised his people to occupy the arable wastelands taken back by the government.[13] He also wrote to a minister in the Hyderabad government about this. After his death, the struggle for the land remained a matter of concern for the Scheduled Caste leadership. N. Sivaraj, president of the SCF, declared he would continue Dr Ambedkar's work. In consequence, a nationwide satyagraha was launched. On Sivaraj's death, Bhaurao (Dadasaheb) Gaikwad offered to lead post-independent India's democratic mobilization of the landless and marginalized, calling on all Indian Dalits to march on parliament on 1 October 1964. This satyagraha proved influential, gathering a nationwide momentum. Through this, the Republican Party of India also attracted Dalit youth who were desperate for an action-oriented form of organization.[14]

However, this success lasted only a short time, for the operations of electoral politics worked against Dalits' interests. The Dalit leadership had to find allies among the dominant, ruling parties, particularly Congress, in order to win concessions. Bhaurao Gaikwad, who had been a close colleague of Ambedkar, struck a deal for a Dalit seat with the Congress. This put the caste-bound and feudal Congress in control of the Dalit political constituency. It also led to divisions among Dalit leaders that continue till today. The bone of contention was about whom one could rely on and whether to make alliances or not. Meanwhile, the Republican Party leadership concentrated solely on party politics, thereby hampering the social movement agenda, which was continued by other Dalit political parties as well.[15]

Already from 1959, the Dalit political leadership centred in western Maharashtra were aware of bitter divisions within the movement. The first was between what were called the *durust* and *nadurust* (correct–incorrect) groups. The *durust* group was led by B.C. Kamble, a well-educated leader and author who wrote the biography of Dr Ambedkar. The *nadurust* group was led by Bhaurao Gaikwad.[16] Class and education played a part in these divisions. Ambedkar's son, Yashwant Ambedkar, was among the first to try to unite the divided leadership, though he met with opposition from Kamble.

In the 1962 parliamentary election, Gaikwad made a pact with Congress to enable him to enter parliament. Although the move did attract poor voters who were inspired by the idea of their leader entering parliament, this came at the cost of overall Dalit representation, as the compromise was regarded as an insult to the radical Dalit consciousness created by Ambedkar.

Divisions over interests and ideologies continued within the post-Ambedkar leadership. R.D. Bhandare, one of the towering leaders of the Gaikwad camp, withdrew from this group, while D.D. Rupwate walked out of Kamble's faction. Whenever the feudal-caste forces or the state attacked the Dalit community, attempts were made to mount a united response, as happened during the 1967, 1970, 1971 and 1974 parliamentary elections. It was difficult for Dalit leaders to cooperate when each of them enjoyed the backing of some part of the community. Within their own constituencies, their vote share remained intact and provided them with political currency.

In Maharashtra, similar efforts to create a unified front proved unfruitful. But the 1985, 1990, 1995 and 1999 elections briefly saw the unity of various factions led by Republican Party leaders who had established separate camps. However, this was not to last, as the conflicts over whom to ally with and contest the elections proved unsurmountable. Whether it was with Congress, Janata

Dal or other regional parties, the radical Dalit movement initiated by Ambedkar was now open to bargaining with other groups. It was not as if Ambedkar had not made compromises in the course of his political career. It was in the nature of feudal relations that democratic practice became inherently caste-sensitive. Ambedkar eventually formed an alliance with the socialists, as they were congenial to his politics and social agenda.

These factions in post-Ambedkar Dalit politics became a feature of the Maharashtra state. At some stage the Dalit literati could not take it anymore. The first generation of educated Dalit youth, who were mostly trained in the institutions established by Ambedkar, such as Siddharth College, Mumbai, and Milind College, Aurangabad, were among the first to criticize the divisive (*gutbaazi*) politics plaguing the Dalit movement. Siddharth College was also a space where the place of literature and the role of Dalits in literary production were discussed. Students here debated topical issues of literature in the Marathi language at a time when the field was controlled by dominant-caste figures. These debates took place under the auspices of a short-lived Siddharth Sahitya Sangh in the 1950s and were published in the weeklies *Janata* and *Prabuddha Bharat*, which had been started by Ambedkar.[17]

The first Dalit literature conference was organized in 1958 in Dadar, Mumbai. Its president was the literary giant Anna Bhau Sathe.[18] The Dalit literary movement provided intellectual guidance to the social and political movements, and it gained widespread support among the general public. Their conferences and seminars were attended in numbers, and books were sold at record speed. Among the scores of festivals and conferences that were organized were Dalit Sahitya Sansad, Dalit Sahitya Parishad, Boudh Sahitya Parishad, Dalit Natya Parishad, Phule-Ambedkar Panchayat, Dalit, Adivasi Mahasabha, Purogami Vichar Manch, Parivartan Sahitya Mandal, Asmitadarsh Sahitya Melava, Dalit

Natya Sammelan and Ambedkarwadi Sahitya Sammelan. They provided sure evidence of the central place that the Dalit literary movement occupied in the Dalit community. They continue to this day.[19]

The Dalit literary movement in Maharashtra has been studied by the sociologists U. Bhoite and A. Bhoite. They argue that it was the "neo-Buddhist elites" comprising "journalists, college teachers, lawyers, etc." who formed the primary membership of the movement. This group was keen on cultural revival by assuming a new identity and discarding the old.[20] When the Bhoites wrote their essay in the late 1970s, the category of "elite" was still evolving, and today one can no longer identify regular government workers as elites. However, if the authors meant influential people, then there were many in the educated class who offered direction to the masses, and these were mainly government employees.

Politically, Dalits could not have an independent role owing to their minority status and their communal location as lower castes. Realizing this, Dr Ambedkar dissolved the All India Scheduled Caste Federation (SCF), which could not bring about the dream of ruling India. Though the SCF acted effectively as a political pressure group, it could not stake a claim on the government. A broader coalition of ideologies was the only way to realize this. Ambedkar thus joined hands with the socialists to create a non-Congress political front.[21] The coalition process, however, did not follow the route Ambedkar had imagined. After his death, many Dalit leaders ended up aligning with Congress to secure election to parliament.

The capacity for self-examination and self-critique helped strengthen fundamental Dalit values. Major criticism was directed against token Dalit politicians who succumbed to the pressure of the dominant-caste political formations. Distrust among the youth, especially about the quality of leadership, erupted in a flood of angry revolt which engulfed everyone. They loosely organized themselves, paving the way for the eventual formation of the Dalit Panther movement in 1972, which was inspired at a distance by the Black Panther Party in the United States.

The Dalit Panther movement was dissolved after five years due to increasing state pressure and in-fighting among its leaders over which ideological direction to take.[22] Some argue it was a party of the moment, which did not long survive. However, the Dalit Panthers remained alive in the memories of the youth and dissenting Dalits. Although the organization's Bombay headquarters were closed down, different chapters of the Dalit Panthers were established in various districts across India, and leadership emerged from various parts of the country. Every leader who believed in fighting against injustice using Panther methods modelled his organization on them.

Dalit leaders who worked with the Dalit Panthers did not welcome the latter's dissolution. Arun Kamble, Bhai Sangare, Ramdas Athawale, S.M. Pradhan, Umakant Randhir and Dayanand Mhaske were among the leading figures who gathered under the new banner of Bhartiya Dalit Panthers (BDP) in 1977.[23] The BDP remained proactive in various struggles and movements for over a decade. They consisted of action-oriented groups who took on the state and the government whenever issues of atrocities and Dalit rights arose. The BDP attracted interest in other states, leading to the formation of state-bound bodies. They organized regular district, regional, zonal and national conferences to keep the flame of their struggle alive. The BDP as an organization was also engulfed in leadership conflicts. It was desperate to represent the cause of Dalits and was not interested in forming immediate alliances with others. The BDP did not appreciate the presence of non-Dalit youth in their struggle, and asked them to leave. Of those who left, some joined hands with opponents of their struggle in Aurangabad, making it a stark Dalit versus non-Dalit issue.[24]

Commentators argue that the BDP also followed the fate of the Dalit Panthers when they dissolved and merged into the Republican Party. Ramdas Athawale, one of the leaders of the BDP and now a central minister, told me in an interview that merging the BDP with the Republican Party of India was a unanimous decision of all the Dalit Panther and Republican factions, as it held out the prospect of a united front.[25] Debate about the Panthers has less to do with the duration of their organizational politics and more about the culture of their leaders and their relations with the Ambedkarite movement. This issue has always invited suspicion among the Dalit community, as Dalit leaders have often been accused of selling out the cause that Dr Ambedkar so laboriously created.

African American literature

Black writers in the United States realized the enduring possibility of literature to create unity by challenging the divisive motifs of boundaries, religion and capital. Through their art and the advantage of the English language's global acceptability, Black literature managed to circulate its ideas in the Anglosphere as well as in other nations that had a kinship with colonial America. Fizzing with lively topics and, at times, conflicting ideologies, Black literature created an international space for Black thought. Drawing on currents of Marxism, nationalism, Islamism, Christianity and realism, African American writers challenged the structural inequities of colour-based discrimination that curtailed the life chances of people of colour in America.

From early on, Black literature became a means of whispering freedom. One of the earlier genres that Black Americans adopted were autobiographies that expressed their real condition in the most graphic form. Many slaves who escaped to the North were helped by pro-abolitionist whites to record the poignant tales of their lives. But this literature was not only an invitation to readers to extend pity in a charitable way, but also an expression of rage and an invitation to protest against tyranny.

Dickson D. Bruce divides the history of African American literature into four phases. The first phase belongs to the period from the 1680s to the 1760s. However, Black literature acquired real shape from the 1760s to 1800s. This phase was notable for the writing of the pioneering poet Jupiter Hammon, the first African American poet to be published in the United States, who appealed in his writing to a Christian faith in God's ultimate judgement. Another prominent writer of this era was Olaudah Equiano, who was born in Nigeria and enslaved in the West Indies and who finally settled in England. His slave narrative was published as a two-part autobiography entitled *The Interesting Narrative of the Life of Olaudah Equiano, or Gustavus Vassa, the African*. It was an instant bestseller that went into nine editions and was translated into German, Dutch and Russian. This was perhaps the first anti-colonial critique rooted in the traditions of Africa.[26]

In the third phase of the history of Black literature, which occupies the long nineteenth century, autobiographical writing was the dominant form of literary expression: nearly a hundred slave autobiographies were published before the American Civil War.[27] The most prominent figure here was Frederick Douglass, who as a 27-year-old free Black man published his autobiography in 1845. His *Narrative of the Life of Frederick Douglass, an American Slave, Written by Himself* immediately gained an audience among white middle-class Americans. Douglass appealed to the genius of Black humanity, which had been denigrated and reduced to the lowest caste, as Douglass put it, "so low in the scale of humanity".[28] A decade later, this man of wise words and convincing oratory revised his autobiography as *My Bondage and My Freedom*, which challenged the belief of Yankee Americans in their liberal and welcoming stance towards Black people. The book was introduced by another famous Black man of the times, the physician James McCune Smith, who wrote of Douglass:

> He is a representative American man—a type of his countrymen. Naturalists tell us that a full-grown man is a resultant or representative of all animated nature on this globe; beginning with the early embryo state, then representing the lowest forms of organic life, and passing through every subordinate grade or type, until he reaches the last and highest—manhood. In like manner, and to the fullest extent, has Frederick Douglass passed through every gradation of rank comprised in our national make-up, and bears upon his person and upon his soul everything that is American. And he has not only full sympathy with everything American; his proclivity or bent, to active toil and visible progress, are in the strictly national direction, delighting to outstrip "all creation".[29]

The turn of the twentieth century saw the emergence of two influential Black leaders and intellectuals, though they championed contrasting ideas. Booker T. Washington produced a guidebook for self-improvement by telling his life story in *Up from Slavery* (1901). This was meant to encourage Black people to find dignity through work, by pulling themselves up by their bootstraps as it were. Washington told the story of how, having been born a slave, he rose to become a schoolmaster and businessman. He emphasized the importance of vocational training and learning a trade, and credited the philanthropy of white people and their generosity for bringing Black people into the economic and social mainstream.

The other intellectual of note was Harvard's first Black doctoral graduate, W.E.B. Du Bois. In his classic work, *The Souls of Black Folk* (1903), Du Bois covered diverse topics affecting the

Black community of America and argued famously that colour and race would become the predominating issues of the twentieth century. In his book, he also rebutted Booker T. Washington's claim that the answer to the problems Black people faced lay in work and industry as opposed to enfranchisement and social responsibility through race pride.

The next influential Black literary tradition in America was associated with the neighbourhood of Harlem in New York, many of whose residents were the direct descendants of slaves who had migrated to the North. Harlem became the centre of a modern American literary and cultural renaissance in the 1920s. The most prominent names associated with the Harlem Renaissance were those of Langston Hughes, Zora Neale Hurston, Ralph Ellison and Countee Cullen, among a host of others. The art and literature they produced became vehicles of the African American political movement. In India, halfway across the world, Dalit writers and activists drew on the inspiration of these writers and produced a slew of articles and books focusing on that tradition. Thus began a one-sided affair between Dalits and Black Americans.

At the same time, one must remember that Dalit literature existed autonomously. The modern Dalit literary tradition developed prior to Harlem, existing in form and shape as journalistic ventures very similar to the African American press. Moreover, there were important differences between the Dalit and the African American literary traditions. This was because of the differing treatment that Blacks in America and Dalits in India received in their respective societies. For one thing, the public sale of slave bodies and the controlling factor of the family system were absent among Dalits. When Ambedkar compared untouchability to slavery, he was more interested in interrogating the nature of the human trafficking that brought with it protection and care given to the enslaved person by the enslaver. In the traditional set-up of *varna*, untouchability, distance and non-ownership defined the nature of caste. Here, the untouchable was an indispensable unit of labour. He could provide his labour without expecting any returns, not even the care a slave owner might give to his slave to ensure his productivity and value.[30]

Dalit–Black cross-referencing

Dr Ambedkar was the first to refer to African American literature from the Dalit side. This occurred in his monumental essay written in the early 1930s, mostly as a response to the Indian revolutionary Lala Lajpat Rai's rebuttal of the American journalist Katherine Mayo's controversial book *Mother India* (1927). Rai had suggested that untouchability was of relative value compared with slavery in America. In response, Ambedkar lambasted Rai in his famous text "Which Is Worse? Slavery or Untouchability?" Ambedkar looked at the dynamics of slavery and untouchability, arguing for the non-value of the untouchable body in the design of the caste labour system.[31]

Ambedkar's essay can be credited as the first Dalit interaction with the African American literary sphere. Perhaps the most prominent twentieth-century interpreter of Black American writing for a Dalit audience was M.N. Wankhede, who earned an MA in 1950 and joined Milind College in Aurangabad as a professor, eventually becoming head of the Department of English. From 1958 to 1962 he served as the principal of Milind College, an influential Dalit educational institution, before going to the United States on a Fulbright Fellowship, where he earned a doctorate from the University of Florida, Gainesville, on "Walt Whitman and Tantrism: A Comparative Study", submitted in 1965. In 1966, Wankhede returned to India to resume charge of Milind College, from where he edited the periodical *Prabuddha*

Bharat.[32] In 1969 he moved to Bombay to become chairman of the Maharashtra Public Service Commission.[33]

Wankhede was a pathbreaker and an originator of many popular ideas that later found a widespread audience. He expanded the meaning of Dalit, which he did not confine to the "Buddhists or scheduled castes" but to "all those who are exploited as labourers".[34] The Dalit Panthers' *Bhoomika* (position document), which charted their goals, bore the influence of this definition and expanded it further. According to the Panthers' definition, a Dalit is a "scheduled caste, scheduled tribe, Buddhists, hardworking people, worker, landless, peasant, poor cultivator, nomadic tribes, indigenous people".[35] The other idea of Wankhede's that spread widely was the need to create a Dalit mythography. He advised Dalit writers to invest in creating myths from the Buddhist past or from the era of Arya-Naga warfare.[36] Arjun Dangle carried forward this idea in his texts.[37]

After his return to India, Wankhede continued his exploration of Black American writing through fresh inquiries.[38] Under his mentorship, his student Janardhan Waghmare followed in his footsteps. When Waghmare arrived as a young graduate at Milind College, he asked Wankhede to supervise his doctoral thesis. Wankhede advised him to work on Black and Dalit literature.[39] Waghmare ended up writing the first-ever critical thesis on Dalits and Blacks entitled "The Problem of Identity in the Postwar American Negro Novel with Special Reference to Ralph Ellison and James Baldwin" (1980), which was submitted to Dr Babasaheb Ambedkar Marathwada University, Aurangabad.

The literary undertakings of Wankhede, Waghmare and others helped educate Dalit audiences about Black American culture and their struggles during the slavery, post-slavery, Jim Crow and Civil Rights Movement eras. Several notable periodicals and journals were launched to carry forward this literary preoccupation among young, first-generation graduates from the Dalit community. One of them was *Asmitadarsh*.

Asmitadarsh

Milind College produced a new class of educated Dalits, who gave expression to their thoughts and feelings through poetry and stories. However, as they were not able to get their work published, M.N. Wankhede started the periodicals *Milind Sahitya Sabha* and *Asmita* (Sense of Identity) in 1967. *Asmita* was launched with Wankhede as its chief editor, R.G. Jadhav as executive editor, and Professor Raymane, Professor Gangadhar Pantawane, Waman Nimbalkar and Sukhram Hiwrale as assistant editors.[40] The December 1967 issue of *Asmita* inaugurated a discussion on the future direction of Dalit literature.[41] Among the topics discussed in the issue were obscenity in literature, higher education and American Negro life and culture, while poetry and commentary were also included. To the editors and others like V.L. Kulkarni, M.P. Rege and M.B. Chitnis credit is due for developing a pathway for the establishment of Dalit sahitya (literature).[42] Reminiscing a decade later, Wankhede attested to the usefulness of a medium like *Asmita* in benefiting many writers and poets, who became well known as a result in literary circles.[43]

Asmita was renamed *Asmitadarsh* due to objections raised by the Maharashtra government. We do not know what those objections were. Juned Shaikh reports that the journal was initially started with some financial help from the Maharashtra state government, which saw the promotion of the Marathi language as a vital way of connecting with the bloody struggle that had led to the state's formation in 1960.[44] When Wankhede had to leave for Bombay, Pantawane was unanimously chosen to take over as editor of *Asmitadarsh*, a responsibility he carried for fifty-one years. It was eventually registered under the Pragatik Vichar Manch Trust established by Pantawane.[45] Wankhede died of cancer on 1 May 1978 in Houston, Texas.

Asmitadarsh gave itself over to experimental writing and publishing. It was a forum for writers, poets, artists, commentators and thinkers. Already associated with some well-known literary figures and founded at a time when there was a need for budding writers to get published, *Asmitadarsh* was considered the "first watershed moment" in the history of Indian Dalit literature.[46] Gangadhar Pantawane, a first-rate scholar, researcher and mentor to many, took over the editorial role in 1968. In the course of his life Pantawane wrote twenty books and edited thirteen more. He died in 2018.

The aim of Pantawane to develop non-Dalit writers, especially shudras and Nomadic Tribes, proved fruitful. Many writers found a home in this Dalit literary establishment. They were welcomed and made part of Dalit literature as Dalits. Getting published in the 1970s and 1980s was considered the highest honour. This was especially true for those people whose parents and forebears were unlettered. To see their name and, even more importantly, their literary creation in print boosted the confidence of many to carve out independent careers in their chosen field. *Asmitadarsh* also carried writings from progressive and Marxist writers and artists who contributed to the quarterly.[47] But, during the effervescent years of the Dalit literary movement (1972–4), *Asmitadarsh* started to move towards the right side (*ujvya toka kade*) of the political spectrum.[48] Divisiveness bred from contending ideological positions could also be observed in Dalit literary circles.

Pantawane's aim in his role as editor was to cultivate a new generation of literary scholars and poets. And the best way to do this was through self-representation. Pantawane became an icon for budding writers, poets and scholars, not least on account of his personality, which demonstrated humility and consideration.

Writers—known and unknown—who paid a visit to his residence or office would be won over by the welcoming hospitality they received. This sense of respectful consideration became rooted in the younger writers. After experiencing their icon first-hand, they carefully took note of his style, demeanour and attitude and carried these traits with them into their lives.

Pantawane indirectly inspired the younger generation to follow the path of humility; with it came responsibility. The responsibility of writers was to carry forward the community's interests. This meant they had to be involved with the public proactively. The large egos of young literati were a well-known phenomenon among Marathi writers. There was also a danger that this might be reflected in wider personal, social and professional milieus, which would harm not only the writers but also the community they represented. To avoid this, Pantawane mentored young writers by exemplifying, in his person, behaviour and leadership, modesty combined with serious work. This came with an unwavering commitment to freedom of speech and thought. Even though the discussions at the annual conferences that he hosted each year might go in contesting, competing directions, Pantawane seldom allowed this to detract from the decorum of the programme. For as long as there was scholarship and deep analysis, critical thinking remained an important feature of the Dalit literary conferences.

Pantawane remained rooted in Dalit culture and the Dalit community. He has been credited with creating a generation of writers involved in the critical analysis of literature and society.[49] He remained loyally devoted to his primary field of investigation—literature—and introduced new scholars, writers, poets and artists to literary festivals.

Pantawane's political thought was inspired by the tradition of Phule–Shahu–Ambedkar (the trinity of Jyotirao Phule, Shahu of Kolhapur and Dr Ambedkar) and their radical anti-caste practice.

In an essay published in 1983 in Barbara Joshi's edited collection entitled *Untouchable! Voices of the Dalit Liberation Movement*, Pantawane sought to revisit and expand the category of Dalit. Dalit, according to him, was a living condition, an archetype of the "exploited men in his country". Dalit was not a caste, but a "symbol of change and revolution". A Dalit was a person who had agency to act and direct his life. A Dalit simply "believes in humanism ... rejects the existence of God, rebirth, soul, sacred books that teach discrimination, fate and heaven". The Dalit does so because, Pantawane added, "these have made him a slave".[50]

For his contributions to Marathi literature and to shaping modern Dalit literature, the Government of India recognized Pantawane's decades-long work and awarded him the civil honour of "Padmashree".

Like Pantawane, Baburao Bagul, another giant of Marathi literature, who is credited with providing an ideological shape to the Dalit Panthers' position document, helped reinterpret the Dalit condition by offering new meaning to the term.[51] He defined a Dalit as someone who seeks total revolution and revival of their pride by relying on the emancipatory resources of the Dalit past.[52] Bagul maintained that the praxis of the Dalit revolution derived from a combination of caste and poverty, the outcome of modern class relations in urban areas. Bagul and Pantawane embodied different strains of political thought, but the literary flair of each carried with it an unmatched, signature style.

These existing tropes of radical Dalit thought, rooted in the humanist vision of Ambedkar, with occasional interventions from the political left, brought into focus new forms of rebellion. This can be seen in the writing and literary thought of Janardhan Waghmare, who was mentored and encouraged by Wankhede to work on the comparative theme of Dalit and Black American literature. This placed him in the school of Phule thinking that underlay the social reform society Satyashodhak Samaj: the latter also found points of comparison between the Dalit and the Black American conditions.

Janardhan Waghmare and the Dalit–Black nexus

Waghmare almost singlehandedly shaped the genre of comparative literature in India. He was born in the village of Kavtha, in the district of Latur in Marathwada, and pursued a career in the region. His writings had as their background Marathwada, which was both separate and isolated from the development of modernity in the rest of the state. The base from which his approach to a comparative analysis of India and the United States began was the hinterlands, where global suffering was imposed on local oppression. Unlike writers from the metropolitan cities who had an urban, ghettoized upbringing, Waghmare's experiences were, like Pantawane's, rural and grassroots. His approach to global politics can be studied through his origins in Marathwada, a region that defied the Government of India's attempt to annex it far longer than any other. It became the last of the kingdoms of colonial India to merge into the Union of India. This region has also seen rigid feudal caste politics, which were taken up by the Muslim aristocracy. In response, the Dalit and Backward castes sought education at the institutions established by Dr Ambedkar. Waghmare was a product of the social movement of the Marathwada region, and he took that viewpoint while writing and also when representing India at the United Nations General Assembly in 2009.

Waghmare wrote numerous articles comparing Black American and Dalit literature, which he called "Negro–Dalit sahitya". Many of them first appeared in *Asmitadarsh* in 1968. A collection of eighteen essays drawing on Waghmare's vast reading of Black literature was published in 1978.[53] Entitled *American*

Negro: Sahitya āni Sankruti (American Negro: Literature and Culture), it was produced by Lokvangmay Griha, a left-wing publishing house in Mumbai.⁵⁴ The book was edited and compiled by Narayan Surve, a well-known poet, who was then working for Lokvangmay Griha. On reading Waghmare's articles in *Asmitadarsh*, Surve offered to compile them.⁵⁵ The book won the Maharashtra State Award in 1983. It came with a preface by Narahar Kurundkar, a leading essayist of the era from Nanded. Kurundkar was a keen observer of caste and religion. His critical essay on Ambedkar's writing brought him a reputation in anti-caste circles.⁵⁶

In an early essay, "American Negro Vangmay: Prerana āni Pravrutti" (American Negro Literature: Motivation and Tendency), Waghmare surveyed Black literature for Dalit readers. Emphasizing its uniqueness, Waghmare argued that because Black people's experiences in America were different and distinct from the beginning, it was natural that those differences and experiences would find their way into Black literature. Even though it was "othered", Black literature won an independent place in American literary culture.⁵⁷ This literature was established and shaped by the descendants of enslaved people who had been uprooted from their motherland and distanced from their culture and religion; it was driven by their quest to uncover their racial history, culture and pride. Through literature Black writers sought to develop new ways of expressing sensibilities, inspirations and attitudes because they wanted to create a new image of themselves.

In his study Waghmare considered the changing landscape of American racial politics and, thereby, literature's poignant role in offering a historical interpretation of the American condition. He describes the post-1920 phase as *prakhar* (intense), leading to the establishment of a new Black literature, also known as the Harlem Renaissance. Among the pioneers of this movement were Claude McKay, Countee Cullen and Langston Hughes. During this phase, three prominent writers gained international attention: Richard Wright, Ralph Ellison and James Baldwin, the latter two being the subject of Waghmare's doctoral thesis submitted to the Dr Babasaheb Ambedkar Marathwada University, Aurangabad. Wright was important because he abandoned earlier forms of writing that Waghmare believed were lacking in "abundance, diversity and depth", the outcome of the historical mischief perpetrated by white Americans who "cut the wings of Blacks, which limited their flight to explore various horizons".[58]

Wright's novel *Native Son* (1940) was, according to Waghmare, responsible for changing American culture. "*Native Son* brought an earthquake to each American, making Wright America's celebrated Dostoevsky," Waghmare added.[59] It inspired the current and next generations of authors—above all, Ralph Ellison, James Baldwin and Zora Neale Hurston—to take up their responsibilities as Black writers. These three were to become leading lights in the protest literature that later emerged in the United States. Waghmare called this a "crescent period" because it was "as short and sweet as a crescent that trails in the dark sky with its silver curve, symbolizing tranquillity of mind".[60]

Waghmare communicated to his Marathi readers how effective literature can be in changing society and influencing culture. Through his citations of African American writers, Waghmare alerted the Dalit community to the need to come to terms with the significance of literature and the extraordinary power of public opinion in bringing about change. Literature was not only a matter of entertainment or leisure but a vector of change at every level of society. However, unlike Black literature, which only became radical over time, Dalit literature emerged at its source as radical because it took the radical Dr Ambedkar as its model and ideal.[61]

Waghmare brought African American life into the Dalit consciousness. Much like his mentor, M.N. Wankhede, he engaged with Black literature as a corpus of writing that had significance for the Indian Dalit community. And, like Wankhede's, his understanding of Black life in America was conveyed through a sensitive and thoughtful reading of Black literature. There were no hyperbolic claims, neither did he indulge in mindless emotionalism. The painful stories and searing life narratives of Black people, including slaves, were presented to the Dalit audience as analogous to their own condition. By conveying the appalling conditions of enslaved people's existence in a simple yet effective way, Waghmare enabled his Marathi audience to relate to the Black experience and to Black writing.

Having described the hellish experiences of slaves, Waghmare presented the history and progress of the Black community through their determination to fight back against oppression. This is how they came to dominate fields such as sports, entertainment and literature. Throughout his analysis, Waghmare maintained a focus on America as a hegemonic oppressor of Black people. He offered a political critique of the system in which Black people were engaged in struggle, juxtaposing the idea of the American Dream with Malcolm X's depiction of the American nightmare.[62]

Waghmare examined America's political dynamics, arguing that the country had a particular interest in exploring its identity. He observed that no other nation or people could compare with America in its enormous concern, even obsession, with national identity.[63] In contrast to India, he believed American diversity, with its settler immigrant population, had given rise to an identity-based society. Uprooting from one culture and region had influenced how Americans perceived themselves. On the other hand, Waghmare saw Indians in general as native groups, despite their mobility and movement across the vast subcontinent.

The American experience was marked by a sense of isolation and unfamiliarity, leading to an identity crisis, as people's identities were almost lost because of mobility, harsh working conditions, and a long period of exclusion.[64] Consequently, the objective became to seek a new identity and invest in the future rather than in the complicated past. All European peasant immigrants had had to assume a new identity as Americans for them to be accepted and noticed.[65] However, America was incomplete without the partnership of the Black population, who were forcibly transported there to work on the plantations in the early modern era. Slavery gave rise to an economy of exploitation and degradation, which remained the cornerstone of American civilization and history.[66]

Dalit and Black literature: a critique

Much of the Dalit interest in Black literature was focused on the issue of caste. In his essay "Negro Vangmay āni Dalit Chalwal " (Negro Literature and the Dalit Movement), Waghmare compared Dalit and Black communities in India and the United States respectively. He observed that, unlike the Black community of America, Dalits were born in India and had firm roots in their motherland. Yet despite this, Dalits couldn't become owners of their land or rulers of their own society. "Even being the inheritor of this country, the [Dalit] couldn't own the inheritance."[67] Waghmare drew an analogy between slavery and the *varna* system; like the former, the latter created a "peculiar institution", that of caste.[68] But Waghmare incorrectly believed that race was a natural division while caste was man-made; a theory refuted by Ambedkar and many social scientists of the twentieth century.[69] Race, like caste, is man-made; both are inflexible formations.

Waghmare identified the broader structural similarities between the Black and Dalit conditions. Both Dalits and African Americans occupy the lowest rungs in the hierarchy of their society. Just as Black Americans are segregated in ghettoes, so are Dalits in caste ghettoes. This separation from mainstream society brought "self-hatred and self-loathing". To retain this unequal structure, the whites of America used myths and stories from the Bible to legitimize their actions, just as the Hindus used the Vedas and the Laws of Manu.[70] In short, Dalit and Black writers portray their situations to the world from their unique perspectives, which can be viewed comparatively. Both sets of writers are in search of a shared reality. Their literary experiences derive from societies built on inequality. Black and Dalit authors write from a perspective of life imbued with social responsibilities, calling for cultural revolt.[71]

Every social movement requires a manifesto for its agenda of liberation. Waghmare argued that the presidential address given to the Maharashtra Bouddha Sahitya Sammelan at Mahad in 1971 could be taken as a manifesto for the Dalit movement. According to the address,

> Dalit literature is not revengeful. It doesn't spread hatred. Dalit literature places importance on human being and advocates for freedom. This is a historical position; thus it assumes a different name. The poetry composed by Dalits or Americans is a poetry first, its pros and cons can be discussed later.

To the charge of standing apart and emphasizing a separate identity from the rest of society, Dalit writers hit back by arguing: "You are the reason for the separation in Indian literature and country."[72] The "you" here is used interchangeably with the nation-state and those in charge of government.

In his preface to Waghmare's book, Kurundkar argued that the influence of Black–Dalit comparison would help introduce

Black life to India, which in turn would help Marathi literature in acquiring shape. This meant that the apathy that had grown up towards Dalit resistance and literature would now receive a welcome antidote because of Black literature's influence among Marathi readers. This argument is important to consider, especially as Dalit life and culture were looked down upon and despised. A foreign perspective would help the Dalit voice to be heard. Through the narrative of Black victims, the Dalit victims would be recognized. However, the danger here is that Dalit humanity may be taken to exist only in tandem with someone else's: Dalits cannot exist as independent thinking and feeling beings. And one can only come to terms with complicity in their sufferings through the figure of an outsider, a white oppressor, but not a Hindu tormentor who identifies with caste as a personality of its own. Even today, Dalits have to resort to adducing Black Lives Matter or borrowing the Black Lives Matter discourse in order to make themselves heard and understood.

Dalit as a second-hand victim

Dalit perspectives often go unrecognized; in other words, they aren't acknowledged or accorded the dignity of human beings. Their suffering doesn't prompt people to reflect on their situation, let alone engage with them. This indifference might change if the oppressor is shown similar actions causing harm to people in a different context. This is where Black American literature can help the Dalit cause. The oppressor castes cannot empathize with the Dalits' condition because they reject their victimhood and do not see them as capable of feeling pain. They believe that any claims of injustice by Dalits are merely pretensions. Given this, conveying a rational Dalit viewpoint is nearly impossible. Hence, showing a mirror by indirectly referring to similar injustices in another society can promote self-reflection—the sign of a mature mind. To restore Dalit humanity, oppressors need to become aware of their own inhumanity. Directly confronting them usually doesn't work since it is common to ignore Dalit discourse in caste-based India. However, exposing a cruel system in another society might help the oppressors realize their role in dehumanizing their fellow citizens.

All the same, there is ample evidence that even after reaching an understanding of oppression in other societies, the oppressor caste does not adopt a critical view of themselves. Instead, it conjures up a fantasy image and calls it anything but Brahmanism. That is how there can be diverse ideologies that fight oppression without criticizing brahmanical supremacy and violence. The Gandhian approach, for its part, patronized people in a demeaning way without realizing the violence it perpetrated upon the victims. For their part, communist and left discourse, although intended to create a revolution, assumed the Dalits formed a class of peasants, thereby neglecting the intersections of caste and class.

Class privilege can be ascribed or acquired, but caste cannot be when the system and society are committed to recognizing castes in rites, rituals and normative affairs. In the same vein, the liberal middle class, though firm believers in the power and efficacy of capitalist expansion, do not see themselves as responsible for the exploitation of poor and working people, but instead look to communalism and secularism as ways of securing the protection of the vulnerable. In none of these various ideologies and systems of thought and belief do the oppressors see themselves as answerable for Dalit victimization. Unsurprisingly, these diverse ideologies do agree in their non-recognition of the Dalit body politic. For them, a Dalit cannot exist as an independent category premised on his or her caste experience. They have to embrace their victimhood through paradigms unrelated to Dalit being.

That is why Dalits were made to put on the mask of poor, rural, illiterate and destitute peasants or workers to satisfy the assumptions of the oppressor castes. They were identified and judged in terms of the artificial categories devised by the entire gamut of academia, media, public scholarship, policy interventions, school education, NGOs and international think tanks. As a result, the articulation of a clear Dalit voice would be caricatured as "radical". Announcing one's identity without reference to the categories imposed by others became an act of rebellion. For Dalits to acknowledge their Dalitness is a call to revisit the improper, nostrum history manipulated and falsely told by the oppressor posing as saviour.

Similarly, by exploring their identities Dalits challenge the unclear definitions imposed upon them. Thus, what it means to be a Dalit remains unresolved and is still evolving. The question arises: can Dalits assert their humanity without relying on another victim's narrative—such as that of the Black American? Must we always view Dalits through the lens of the Black struggle for humanity? Or should Dalits reject any projections of their co-dependency on others, whether Black Americans or an internationalist movement, and simply articulate their own case with confidence and style? Will this assertion require the use of Western terminology to satisfy the editorial standards of Global North gatekeepers in funding agencies or academic departments? These questions are raised by those deeply affected by caste experiences.

The notion of Dalit modernity can be analysed in two ways: through a serious examination of the past and by utilizing modern tools to secure a place for them in the future. The influence of the Dalit Panthers, as discussed in the previous chapter, is still present because, even though the Dalit Panthers have disbanded, they have created surrogates. Many Dalit Panther organizations were formed in the past, and some continue to emerge to public recognition. Much of the Republican movement has been carried on by its successors through the Panther project. Therefore, we cannot consider the Dalit Panthers as just a moment, but as a movement. It has been navigating a tortuous path, desperately trying to find a space in the caste politics of India.

Viewing Dalits solely through the Black lens places undue responsibility on the already victimized Black person. For the most part, the Black body is recognized when it is criminalized or stereotyped, and in this way Black oppression is perpetuated. Thus, for Dalit humanity to be acknowledged, it often relies on Black death as a way of recognition. New efforts need to be made to change this fatal possibility and break the chain of oppression. One way of doing so is by returning to the roots of both Dalit and Black humanity in the past, so as to reimagine and reconstruct new images for the future.

The World Marathi Literary Conference

An important moment in the history of Dalit literature occurred when Gangadhar Pantawane was elected president of the First World Marathi Literary Conference held in San Jose, California, from 14 to 16 February 2009. This moment marked the culmination of a long-standing dialogue between the Black American and Dalit literary worlds, which formally began in 1869 in America with Charles Sumner's famous speech on caste (though we find references to caste in America dating back to the eighteenth century),[73] reciprocated by Jyotirao Phule with his book on slavery in 1873,[74] and which was amplified by Ambedkar's comparative studies in the first half of the twentieth century.[75] Only someone of Pantawane's stature could have presided over such a historic occasion of shared solidarity, for his entire career had been invested in advancing such notions of international dialogue.

In his presidential address, Pantawane sailed through the ocean of literature, demonstrating his mastery of the Marathi canon. He expressed admiration for the capaciousness of Marathi literature and its rejection of Vedic values by quoting poets, saints and writers of the Bhakti era, especially those of the tenth to thirteenth century, as well as modernist writers. In his twenty-eight-page-long address, Pantawane touched on many topics, including Black literature. He had long been observing developments in that field closely, especially through his journal *Asmitadarsh*. Almost everyone working in the field of Marathi and especially Dalit literature was familiar with the "Negro Sahitya".

Pantawane attributed the emergence of Dalit literature not to Black or Marxist thought but to *Ambedkarwad* (Ambedkarism), because "Ambedkarism is Indian. It is self-enlightened and innovative. Ambedkarism anticipates a bondage-free humanity and society."[76] Pantawane went on to define and theorize Dalit literature. "Dalit literature is a literature of self-discovery ... it rejects the dominant castes. It analyses the condition and finally attempts a self-disclosure." As a result, Dalit literature "interprets society in newer forms. It rejects cultural terrorism to promote human equality, social justice and liberty. This is the positivity of rebellion. It belongs to India's land, Indian life, and thus belongs to the transformational culture of India."[77] It is noteworthy that Pantawane emphasized the originality of Indianness in drawing upon Dalit thought. He forcefully attempted to recover the Dalit in the world of words. "Those who were denied humanity, once they found words, made the words appear as rebellion."[78]

In his survey of Indian literature Pantawane was adroit in paying attention to the voices of Dalit writers and poets from non-Marathi regions. Thereafter he directed his attention to global literature, for it was important for Marathi writers to develop a world view. Pantawane then turned to the work of African American intellectuals, especially W.E.B. Du Bois, spending some time talking about Du Bois's work and literature. He recognized Du Bois as a "heroic, courageous seer" and Black intellectual who started the "Niagara movement that created an abode of intellectualism amongst the youth". Du Bois, Pantawane further added, "went to the intimate depths [of his people] and psychoanalyzed them".[79] Donning the hat of literary critic, Pantawane recognized Du Bois's *The Souls of Black Folk* as a source of inspiration in terms of its "ideas, language and literature". This was a pioneering piece of literature that paved the way for others to follow. It provided a new consciousness by shaping the nature of thought and enlightenment. "This transformational literature was different from the American literature." Through literature, Pantawane assured his listeners, Black people achieved new dreams with self-confidence, a confidence that came from the rejection of their inferiority. He wanted his audience to keep that strain of politics in mind, as we shall see.

The source of this inferiority came from the literature and history written by whites. That is why Du Bois is the anchor of Pantawane's interest. Pantawane echoed Du Bois in counselling his people not to rely on history written by whites. He interpreted Du Boisian ideas for his Marathi readers in the United States as well as back home in India. "The whites have written our distorted history. They made us feel inferior and uncultured. They kept us away from the mainstream."[80] By invoking this theme of inferiority and distortion, Pantawane was gesturing to his condition as a Dalit, one who was trying to break the mould of his image shaped by the dominant castes of his own society.

Pantawane then quoted Langston Hughes's 1926 essay "The Negro Artist and the Racial Mountain" on protecting and preserving the Black soul from the impositions of whites.

> We younger Negro artists who create now intend to express our individual dark-skinned selves without fear or shame. If white people

are pleased, we are glad. If they are not, it doesn't matter. We know we are beautiful. And ugly too. The tom-tom cries and the tom-tom laughs. If colored people are pleased, we are. If they are not, their displeasure doesn't matter either. We build our temples for tomorrow, strong as we know how, and we stand on top of the mountain, free within ourselves.[81]

This essay is especially poignant because in it Hughes pushes back against Black inferiority and Black impersonation of the white world. He said he felt sorry for a Black poet who once told him that he wanted to be "a poet—not a Negro poet". Hughes took this as the poet's desire to abandon Blackness and embrace the white world: in short, "I would like to be white."[82]

It is significant that Pantawane chose Hughes and especially this essay, which affirmed a strong Black character. Hughes laments that middle-class Black people snubbed the art produced by Black people, as part of an attempt among an emerging elite in the 1920s to whiten their souls. The responsibility, Hughes suggests, lies with younger artists: they should convey and instil pride. "Why should I want to be white? I am a Negro—and beautiful."[83]

In this profoundly compassionate account of how to write and embrace yourself, written almost in anguish, Hughes draws impressive analogies to bring home his point. Hughes is "ashamed" of the poets, artists and academics who run away from their unique position and role. There is no doubt that Pantawane, Hughes's equivalent in the Dalit literary sphere in terms of guidance and editorship, wanted to tell his pupils and colleagues to embrace what was theirs—their self.

In his admiration for the Black world, Pantawane captured the beauty of Black people and their writing. "Black literature has made the world great." As a departing thought, Pantawane theorized beauty and its importance. "Beauty is like a flower of the mind. Beauty is expressed through various emotions, ideas, mental transformation." This idea of beauty is not merely poetic and metaphorical, but is meant to serve a purpose—whether large or small. Beauty, after all, is a rebellion. It is a declaration of owning oneself, all the while celebrating the people of whom one is part. In addition to Hughes, Pantawane acknowledged the works of Richard Wright, Ralph Ellison, James Baldwin, LeRoi Jones (Amiri Baraka), Alex Hayley and Eldridge Cleaver. His editorial work at *Asmitadarsh* came in handy in combing through the diverse literature from America.

Transformation is another theme that dominated Pantawane's speech. He observed, "Social justice and equality are the two eyes of transformation."[84] Transformation from social oppression and material conditions was the purpose of revolutionary culture. Pantawane argued that the idea of transformation needs to take root in society so that it becomes part of individual life.[85] To achieve this in its own world, Dalit literature needed to take a leading role.

Theorizing solidarities

The purpose of solidarity is to support the cause it aligns with. It is based on shared goals, even if the groups involved don't communicate with or know each other. What drives the solidarity agenda is the desire to end oppression and create a better world. Solidarity shows appreciation for others and involves taking risks by sharing burdens. It is a voluntary act that speaks out against collective oppression. Those showing solidarity may feel powerless, but through their actions they reclaim power and a role in the process.

While Dalit intellectuals created a space for ontological mapping through literary expression, there were also many avenues they couldn't explore. This was partly due to the restrictions on their expression and their radical reinvention of self. Language and cultural barriers played a role here, but they weren't the only reason. Many global solidarity movements were not well led or directed. Staying true to the purpose of literature, many writers engaged in critical self-reflection. This paved the way for the emergence of groups of creative writers and thinkers who were sometimes hostile and antagonistic to each other. While this meant the development of vibrant, colourful schools of thought that experimented with diverse ideas and interpretations, it didn't translate into informing the outer publics, beyond the boundaries of the Dalit world.

What would it mean to bring Dalits and Black people together to communicate with each other? The first task at hand is to define solidarity and then theorize its existence. Solidarity in the Dalit–Black context involves, first of all, clarifying their conditions in relation to each other as well as independently. After recognizing their independence as a temporary state, the oppressed must identify their enemies. Exposing these enemies is a process of celebration, reducing burdens and providing relief by showing up those who have warned their subjects not to declare their identity. Once familiarity with each other is established through the exposure of individual enemies, the next task is to find the connection between these separated yet closely linked enemies and their sources of action through the intimacy of capital, networks and the geographical necessity of being in transit.

The enemies of the oppressed in the current unequal world order are those collaborators who create new policies for global control. They do not target single subjects but extend their control in all directions to diverse others. As a result, caste oppression is no longer geographically isolated. The oppressors in the diaspora have established a template for control and rule. They have expanded their dominion to uncharted territories with similar conditions. For the oppressors, land, tribe, law, nation, hierarchy, capitalism and culture are universal sources of control. Traditional institutions that have regulated societies worldwide now face new oppressors, not necessarily with identical colonial faces or names. While the nature of oppression has remained the same, its shape and identity have changed. The universalized brahmans and Baniyas from India and their counterparts in other regions are now united in advancing their global caste project.

In the present day whites as an oppressor subject in various Western societies have selected candidates from diversity quotas to create a multiracial front to advance their agenda of strengthening the empire. The American empire is devoted to maintaining its racial-caste capital order under the pretence of creating equity for its own people, but at the expense of its own people. In simple terms, it cherry-picks a few individuals from the same socio-racial group that it plans to target with its abusive politics and policies.

Once the deceitful nature of these oppressive structures is known and their disguised locations are exposed, it becomes the responsibility of the oppressed to reveal and highlight them, making their disguise and hidden nature intolerable for the oppressors. The oppressed have an opportunity to communicate with each other to uncover the secrets of their oppressors, who have managed to evade accountability and responsibility by pretending to be non-partisan and even-handed.

As in the imperial era, when the oppressor white caste was challenged by non-white and poor white groups, there is an urgent need in the present era to dismantle ruling regimes. In forming Dalit–Black solidarity, it is crucial to recognize early on that it is engaged in a twin struggle—both local and global. It is an interconnected story in today's world. Therefore, critiquing the local landlords who have boycotted the Dalit communities in Pimpalgaon, Nanded, also involves articulating this within an international human rights framework, appealing to the protection of international conventions. Similarly, the response to the murder of George Floyd should involve an appeal to the world to recognize the dehumanization of oppressed communities worldwide who also struggle to breathe.

Solidarity is thus multi-caste, multi-colour, international, cross-cultural and even interspecies. The conduct of twenty-first-century solidarity must be directed at altering power relations in the process of negotiating the identities of various oppressed groups worldwide.[86] Such informed global projects are ethical instruments to guide the political ideas of nations. They serve to counter suspicions of having to engage in politics and compromise with corruption in the state. This pragmatic response is necessary so as to deal with the various dimensions of state functioning that keep the lower castes in a state of perpetual victimhood. That is why solidarity as a moral project involving state capacity can contribute significantly to constructing a new nation. What is new is the cause of universal justice and support for the vulnerable. The official stance of South Africa towards Israel's occupation of Palestine is one such example, though an imperfect one. However, this state-centred solidarity is directed at another state. What happens to the future of solidarity between the subordinated nations of Dalit and Black peoples? They become part of a class trying to negotiate ownership of their bodies and their value.

Fighting against the structure rather than the state

The literary sphere of Dalit activism was a deeply collaborative effort. It drew on various genres and invited scholars, writers, poets and performers to share and co-develop a repertoire of knowledge and make it available to the general public. The practitioners of Dalit letters and social change did not limit participation to a few castes but opened the field to many who could find a purpose in it. That is how non-Dalits also made the fight against caste their goal and purpose. The Dalit literary tradition has been active since the nineteenth century. With the print media as an entry point, it succeeded in capturing the attention of the state and the ruling class. Its aim can be broadly defined as threefold. The first was to produce original writings for the Dalit publics; the second was to characterize the state as an oppressive, casteist order; and the third was to form a political consensus on Dalit liberation and anti-caste practice.

The Dalit Panther movement was not just a literary response but a political one as well. Its approach was located in Ambedkarian practice. It did not take a strong, militant position against the state but held the elected government primarily responsible for the pitiable condition of the Dalits. Their assault on brahmanical cultural nationalism was forthright and so intense that it united many fragmented lower-caste groups who had been victims of majoritarian nationalism. By not identifying the state as a machine of oppression, the Dalit movement, through art, culture and protest, succeeded in attacking internalized structures that supported the hegemony of the state. They realized the ineffectiveness of an anti-state position, which would put them in the company of those wanting to wage war against the political state. On the whole, the Dalit literary movement did not give way to the leftist ideas of revolution and popular revolt, though a section remained committed to left ideas, bridging the gulf between these ideological camps

The Dalits, inspired by Ambedkar, looked at the state as an instrument to implement their ideas without destroying its edifices. One option was capturing political power through the ballot; another was protecting political and social rights guaranteed under the constitution by force of arms. But what the movement largely attempted to do was to restore faith in people's own ability, and not that of someone else, to bring about change through government. The state had been captured by brahmans, Baniyas, Thakurs and the capitalist class, who were working against the majority (Bahujan) of the population, and so the latter had to pull together if it was not to be permanently oppressed. By joining under a common political programme, social and cultural movements helped limit the dominance of brahmanical ideals and politics.

The most effective tools to carry out the programme of social and political justice were literature, art and activism. At the same time, these modes of Dalit expression worked to push their own politics and culture into the mainstream. These forms of articulation, which were otherwise condemned to marginalization, served to instil confidence among the working- and middle-class salaried Dalits to make a call for change. At the same time, these methods can be seen as those of an elite reposing faith in modernist virtues. Modernism argues for equality and rights.[87] Yet the Dalit programme of rebellion did not consider other methods of modernist pushback against power and colonization evident around the world in the past hundred years.

Conclusion

Largely through the networks of the Indian diaspora, Dalit literature and the anti-caste tradition reached beyond India to various parts of the world. During the twentieth century, the Dalit community acquired an anglophone champion who could communicate with the colonial state and the wider world in the person of Dr Ambedkar. Ambedkar wrote for an international audience, being aware of the broader support he needed for his cause. His strategic choice of working in the English language and his sensibility towards the Black struggle are evident in his citations of Black scholarship and writing in his texts.[88] This spirit was carried forward after his death, when his successors not only continued to draw directly from Black writing but also referred to it as part of their struggle for justice. The birth of the Dalit Panthers was an acknowledgement of the internationalism existing among Dalits.

However, this appreciation shown by Dalits for the Black literary culture was largely one-sided, as the Black cultural world especially after the 1960s remained mostly unaware of developments among Dalits. This had not always been the case. An earlier generation of Black intellectuals had paid attention to the Dalit movement. Prominent among them were W.E.B. Du Bois, Martin Luther King Jr. and George Schuyler. Among the next generation, the Black Panther Party and its members did acknowledge the existence of India's Dalit Panthers in their newspaper, the *Black Panther*.[89] But there was no active reciprocation or understanding of the cross-national, intercultural Dalit movement. As a result, the possibilities of sharing were limited. One major reason for this was the absence of a common language. The Dalits wrote in Marathi, Hindi, Tamil, Gujarati, Telugu, Kannada, Malayalam and Bengali. Their writings were not translated into English at the time and it took four decades before this began to happen.

One of the limitations of solidarities is that they rely on mutual understanding and shared beliefs, which need to be substantiated by sharing space and facilitating discussions. In the absence of state-sponsored support or the interest of private entities there was little possibility of cross-language dialogue between the Black American and Dalit movements. Solidifying narratives into a common agenda could have been mutually beneficial. But solidarities built on inspiration and affection last only in literary works and poetic imaginations.

3

RACE AND CASTE
IN THE AGE OF DALIT–BLACK LIVES MATTER

This chapter deals with the complexities of the Dalit and Black movements in India and the United States respectively, and the possibilities of their similarities and solidarities as framed in both academic literature and the popular media.[1] Though appealing, such a comparison exaggerates what both movements stood for. To begin with, the positions of the Dalit and Black movements, generally speaking, were divergent. In America, from the 1960s there were radical uprisings among the educated Black youth, who were unfair targets of police harassment and brutality. For the Dalits in India, whose status was that of a subordinate minority and untouchables, any demands they made for equality as enshrined in the Constitution were met with localized violence, either committed against individuals or the Dalit ghettoes. Dalit women were a particularly vulnerable target.

Through media coverage of Black atrocities in the United States, Dalits in India became aware of the situation faced by the descendants of slaves in white-ruled America. Reports in the American media made their way to the larger Indian cities such as Mumbai, where they were picked up by the Dalit literati, who read *Time* magazine, the *New York Times* and *Newsweek*, and discussed the reports with friends in literary circles drawn from diverse castes. What happened in America resonated with Dalits in India. They read of the American state going rogue against Black people in a spate of racial attacks. In one incident, which took place on a Wednesday evening in July 1967, two white police officers dragged a Black taxi driver, John William Smith, into their precinct building in the city of Newark, New Jersey. Smith, a taxi driver, had just been arrested for the alleged crime of improperly passing the officers' car, and was beaten so brutally that he could not walk. Residents of a nearby housing project saw him being dragged inside the precinct, and a rumour was set off that the cops had killed another Black man. A crowd formed and resorted to attacking the police station. For five days, violence tore through the city, with a toll of over two dozen lives. Some called it rioting, others a rebellion.

That was just one flashpoint in what came to be known as "the long, hot summer of 1967". The United States witnessed over 150 "race riots" that season, with police brutality against Black people a common spark, extending a long lineage of rage—Detroit in 1967, Hough in 1966, Watts in 1965, Harlem in 1964 and 1943, Chicago in 1935 and 1919, and so on. This has been termed a rebellion of the urban class of America, with 1967 the pivotal year.[2] The US president Lyndon B. Johnson, already battling public anger over the invasion of Vietnam and faced with a fresh crisis, formed a committee to answer three questions: "What happened? Why did it happen? What can be done to prevent it from happening again?"

The Kerner Commission, under the chairmanship of Gov. Otto Kerner Jr., was formed. As part of its work, it hired a group of social scientists to bolster its research. Their draft submission to the commission echoed the radical language and ideas of the rising Black Power movement, and came to some alarming conclusions. Under the present course, the researchers wrote, the United States was headed for a full-blown race war, involving "guerrilla warfare of Black youth against white power in the major cities of the United States."[3] It foretold civil war on the streets, which would turn American cities into "garrisons".[4] Gillon quotes David Ginsburg, the commission's executive director handpicked by President Johnson, to have buttressed the point about "white power, white racism and white repression" as representing the police system.[5]

The only way out of this impending war was a radical programme to tackle the poverty and socio-economic stagnation facing Black communities, to reform the police and other institutions that plainly discriminated against Black people, and to make drastic changes that went far beyond the "token concessions" offered to the community till then. "There is still time", the researchers added, "for one nation to make a concerted attack on the racism that persists in its midst." If it did not, "The harvest of racism will be the end of the American dream."[6] The document was entitled *The Harvest of Racism*.

This preliminary report did not give comfort to the Johnson administration. In reaction, the document, with "Destroy" scrawled on its front page, was consigned to oblivion, until it was discovered in an archive and published half a century later.[7] The social science researchers were all dismissed. Still, as the historian Julian E. Zelizer notes, much of the data they collected survived in the commission's final report and contributed to its findings. The commission's basic conclusion was this: "Our nation is moving toward two societies, one black, one white— separate and unequal."[8] The report rejected any notion that the riots were part of some grand conspiracy, and asserted that the people on the streets were just ordinary people tired of waiting meekly for change. It did not place much hope in Johnson's social programmes, as the president had hoped it would, or lament the crumbling of the "Negro family" in line with an earlier government study, the Moynihan Report.⁹ Instead, it located the causes of the riots in police violence, institutional exclusion, unemployment and segregation, and called for "a commitment to national action—compassionate, massive and sustained, backed by the resources of the most powerful and the richest nation on this earth". And while the causal factors were complex, "certain fundamental matters are clear. Of these, the most fundamental is the racial attitude and behavior of white Americans toward Black Americans. Race prejudice has shaped our history decisively; it now threatens to affect our future."

Although Johnson effectively disowned the report, he could not stop it from becoming public, which it did in March 1968. For many Black leaders, its frankness was astonishing. The civil rights activist Floyd McKissick thought it was a historic landmark: "It's the first time whites have said, 'We're racists.'" Martin Luther King Jr. described the acknowledgment of white racism as "an important confession of a harsh truth". King himself was assassinated the following month while Johnson was replaced in the White House by Richard Nixon. The new president would not hear of "national action" to curb racial discrimination and inequality. He instead talked up "law and order", of meeting "force with force", thereby pandering to white fears of increased Black assertion. Nixon's response to the Kerner Commission's report was that the report blamed everyone but the "perpetrators of the riots".¹⁰

Nixon's approach, with occasional exceptions, has survived for half a century. Though the Kerner report was a runaway bestseller when published, the country clearly did not take its message to heart. And generations later, with the police killings of Breonna Taylor and George Floyd in 2020 and a rebellion in the streets, the United States had to confront the same ugly truths.

Many today have begun to look back to 1967 and 1968 in an effort to make sense of the present, perhaps to wonder what might have been. There are parallels, and there are differences. One contrast stands out: the number of non-Black people standing up and speaking up to say that Black Lives Matter. Black people had allies across racial lines in the 1960s and earlier, but never on the scale seen in the summer of 2020. Today, Black people remain the main power behind the protests, but conspicuous alongside them in the streets as well as online are young white people, Hispanic people, South Asians, East Asians and many others—not to mention people from across genders, sexualities and religions. This diversity is testimony to the work of the activists who fought, especially through the years when so few were listening, to expand the American conscience.

This wide support nevertheless requires a critical view: many are not yet fully confident about white protesters' "performative solidarity". As the writer Stacey Patton has asked, "Are white people protesting because they are in honest solidarity—or because it helps to soothe their own conscience or assuage their guilt?"[11] Yet, whatever people's motives may be, the flood of public statements of support has been unprecedented. Across the United States, people—most often white people, of a certain liberal bent—are confessing that they have not done enough, and pledging that they will do better. Few will speak the bluntest truth, but its echoes are clear in what has been said. America—white America, where white people control power, wealth and the country—is racist.

Black lives beyond Black lives

The power and momentum of the Black Lives Matter movement has taken it far beyond the United States. Demonstrators were galvanized in Britain, Germany, Belgium, Australia and many other countries with racist pasts and presents. They came out on the streets to send strength to those marching in the United States but also, crucially, to press their own societies to settle historical accounts. The #BlackLivesMatter hashtag, if not the protests, arrived in India too—but here the movement barely prompted any self-examination at all.

Of the Bollywood stars who posted against racism, several had endorsed skin-lightening creams in the past. Of the media outlets that carried news of the protests, all except a very few did little to hold the police to account for their role in the anti-Muslim riots in Delhi just months before the George Floyd lynching, or to call out the ruling government of Narendra Modi for presiding over a spike in atrocities committed against the country's oppressed castes and ethnic and religious minorities. The Ministry of Home Affairs' National Crime Records Bureau data revealed that cases of atrocities against Dalits grew from 45,961 in 2019 to 50,900 in 2021.[12] Many of the global corporations that came out against racism have extensive operations in India, but none has ever taken a stand on behalf of the rights of Dalits. Nor have any of India's own corporations, which is unsurprising. It is no exaggeration to say that the case of George Floyd received more attention in India among the urban middle classes than any of the recent incidents in India's endless onslaught of caste crimes. In the state of Uttar Pradesh, a young Dalit, Vikas Kumar Jatav, was shot after he dared to pray at a village temple, and the Dalit politician Chhote Lal Diwakar and his son were shot after an argument over land. In both cases, the murderers were dominant-caste men. In Kerala, a young Dalit man had his hand hacked off by the brother of the dominant-caste girl he loved. Government records show that several hundreds of Dalits lose their lives to caste crimes every year.

Some commentators and social media users cared enough to point out this hypocrisy, and to ask the obvious question: when will India have its equivalent of a Black Lives Matter moment, a realization that Dalit lives matter, that Adivasi and Muslim lives matter, as well as the lives of all those pushed to the margins of Indian society? They pointed correctly to the symptoms, including caste, race and religious hatred. But when it came to placing responsibility where it really belongs, they missed the mark.

The tendency in this moment, as in many others, is to speak of India as a unitary society. Of course it is not, and the largest share of those writing, posting and reading about Black Lives Matter represent a very specific part of it. That part is fluent in English, digitally savvy, and well-versed in US politics to understand the issues at hand—a combination of characteristics almost wholly exclusive to the country's social and economic elite. And that elite is almost wholly drawn from a narrow set of "twice-born" *savarna* castes that form the three highest tiers of the four-tiered Hindu *varna* system—the brahmans, kshatriyas and vaishyas. These castes constitute a minority of the country's population, yet in all the institutions of social, cultural, political and economic power, they are the dominant majority. They are the people who run the country.

It was a strange sight for me, a Dalit—a person outcasted by society—to see the dominant castes decry "Indian" racism, casteism and religious prejudice. The country is not innocent of any of these things, but the problems, especially when it comes to these castes, are not so "Indian" after all.

Consider the example of the United States. It is easy to speak of racism as an American problem, but framing it this way obscures a more specific story. In the United States, racism is a white instrument that holds down Black people: what is involved here is a matter of colour castes. Colour castes draw on the power attached to the lineage of one's birth and to societal beliefs: one is born into an unbreakable, rigid caste structure.

In America, an individual's status is largely defined by two main factors: their birth into a certain caste rank and their class. This dual recognition becomes a means of determining a person's status. Often, those in the dominant caste do not appear to be the power-holders, as they conceal their presence through state structures and societal institutions. Conversely, oppressed castes are made visibly apparent, engaging constantly with the state either to demand their rights or claim their share in state operations. In this context, colour castes are regarded as organizing principles necessary for any normal society to function. This normalization downplays the significant influence caste has on society's mindset and functioning. Every significant shift in the history of American stratification, although imperfect and incomplete, has necessitated a change in white caste beliefs and behaviours, both voluntary and through state enforcement.

The nation, founded by men of the white caste, was never meant to be universally democratic and equal—the continuation of slavery was taken for granted. While Black people never needed to be convinced of the evils of slavery, white people did. The American Civil War was their moral reckoning with it. Even after slaves were freed, the white elite found ways to strip Black people of their rights, their intelligence and their character. Decades of Black activism forced white America to reconsider legalized segregation and secured the Civil Rights Act of 1964, which prohibited discrimination in terms of race, colour, religion, sex or national origin.[13] Yet the exclusion and marginalization of Black people continued. More than half a century since the Civil Rights Act, Black people remain in an economic stranglehold that maintains a yawning gap in wealth and opportunity between them and whites. Redlining policies pushed masses of Black people into ghettoes, and biased police officers and courts pack Black people into prison at a rate five times higher than for white people.[14] Black Lives Matter has forced another moment of truth upon the white-dominated country. This is why the movement holds real promise—though it is essential to remember Khalil Gibran Muhammad's caution that "Americans have short memories and long appetites when it comes to racism".

In India, sweeping talk of "Indian" prejudice advantageously shields the real architects of the social order from responsibility. The forces that give life to caste are apparent. The brahmanical-Hindu "holy" books, which enshrine the *varna* system, have been preserved, ameliorated and propagated for millennia by the brahmans, who exercise monopoly over the priesthood and vast power over social thought. The other dominant castes have surrendered their minds to brahmanical beliefs, and have joined the project of translating these into reality. While the equations between the dominant castes have seen various configurations over time, as have their relations with changing political rulers across historical periods, their collaboration in shaping the present state of affairs is indisputable.

Religious and social hatred is deeply enmeshed with caste belief. According to the rules of caste, all those not born into the *varnas* are subhuman, and their mere proximity or touch is a source of spiritual pollution. This explains the ostracization of many of the country's ethnically stratified minorities—most notably the indigenous Adivasis, who are ranked alongside Dalits in the brahmanical hierarchy. Huge numbers of Indian Muslims, Christians, Buddhists and Sikhs come from these outcaste groups, having converted to try to shake off the stigma they carry in Hindu eyes. But the dominant castes do not forget that stigma so easily, and brand them with an added mark for the supposed sin of abandoning the Hindu religion. Even in their new faiths, which espouse human equality in the eyes of God, Dalit and Adivasi converts find that a narrow elite, often converts from higher castes, continue to shun them.[15]

Colour comes into the picture too, even if skin tone does not set oppressors and oppressed as neatly apart in India as it does in the West. A common belief, though not always true, associates darker skin with lower caste. Slurs of caste and colour overlap and are paired together in Indians' vocabularies. Darker groups—South Indians, Siddis, Africans and others—face rampant discrimination.[16] Generally, people with the privilege to determine their treatment—police and government officials, landlords, employers—come from the dominant castes. So do those in the media, film, advertising and other cultural industries with the greatest power to shape physical and cosmetic ideals. While it can be argued that the local fetish for fair skin owes a good deal to the complexes left behind by colonial rule, this cannot be used to deflect attention from indigenous prejudice; varna literally translates as "colour-based hierarchy". The Indian elite make much of the fact that they have been subjected to racism by white people, whether in the past or the present, and on this basis claim solidarity with Black people. But, whether in India itself or in the Indian diaspora, this is the only form of discrimination they are willing to critique.

Casteism, colourism and religious hatred in India are brahmanical instruments of the dominant castes for holding down Dalits, Adivasis, Muslims, Christians and many others. The refusal by the dominant castes to acknowledge this is what keeps movements like Black Lives Matter from having any real impact here, and prevents any national introspection on how this society debases the lives of its oppressed ethnicities and castes and religious minorities.

The evil genius of the caste system lies in what Dr Ambedkar described as its "graded inequality".[17] The brahmanical order thrives on a seemingly infinite fragmentation of castes and subcastes, the position of each being dependent on its discrimination and violence against those it claims superiority over in the endless quest to defend and improve its rank. It is a near-perfect guarantor of hierarchy—self-enforcing, self-expanding and self-perpetuating, with a built-in mechanism against the unity of the oppressed. The system has survived for thousands of years without any major change to its essential structure. It is impervious to political revolutions and ideological challenges, and is able to transplant into new religions and lands.

If the elite castes ever care to confront religious hatred, racism and casteism, they will very likely have to find the political morality to attack the foundations of caste. The foundation stone itself, as Ambedkar pointed out, is the brahmanical Hindu religion, Hinduism, which is so centred on the *varna* system that it cannot survive without caste—or, put another way, the annihilation of caste would depend on the dismantling of the *shastras* (holy books) upon which Hinduism stands. To vainly wonder when Dalit, Muslim, Adivasi and so many other Indian lives will matter, while glossing over this reality, is an obfuscation of the Hindu religion and of Indian history.

India's caste-oppressed communities have taken inspiration from the anti-racism struggle in the United States for over a century, seeing parallels between the evils of caste and of race, yet dominant-caste thinkers have usually tried to undermine claims to solidarity and shared experience—with the notable exception of Vijay Prashad, who authored a few articles along these lines.[18] Before and since the creation of an independent India in 1947, the oppressed castes have repeatedly asked the dominant castes to recognize their plight, acknowledge their part in it, and redress the injustice. Yet at every step the dominant castes have refused them empathy and undermined their efforts at change. In the United States, in the wake of George Floyd's killing, Black people asked white people to hold themselves accountable, and they are being heard through institutions and organizations by the white power-brokers. In India, the

Dalits have been asking the same thing of the dominant castes for a long time. The response they get in return is dismissal or silence.

Dalit Panthers

There have been many theories and debates around the word Dalit. One camp argues against the use of the term while the other prefers to keep it. The argument for its non-use is that the term evokes a sense of inferiority and indicates people's lower-caste position. Since India has gained independence and abolished untouchability, we do not need to subscribe to the idea of a lower identity. Meanwhile, the other camp believes that Dalit identity is an existential one, which cannot be wished away by negating the term or by ignoring the experience it embodies.

Dalit, in its prevalent meaning, is a caste-specific term of assertion for those once called untouchables and now officially designated the Scheduled Castes. When it first emerged in Marathi in the 1920s, "Dalit"—literally, broken people—was reserved for the untouchable castes, but the word has taken on a wider meaning over time. Gopal Guru considers the conceptual ability of the term dalit (lowercase) as an ontological and material logical parallel to terms such as Buddhist, Bahujan, or subaltern. According to him, they are mutually co-constitutive as "they share the same positive utopia of creating a society free from coercion, exploitation and thus, dehumanization of people".[19] Anand Teltumbde has observed that Ambedkar "used 'Dalit' as a quasi-class term", which included "within its ambit the downtrodden and poor".[20] But Ambedkar often preferred other terms for the oppressed—underscoring the difference between touchables and untouchables. He at times used Depressed Classes—later, he disowned this term. Along with his colleague at the Round Table Conference, Rettamalai Srinivasan, he petitioned the government to replace the use of the term as it was "degrading and contemptuous". Instead, they proposed several options, such as "Non-caste Hindus", "Protestant Hindus" and "Nonconformist Hindus".[21] While the identity of untouchables underwent many changes bureaucratically, the term Depressed Classes remained in use. When Ambedkar started his political party, the All India Scheduled Caste Federation, it was also widely known and described by him and his partymen as the Dalit Federation. The term Dalit remained in circulation but did not create a pan-Indian movement until the 1970s, many years after Ambedkar's death, when the use and political gravity of the term Dalit suddenly took off.

Credit for this belongs to the Dalit Panthers, the radical anti-caste organization which was founded in Bombay in 1972, distantly inspired by the Black Panther Party in the United States. Their legacy, though largely ignored by mainstream Indian histories, is hugely relevant today, beginning with their definition of "Dalit". As defined in the Dalit Panthers' *Bhoomika* (position document), the term embraces not just the oppressed castes, but also the Adivasis, or Scheduled Tribes, and "the working people, the landless and poor peasants, women and all those who are being exploited politically, economically and in the name of religion".[22] Part of this definition is explained by the Panthers' avowal of socialism, but the acknowledgment of injustice based on gender and religious identity challenged the class-bound programmes typical of socialists and other leftists of the time.

Dhasal noted that he did not want the ostracized Dalit community to be further alienated. To bring that community to the mainstream he expanded the definition so it is inclusive of other vulnerable groups. However, the antagonistic forces" in the Dalit Panther pointed it to be an influence of communists.[23] This led to Dhasal's ousting which he pointed out to Naipaul during the interview with him.[24]

If seen from a political solidarity, the term Dalit was not different from Bahujan—the subalterned majority. It was analogous to the definition of the Black Consciousness movement in South Africa that adopted black as a non-white and emancipatory identity open to diverse races arrested in the suppression of the apartheid regime.[25]

The founders of the Dalit Panthers were ideologically divided. One group looked at the socialist camp with suspicion and discomfort, as they saw it as being close to the Maoist insurgent ideology of the Naxalites. They preferred to contemplate liberation through Buddhism, as proposed by Ambedkar.[26] Yet the *Bhoomika*, it has been argued, also bore signs of Naxal influences.[27] J.V. Pawar, one of the leaders and chroniclers of the Dalit Panthers, has said that the *Bhoomika* was issued by Dhasal without the approval of the Panthers' monthly meeting.[28] Scholars state it was written with the help of Anil Barve, a communist activist,[29] who was later ejected from his Dalit Panther group.[30] The *Bhoomika* largely adopts a left-oriented position on class oppression, caste discrimination, and the question of landless labourers. It also refers to the failure of the left parties after India's independence to capture political power in general elections.

As a relatively small group founded in reaction to caste-based violence and injustice, the Panthers centred their praxis and rhetoric on furthering oppressed-caste unity, organization and pride. The wider coalition suggested by this aim never eventuated under the Panthers' watch. Yet its foresight and importance remain undiminished.

According to the criteria of economic and political exploitation, the Panthers' understanding of "Dalit" also includes large numbers of the Adivasis, Minorities and shudras, the last-mentioned largely grouped under the Other Backward

Classes (OBCs), who form the last of the four tiers of the *varna* hierarchy. Shudras are looked down upon by the dominant castes and are confined to the middling ranks of society and power,[31] but are ranked above the Dalits and Adivasis, who are considered to belong to no *varna* at all. At least one government survey has put the OBC population at 40 per cent. By the official reckoning of the Mandal Commission, which in the early 1980s wrote a landmark report on the social condition of the OBCs, only a small minority of this highly stratified group belongs to "upper" shudra castes with significant wealth and power. The rest have little of either.[32]

Though the exact demographic weights of all these communities are debatable, there is every reason to think that Dalits, understood as the Panthers defined them, form more than three-quarters of the Indian people. The Mandal Commission estimated that the dominant castes account for barely more than 17 per cent of the population—roughly a sixth of the total. It is in this light that Indian society must be understood. The huge majority of castes and ethnic and religious minorities are held subordinate by a small religious and caste elite. In the United States, by contrast, Black people account for under a sixth of the population, and white people for almost three-quarters. There, the dominant majority is being made to acknowledge the wrongs done to the minority. In India, the dominant minority holds such disproportionate privilege that it can still comfortably ignore or turn away from the damage done to the oppressed majority.

The Panthers' definition of Dalit laid the groundwork for the political imagination necessary to challenge this state of affairs. Others would go on to prove the power of the oppressed majority in electoral terms—most notably the Dalit leader Kanshi Ram. After first organizing the Dalit Shoshit Samaj Sangharsh Samiti—the Dalit and exploited people's struggle committee—in 1984, Kanshi Ram founded the Bahujan Samaj Party (BSP).[33]

This meant an expansion of the group he wanted to bring together, with strong overlaps with the Panthers' definition. The Bahujans—literally, the subalterned majority or the many—included not just the oppressed castes, but also Adivasis and converts to minority religions. By courting voters and alliances across these lines, the BSP has risen to power multiple times in Uttar Pradesh, and is expanding its strength and presence across the country.

The Dalit Panthers' pioneering efforts hold other lessons in political imagination and solidarity too. They imagined a fruitful connection between the Black American and Dalit struggles—even if, as throughout much of the last century and a half, that connection was never made material.

The precedent for this connection goes back to 1873, when Jyotirao Phule, the iconic shudra thinker and anti-caste reformer, wrote the book *Gulamgiri* (Slavery). In it, Phule attacked the scriptural bases of the *varna* system and described the condition of the oppressed castes as a kind of inherited slavery. He also weaponized the English language, understanding as he did its power to carry his message beyond the confines of India's vernacular tongues, where the dominant castes jealously policed ideas. *Gulamgiri* was published in Marathi, but to make sure its point was not lost to English speakers, the book carried an English translation of its full title—*Slavery, in the Civilised British Government under the Cloak of Brahmanism*—and an English dedication and preface. The dedication read:

> To the good people of the United States as a token of admiration for their sublime disinterested and self-sacrificing devotion in the cause of Negro Slavery; and with an earnest desire that my countrymen may take their noble example as their guide in the emancipation of their Sudra Brethren from the trammels of Brahman thraldom.[34]

Phule was writing less than a decade after the United States adopted the Thirteenth Amendment, which abolished slavery in 1865, and before the country's restored regime of racism could dampen his admiration. Still, the spectacle of legislative action against an abhorrent and pervasive system of inequality was a legitimate cause for wonder in a land where the caste order flourished without hindrance. When India got its chance after independence in 1947, it passed a constitutional ban on the practice of untouchability but never outlawed caste itself.

Phule had no open avenues of communication with the United States, and could only draw inspiration from afar.[35] Ambedkar, born in 1891—the year after Phule's death—got to know the country more intimately, spending some of his student years in New York City. Decades later, after he had returned to India, Ambedkar exchanged letters with W.E.B. Du Bois, the towering Black intellectual and civil rights leader. "I have been a student of the Negro problem and have read your writing throughout," Ambedkar wrote by way of introduction. "There is so much similarity between the position of the Untouchables in India and the position of the Negroes in America that the study of the latter is not only natural but necessary." He asked Du Bois to share a copy of a petition submitted to the United Nations on behalf of Black Americans, since the "Untouchables of India are also thinking of following suit".[36] Du Bois obliged, and in a letter dated July 1946 he replied, "I have often heard of your name and work and of course have every sympathy with the Untouchables of India. I shall be glad to be of any service I can render if possible in the future."[37] This communiqué represents the meeting of two groups whose common fate was tied to their shared experiences. The interchange could not proceed further due to logistical and organizational limitations. As far as known records show, the correspondence between Ambedkar and Du

Bois ended there. But Dalits once again drew inspiration from the Black struggle with the emergence of the Dalit Panthers.

Ambedkar's death in 1956 left the Dalit cause adrift. As we saw in Chapter 2, many Dalit leaders were drawn into party politics, where they succumbed to infighting or were co-opted by the ruling establishment, most prominently in the form of the Indian National Congress.[38] Atrocities against the oppressed castes continued on a massive scale—rapes, murders, whippings, deliberate contamination of their water sources—without any political or official pushback. This was acknowledged by the Elayaperumal Committee, appointed to look into untouchability and the condition of the Scheduled Castes, in a report submitted to the government in 1970.[39] By 1972, continuing reports of the ostracization of Dalits and attacks against them—in one case, two Dalit women in a village in Maharashtra were stripped and beaten for attempting to drink from a well reserved for the dominant castes—were provoking violent outbursts among young urban Dalits, including against the existing Dalit leadership. As a result, the Dalit Panthers were formed in Bombay to try to channel popular anger towards real change. They were led by a bold group of Dalits including Raja Dhale, Namdeo Dhasal and J.V. Pawar. Pawar joined as a seasoned activist who had started working in the Republican Party of India as an assistant secretary of ward 29 in Kamathipura, Mumbai, in 1957. Being well educated, he was enlisted to take notes and write letters. But Dhale and Dhasal had created the literary marvel that was giving Dalits a bold and powerful voice that they desperately craved.[40]

There are some parallels here to the emergence of the Black Panthers. That organization was born, in 1966, out of a frustration with the limitations of the civil rights movement. The movement's non-violent activism had delivered the Civil Rights Act, but it seemed powerless in the face of the unrelenting economic inequality and racial violence that fuelled the riots in its aftermath. The Black Panthers made it clear that enough was enough, and proposed radically new methods of Black assertion.

Dalit-land, or Dalitsthan

The Dalit Panthers acknowledged their debt to this spirit of radicalism in the choice of their name, and also in adopting the American organization's symbol of a snarling black panther as their own. Of the eleven sections in the Dalit Panthers' *Bhoomika*, one was entitled "The relations between Dalits of the world and us". It was clear that the intention of the Dalit Panthers was to internationalize their agenda and connect with the rest of the world. It was not an insulated or overtly ideological position. They did not adhere to either communist or capitalist ideology. While the Cold War era often compelled movements to align with one or other ideology, the Dalit Panthers stood apart and crafted their own vision and defined their own enemies. The enemies were as follows: 1. Power, Wealth, Pride. 2. Landlords, capitalists, money-lenders, and their lackeys. 3. The political parties who uphold communal values, casteists, and the government who backs them.[41]

When Dalits saw the Black Panthers fighting for their rights in their own country, which professed democracy, the imagined kinship found meaning. In the *Bhoomika*, they wrote, "From the Black Panthers, Black Power emerged. The fire of the struggles has thrown out sparks into the country. We claim a close relationship with this struggle."[42] There were other similarities too: mass gatherings, fiery rhetoric, the broad goal of liberating oppressed people. Significantly, both groups responded to their governments' abject failure to stop the violence against their communities, and the same governments' frequent complicity in the attacks against them, by trying to take their defence into their own hands. The Dalit Panthers' founders even drew on some slivers of the same cultural heritage as the Black Panthers—Dhale translated numerous Black poets, including Langston Hughes and Robert Hayden, into Marathi.[43]

The Dalit Panthers claimed to draw inspiration from the third world: "Vietnam, Cambodia, Africa, etc. are our influences whom we look up to".[44] By imagining a global presence of Dalits outside India, the Dalit Panthers refused to be confined to a singular narrative of their experience. They also broadened their scope internationally so that solidarity groups could offer their support and attention.

In many ways, the Dalit Panthers and the Black Panthers were actually more different than they were alike. Where the Black Panthers were a political party—originally the Black Panther Party for Self-Defense—the Dalit Panthers were not. The Black Panthers aligned with Marxism-Leninism, while the Dalit Panthers were never wholly taken by or committed to any political ideology other than Ambedkarism. And while the Black Panthers had many formidable women in their leadership, such as Kathleen Cleaver and Angela Davis, the Dalit Panthers had none—a serious impediment to their politics and outreach.

Moreover, the Black Panthers were proponents of Black nationalism, while the Dalit Panthers had their own Dalit nationalism. But beyond the shared ideal of self-respect, Dalit nationalism took a very particular shape. Earlier, Ambedkar had proposed the establishment of separate settlements for Dalits where they could be free from dominant-caste oppression and own the land.[45] This was not a separatist project but was to be achieved within the framework of the Indian Constitution. When I spoke to J.V. Pawar, he told me that when the Dalit Panthers raised demands for a "Dalitsthan", they had in mind settlements along Ambedkar's lines, as a way to guarantee Dalits' economic and social development in pursuit of a casteless society.

The Black Panthers put great emphasis on social assistance—most famously through their scheme of free breakfasts for children. The Dalit Panthers, though a social organization, had nothing similar, and never obtained the resources or organizational scale required for such action. They had to confine themselves to changing hearts and minds and protesting against injustices without making the material conditions of Dalits their agenda.

Another stark difference lay in the origins of the violence and oppression the two suffered. In the United States, the Black community faced the direct state violence of the police upon the Black community. For Dalits and Dalit Panthers, on the other hand, the source of violence was extra-state actors, such as landlords and caste-dominant groups, though there were incidents of state violence in episodes of the Dalit movement's suppression.

When it came to self-defence, the Dalit Panthers put together some bands to resist dominant-caste violence, but these were typically loosely organized and barely armed. This could not compare with the uniformed organization and the almost military discipline that became synonymous with the Black Panthers, or the gun-carrying squads they sent out to deter police violence in Black neighbourhoods, exercising the right to bear arms under US law. However, the Dalit Panthers did have a defence minister and an armed unit.

Why did the Dalit Panthers not become full-scale militants like the Naxalites of India or Umkhonto we Sizwe of South Africa? For one thing, the Dalit Panthers did not seek to subvert the Indian state but to obtain rights for themselves within the existing state formation. Secondly, possessing unlicensed firearms is a crime in India. The Dalit Panthers had to fight the feudals and their subordinates in street-fighting mode. They could not take on the might of the state as an armed group, because they were localized and not pan-Indian, and most importantly because their ideological convictions lay in Ambedkarism, which promoted democratic participation in the state.

The differences between the Dalit Panthers and the Black Panthers are in fact not surprising. There was no real relationship between the groups, no two-way exchange. Each worked separately and independently, responding to the specific and divergent circumstances of India and the United States. Yet the Dalit Panthers, to a greater degree than Phule and Ambedkar before them, showed the potential the Black movement had to pollinate ideas and inspire action in the struggle against caste. There was possibly much more of this potential than was realized, but the time to explore it soon ran out. The Dalit Panthers were disbanded in 1977, undone by a mix of repression and the jealousies and ideological quarrels of their founders. Even in their brief heyday, they never gained a strong presence outside the state of Maharashtra, let alone internationally.[46]

For their part, the Black Panthers, repressed by the US government and rocked by internal schisms and violence, dissolved in 1982. They managed to establish some international chapters and develop ties with several foreign governments—the communist regimes in Cuba, China and North Korea, for instance—but paid little attention to India. Because the budding Dalit understanding of the resonance between the Dalit and Black struggles for dignity was not reflected in the Black Panthers' worldview, they had no reason to try to establish contact. Only on one occasion do we see the newsletter of the Black Panther Party, the *Black Panther*, "greeting" and acknowledging the work of the Dalit Panthers. This was in an article published on 11 May 1974, entitled "BPP Greets Dalit Panthers of India's Untouchables", which chiefly drew information from an article published in the *LA Times* on 29 April 1974. In it, the Black Panthers extended their revolutionary greetings and "profound love" to the struggle of the Dalit Panthers.[47] However, there remained clear differences and unestablished relationships between these two organizations.

Casteism in diplomacy

As with everything they did, for the Dalit Panthers to imagine common ground between Black people and the oppressed of India involved defiance of the Indian government. This was because the terms of international cooperation established by the brahmans of India's foreign policy after independence did not allow for any solidarity between the victims of racism and the victims of caste.

When Jawaharlal Nehru became the first prime minister of India, he also assumed the post of foreign minister and held on to it for the rest of his life, until 1964. For all of this time, his sister, Vijaya Lakshmi Pandit, led India's delegation to the United Nations.[48] Nehru and Pandit charted a diplomatic course based on neutrality towards both the United States and the Soviet Union, and put India at the forefront of the "non-aligned" countries—the so-called third world. India's main partners in this bloc came to include Ghana, Indonesia and Egypt—"key regional leaders in South Asia, the Middle East, and sub-Saharan Africa"—and its diplomacy was premised heavily on the unity of the formerly colonized and racially oppressed.[49] Nehru became the darling of the post-colonial world.[50]

The reality that vast numbers of Indians continued to live under caste oppression, their socio-economic position dictated by birth just as in any racist colonial regime, did not sit well with this project, and any discussion of it on the global stage was anathema to India's elite. For both domestic and international consumption, overwhelmingly dominant-caste officials, scholars and businessmen cultivated a romanticized picture of India where caste was not a problem—an act of subterfuge that continues today.[51] The petition to the United Nations that Ambedkar was considering when he wrote to Du Bois never materialized, but if it had, the Indian government would not have welcomed it. When Ambedkar resigned as the law minister in Nehru's cabinet in 1951, one of his complaints was that he had been frozen out of key cabinet committees, including the one on foreign policy.[52]

In the second half of the 1940s, India gained acclaim at the UN for leading the charge against South Africa as the country's system of segregation hardened into the policy of apartheid. India's specific complaint was the discrimination against South Africa's Indian-origin population, who were racially segregated and denied full citizenship, and not the similar subjugation of all non-white peoples in the country. In return, South Africa developed a habit of calling out caste-based violence and discrimination in India, which it described as racism in another form. India denied any comparison—setting a precedent it has stuck to furiously ever since. The inconvenient fact that Phule and Ambedkar had thought the comparison to be valid and relevant was disregarded.

In September 1949, before the UN General Assembly, India called for UN intervention in aid of Indian South Africans. Meanwhile, Ambedkar pointed out before the Indian parliament that the "tyranny and the constant and shameless resort to violence by Hindus" made the position of Dalits "far worse than the position of Indians in South Africa". He punctured India's grandstanding on racism: "South Africa is replicated in every Indian village."[53]

Despite diplomatic deadlock, India managed to pressure South Africa to enter preliminary talks on the issue. With the General Assembly still in session, B.N. Rau, India's permanent representative to the UN, approached his South African counterparts to propose a compromise, with the Indian government's permission. The South Africans reported the conversation to their government in an astonishing "private and secret" memorandum recently uncovered by the scholar Vineet Thakur.[54]

Rau, who had worked with Ambedkar to draft the Indian Constitution, lamented to the South Africans that "the feverish attempts in his country to destroy all caste inequalities were resulting in what in actual practice amounted to discrimination against the erstwhile ruling castes such as the brahmans, to which he belongs".[55] He added that the Indians who had moved to South Africa—primarily indentured labourers from the Dalit and shudra castes—"did not belong to the best type". He thought South Africa's treatment of them "might be fully justified and that in fact India would not mind discrimination against our local Indian community if only it was not based on racial lines". Rau proposed that South Africa offer citizenship to "a small number, say ten, of the cultured and best type of Indians"—likely from among the higher-status, non-labouring "passenger" Indians— "as a token to the world that the racial equality of Indians was recognized".[56] In effect, as Thakur has pointed out, India wanted a casteist solution to a racist problem. South Africa did not take this idea forward.

By the time of the Dalit Panthers, India had aligned itself firmly with the Soviet Union. This lay the ground for alliances against American imperialism—together with numerous African nations, for instance—but the framework also left no room for connections between anti-racist and anti-caste struggles. India was ready to admit to the problem of mass poverty, but not to the problems of caste discrimination. In the world of Indian diplomacy, Dalits as an oppressed category were not supposed to exist. The Panthers dared to think internationally anyway, connecting themselves with a larger struggle for universal human dignity even while they fought localized oppression. In their *Bhoomika*, they claimed membership of "the Third Dalit World, that is, oppressed nations".[57]

Other Dalits have since tried to do what Ambedkar and the Panthers never achieved—to bring the issue of caste to international attention and connect it to global anti-racism struggles. In 1965, the UN adopted the International Convention on the Elimination of All Forms of Racial Discrimination. India signed and ratified the document, which defined racial discrimination as "distinction, exclusion, restriction or preference based on race, colour, descent, or national or ethnic origin which has the purpose or effect of nullifying or impairing ... human rights and fundamental freedoms in the political, economic, social, cultural or any other field of public life". But the treatment of India's caste-oppressed groups was not considered to fall under this definition. Dalit activists objected, and several of them put their views across to UN bodies in the following years—E.V. Chinnaiah in 1968, Laxmi Berwa in 1982 and Bhagwan Das in 1983. After decades of lobbying, the UN finally acknowledged the oppression of Dalits and Adivasis in 1996, when the Committee on the Elimination of Racial Discrimination (CERD) accepted that the conditions of the Scheduled Castes and Scheduled Tribes fell within the scope of the convention. The Indian government continued to protest against this.

In 2001, in Durban, the UN convened the World Conference Against Racism, Racial Discrimination, Xenophobia and Related Intolerance. Its goal was to identify and recognize forms of discrimination so far excluded from the ambit of the UN's work, especially those based on criteria that did not fit within Western notions of colour and race. A large contingent of Dalit leaders and intellectuals headed to Durban to insist on the recognition of casteism alongside racism, and to challenge the Indian government's downplaying of caste discrimination before the world.

The Indian government stayed true to form. Before the conference, its foreign minister, Jaswant Singh, said that caste-based discrimination was "not a matter for any international initiative or intervention". Omar Abdullah, a minister of state in Singh's ministry, declared, "You cannot equate casteism with racism."[58] The official delegation to Durban—led by India's attorney general, Soli Sorabjee—stuck to these points through the bitter feuding that followed at the conference, and opposed any mention of caste in its programme.[59] Between Singh as a dominant-caste Hindu, Abdullah as a Kashmiri Muslim of brahman ancestry, and Sorabjee as a member of Mumbai's Parsi religious minority, none of those shaping the official Indian position came from Dalit backgrounds. The final declaration and plan of action agreed by the conference made no reference to caste-based discrimination.

Even so, in the following year, the CERD in its general recommendations on article 1 of the Convention, "strongly" reaffirmed that "discrimination based on 'descent' includes discrimination against members of communities based on forms of social stratification such as caste and analogous systems of inherited status".[60] It made it clear that such discrimination violated the 1965 Convention.

There have been voluminous debates on the similarities and differences between race and caste. The two are not exactly alike, but they share one overriding similarity: both form the foundations of systems of discrimination, propped up by socially constructed notions of unequal human worth, in which the targets of prejudice are selected on the basis of biological descent. As the National Campaign for Dalit Human Rights noted after the Durban conference, "Whether or not caste is the same as race, the reality is that caste is a basis for discrimination on par with racism and apartheid and severely reducing the quality of life for at least 160 million of India's own citizens." The crucial choice was either to foreground these similarities and commit to global and local action to eradicate both these notions, or to fix on the differences as a distraction and so shield casteism from the same scrutiny and censure as racism.

The Indian government, just like countless dominant-caste leaders and thinkers, prefers the second option. In a submission to the UN Special Rapporteur on Contemporary Forms of Racism in 1997, the government wrote, "There is ample evidence of persons belonging to different castes having the same racial characteristics ... Persons who belong to the Scheduled Caste communities are today considered different from others because of their social, economic and educational backwardness, not because they belong to a separate 'race'."[61] What went unsaid is that one's social position is predetermined by the caste one is born into, and caste identity then dictates the degree of access one has to educational and economic opportunity. The *varna* system does not allow for any caste mobility—a person is meant to die in the same social rank they were born in, no matter what they achieve in life, akin to the caste experience of Black people in the United States.

The government also stated that caste "has its origins in the functional division of Indian society". It did not say that this so-called "functional division" forces the oppressed castes, as part of their supposed spiritual duty, to provide manual labour to the dominant castes and perform the most degrading tasks—such as cleaning human excreta with their bare hands.

In 2007, an official Indian delegation met with the CERD to again press the case that caste discrimination does not fall under the 1965 UN Convention. The delegation included the sociologist Dipankar Gupta, who presented academic arguments for why caste discrimination is not racial discrimination. The scholar Balmurli Natarajan later deftly punctured these arguments in the magazine *Seminar*. Natarajan noted that by "framing the discussion as 'caste is not race'", Gupta had constructed a straw-man argument.[62] When it came to the real question—"How similar are the discriminations based upon caste and race?"— Gupta had nothing to say. Gupta's claims included the absurdities that "caste is not about descent" and that "each caste equally discriminated against other castes". As Natarajan wrote, "While it is quite feasible to argue that in a casteist (or racist) society, everyone can be prejudiced, it is simply not true that everyone's prejudice has equal impact. Would Professor Gupta equate the daily humiliations, lynching, and rapes of Dalits by all castes who wield power over them, with the presumed prejudice that Dalits might hold against other castes?"[63]

In 2009, the UN held a conference to review progress towards the goals agreed on in Durban. A statement by several Dalit and human rights groups noted that even if caste had been excluded from the Durban Declaration, the CERD's subsequent affirmation that discrimination based on descent included caste-based discrimination meant that it qualified for scrutiny at the review conference. India disagreed, and all consideration of caste was blocked, as it was again at another follow-up conference in 2011.

In 2010, anti-caste activists won a major victory when Britain's House of Lords passed an equality bill that recognized caste discrimination as a form of racism.[64] The Indian government and Hindu groups protested, and in 2018 the British government announced that it no longer planned to bring the bill into law. Dalit activists campaigning for caste discrimination to be punished under existing anti-racism laws in the United States have been frustrated by similar opposition. But in June 2020 the government of California took the technology giant Cisco and two of its dominant-caste employees to court for alleged discrimination against a Dalit engineer. In this landmark case, the government argued that Cisco "engaged in unlawful employment practices on the basis of religion, ancestry, national origin/ethnicity and race/color". This has prepared the way for an eventual showdown over caste and descent-based discrimination in the US courts.[65]

Over the last decade the UN's secretary general and high commissioner for human rights have spoken out repeatedly, in UN reports and global forums, about the need to stamp out the evils of caste.[66] The Indian government's opposition to action against caste discrimination on the international stage remains unchanged.

Myth of a universal solidarity

The era of decolonization saw the emergence of the myth of a universal solidarity between Black and "brown" people as a programme of third world solidarity. In India, the myth has been exposed by the degrading treatment there of Black people. African students frequently experience harassment and physical assaults in India. The West Indian cricketer Darren Sammy recently spoke out about how, during his time with a franchise in the Indian Premier League, some of his Indian teammates used a slur referring to his colour as his nickname.[67] Such behaviour is so normalized that few in India see it as a problem. Across the country, Black people are stereotyped as "Nigerian" drug peddlers or sex workers, and are the targets of unwarranted public scrutiny and police attention. Celebrities and government ministers sometimes condemn such racism, but their words are never followed by concrete action or change.

It is only outside India that the sense of solidarity, established on the principle of universal human dignity, survives. That this is possible is due to ignorance of India's social realities and the pervasive nature of caste, even among the Indian diaspora, which undermines social equality. Justice for the oppressed may be the true shared goal, but the spokespeople of the brown world, who derive almost exclusively from the dominant castes, are often excused from acknowledging the monster of caste within. As it stands, the dominant castes, acting on an ingrained exceptionalism while professing progressive values, have been happy to benefit from Black activism, which has challenged their own mistreatment under racist systems, while simultaneously undermining the solidarity of Black people and the caste-oppressed.

In the United States, the Indian diaspora owes a huge debt to the Black struggle. The arrival of Indians in significant numbers in that country was only possible after 1965, when a new immigration law barred discrimination on the basis of race, sex, nationality, place of birth or place of residence. The Asian American Commission of the Commonwealth of Massachusetts, in a statement of solidarity with Black Lives Matter, acknowledged that this breakthrough "was shaped by other Black-led civil rights victories", and also recognized the roots of a shared history in how "the Dalit Panther Movement found inspiration from the U.S. Black Panthers".[68] Indian Americans have also benefited from other victories for racial equality that could never have come without Black activism—including the policies of reservation quotas, which have opened the doors of employment and education to so many of them.

Yet the Indian diaspora's relationship with Black people has been ambivalent and often hostile. The Black novelist Toni Morrison once said that when European immigrants arrived in the United States, the moment "they got off the boat, the second word they learned was 'nigger'". Without Black people, she explained, "immigrants would have torn each other's throats out, as they have done everywhere else". Taught to share a common hatred, they "could all say, 'I am not *that*.' So in that sense, becoming an American is based on an attitude: an exclusion of me. It wasn't negative to them—it was unifying."[69] Indian Americans have been part of the same process, and Morrison could just as well have been talking about them too.

Indian Americans, after no more than a few generations in the United States, are now identified as a "model minority"—highly educated, renowned for their work ethic, having a considerable political footprint and the highest median household income of any ethnic group in the country. Black people, on the other hand, after centuries of exploitative toil, have the lowest median household income, and are very often denied decent education, employment and healthcare. The model minority—given this tag by white people because it has modelled itself on white people—chooses to look away from this awkward scene. The diaspora has not used its growing capital in the service of justice for Black people. Indian Americans are plentiful in the tech companies and corporations where Black people barely find room. In numerous cases, they are leading or managing them.

For an affluent group to craft a model minority status serves to undermine the majority, who are marginalized for being perceived as not good enough. This majority includes Blacks, the poor, Hispanics and immigrants. By highlighting the well-off and content Asian groups, the model minority myth reflects the merit-based claims of the dominant castes in India and is reminiscent of British colonial practices in the past.

The privileged model minority extends an invitation to conjoin with the capitalist forces of America by creating more opportunities for itself. And these minorities are models because they have a non-African history. Thus, the benefit of a model minority lies in their occupying a space where they cannot be questioned for their elite position or for not being white. Their inherent racism is a direct reflection of their surreptitious sense of superiority modelled on the caste hierarchy that they are used to and comfortable with.

It is important to understand the socio-economic background of the diaspora. Especially during the earlier waves of immigration, the largest numbers of new arrivals came from the dominant castes. With few exceptions, India's oppressed castes and ethnic minorities, as well as the marginalized converts to non-Hindu religions, did not have the wealth to fund such a move or access to an English-language education that would ease the way to integration and employment in the United States. Nor were they welcome in the family and caste networks that quickly took shape in the diaspora and facilitated the arrival and success of more and more dominant-caste Indians.

Much of the diaspora's community life came to centre on temples run by brahman priests who recited religious texts extolling caste, and on festivals celebrating gods and classical art forms that the dominant castes had monopolized for centuries. Social inequality and segregation, celebrated as part of the dominant-caste tradition, were accepted in the new country as in the old one. The only oppression the dominant castes would not tolerate was their own. The number of oppressed-caste immigrants from India has gradually grown in recent decades—especially since the 1990s, when reservations in public education and the liberalization of the economy gave them some new opportunities—but the casteist shape of diaspora society remains unchanged. The Indian American identity leaves almost no room for Dalits, Adivasis, Muslims, Christians and Sikhs.[70] It is embodied as a dominant-caste Hindu identity. The diaspora sees it as a victory that Diwali is now celebrated in the White House. It does not care that this celebration of the "good" Hindu goddess Durga's killing of the "evil" Mahishasura is offensive to many Dalits and Adivasis, for whom Mahishasura is an ancestor.[71]

The Indian diaspora in America has not looked kindly on caste inclusivity and diversity within, while at the same time it has taken advantage of racial diversity. Universities admit dominant-caste children and corporations hire dominant-caste workers to increase racial diversity in their ranks. When Indian Americans call for the promotion of their fellows in public and corporate life, it is most often a case of the dominant castes cheering on their own. Meanwhile, large sections of this same diaspora are hostile to India's limited system of affirmative action for the caste-oppressed in public education and employment, thus mirroring the attitude of the dominant castes in India. They are also opposed to any demands for equal rights from the country's Dalits, Adivasis, Muslims and other oppressed groups.

Even within the United States, the Indian American fondness for racial diversity has its limits. Harvard University lost the battle in the Supreme Court over its affirmative action policy when challenged by an Asian American coalition. Their petition had claimed that Harvard's admission policies discriminated against the growing number of highly qualified Asian American applicants in the effort to promote greater racial diversity in the student body. Numerous Indian American groups were part of the coalition, with little concern for the heavy cost that an end to racial considerations in university admissions would bring for the most disadvantaged racial groups—especially Black and Hispanic people—who already struggle to get a chance at higher education.

This challenge against the state's efforts to uplift marginalized groups is not new in America. In the late 1990s the Indian American Forum for Political Education in North Carolina looked at the policies of affirmative action not as a mechanism for correcting historical wrongs but to advance their own position in the light of ethnic diversity.[72] Ajantha Subramanian questions the meaning of diaspora as applied to Indians in North Carolina. She argues that the creation of a diaspora ordinarily entails loss or displacement from the centre of a motherland. In the case of the Indians whom she studied in North Carolina in the 1990s and 2000s, Subramanian argues that state-funded quality education in India produced a global class of professionals who sought opportunities in world markets that were favourable to their advancement. However, when these immigrants arrived in North Carolina, they dominated the non-white groups by virtue of their class and education, even "marginalizing poor Black and white residents".[73] This dominance was mitigated by the promotion of a type of multiculturalism that was presented as class-neutral and non-caste, at the expense of historically marginalized groups.[74] This new identity of Indians as a distinct transnational group was intended to enable them to self-segregate and establish themselves as an enterprising dominant group or "model minority", fitting the classic notion of the capitalist American dream.

Yet the story of Indian immigrants as a non-white group represents a process of social identification sans social justice. Many Indians saw affirmative action in America as a means to rise to the upper echelons of the corporate world—not as a way of identifying with the experiences of Black and Hispanic people. This is a form of "misidentification" whereby other minority groups' experiences are used as an inspiration to advocate for one's own economic and political advantages, and not as a shared structural position in the hierarchy of colour in America.[75] Essentially, the Indian experience in America is presented as one of a culturally distinct superior caste or group that needs to establish its "cultural difference" as a minority class for purposes of social mobility and success, thereby reinforcing the myths of colourized-racial solidarity among US ethnic groups.[76]

Gandhian episodic intervention

The myth of Black and brown solidarity does not need to remain a myth. The Black movements can assist this process of demystification by better understanding caste and its consequences. A major hurdle to this Dalit–Black solidarity came in the form of an airbrushed image of India, and of Hinduism, that many still hold. One clear symptom of this is the esteem reserved for Mohandas Gandhi.

The uncritical admiration of Gandhi owes a lot to his valorization by Martin Luther King Jr. and the American civil rights movement. King saw Gandhi as the world is used to seeing him—as India's non-violent saviour from colonial and racial domination, and an exponent of Hinduism's supposed belief in universal respect and peace. But this image, cultivated by Gandhi and now tended by the Indian state, obscures many of Gandhi's beliefs and politics.

Though Gandhi opposed untouchability, he defended the caste system itself. Just like many dominant-caste thinkers today, he idealized traditional Indian society and the ancient values that were sentimentally casteist in formulation. The caste system for him was a legitimate method for the division of labour and an irreplaceable part of the supposed harmony of Indian civilization. During colonial rule, when Indians could elect their own representatives to provincial legislative councils, Ambedkar championed separate electorates for the oppressed castes, to guarantee their political representation and autonomy in a system where they were otherwise frozen out by the dominant castes. When the British government agreed to this in the early 1930s, Gandhi began a fast unto death. Ambedkar described this as a form of blackmail: there was a great risk that if Gandhi died over the issue, the dominant castes would hold the oppressed castes collectively responsible and initiate mass slaughter.[77] Ambedkar backed down, and Dalits have had little more than non-autonomous token representation in Indian legislatures ever since. Ambedkar lamented this episode, known as the "Poona Pact", till the end of his life.[78]

Ambedkar continued to see Gandhi and the Congress party as adversaries of the oppressed castes. When freedom from British rule was achieved, he still regarded the liberation of India's people as an unfinished project. Ambedkar spearheaded the writing of the Indian Constitution, but, stymied by a largely dominant-caste constituent assembly, he could include only limited safeguards against the caste system. Just as the Constitution was coming into effect, he warned presciently that

> we are going to enter into a life of contradictions. In politics we will have equality, and in social and economic life we will have inequality. In politics we will be recognizing the principle of one man one vote and one vote one value. In our social and economic life, we shall, by reason of our social and economic structure, continue to deny the principle of one man one value.[79]

Before he rose to prominence in India, Gandhi made a name for himself by confronting the British colonial government in South Africa. His quarrel there was not with discrimination against all non-white people, but with the treatment of Indians—especially dominant-caste and "passenger Indians"—as inferior to the whites.[80] India's post-independence diplomacy followed his example.

Gandhi bought into the colourized racial theory that white people came from a superior Aryan stock, and was convinced that the dominant castes shared the same Aryan blood too. His own writing signals to anti-Black racism—a more recent realization that has sparked a belated reassessment of his legacy. In 2015, during student demonstrations in South Africa, a Gandhi statue in Johannesburg was vandalized in protest. A statue of Gandhi gifted to the University of Ghana by the Indian government was removed from the campus in 2018 following protests by students and faculty.[81] During the Black Lives Matter protests, the word "racist" was spray-painted at the base of Gandhi statues in London, Amsterdam and Washington DC, and there were calls to remove his statues in numerous cities in the West. Gandhi's statue continues to be a site of vandalism outside India.[82]

Admiration for Gandhi goes hand in hand with a lack of awareness of anti-caste thought. Ambedkar and other anti-caste thinkers are not adequately read in the United States, not least among the Black intelligentsia. When I met Bobby Seale, a founding member of the Black Panthers, he told me he was aware that the Dalit Panthers had existed, but did not know much more about them. I later established contact with him during the Dalit Panthers' Golden Jubilee celebrations, inviting him to India in 2022. He responded positively, but his health didn't allow him to undertake the long journey and his speaker's fee was beyond the pocket of the Dalit Panthers in India.

Angela Davis, also a former Panther, admitted during a lecture in India in 2016 to a profound misreading and reductionist understanding of the Dalit cause by the Black movement. One instance of this, she said, was Martin Luther King's endorsement of India's ban on untouchability without holding the government accountable for its broader tolerance of caste. Another was the Black Panthers' understanding of the Dalit struggle as one against racialized colour oppression—"as if that is the only way that connection becomes legible".[83] Such misconceptions are to be expected in the light of the circumstances of both movements so far and the powerful forces that have always resisted their growth. However, the minority presence of Indian and Dalit groups in the United States should have allowed for some connections to be made.

Dalit diaspora activism in the US: a brief history

Some examples of the Dalit presence in America might have pointed the way. One of these was VISION—Volunteers in Service to India's Oppressed and Neglected—a pioneering multi-caste, multi-religious organization formed in 1976 and led by Dalit professionals who sympathized with the African American liberation struggles.[84] They included a number of notable Indian men and women. Dr Shobha Singh was a Fulbright scholar at Johns Hopkins University who earned his PhD in 1957 and worked for AT&T Bell. Yogesh Varhade, a German-educated engineer, ran a successful business in Niagara Falls, Canada, and visited America frequently. Dr Laxmi Narain Berwa, an oncologist and veteran of the US Air Force, pursued a career in public service and social life in the States.[85] Ranveer Singh worked for the US Federal government.[86] This loosely knit group of North American Dalits from various walks of life, all devoted to the ideology of Dr Ambedkar, met at Ranveer Singh's Woodbridge house in Virginia, where a proposal was made to start a Dalit rights organization. Out of this emerged VISION.[87]

VISION lobbied the US government and international bodies, and organized conferences and protests to highlight the issue of caste oppression. Such lobbying proved fruitful when Dr Shobha Singh received a letter of support from Senator Dan Rostenkowski, who had raised Dalit rights issues in Congress. Dr Berwa reminisced during an interview: "A copy of this letter of solidarity from Senator Rostenkowski was with Dr Shobha Singh, who was very proud of this."

VISION also took the Indian government to task for not doing enough to curb the atrocities committed against Dalits. After the Bangladesh War (1971), when relations between America and India were strained, Indira Gandhi visited the United States. However, her trip was rocked by protests from the Indian diaspora Dalits in both the US and Canada, who had requested to meet her and inform her of their concerns about growing Dalit atrocities. On failing to receive any positive response, VISION members, primarily Dr Berwa, started to lobby US Foreign Relations Committee members like Paul S. Sarbanes and Charles McC. Mathias Jr., who promised to take up the matter with Mrs Gandhi. In their separate letters addressed to Berwa, both

Sarbanes and Mathias applauded him for bringing the concern of untouchables in India to their attention.[88]

Newspapers such as the *Washington Post* and *New York Post* carried news items on the Dalit protests in the US in July 1982.[89] An irritated Mrs Gandhi sent a letter to VISION, which Berwa has kept to this day. "It does not help for those who are living in affluence abroad to comment on situations about which they have little knowledge," she chided.[90] This angered the members of VISION. Laxmi Berwa, then president of VISION, hit back with a letter calling out her "meanness, arrogance and indifference". He condemned her "callous attitude towards the Scheduled Castes" and declared her a "selfish manipulator, egocentric leader" whose "arrogance and dictatorship" would hurt her and many others.[91] The furious VISION leadership didn't hold back and made references to the support she had received from the Scheduled Castes and Tribes in her electoral victory.

While the group focused on its main mission of promoting the ideals of Ambedkar in North America and protesting against caste atrocities in India, it also forged some early links with the Black community, despite the obstacles. Yogesh Varhade, one of VISION's founders and leader of the Ambedkar Center for Justice and Peace (ACJP), told me that the group had been "keenly observing the Black movement and saw apparent parallels".[92] But many Black activists at the time were being watched and harassed by the US government, and Varhade and his colleagues hesitated to reach out. "We were trying to establish ourselves and could not risk anything," he explained. "We were new to North America and many of these people [Dalits] who were living here were afraid to get involved with the Black movement due to the FBI intrusion. Everyone had a family and their roots were not that strong. The issue of the Black Panthers and its following movements was complicated by its own intra-US politics. We couldn't think of making inroads because we were preoccupied with our struggle that was already sore in the eyes of many."⁹³ But the group did what it could.

Barring a few occasions, relations between Dalits and the Black movement did not solidify in the United States. Once Dr Berwa spoke about caste issues to a patient of his, Petey Greene, the TV host of a popular talk show, *Petey Greene's Washington*. This led to Dr Berwa being introduced to a network of African Americans. He subsequently made numerous media appearances and talked at meetings and conferences where he introduced audiences to the Dalit struggle.

Years later, Sulayman S. Nyang, a professor of African studies at Howard University, Washington DC, introduced Berwa to Randy Short, a graduate student with an interest in the Dalit cause. Short had been intrigued by India and its "evil" caste system from an early age. His attention to Dr Berwa was drawn by a *Washington Post* story that covered Berwa protesting against Indira Gandhi outside the White House. Short and Berwa connected and in 1998 they organized an event to mark Ambedkar Jayanti at Howard—the first such commemoration of Ambedkar's birthday on a historically Black US campus. A poster made for the event introduced Ambedkar as "India's Martin Luther King, Jr." and called for unity with Dalits to "break casteism's 3,000-year grip". The event was hosted at the Ralph Bunche International Center in 1999 and co-sponsored by the Graduate Student Council, Caribbean Students Association, African Students Association, International Students Association and Haitian Students Association. A similar effort to host Ambedkar at the southern Black university of Fisk had been made in the 1950s.⁹⁴

While they were building such alliances, anti-caste organizations such as VISION also campaigned to bring caste oppression to the attention of international bodies—Berwa was among the first Dalits to approach the UN—and the US government.

Dalit–Black Lives Matter

Another example of building solidarity is provided by Raju Kamble, the founder of the Ambedkar International Mission in the United States.[95] Kamble gained recognition in Ambedkarite circles for building up a network of Dalit activists across the world, but what is less well-known is that he also established ties with Black activists in Texas, where he was based. A growing number of young Dalit activists now follow in Kamble's footsteps. I helped facilitate a symposium on the Black and Dalit struggles in partnership with the Boston chapter of the Black Lives Matter movement in 2017. After the killing of George Floyd, several Ambedkarite groups issued statements in support of the Black Lives Matter protests.[96]

Overall, however, the Dalit leadership of Ambedkarite organizations in America did not seem overly concerned about what was happening in the country. In a Zoom call that I set up in the summer of 2020, I tried to understand this reaction. Respondents revealed that they did not have connections with Black movements or non-Indian movements, and thus couldn't find avenues to express their concern. When I proposed that they release a statement offering support and donations, the organizations' leaders came forward, albeit with reservations. Moreover, there wasn't an active interest on either side to communicate and build solidarity. Raju Kamble was an anomaly in that he had come from a diverse, international work experience. Besides, his stint with BAMCEF had prepared him to seek out difficult and unmoderated spaces to create networks. Another legendary figure in the tradition of Dalit and Black solidarity was Dr. Velu Annamalai, a PhD in Engineering who established contacts with Black activists and scholars of America. He espoused the racial view of Indian untouchables, aligning with Black scholar Runoko Rashidi. A lengthy review of Annamalai's work is due that would open the dimensions of Dalit and Black movement's history making in the US. The current Dalit leadership in America comes primarily from a middle-class background whose concerns are class-oriented and who are comfortable with ready made activism. Their situation resembles those of the brown folks of middle-class "model minority" America, but their disposition comes at the cost of hindering Black liberation and perpetuating the anti-Black racism practised by their fellow nationals.[97]

In India, on the other hand, there have been active attempts to develop reciprocity and solidarity. Recently, the Tamil Buddhist activist Dr Bharathi Prabhu has been responsible for organizing special graduation ceremonies in Chennai for Dalit and African students, emulating the tradition of Black graduation ceremonies in the United States. These events celebrate icons of the Black struggle side by side with Dalit heroes and invitees have included Barack and Michelle Obama, Cornel West and Keeanga-Yamahtta Taylor, amongst others.

Another inspiring example is Dalit History Month, an effort to highlight the Dalit movement with events across the world every April. It is modelled on Black History Month, which has been celebrated every February in the United States since the 1970s. First conceived in the early 2000s by D. Ravikumar, a literary intellectual and current member of parliament from Tamil Nadu, Dalit History Month originally ran from Ambedkar's birthday on 14 April to the birthday of another anti-caste hero, Iyothee Thass, on 26 May. This effort builds on the Ambedkar Melas started in the 1980s by Kanshi Ram, which criss-crossed the north of India for two months after Ambedkar's birthday every year, celebrating Dalit history and spreading Dalit thought.

Dalits are invested in protecting Black lives because they see their suffering reflected in that of other oppressed people. They empathize with the pain Black people express and the constant diminishing of their humanity by the skewed standards of dominant groups. The demands of Black people for human rights are viewed as an affront by the dominant-caste society in America and worldwide, where Black people are a minority. Dalits' concern for Black people extends to the analogous scenarios they face. For example, Black people cannot be angry because they are then seen as overreacting; cannot protest because they are then accused of rioting; cannot demand a fair share of wealth because they are then labelled freeloaders; and cannot talk about the past because they are then accused of self-victimizing. They cannot cry because they are thought to be faking; cannot laugh because they are considered loud; and cannot be expressive for fear of being seen as annoying—even when their family members are being killed in the streets. All these are also facts of Dalit life and their survival strategies.

At a systemic level, the US criminal justice system's biases against Black people are well documented and remains a reality. Police brutality against Black people has gone on for centuries, with impunity even for police officers with long records of violence.[98] Numerous cases have emerged of avowed white supremacists infiltrating the ranks of law enforcement. In India, Dalits, Adivasis and Muslims—who account for significantly less than half of the population—made up just over half of all prisoners in 2018. Police brutality, including torture, is endemic in India. The National Human Rights Commission reported more than 2,150 deaths in judicial custody and 155 in police custody in 2021/2—at a rate of over five deaths per day.[99] Most of the those who died were Dalits, Adivasis and Muslims.[100] Besides, atrocities committed against Dalits number over 50,000 per year.

From personal to social action: the demise of the Dalit Panthers

According to J.V. Pawar in his book *Dalit Panthers: An Authoritative History*, it was the communists who were responsible for destroying the Panthers. "The communists had tears of happiness in their eyes. It was their jubilance to destroy a fiery organization." In a telephone interview, Pawar mentioned that the communists took an active interest in the affairs of the Dalit Panthers from 1974 and eventually began to influence them. The communists, largely consisting of non-Dalits, started to change the "colour of the Dalit Panther organization".[101] Their show of solidarity came with forms of mutual assistance: with their networks, communists helped the Dalit Panthers in legal matters as the latter did not have the resources for instance to secure bail in court cases.

However, the real reason for the split and later dissolution of the Dalit Panthers was a clash of different agendas. Namdeo Dhasal, one of the founders, went over to Congress, then later Shiv Sena, and worked under their patronage. Another founding member, Raja Dhale, disowned the Panthers and started his own organization called Mass Movement. He did not want anything more to do with the Panthers. According to Pawar, Dhale became so anti-communist that anything that smacked of communism would be shunned by him. Inevitably, the split was less one of ideology and more one of growing jealousy between the leaders.

In our conversation Pawar took me back to the years when the Panthers were active. He observed that two blocs were created within the Dalit Panthers. One was led by Dhale and the other by Dhasal. Both these leaders were charismatic and brave. Dhale was educated and suave while Dhasal was a working-class man. The supporters of each man would champion their leader at events and functions, creating friction and animosity between the two.

Then the divisions started to become personal. Dhasal's drinking habits and his lifestyle were reckoned unbecoming of a traditional Buddhist householder, which set him apart from those who preferred a pious leadership. Dhale, on the other hand, was bent on following a Buddhist approach that would mean making a moral cause in politics. However, the split was further exacerbated along educational lines. Those who had some degree of education were often put off by the brashness of the uneducated group.

V.S. Naipaul toured India in the 1980s. His first stop was Mumbai. There, he was taken by the Dalit community's presence. Thus, he sought out the Dalit Panthers, about whom he had heard of previously. He spent time with Dhasal and also interviewed Malika Ambar Shaikh, Dhasal's wife, who had written a memoir expressing the torments of being the domestic partner of a poet and Panther. It did not paint Dhasal in a positive light. His illness and drinking habits resurfaced.

Dhasal, for his part, was pained and psychologically wounded after the Panthers' demolition. He found his pathway outside the literary realm, in politics. Naipaul reports the state of Dhasal's life and what the Panthers' divisions did to him. However, had Naipaul been introduced to the other members of the Panthers' leadership, his review of the Dalit Panthers' movement could have been composite.

While it was active, the Dalit Panther organization unleashed a *kshankaal vaadal* or "momentary storm" in the social, political and cultural life of the Maharashtra state.[102] Some consider it not as significant an organization as it is given credit for. Owing to its rapid rise within two years, new entrants could not be trained properly in ideology and strategy. The leaders, meanwhile, took independent decisions without due process and consultation.[103]

In addition to the ideological divisions, the state played a significant part in dismantling the Panthers by using police machinery to drag Dalit Panther activists and leaders to court. Nearly 350 cases were registered against Dalit Panther cadres who were victims of state violence. Dhasal blames state intervention in loosening the Panthers' organization.[104]

The Panthers also suffered because their programme did not seek to make a claim for political power but instead stuck to social change as their agenda. Pawar clarified this by quoting a letter from the Dalit Panthers' leader in the UK, Krishna Gamre: "Dalit Panthers is a social organization; it wants to make change in the Indian society. We are not interested in political transition."[105] The belief in social change through mobilization and protest was somewhat naive, and it placed the Dalit community on the defensive. This resulted in many defections among the Dalit youth. That political avenues and options were self-centred and needed to be condemned was a widespread belief among the leaders.[106] They held the view that politics were untrustworthy, as many leaders of the community succumbed to the political pressures of the ruling castes. Many Dalit Panther leaders did not think of political power as the next step after social organizing. To exercise power required compromises, which the Dalit community was unable to contemplate, as the extent of the atrocities and injustices the community faced needed a firm commitment. Nevertheless, all the leaders later moved to political organizing, making alliances with those parties they had previously condemned.

Though the Dalit Panther organization discontinued, it never died. Many Dalit leaders took on the cause of the Panthers. They started their own version of the Panthers: Bhartiya Dalit Panthers, Dalit Panthers of India, and so on. The spirit of fighting against injustice and atrocities continues to ignite the minds of disgruntled youth. And whenever atrocities befall the Dalits, there is a strong urge to bring back the Panthers. A former Panther leader and currently a central minister in India, Ramdas Athawale, told me that the attraction of the Panthers continues, and its purpose is still felt whenever atrocities arise. "We're thinking of restarting the Panthers."[107] He is not alone. Several meetings took place in 2022, led by Dalit Panther veterans who wanted to erect a stand-alone Dalit Panther organization. The yearly reports of the National Crime Records Bureau documenting atrocities and instances of violence against Dalits are replete with casteist overtones. These incidents unify the Dalit community in protesting against the state and society.

There are many groups currently who identify with the Dalit Panthers and who are inspired by their work and activities, especially the youth. My research has found that many Dalit youth groups around India, especially in Maharashtra, sympathize with the Panther ideology of revolt and resistance. For instance, to celebrate the fiftieth anniversary of the founding of the Dalit Panthers, the Yuva Panthers in Nanded hosted a Golden Jubilee event, honouring the veterans.[108] Black Panthers from the Illinois Chapter were the guests of honour.[109] I curated a special number for the *Outlook* weekly commemorating the Dalit Panthers with the intention of recording the past and reflecting on the contemporary reaction.

Conclusion

Laxmi Berwa, who is now approaching his eighties, told me that as people get older, they become conservative. "I am that person now." Though his commitment to Dalit liberation is unwavering, his oft-repeated phrase is that he wants to "contribute and continue the work of his idol, the great Dr Ambedkar". He keeps up to date with his reading. He had just completed reading a thick biography of Ambedkar, which he found impressive. When I met him, Berwa also brought me printed online articles that espoused his new viewpoints. He was critical of Hamas, a view that informed his understanding of the Israel–Palestine war. His sources were Fox News and the *Washington Examiner*, both conservative right-wing outlets. A year later, in 2025, at his house in Virginia, his desk was full with books on topics ranging from

Buddhism to Caste, Ambedkar, and RSS. He also had printed copies of Masters and PhD theses on Buddhism submitted at US and Canadian universities. He defended President Trump's policies for hours altogether.

Recent global political developments have cast doubt on the viability of democracy and highlighted its susceptibility to capture. Leading democracies are increasingly influenced by individuals with inclinations toward ethno-nationalism and capitalism. Consequently, the phenomenon of "othering" has emerged as a central theme in the political agendas of ruling regimes. While formerly marginalized groups based on caste, colour, religion and gender have ascended to positions of titular power, instances of discrimination and violence persist under their rule. This is because modern politics tend to prioritize group representation over the interests of subgroups, particularly those belonging to persecuted rather than privileged minorities.

Celebrated movements like Black Lives Matter carry within them the seeds of their own failures and defeats. BLM was embroiled in scandals involving its founders and leaders profiting off the movement.[110] Old-school, traditional activists had seen this coming and thus had exercised caution. However, when the movement held the US nation's attention in 2020, even the naysayers jumped on the bandwagon. Personal charges aside, the sudden emergence of a disorganized group in rallying people to call for justice was welcomed by all.

The success of any movement now depends on how one overcomes the limitations of activist networks. It is this crucial and significant constituency that has the power to shift the direction of the predominant ideas of liberation. It is not their intellect or ideology that will bring this about, but their sheer numbers and their influence across various spheres.

4

THE DALIT REPUBLIC OF DIASPORA
A CASE STUDY OF TRINIDAD

When we speak of caste and its presence worldwide, the conversation is often confined to the contemporary rise of migration and caste in the West.[1] Most often the dialogue is restricted to the diasporic Dalits resident in the West. One can hardly find a comprehensive study of castes in locations outside the Western episteme. When I went to South Africa, one of the urgent projects that I had intended to study was caste among Indians and non-Indians in Africa. I was advised instead to focus on contemporary Indian migrant labour.

During my research, I found out that major studies of the history of indentured labour, the sociology of political movements, and the economics of social classes in India did not feature caste as one of the subjects of analysis. There are various reasons for this. But the three most important are that caste was forgotten during the era of the indentured system; people gave up caste owing to pressure from the colonial regime; and Indian identity was mostly divided because of regional and religious

(Muslim–Hindu) differences. While these reasons partly explain why, they do not give a complete picture.

In my research I found out how both Hindus and Muslims, the South Indians and Gujaratis, had retained their own cultural practice of caste through the recounting of memories of their ancestry. This was reflected in the way the socialization of families took place and the remembrance of their heritage. Though the current generation does not adhere to caste norms and beliefs, there is a recognition and also a disowning of castes among the older diasporas. Caste, as we shall see in this chapter, has evolved and accommodated itself to local practices and state norms. We cannot speak of caste as a common ancestral practice that originates in one country and replicates similarly elsewhere. To do so is to ignore the ability of caste to reproduce itself as a system that accommodates itself to local customs and introduces its hierarchical logic as a justifiable practice of old. Thus, caste develops in different forms and takes on localized manifestations embedded in the practice of tradition and faith. Even though it faces opposition, it nevertheless assumes a position of importance as a recognized element of the spiritual order.

In this chapter we will take a look at Trinidad and see what caste has meant to this island nation whose population is nearly 40 per cent Indian. Most Trinidadian Indians are of subaltern caste origin. What has this done to the intellectual retelling of the Indian story of Trinidad and what does it tell us today? More specifically, can Trinidad be regarded as a satellite Hindu society without Dalits? As my research explored the archival history of Trinidad, it also engaged in deep empiricism. My fieldnotes from my first trip in 2022 were lost but then miraculously reappeared in late 2024 in a trunk I had left in Europe. However, it was the data I had collected in the summer of 2024 that became the source of much of my analysis. I had written down broader summaries of the 2022 visit. What changed in these years was the confidence I acquired from my informants who had taken a bold and critical political stand on the caste question. This encouraged me to produce a proud and complex story of the Trinidadian Hindu community.

Trinidadian Hindus, like many in the diaspora, live in the complex conditions of a post-independent, racialized democratic country while also being a prominent, indeed dominant, player in its economic affairs. This has brought them closer to Western modernity. Nevertheless, their faith in their ancestral heritage takes precedence over their transnational outlook. For many of the elites whom I met and interviewed in Trinidad, their ancestral land is but a figment of their imagination. Some are nostalgic and hope to visit India, but many are content with what their home country of Trinidad offers them. Their Hindu and caste identity was and continues to be primarily shaped by brahman-centric forms of ritual. There is some opposition to this brahman centrality by non-brahman Hindus and some progressive brahmans. These, however, do not take account of the changing landscape of caste.

The important historical role of Brahmanism in defining Hindu identity as an ethnic group still continues today.[2] In this respect, the research findings of Peter van der Veer and Steven Vertovec from the 1980s broadly align with some of my own. In India, the concept of a single Hindu identity, as opposed to plural definitions, was promoted to create one ethnic community, especially after independence and the establishment of a democratic republic. Subaltern cultures and traditions were subsumed into the dominant brahman caste rituals, sidelining lower-caste gods and their cultures. This was evident in practices such as *kathas, yagnas, mandir havans, bhajans,* marriages, funerals, and night-long recitations of the Ramayana. The stereotype of the brahman as a learned pandit persists in religious circles, where he is expected to be a brahman "religious specialist".[3] This confers legitimacy on rituals and authority on religious functions. Brahman dominance became a part of Hindu life, though not without opposition. Nevertheless, brahmans have succeeded in maintaining their control.

After taking over Hindu institutions, brahmans began to manage the affairs of temples and religious organizations, and broker deals on behalf of Hindus to secure political alliances. Hindu ethnicity as a religious category is recognized in the constitution of Trinidad and Tobago. Van der Veer and Vertovec, like other scholars, argue that brahmans were instrumental in making Hinduism an ethnic identity. Hindu practices in the Caribbean provide an interesting study of the future development of castes in the diaspora. Many who left their homes as indentured labourers envisioned a new future for themselves, and what we find today offers a glimpse of potential developments in the evolution of caste and identity. Hindu practice in the Caribbean society makes for an interesting case study of the after-life of castes in the diasporic imagination.

Investigating caste in the diaspora

Caste has achieved its purpose of segregating and further dividing various cultural groups into subcategories and groups as *jatis*. Though *jatis* do not exist in their innate forms, they operate in interpersonal relationships and reproduction. One of the prominent routes proposed by Dr Ambedkar to escape caste was by intermarrying and by destroying the beliefs of caste promoted in the Hindu *shastras* (scriptures).[4] In addition to reformation, Ambedkar also proposed conversion out of the religion that maintained caste.[5] Given the violence in the rural agrarian political economy, Ambedkar exhorted his followers to migrate to urban areas, where the intensity of caste practice was relatively mild. Migration out of caste was a way to challenge caste. Migration was a form of dislocation as well as a voluntary exodus.

Have there been attempts to test the migration-out-of-caste proposition in the context of transoceanic mobility? Studies of the Indian diaspora do not pay much attention to caste, for two major reasons. The first is the non-availability of easily accessible data on caste as opposed to the noticeable ethnology of Indian religions in the diaspora. The second is the paucity of information in the colonial archive about caste,[6] and academic studies of caste experience are far too scant.

To investigate caste in the diaspora, we need to look not only at the peculiarities of caste institutions. We cannot, for example, expect caste to exist in the same form as we find in India. Although the practices of Dalits and their cultural artefacts have continued in one way or other in the diaspora, caste has not migrated unchanged. Over the years, it has moved away from being a strictly cultural institution to becoming an assimilated part of life in which outcastes exercise agency. Caste has undergone a creolization of sorts. It might even have become an institution that is reborn in a new shape with every generation.

Owing to the intermixture of Indian indentured labourers with other caste groups and racial ethnicities, caste now operates as a distinct element of observable belief in host society. The question remains whether caste exists as a system in diasporic societies or whether, simply, castes exist. In Trinidad, my research shows that caste does not exist as a system of strict rules enforced by public support and institutional sanction. However, caste does exist as a personal or associational feeling bound up with identity, prestige, ritual and endogamy. For a caste system to exist, a ritual background is necessary, while castes can exist outside the purview of religion in a secular society.

Trinidad has retained an attraction for anthropologists and sociologists since the 1950s. Various researchers have visited the island nation to understand rituals, endogamous practices,[7] creolization,[8] the West Indian and East Indian grouping of its African and Indian population,[9] ethnic castes and cultural practices.[10] There are also various sociological studies of Trinidadian Hinduism, which through social acculturation became stabilized in the regular practices of diverse castes.[11] This is what also took me to Trinidad. The existing research studies came to my attention when studying the Indian diaspora in South Africa. The rapt attention these paid to caste and ritualism among Indians in Trinidad made a strong impression on me. It was because of this that I returned to the region and its practices.

After the abolition of slavery in all British territories by the British Parliament in 1838, the Empire looked at the indentured system as a way of providing bonded labour in the plantation colonies. To give indentures a separate status from slavery, contracts and records were kept and formal processes of recruitment were observed. As a result, many lower-caste Indians and a few from the dominant castes took the route of the much-dreaded *kaala paani*—black waters—a metaphor for the dangerous oceans. Ritually, it meant that one would lose one's birthright to one's caste. All the same, 143,939 indentured Indians landed in Trinidad, with 90 per cent returning to India after the completion of their contracts (the actual numbers of returnees vary).[12] Of these, 88 per cent practised Hinduism.[13]

Becoming brahman

As the General Register of Indian Immigrants makes clear, the Indian indentured labourers who were recruited for the plantations of Trinidad left their villages and travelled abroad in batches.[14] Naturally, their social relationships and social circles were based on their caste, village, and language similarities.

This made it possible and likely for them to reproduce caste in Trinidad. Over the years, however, the material conditions in their newly adopted land did not prove conducive to the maintenance of the caste system as they had known it in India. Moreover, because their work was secular in nature, requiring hard labour in the canefields, the economic and occupational basis of caste was "eliminated almost completely" in Trinidad.[15] Yet despite the argument that caste dissolved after two or so generations, the power and authority of ritual and the hold of a brahman-centric theology continued to shape people's lives. Caste became part of people's Hindu identity, being revealed in their practice of religion and their reverence for the hierarchical order.

Many of those considered lower or outcaste Indians who arrived on the shores of Trinidad aspired to a superior status and adopted a new identity in the hope of climbing up the ladder of the caste hierarchy. Reinventing themselves and their status was clearly an advantageous and attractive move for those untouchables who were ritually outside the ranks of the brahman *sramanas* (ascetics or hermits). Becoming a brahman automatically provided one with a prominent position in the society of indentured labourers. Some people touched their feet as a mark of greeting. brahmans were also served food first and they were assigned the title of "panditji" (educated priest). This public practice of recognizing brahmans and their position of superiority was indicative of the widespread acceptance and prevalence of caste among the Indian community in Trinidad. People also usually preferred a brahman over a non-brahman for conducting religious ceremonies. Given the ceremonial authority that brahmans wielded, temples became a space for exercising power and demonstrating status in the community. Caste is, after all, a ritualized, ceremonial practice in the Indian Hindu caste order, which receives social sanction as a result of the influence of the *shastras* (holy texts), mainly the *smritis*.

The caste origins of the many orthodox brahmans in Trinidad thus remain suspect. Though many claim that they can trace their ancestry through memories passed down from their grandfathers (*aaja*), their authenticity is not quite on a par with that of the brahman *sramanas*. Today those who claim a brahman identity in Trinidad face some hurdles in asserting a superior identity.

In his pioneering study of Trinidadian caste formations, Colin Clarke noted that two prominent castes of brahmans were recorded on the island: Gosain brahmans and Maharaj brahmans. It was commonly accepted among brahmans that the former, who were considered hermits or ascetics, formed the highest caste.[16] The Maharaj brahmans were dominant in the town of San Fernando, the most populous city on the island. Part of the reason for this is that Maharaj is not a subcaste of brahmans but a title that refers to royalty or the ruling class. Many socially mobile and aspirant Indians took this name in the hope of enhancing their status, and thereby ascended from non-brahman castes to brahman.[17] That is why one could find a pork-eating Maharaj in Trinidad.[18] A second reason for the number of brahmans in the biggest town of Trinidad could be related to the salience of class over caste in a modernizing multiracial society. Clarke reports families who graduated to the brahman caste regarded it as a "secular" status quite distinct from that of the retrograde, ritualistic brahmans.[19]

An important part was played in the reproduction of caste in Trinidad by the Ramayana and other Puranic stories, which acquired a heightened value and significance among all believers. Ram became the Ram of everyone. As soon as the lower castes— the East Indian Trinidadians—started claiming positions of leadership by virtue of Ram—the lord of displaced nations—they became respected representative figures. Their understanding of Ram was informed by the writings and teachings of the accessible and egalitarian fifteenth-century mystic Kabir. One of the earliest

Indian organizations to be formed in Trinidad was the Kabir Das Kendra, which represented Ram as a virtuous figure.

Untouchability

In her ethnographic study of Indo-Trinidadians, Tejaswini Niranjana states that untouchability among the Indians in Trinidad disappeared as the indentured communities underwent complex changes.[20] There is, however, no detailed explanation of what happened. There were certainly complex relationships between assimilation, enhancement of status, and economic possibilities that offered change. Change indeed eroded caste identifiers, as was the case with the majority of the nineteenth-century Indian diaspora, most of whom consisted of vulnerable caste communities.[21] Yet caste continued to be practised on the plantations, and special demands were made by brahmans on account of their caste.

While conducting research in 1964, Clarke found that only 20 out of the 149 Hindus whom he surveyed knew about their caste.[22] Yet after interviewing people across castes, Clarke concluded that "Brahmanism has increased and not decreased in importance", contrary to what was often assumed.[23] The outcastes were mistreated when food was served. For example, a labourer from South India, referred to as a "Madrassi", mentioned that a Kurmi-caste woman didn't offer him food on a plate but on a leaf because of his low caste position. Caste even operated among the dominant castes: one Indian-born brahman informant reported to Clarke that caste arrogance existed among the upper echelons. "The high castes are arrogant," he lamented.[24]

As can be observed from this, caste plays a role in diasporic Indian society. As an occupational category it exists among the Indo-Trinidadians.[25] The Pandits' Council of Trinidad and Tobago, which is the accredited body of 500 pandits who are brahmans, controls the religious aspect of the Hindu community. For a non-brahman member to obtain membership and become a priest is almost impossible because of caste restrictions. This also applies to the work of brahmans in officiating at religious ceremonies and at marriages. An absolute control of the vocation was accepted by the Government of Trinidad and Tobago. When a non-brahman tried to secure membership of the Pandits' Council, he was refused by the community, which organized a public hearing in the square reminiscent of the *panchayats* in Indian villages.[26]

Non-brahman groups, mostly shudras, have taken offence at brahman exclusion. Their support of Hindu organizations and institutions derives from their shared faith. However, they are at odds with the ritualistic exclusion of non-brahman castes. An Ahir-caste middle-class youngster, Bisram, charged the brahmans with reproducing Brahmanism in Trinidad. He accused them of isolating the religion from the rest of the non-brahman community and not giving due recognition to the faith of believers. "They have not taught the people about their religion; in fact, it has been in their interest to keep the people ignorant and superstitious," lamented the Ahir-caste informant to Clarke.[27] Similar sentiments can be noticed among reformers and radical activists in India, who have all argued for the rights of shudras.

Bisram made several attempts to reform Hindu religious practices in Trinidad. But applying a similar pattern of protest seen in India did not succeed in breaking the closed sanctum of brahman supremacy. Bisram was a Sanskritized Hindu who spoke Hindi and followed a brahmanical ritualistic lifestyle. He didn't smoke or consume alcohol, he was vegetarian, and adhered strictly to Hindu practices, yet his campaign to realize an ideal brahman was unsuccessful.

The right combination of caste, class and occupation is a distinctive requirement in securing employment and managing the affairs of the Hindu community as a whole. Caste can provide an attractive means of transcending class, especially for poor brahmans, who manage to secure honour and respect as brahmans even though poor. However, the same is not possible for a Chamar, whereas a poor brahman can obtain a position in the social circles and councils of higher-caste wealthy brahmans. This phenomenon presents a challenge to the theory of caste as a religiously sanctioned graded class system. The higher in the caste and subcaste one goes, the more respect is given, but for poor, low-caste brahmans, that is a distant possibility. In India, with over 1,880 subcastes among brahmans, those lower-caste brahmans who are treated with contempt by the public are the ones who have frequent interaction with non-brahman castes. They receive scorn from the general public for cheating and deceitful practices. These lower-caste brahmans do not receive the same respect from higher-caste brahmans, and neither do they obtain preferential treatment among the majority shudra, Baniya and Dalit groups.

To examine the relevance of caste among the diasporic populations, we need not confine ourselves to the oppressed subjectivity only. We need to examine the dominant castes who have managed to reproduce and retain the institution without much opposition. The *gurudwaras* (places of Sikh worship), temples, social organizations and nationalist cultural groups are all riven by bitter caste divisions. The expressions of caste warfare don't find their way into the media nor are they the subject of inquiries by policymakers. However, caste has remained part of Indian culture.

Caste has been corporatized in the form of cultural institutions, subcaste associations and religious bodies. For ritualistic purposes, caste is pervasive and one of the most reliable markers of difference. Here notions of purity and pollution are central to the caste order. Food-eating habits such as vegetarianism and the preparation of food by acceptable dominant castes are normative. The same might not be reflected in secularized spaces, where people prefer to order food from delivery services or eat in restaurants. Many brahman and other dominant-caste households have supported and developed private food delivery services to satisfy the *sattvic* dietary requirements of brahmans, who prefer brahman-cooked food. I witnessed the informal organizing of food delivery in South Africa and America. At the other end, the lowest castes, who are regarded as impure and dirty, consume meat like Muslims and Christians.

Caste, then, is not only a ritualistic Hindu category but is present in other religious identifiers. Many Dalits in the diaspora converted to Christianity and Islam in order to escape caste oppression. As the brahman category was not easily accessible to the outcastes, other religious identities which put them on par with higher castes were assumed. Thus, caste existed among Indians of other religions. Castes among Muslims are also a feature of Islam in South Asia, especially so in India. The influence of caste is visible in the practices of marriage among Muslims and the pride they carry in their last names. Many of the younger generation of Indian Muslims carry their caste rank with pride without knowing much of its deep history.

Racialism and Dalithood

The relationship between Black people and Dalits in Trinidad is quite striking, not only because of the common history of oppression and marginalization but also because of the characteristic nature of their status in society. Whites and brahmans, for both Blacks and Dalits, represent oppressive structures of control. The solidarity between colonial whites and brahmans or dominant castes is well known from various episodes during the era of the British Empire in the subcontinent.

However, there is an equivalent history of solidarity between Dalits and Blacks, starting in the nineteenth century and continuing into modern times. We have analysed this solidarity between American Blacks and Indian Dalits in previous chapters. However, similar solidarities exist in the global South, especially among the outcastes of society.

When I started investigating this solidarity in the Caribbean, the people who reached out to me from the islands were of lower-caste heritage. Many of them had mixed over several generations, but remembrance of their past formed part of their family history. The lore that was passed down from generation to generation spoke of their triumph in transitioning from an outcaste to a successful person in the Caribbean. However, this was not always the case. Others chose not to prioritize their identity. There were several reasons for this. One was the lack of written texts demonstrating caste pride and discourse. Much of the literature related to India was religious or political in nature. The Bhagavad Gita, which was widely available to Indians on the island, does not grant pride to the lower castes. Moreover, anti-caste, critical hermeneutic literature written in English did not find a place on the shelves of public and private libraries. What were often available were political studies of Gandhi-inspired activism and social organizing.[28]

An exception to this was in the Southeast Asian countries, where the Tamilian labour forces gained access to Tamil literature and news updates from the homeland, given the proximity of the two and connectivity within the region. Rettamalai Srinivasan's weekly *Parayan* was read by Tamil labourers in British colonies in the region.[29] The social activist Periyar's Self-Respect Movement had branches in Ceylon (Sri Lanka), Burma and Malaya in the 1920s. They were an active force that contested caste discrimination. Periyar argued that the Tamil people had fled to faraway lands to escape caste discrimination at home.[30] By this he largely meant the landless working-class Dalit labourers. Their descendants were instrumental in organizing the first World Dalit Convention in 1998 and the second in 2024, at which the prime minister of Malaysia, Dato' Seri Anwar Ibrahim, was the chief guest. According to Vivek Kumar, the Dalit Tamils of Malaysia came together with non-Dalit Tamilians to show solidarity as Tamils.[31] But they eventually broke off and started their own political organization in the Indian Progressive Front. This demonstrates that the Dalit population was sizeable enough to establish a political party in Malaysia (more in Chapter 5).

This was not the case in the Caribbean. But given their common social position, the two groups on the island, Black and Dalit, began putting out feelers and entering into conversations with each other. One example in Trinidad is provided by Nanan, a higher-class civil servant Chamar who became the secretary of the Gandhi Service League. Until 1963, the president and treasurer of the League had been a brahman.[32] Nanan was supportive of the Black-led government at a time when the Indian and Black communities of Trinidad were mutually hostile. Nanan tried to break down the barriers: he associated with the Black community and participated in the multiracial events in San Fernando.

Because of Nanan's progressive position, caste Hindus scorned him, yet a few brahmans who took a similar position to Nanan's and supported his initiatives were not subjected to similar hostility. For interacting with Black Trinidadians, Nanan was charged with breaking community rules and not adhering to a commonly accepted norm.

Trinidadian Hindus

It seems that Indo-Trinidadian Hindus are in the process of forming an identity, rather than adhering to a settled doctrine.

Their Hindu identity is as much a political act as it is a reaction to the dominance of Catholic and Muslim religions. As can be seen in the Indian context, the construction of a Hindu identity often comes about in opposition to the proselytization conducted by Christians and Muslims. Non-Christians and non-Muslims commit to a faith that does not subsume their heritage.

As the Trinidadian academic Kusha Haraksingh has said, his Hindu identity is "absolutely essential" for him. The first reason he gave was that he could ward off the Christian missionaries who knocked on his door trying to convert him. His gods look like him, he said, unlike those depicted in Christianity ("blue eyes and blond hair"). Being a person with caste privileges, he is aware that the Hindu faith is a religion that grants him access to his past. He is also proud to share his festivals and ceremonies with his non-Hindu friends so they can experience his culture. However, Haraksingh is opposed to theocracy. He wants the rituals to be free from orthodoxy. Haraksingh is emblematic of the majority of Indo-Trinidadian Hindus.

Over the past century, Hinduism functioned as an identity. It was, and continues to be, a performance of one's equal stature in a democratic, multi-ethnic, historically contested Trinidad. With it comes the idea of India, which is secular and embraces all those whose ancestry is Indian. Many Indians who converted to Christianity or Islam retain an Indian identity. It is practised as a robust acknowledgement of belonging to an ancient civilization. Brinsley Samaroo, a historian and politician of Trinidad, wrote that for Indians like Adrian Cola Rienzi, a labour unionist, the Indian connection provided them with an "alternative, non-British source of strength and confidence".[33] Similar sentiments are shared by others who have assimilated in the melting pot of Trinidadian society.

Hindu identity is an identity of the displaced and a memory of one's ancestral heritage. In the political economy of the plantation and later in post-independence Trinidad, society was riven by intra-racial tensions. The Indians felt they were not being given adequate respect, and that is why, for instance, as a protest, they supported the Indian cricket team whenever it visited Trinidad, at a time when the West Indies team did not have any Indian players.

Most Trinidadians who identify as Hindu are liberal in their politics and faith. Among the educated, there is an absolute detestation of the "bigot pandit" or "hypocrite brahman"—two terms often used by brahmans and kshatriyas alike. Trinidadian Hindus have a reverence for their Hindu identity, but only in so far as it provides them with respect and dignity in the extra-religious arena. Though they are Hindus, they are also aware of their caste. Caste goes along with Hindu identity. People are open to talking about it. They can easily relate to their caste by tracing their lineage, and they are well aware of their caste location. When I met them, they certainly appeared hesitant and cautious not to disrespect me or my caste location.

"The pandits con people here and demand money," said an octogenarian brahman who appeared unhappy with the way religious life was conducted on the island. "We should ban the pandits from being a brahman, they bring a bad name to the brahman," he continued. "Dharma is duty, but they make it a religious activity." The elderly brahman was a follower of Gandhi. His house was decorated with Gandhi's photos and quotes, reminiscent of post-independence Indian households that displayed the photos of national leaders. Every so often the anguished elderly gentleman would come and confide in me his strong views on caste and his distaste for it. "If someone advocates or talks about caste in Trinidad, I will fight back," he said. Upon my asking how he would do that, his response was that he would "cuss and insult them" so as to put them in their place. Increasingly, he appeared unconvinced about his own caste status. Though he had a Maharaj name, which designates the brahman caste, for him it was a mere title.³⁴ He said it was just a name and meant nothing to him.

I was informed by Sam Maharaj, a veteran labour unionist, that the Hindu faith in Trinidad inclined towards a community faith. A non-brahman pandit of a temple said the same. Increasingly, the number of people entering the temples was decreasing, and the youth were not paying attention to their ancestral faith as much as in the past. Sam Maharaj is among the many middle- and upper-class Indo-Trinidadians who express anguish about the practice of Hinduism in their country. "*Bhakti* has been gravely misunderstood," Sam said. "*Bhakti* means service. Not the kind offered while sitting in the temple and worshipping something. Nothing wrong if anyone wants to do it. But *bhakti* to me is service to the underprivileged. It is nothing else." Then the Gandhian Sam added with some humour, "Service to the underprivileged is alright but not to those who are lazy underprivileged, then your points get decreased."³⁵

Many were aware of their caste background, yet they carried out their activities as upper castes without receiving much pushback. There were many reasons for this. First, the plantation economy and the social life of indentured workers did not offer much opportunity to retain caste. However, in some instances, those with dominant-caste names could use their influence to gain favours from the planters or navigate the system of repression.³⁶ As a result, a caste binary was created: brahman and Chamar, which came to characterize caste in Trinidad. The brahmans remained the leaders and the Chamars the followers. However, case studies do show that many Chamars, like other labourers, rose in the hierarchy by gaining better economic positions.

In the plantation era, the brahmans, who were perceived as the "carriers, interpreters, and transmitters of Hinduism within the Caribbean",³⁷ could not establish their credentials as they were unable to read Sanskrit, carry out rituals, or engage in *pooja* (ceremonial offering).[38] What the brahmans were respected for was the cultural support they provided to the identity of Indians against the incursions of Christian missionaries. This position naturally gave them status and rank. But it also opened opportunities for others to consider this option. The role of the brahman was to administer a ritualist role. This could be learned by anyone interested, and thus many brahmans pursued an independent vocation in the priesthood. Those without brahman ancestry were anxious about their non-brahman caste, but over the generations they have acquired a belief in themselves. By being able to recite the religious texts, they make a case for their competency.

There is a sense of recognition among Trinidadian Hindus about their caste. They might shy away from discussing or emphasizing it unless they are brahmans. Yet caste has been part of the Hindu consciousness in Trinidad. Many people know about their ancestors though sometimes they have uncomfortable feelings about describing their caste as it is made up of many stories and legends. I asked a person of brahman background about the validity of his caste. He said his grandfather told him, which is why his family are brahmans. He added that one cannot prove it since everything was mixed in Trinidad. It is a challenge to establish one's caste. The brahman wears the *janeu* (sacred thread worn by Hindu men), but it has become a marker of ritual relations only. He does not wear it every day. Only when it comes to observing certain rituals or festivals does he don the thread. He told me that people make it a business to show off their *janeus*.

How does caste, then, become a topic of conversation if it only concerns priestly activities? A Sanskrit teacher told me that caste only matters when it comes to brahmans. However, this has been challenged by the growing influence of liberal Hindus, Arya Samaj and other radical factions who parted with the Sanatan

Dharma Maha Sabha (commonly known as the Maha Sabha), a brahmanical Hindu organization founded in 1952, over their religious orthodoxy in believing in birth-based caste as opposed to karma.

Lamarsh Roopnarine argues that the brahmans' birth-based right to special status has been diminished, which is generally true. But there are certain influential Hindu groups run by brahmans who feel otherwise. This has remained one of the primary issues of dispute and disagreement in Trinidadian Hinduism. Various Hindu temples and institutions have established their own organizations because of their differing views of caste politics. In Trinidad one hears talk about "brahman by boat" instead of "brahman by birth". At present, people are hesitant to call out the caste of others who they think might have received it from their socially mobile ancestors. However, there exists a group that believes caste is assigned at birth, and one has to commit to it in this life. This is SWAHA, an offshoot of the Maha Sabha.

Sanatanists of the Caribbean

A few Sanatanists, who believed in the eternity of their dharma—their brahmanical ritualistic faith—came together to form a body propagating and preserving the values of their faith. In the 1970s, under the leadership of Pandit Hari Prasad and his six sons in Aranguez in north Trinidad, they initially organized as the Gyaan Deepak Kirtan Mandali (GDKM) to serve the Trinidadian community. Having a commitment to the Sanatan ideology, the GDKM took the next step to formally associate with the Sanatan Dharma Maha Sabha in the 1980s. They were advised by a professor of Hindu studies from Banaras Hindu University, L.N. Sharma,[39] who was one of the consultant editors alongside Kusha Haraksingh of *Nidān*, a journal published by the Department of Hindu Studies at the University of Durban-Westville. With his expert advice and that of the leadership, GDKM prepared itself for the twenty-first century's needs. It set up SWAHA International to facilitate cooperation between Trinidad and the Americas.[40]

SWAHA is supposedly named after the ending of the religious verse in the Hindu practice of *swaha*. SWAHA is known for its activism in the Indian community to encourage religious practices as the ritual order of Hindu society. It is registered as an international non-profit in Trinidad. The introduction on the organization's website states: "We are a Sanatanist Hindu organization following orthodox Hindu traditions. Though Hindu based, the people of SWAHA engage in the service of humanity."[41] Being a Sanatanist involves working towards five Ps: "The Pundits and the People working in a Partnership for Progress in the pursuit of Paramatma."[42] Their work is informed by the values of "truth, cleanliness, compassion and integrity".

SWAHA operates educational institutions, cultural centres and religious organizations. They claim to have fifteen centres and branches in three countries: Trinidad and Tobago, Canada and India. Alongside, there are twenty institutions operating under SWAHA International. Eight additional branches act as community centres and religious organizations. There are four schools, a Hindu college, and a children's home where the children are taught the Hindu faith and ideology. The Sanatanists tend to concentrate on the younger generation proactively by organizing sporting events and youth camps and preparing them for voluntary service in temples known as *mandir sewas*.

I met a young person in his early twenties in the central part of Trinidad who was now leading prayers at a temple as a priest. He had started by attending a youth camp, where his interest in the faith was first kindled, and he then moved on to formal religious training. When I asked him about his experience of becoming a young priest, he shyly responded that it was good for him.

There were not many like him. Since becoming a pandit, he has had to abide by the rules of the faith. He cannot date whomever he likes. He cannot partake in activities that are not considered moral or ethical. He cannot consume alcohol or smoke. He cannot be seen by people in a negative light. His behaviour and attitude towards his religious duties were largely driven by his sense of responsibility as a priest. He said he was supported by elders in the community. In particular, Pandit Amar offered him support, acting as a kind of mentor. Another important fact was that the young priest was not a brahman and was aware of caste distinctions.

The institutions under SWAHA operate in terms of a broader Indian and Hindu identity. Preserving their cultural heritage is essential to their existence. The annual *Swadeshe* event to commemorate the arrival of Indians in Trinidad confirms their presence in Trinidad and Tobago society and politics. It also affirms their ancestral motherland, India, from which their faith and belief in righteousness originated. Alongside this, Diwali celebrations, youth camps, religious teachings, and instruction in Hindi and *bhajans* help keep the younger generation grounded in their tradition and history.

SWAHA also operates a community outreach programme using various media. They have an elaborate media centre adjacent to their schools. One community radio centre hosts many people. SWAHA is currently run by a young marketing professional and teacher, Jaidath Maharaj. Jaidath looks after the running of the temples, does the panditry, sings *bhajans*, and facilitates community visits to India. He is in his forties and has somewhat complicated views about his faith and practice. He identified himself and, thereby, his organization as orthodox. Upon being asked what this meant, he said he believes in the authority of the *shastras* as opposed to the supremacy of the Vedas. *Shastras* offer a doctrinal basis for Hindus, so Jaidath subscribes to the *smritis* and *shrutis*. As for the *smritis*, he feels they are vital for the conduct of a Hindu society. That is why Manusmriti is an important text in his practice. This means he does not believe people who are not born brahmans can be religious authorities. Their karma gave them a non-brahman life, and they should commit to their dharma. Since brahmans are born, there has been no question about non-brahmans taking over the affairs of Hinduism. He holds similar views about women. They cannot embrace the priesthood, and it is against their dharma. This, and not so much the earlier issues, has put SWAHA at odds with other Hindu organizations in Trinidad. However, SWAHA has held to its position, justifying it from the Hindu holy texts.

Jaidath cited chapter and verse from the Gita in which Krishna himself announces that he is the creator of the caste system. He also refers to the Puranas, especially the Gita Puran, to make his case. Jaidath believes in the value of texts written "so many thousand years ago by the sages".[43] Though he holds this belief himself, he is not quite ready yet to impose it on others. Part of the reason is that his organization is not strong and does not have many resources. With approximately 17,000 members nationwide, Jaidath wants SWAHA to continue to exist as a separate body.

His organization is a topic of disagreement and debate among Hindu and non-Hindu Trinidadians. Jaidath also has views about LGBTIQ+ communities. He does not see gay pandits as necessarily a bad thing. He knows a few of them in Trinidad. When asked what is orthodox about his faith, Jaidath said that he is orthodox in the circles of his faith. This does not mean that orthodoxy can be assumed in a secular setting. His actions are orthodox for as long as they concern his privately held faith, but they might not reflect secular orthodoxy. Like many Hindu leaders of Trinidad, Jaidath is aware of living in a multicultural country with a common law which everyone has to abide by, irrespective of faith.

What does it mean to be a Hindu?

The distinguishing aspects of the Hindu identity in Trinidad are dietary habits (both vegetarian and non-vegetarian),[44] sacred rituals and ceremonies. As far as the first are concerned, the sanctity of beef is universal. Many who converted out of Hinduism to Christianity also find eating beef or pork repugnant. If a family member wants to eat beef or pork, they are not allowed to cook in the same utensils. However, chickens, eggs and fish do not arouse the same disgust. Goat meat is widely appreciated, demonstrating that the majority of Hindus are meat eaters. "Hindus who subsist entirely on a vegetarian diet are rare."[45]

It seemed to me that Indians identified as Hindus because, for them, it didn't mean anything more significant than attending some rituals and keeping hold of their ancestors. Hinduism can be practised as much in private as in public. Indians follow the cricket, Indian TV series, and the culture that it espouses. Hindi TV series mostly have a brahmanical-Hindu narrative that embraces Indian Hindu culture. In day-to-day life, *bhajans*, *satsangs* or *poojas* are played in the background in households.

The question then arises: what does it mean to be a Hindu? It means many things, and, depending upon the various sects, organizations and groups that subscribe to a Hindu identity, its meaning can assume different dimensions. A *dharmacharya* (religious teacher) of a Hindu organization told me that the individual practices of various groups depend upon their own organization and beliefs. Hinduism is ever-expanding, and everyone can be part of it. "If one is practising the Hindu faith in a different *sampradaya* [sect], then they have the right to do so; I may not have any stakes in it. I go to other Hindu gatherings here whenever they invite me."⁴⁶ The *dharmacharya* suggested that though differences exist among the 240,000-odd Hindus of Trinidad, and he might not officially affiliate himself with any of the organizations and their sets of practices, he will still attend because they are Hindu. He did not rule out the differences that exist organizationally, which set them apart.

Hanuman in Sitaram

The common greeting among Hindu Trinidadians is "Sitaram" and "namaste". The influence of Ram through Tulsidas's sixteenth-century epic poem *Ramcharitmanas* is unmistakable. No other versions of Ram are recited or revered among the sects of Hindu believers. Part of the reason could be that their heritage derives from Uttar Pradesh and Bihar, which assiduously adhere to a particular version of the Ramayana. Hindu organizations and temples in Trinidad also keep in touch with their Indian counterparts, and are guided in their activities by them. Most rituals and religious practices follow the Indian tradition, and the temples in Uttar Pradesh and Bihar are preferred sources of guidance in Hindu interpretation and practice.

In the Ramayana, Ram is the god that everyone looks up to. However, the deity Hanuman is the main object of people's interest of devotion not least for his important role in the life of Ram and Sita and his dedication to the ideal of Ram. A pandit in Trinidad told me that Ram's inheritance was transferred to Hanuman and that he was instructed by Ram to become his representative after his death. The pandit, who was inspired by Hanuman, had a non-brahman background.

The devotion to Hanuman among Trinidadians is widespread and profound. However, no one greets with Hanuman's name but instead announces Sitaram when meeting others. The form of prayer used is the *Hanuman Chalisa*, in honour of Hanuman, and readings are drawn from the Gita and Ramayana, varying according to the occasion. The Ram Navami festival in honour of Ram's birth is not celebrated with as much ceremony as the Hanuman Jayanti or Ganpati festivals. The priest in Trinidad told me that though Hanuman is the preferred deity, temples without exception worship Shiva because he represents *shakti* (divine energy or power).

The practice of Hinduism is led by pandits who perform various roles and conduct various services, as "gurus, *acharyas*, scholars, and astrologers". However, the rank and caste of the pandit are not always related. There can be pandits from a non-brahman background who are still revered, but they minister to congregations separate from those dominated by caste-believing Hindus who identify themselves as *sanatanis*.

Scholars have argued that owing to economic activity and opportunities for upgrading one's status, the caste system dissolved into a class system of indentured Indians in Trinidad.[47] This is on the whole true. However, marriages, alliances and even temple leadership are significantly caste-sensitive and conscious of caste. One of the Hindu female leaders, a brahman herself, told me that while caste was important to her father, it was less so for her and, as for her children, it didn't feature in their minds at all. But on the issue of caste status in Trinidad, she said, "Caste has not gone. It has improved a lot."[48] She referred to a relative who married someone from a Chamar background. Whenever there arose a conflict between the couple, the brahman woman would shout her husband down with expressions like "You Chamar!" "Chamar" is considered derogatory, and even though people might not use it much now, it "still exists in their mind", she confided. She narrated an incident in which the word "Chamar" was used in caste conversations, and not in a positive light. A similar incident was recorded by Arthur Niehoff in his study, in which he heard the word "Chamar" used as an insult.[49]

When asked what she meant by caste improving a lot, she said that it meant that caste conversations were not taboo anymore. I had also noticed this among the Indo-Trinidadians. Many still felt uncomfortable announcing their caste unless they claimed a brahman or kshatriya identity. While caste has largely given way to class as an identity and organizing social principle, the power and significance of caste has not entirely disappeared. In fact it has assumed a new role and pattern that accommodates the standards and possibilities of the host society. The brahmans still occupy a recognized rank, and people acknowledge their superiority, while the term "Chamar" remains a slur and people are afraid now to use it. The Trinidad case is a peculiar example of how caste evolves and changes its forms. Its everyday impact is not as visible as in the past, but it does remain in memories and practices, particularly in the context of religious and, less so, communal and interpersonal activities.

Who is a brahman, and who is not?

Brahman is still a contested identity in Trinidad. Sometimes, it becomes a source of discontent and conflict while at other times it is the subject of jokes or its mention is greeted with a sarcastic smile. The identity of brahmans as a ritual elite comes with the added advantage of their being regarded as arbiters of social conventions. brahmans naturally assume leadership positions. Consequently, leading figures in the social, political and cultural fields have brahman names. The prime minister of Trinidad Basdeo Panday, for instance, was a sworn brahman. However, it is not certain whether every person's origins are truly brahman. Over the years, disputes have arisen between the ritual brahmans and others, who have been accused of not having an inherited superior position.

The Kabir Panth Association (KPA) is a group that holds the fifteenth-century holy man Kabir as their deity. They follow Kabir's spirituality, thereby undermining the assumed dominance of the brahmans. They are a non-brahman Hindu spiritual group that doesn't subscribe to the conservative values of their counterparts from the Hindu Maha Sabha. Their Hinduness is driven by the Kabir religion. The leader of the KPA mentioned the stark difference between his organization's approach to the Hindu religion and that of others. They did not support or endorse religious and caste differences, though he did acknowledge caste as a system and was forthright about his disagreement with it. Their non-caste, non-brahmanical agenda was attractive to the majority of Indian indentured labourers in Trinidad, among whom they began missionary work in the 1880s. Most members of the KPA have inherited their faith from their ancestors.

In 1932 the Kabir Association was officially incorporated and in 2019 it amended its name to the Kabir Panth Association, signifying its status as an independent sect in Trinidad.[50]

Like other Hindu organizations, the KPA runs a number of schools. Schools are a significant way of providing children with community-based values and education. Trinidad has many faith-based schools, which were historically started and run mainly by missionaries. In addition to education, the KPA also hosts religious events, facilitates cross-religious marriages, and participates in the religious programmes of Trinidad.

Non-brahman pandit

Before my arrival in the field, I was alerted to the existence of a head priest of a Ram temple in central Trinidad who held a certificate for officiating at Hindu festivals and rituals. Yet he was looked down upon because he was a non-brahman Kurmi (a non-elite agrarian caste). Pandit Amar Sreeprasad is a non-brahman pandit who is objectionable in the eyes of many. His temple's devotees are also mostly non-brahmans, who do not mind one of their kind leading the procession and chanting the holy mantras every Sunday.

The story of Pandit Amar Sreeprasad is one of resilience and spirituality. He grew up hoping to commit to dharma. His life story is that of a faithful truth seeker trying to find a respectable place in Hindu society, yet he kept meeting obstacles—not only on account of his caste but also because of his approach to reforming traditional practices in society. Pandit Amar comes across as a devout Hindu who is invested in the religion of his ancestors. Despite the obloquy he has received at the hands of dominant-caste pandits and their Hindu organizations, he has not shunned his faith or calling but has become even more resilient.

When I reached out to him, he was curious to meet me. He patiently listened when I told him about my research and why I chose Trinidad as a field site. He was happy to hear of my interest in Trinidad and the caste story of the country. He opened up and started to share the story of his life as a Hindu, but the scars of being looked down on as a non-brahman, of lower caste, remained unstated. He preferred to talk to me while taking me to places of historical and religious importance, introducing me to the nuances of the story behind important episodes in the history of Hindus in Trinidad.

Pandit Amar invited me to attend the Sunday *pooja* and participate in the ritual. There he was transformed into a priest. He wore a long *rudraksha* necklace, a kurta and a dhoti. I asked him what made him a priest. His response was that one must know the scriptures and pass an exam. He was young when he decided to pursue this life. It so happened he was exposed to temple culture through his family. His father, Roopchand Sreeprasad, was a labourer and a devout Ram *bhakt* (devotee) who used to participate in *satsangs* at people's houses and give expositions on the Ramayana. He had read the Ramayana in its entirety. His interest in engaging with the text brought him into contact with like-minded people. In this way a number of devotees came together in the 1950s to start a temple to cater to the needs of the Hindu community. The story goes as follows.

A swami from Bharat Sevashram Sangh came from India and started to teach ordinary people Gayatri Mantra at the Campu Temple in Cunupia. When the brahman pandits at the temple opposed his efforts, the devotees decided to part ways and, along with eleven others, Roopchand brought a plot of land next to the Cunupia river in the 1950s for the temple. Thus began a new form of worship for Hindus in which the swami would offer *havan* every Thursday evening. This is the same temple that Pandit Amar inherited in 1979 when he took up the temple's presidency. He remains the president and head priest. After assuming charge, Pandit Amar finally chose to follow his long calling and enrolled in the course for *panditai* at the Academy of Hinduism in the 1980s. "Those days it was not very formal, and the course was not serious," he said.

The title of pandit came with a certain standing and status. Even though he was president of the temple, people started to refer to him as "pandit" and asked him to officiate at religious functions. He became the guru to those who wanted to be initiated as priests. Becoming a pandit gave him an authority and provided him with legitimacy for his work. He was now given due recognition by his people, who called him to their homes and acknowledged his authority.

After becoming a pandit, he was ready to pursue his career, but caste kept raising its head, sometimes confronting him directly but often remaining in the background. But Pandit Amar was defiant. He was well versed in the scriptures and had studied the Hindu community carefully so as to establish himself. He had connections with people across the Hindu organizations and temples who noticed him and acknowledged his work.

Given the association of superiority with the Hindu brahmanic faith, many in the diaspora tried to emulate the character and habits of the brahmans. However, there isn't an ideal brahman who can be identified easily. Those who are priests also have to balance being a Trinidadian and a Hindu while trying to be the archetypical brahman in the eyes of their followers. For instance, Pandit Rampersad Parasaram is a physician with a degree from India. He spent time in India and became familiar with Sanskritized Hindi. His educational qualifications, the bureaucratic position he once held as a chief medical officer, and his core competency in reading religious texts eminently qualified him to become the patron pandit or *dharmacharya* (religious head) of the largest Hindu organization in Trinidad, Sanatan Dharma Maha Sabha. The Maha Sabha has over forty-two primary and high schools throughout Trinidad, exposing students simultaneously to religion, culture and pedagogy.[51]

Before turning to religious work full-time, Pandit Parasaram was founding chairman of the United National Congress party. He speaks fluent Hindi and has a command of Sanskrit. In his lectures, he easily switches between Hindi, Sanskrit and English. While giving a speech, he can deliver a *bhajan* (devotional song) and add musical flavour, as happens at *satsangs* in North India. Pandit Parasaram struck me as someone who practises certain traditions of austerity in his personal interactions. He preaches purity in practice.

Pandit Parasaram is proud of his brahman lineage. When asked if he can prove it, he replied that he had gone to the land of his ancestors, traced his people, and found that he was indeed a person of brahman caste ancestry. He is a man with gentle attributes. He holds some strong views but does not air them with similar intensity. In fact, he owns up to the trait of "Hindu politeness" when interacting with the modern forces of civic society—that is, the values of democracy.[52]

At the same time, Pandit Amar is searching for equality amidst discrimination and mistreatment. His Sunday sermons and religious events in private and public places keep him busy. Those who subscribe to his ministry are mostly non-brahmans. Pandit Amar is, in some ways, a challenge to the moral order of the conservative Sanatan Hindus. He has cordial relations with other sects. He took me to the Chinmayananda Ashram for a vegetarian lunch. The ashram is a training school that accommodates temples and rituals.

Pandit Amar is succinct and sombre when the topic of caste and politics is discussed. He was keen to learn about what was happening in India. When he heard about the various reform movements in India, he smiled. He said he was on a similar path in Trinidad. He is also keen to gain recognition from other dominant Hindu groups. Though there is strong disagreement about their working style and politics, Pandit Amar tries to keep the conversation channels open. He is not overly upset by the treatment he receives from others, but he is interested in challenging the exclusionary order of caste in so far as it influences people's faith.

Pandit Amar has a "very low regard" for the brahman pandit.[53] They look down upon people, he said, whereas his life is about working with them. One can notice how hands-on he is in his work at the temple and around the community. On the occasion of a Sunday sermon, I saw him picking up the table and organizing chairs once the *pooja* was finished. He pointed out that brahman priests would usually retire to a special room and dissociate themselves from such manual work. "They became Bhagwan [God] on earth!" he says, adding in a tired tone, "This is very sad."

He mentioned one incident when a devotee invited a few brahman pandits of the Maha Sabha. Once the two-hour-long event was finished, all the brahman pandits were first in line for being served with food while others were equally hungry. "I don't believe in that form of pandit superiority. The children should get the food first, and I believe that they should be a priority ... The pandits should be part of the people and they should eat with them. I usually spend time with devotees in the kitchen and other places. We don't need differences between the pandit and the common people. They are also humans. They are special only when they are officiating and on *singhasan* [throne]; but when they are not on official duty, they should be spending time with the people."

Pandit Amar is cognisant of the caste discrimination he faces when fellow brahman pandits don't address him as pandit. Though he calls them pandit, they merely address him by his first name. He notes that caste is fortunately not a concern for many. "We treat everyone as Hindus." Of the 240,000 Hindus of Trinidad, he notes, only 50,000 are active believers. So caste as a principle is not a priority for them, though it is of relevance in exercising leadership and gaining people's attention.

The Sanatan Dharma Maha Sabha is the most well-resourced Hindu organization in Trinidad and is also more traditionally caste-conservative. Their network of schools and radio and TV stations provides an excellent means for reaching out to people. "Whenever anyone wants to listen to *bhajans* or seek spiritual content, they tune into the radio or TV show. That is how they can have a number of devotees in their fold, which makes them predominant in the Trinidadian Hindu community." However, this has not prevented disagreement and criticism of the Maha Sabha's activities or its forceful assertion of dominance in the Hindu community by other Hindu organizations and individuals.

The situation of Pandit Amar can be looked at in two ways: firstly, the issue of faith and, secondly, the rootedness of caste. Even if he avoids caste and looks ahead, he still faces discrimination based on his ancestry. His ancestors were known for their Kurmi caste background, yet they participated in the religious tradition of Trinidadian Hinduism. Pandit Amar has a calling to serve the dharma of his ancestors, which the brahmanical Maha Sabhas interpret differently. Each group derives legitimacy from their ancestral inheritance: the Maha Sabha with its textual interpretation of brahman superiority, while Pandit Amar followed his father in pursuing the call of devotion and faith.

Pandit Amar has not travelled to India but has ensured that his son did. He is always keen to follow the news about his ancestral homeland. He navigates his faith with a strong belief in his practice of faith and by serving his congregation. He is aware of the challenges ahead but is also uncompromising. He has faced the brunt of discrimination, and that is always at the back of his mind as he preaches the word of dharma.

The turn to the right

There are many Trinidadian Hindus whose identity as Indo-Trinidadians has coalesced with their religion and who have held on to their culture as a defiant statement. This is often not so much against the past as about the present and the future. One such is Ravindranath (Ravi) Maharaj, who grew up as the son of a brahman. Curious about the world beyond him, he wanted to leave Trinidad after school and go to India to learn Sanskrit and study the holy scriptures. An opportunity arose when in the early 1970s S.S. Apte, the founder and general secretary of the Vishwa Hindu Parishad (VHP), the right-wing Hindu nationalist organization, came to Trinidad. Ravi was tasked with facilitating the meeting. It was successful. Moreover, the convention opened his interest in his faith and directed him to his calling. Apte noticed the young man and the work he had performed, and asked Ravi if he wanted to visit India. "This was divine. I was expecting it for a few years and now in 1972 I was offered to go." He arrived in Bombay.

As a young Hindu brahman, Ravi realized that it took more to be a Hindu than merely participating in Hindu rituals and prayers. He slept in the offices of the Rashtriya Swayamsevak Sangh (RSS), a Hindu nationalist volunteer paramilitary organization, in Mumbai, Bangalore and Delhi, before finally settling in Benares (Varanasi). Here he enrolled for an elementary course in Sanskrit at the Sampurnanand Sanskrit Vishwavidyalaya.

While growing in the discipline of the RSS, Ravi was exposed to various aspects of Indian society. He was also encouraged to study. Finally, after some years he was admitted to a doctoral degree in religious studies. In the process he learned about the relations between dharma and politics. He spent a decade as a Hindu missionary, supported by local Hindus. They fed him and offered him support whenever needed. He kept in touch with his family back home via letters.

It was not until he was obliged to conduct fieldwork for his doctorate that he returned home to Trinidad. Upon his return, he became a respected patriarch who could advise the younger generation of Hindus. He became a point of contact between Trinidadian and, by extension, Caribbean Hindus, devotees of African religious traditions in the Caribbean (the Orisha faith), and Indian Hindu organizations. He founded Hindu Prachar Kendra, which organizes religious festivals and the observance of important days in the Hindu calendar. Ravi is often the officiating head at these events. At temples across Trinidad, it is common to recite mantras and *bhajans*, play Indian musical instruments such as harmonium and tabla, and listen to lectures by pandits or learned people. Along with leaders of the Hindu Trinidadian community, Ravi has been trying to bring people to a focused political and spiritual reckoning by means of faith in Hindu dharma. Here, "dharma" stands for a common Hindu identity. However, not all align with the Hindu Prachar Kendra's politics. The differences are caste-based and stem from the hierarchies of the various Hindu organizations. Some conservative institutions do not countenance reform, while others feel affronted by it. The innocent devotee is thus often someone who has built a strong political Hindu identity outside of organizations. This makes it difficult to generalize about intra-Hindu dynamics.

When we met on 23 May 2022, Ravi was nostalgic about his days in India. He recounted the time of his activism as a *swayamsevak*. He was particularly attached to Benares, where he learned about responsibility and action. The reference to Ahilyabai Holkar made him emotional. Holkar, a shepherd-caste noble queen of the Maratha Malwa kingdom of the eighteenth century, is credited with restoring Benares to its status as a Hindu centre. Her work in rebuilding the Kashi Vishwanath Temple in 1776, which had been desecrated over many centuries, is a reminder of India's troubled past.

As a non-Muslim monarch, Holkar worked towards reinstating the legacy of the Hindus, and this meant awakening faith in the public by investing in the building and rebuilding of temples. Repairing demolished sites was a dream of the Maratha empire, for not only was it an attempt to undo the legacy of the Islamic kingdoms but also a way to bring pride to the native people who were attached to these sites of worship. It was a means to establish their agency.[54] Holkar was nevertheless challenged by the brahman Peshwas, who invaded her kingdom. She carries an honourable mention in the history of Hindus, especially among the RSS. This is evident from the recent installation of Holkar's statue at the Kashi Vishwanath Dham.

Prime Minister Modi, who inaugurated it, was widely credited as "silently following in the footsteps of Devi Ahilyabai Holkar".[55] Ravi feels the government has not done enough to preserve her name and legacy, partly because she was a woman and belonged to a lower caste.

Ravi pursued his agenda of uniting the Hindu community in Trinidad and the Caribbean. Thus, it is no surprise that he became a source of inspiration for many Hindu right-wing cadres. When he returned to Trinidad in the 1980s, his social activities coincided with his religious work. This drew the attention of the Hindu community. He was profiled by *Hinduism Today* for their January 1990 issue.[56] In that article, he explained that his ideal was to fulfil the unfinished mission of the Hindu dharma. However, he preferred to exercise patience and work towards his goal without competing with existing faiths in Trinidad. What he meant was that his work had begun, and it required a great deal of effort and compromise to start something new when conditions were not favourable. To remedy this, he managed to raise scholarships from the 1990s onwards for Hindu students to go to India and the United States to study "Hindu sculpture, the Ramayana, the Mahabharata, the Gita, the Shastras, Hindu arts and crafts".[57] The people he has mentored are an interesting mix. They look at him as an advisor. Ravi told me that he doesn't get involved in the affairs of the organizations he has established but lets the younger folk run the show. Whenever they call upon him for advice, he makes himself available; at other times, he says he prefers to stay put and devote his attention to his ailing wife and his own health.

He is looked upon as a "great Hindu teacher, leader & visionary [who is] regaled as one of T&T's [Trinidad and Tobago's] most iconic Hindus, having made an indelible and irreplaceable mark".[58] People in general have a favourable view of him, but there are many Hindu progressives who find his close association with the

RSS and the Hindu right of India problematic. One informant in his late seventies told me that Ravi has made money from his connection with the RSS. Otherwise, "on meagre earnings, how could he afford the lifestyle?" Such personal accusations do make the rounds. The Hindu community and Indians in general are aware of his work owing to his influence among wider circles in Trinidad. Ravi has been instrumental in bringing the Hindu community to the political forefront by making them active in the project of nation-building in Trinidad. His commitment to the land of his birth is apparent for all to see. This is the same place that Ravi found astounding upon his return in 1983. Perhaps his primary work has been to develop future leaders of the Hindu community in Trinidad.

On being asked his views about the future of the Hindu Trinidadians, Ravi said that he is concerned that they are not involved in practices that will bring them glory. He accused them of embracing modernity while forgetting their roots. However, this is not true of all. Many follow the dharma and learn constantly about their faith. Notwithstanding the bitter divisions among the Hindu organizations and temples, he feels that there is a common effort to transmit the legacy of the Hindus.

When asked about his opinion of the politics of Trinidadian Hindus and Indians in India, Ravi was sombre but hopeful that things would change for the better. He did not mention this, but I was made aware of the fact that he is a good friend of Prime Minister Modi. When I probed him about this, he cautiously but casually mentioned that he had worked with Modi. They share a past and are on talking terms. When asked if he was in touch with Modi, he replied in the negative. Two years later I asked him again and he explained they had spent time together in the Hindu nationalist student organization Akhil Bharatiya Vidyarthi Parishad (ABVP).

Modi was always curious. He was a listener, which made him a learner. He would ask me questions about Trinidad and hear my response. I was shocked to learn that he entered politics. He was an organizer and not a talker. Whenever the conferences of VHP were organized, the RSS deputed Modi also; thus he had visited the country twice. He learned about the religion here and would reminisce about Bharat [India].[59]

Modi and Ravi interacted a few times in India and Trinidad at the World Hindu Conference in 2000. Ravi had connections with high-ranking VHP and RSS leaders. His home became a rest house for visiting political leaders of the Hindu right from India. Ravi preferred not to delve further into this. He wanted to cast more light on his role as a benevolent veteran leader. He was still keen to describe the future of the Hindu dharma as a political project. His organization is involved in creating younger cadres and training them to become responsible Hindus.

The way in which Trinidadian Indians experience patriotism is complicated by racial dynamics. The African community makes up over 34 per cent of Trinidad's population, while East Indians constitute over 35 per cent, yet the African community has almost always taken the lead in forming the government in Trinidad. An important factor in the political demography is the "mixed" (biracial) category of people, who constitute close to 22 per cent. Of the eight premiers of the country to date, only two have been Indians. This has created strong objection and antipathy among the Indians in the Indian political party. There are often racial undertones in the discourse on both sides. The African community would often categorize Indians in a way that emphasized their lack of trust, while Indians would casually stereotype Africans as incapable of running the state and call them racist for not giving Indians adequate opportunities.

THE DALIT REPUBLIC OF DIASPORA

As our conversation proceeded, Ravi became more casual and relaxed. He began to discuss Caribbean Hindu nationalism, which can be described as a satellite Hindu nationalism that operates in various diasporic countries. Belief in the immortal words of the sacred texts composed in India carries a sense of longing and belonging on the part of the Indian Hindu community. That is why their investment in India is so deeply cultural; it is also an opportunity for them to assert their historical superiority by declaring their civilizational superiority to white people, Africans and other ethnic communities. This form of nationalism provides an unbreakable bond for the separated children of the holy motherland, which is not just an ancestral home but also a civilization of world renown. Despite their transplantation to Trinidad, their Indian identity was not unmade. This is a strong force in their existence. While many are unable to take the costly journey to India, all are sustained by their imagination of their devotional land, which is constituted by the locations mentioned in the Ramayana, the Mahabharata and the other epics they read as part of everyday rituals. In the retelling of Ramayana, the most famous text of Hindu Trinidadians, the stories and the allegories carry a strong locational aspect which evokes strong sentiments among devotees. The longed-for land—Bharat Varsha—with its mystical past and energizing spirituality, is a place of great attraction. (The reality, which only a few can afford to visit, is often the cause of great disenchantment.)

On arrival in Trinidad, Indians sought to recreate their motherland in their new home. This is especially true of the older diaspora as opposed to those who arrived post-1990. The older diaspora established various institutions and religious sites to emphasize their sense of belonging, not only to Trinidad but also to India, trying to ensure they were similar to those of the original faith in the motherland. Thus, Trinidadian Hinduism is an assimilated form of the Hindu faith that compromises with local traditions and practices. Something similar was observed by Shobana Shankar in her ground-breaking work on African Hindu priests in West Africa.[60] This desire to open up the Hindu fold by embracing native practices is often looked upon with suspicion by the conservative Hindu community.

Ravi bemoans the conservatism of the Maha Sabha. They did not welcome him when he returned to Trinidad. They insisted on pushing their own values, which were not amenable to change. But he does credit the RSS for what he is today.

> I organized children, created *shakhas* where they can play, do yoga, socialize, talk about ancestral history, and train as a scout. They are the third generation of leaders of the Hindu community. I am now organizing the Hanuman Chalisa recitation where 15,000 people are expected to attend. I am inaugurating the function at the hands of a local indigenous chief, Orisha faith leaders. I have been working since 1983 and it took this long to come to this. The path that Sangh taught me was to nurture. Don't force anything upon anyone, but let it become.[61]

He showed me WhatsApp text messages with Chief Ricardo Bharat, in which they shared pleasantries and solidarity. Ravi referred to the subjugation of the indigenous people since the time of Christopher Columbus. Chief Bharat replied in a spirit of mutual recognition and invited him to support their initiatives. The conversation between them had to do with the common experience that India and Trinidad shared of colonial subjugation.

> I grew up in this country thinking I was weak. The culture was anti-Indian, the colonial government forced us into the indentured life, and the African majority did not consider us as equals. When India was defeated in cricket it would shame us. We did not read anything about India or Africa in our curriculum. We read British history. Whenever the newspapers talked about India they talked about famines and

droughts, portraying a negative picture of the country. But I am not an Indian nationalist only, but I am also a Trinidadian nationalist. Do you know where this comes from? I draw this from Ramayana when Prabhu Ram says that the motherland is greater than heaven. My god presents this possibility.

True to these words, he wore a kurta pyjama made out of a Trinidadian flag. He is a Hindu nationalist of Trinidad who wants to stake a claim to the country of his birth. Yet he spends at least two hours daily glued to YouTube, watching news related to India. "All I do is to the credit of Sangh," he observed as he charted his lifelong venture in Trinidadian Hinduism. One of his great achievements was creating a cadre of *swayamsevaks*, people in their twenties and thirties who surround him and support his work. I noticed them preparing for the Hanuman Chalisa event in the boardroom, where Ravi held the interview. Many of them were tech-savvy, and I doubt whether they were fundamentally driven by the desire to establish Hindu supremacy. They appeared to be ordinary educated Hindu youngsters who were devoted to their faith and who looked up to their mentor, "Raviji", who welcomed them with warmth and supported their ideas. They were accountants and business management experts who were conducting financial deals with the businesspeople who set up shop at the venue for the event.

The day of the Hanuman Chalisa event finally broke. As anticipated, the entire area I had visited three days previously was now covered by a sea of red. The participants donned red clothes, including the former prime minister of Trinidad and now leader of the opposition, Kamla Persad-Bissessar, who was in attendance. The red dress that Ravi had donned when I interviewed him was now worn by everyone at the event as if to demonstrate his leadership. He explained the reason for red in a press release. Red was the colour of Mars (*Mangal Graha*), which is associated with

Hanuman, who is a Rudra—"the mightiest of the mighty". Red therefore represented "the fiery strength of Mars".[62] Tuesday, *Mangalwar*, is also the day of Hanuman. Cleverly, through the colour red, Ravi also adverted to the Trinidadian national cause.

During the event *poojas* were performed by people in a big *pandal* (marquee). The priests occupied tables spread out in great numbers to cater for the devotees, who had come with their families. It reminded me of the village *yatra*, when people undertake a pilgrimage to fulfil their promises to the gods. Those attending were familiar with the Sanskrit verses that were sung from the stage.

As the chanting began with a *doha* (couplet) from the epic poem *Ramcharitamanas*, the screen projected scenes from the Ramayana. The crowd was swept into a trance to the singing of about thirty vocalists, eighteen female and twelve male, including the musical artists. The base provided by tabla and dholak (drum) kept the tempo steady. One could see that the crowd knew the verses and were quick to join in the choruses. A visiting priest from Guyana broke into tears. A motley group dressed as Ram, Lakshman, Sita, Hanuman and the entourage of Ram's army walked through the audience of around 15,000. They kept appearing to enliven the stories from the people's favourite epic.

At the event leaders from the Orisha faith offered prayers in their own language,[63] while the mayor of Chaguanas, Mohammed, presented his greetings and elaborated on the history of the region and of Hindus in Trinidad. He emphasized that as a Muslim he was respectful of the Hindu faith. India's High Commissioner to Trinidad also spoke. He announced that the *prasad* from the Ayodhya Temple in India would be given to the devotees in Trinidad. He also chanted a prayer and expounded on his belief in Hanuman. A member of the organizing committee had to indicate for him to end as he had gone over time. Ravi then took over the stage to conclude the event. He started his speech by asking everyone to stand and offered prayers. He announced that the prayers of his ancestors and their vibrations were still felt in this country. He also made special mention of Trinidad and Tobago, hinting at the political interest of Indians in the government, and ended his speech with "Jai Trinidad and Tobago", to which a few members in the audience replied with a chorus of "Jai".

The salutations of Hanuman or Ram and appreciation of the Ayodhya Temple are not the same as the mass politics of the RSS and BJP in India. In Trinidad, reverence for Ram or Hanuman should be understood in the context of religious devotion and the long memory of people's ancestral heritage. The construction of the Ayodhya Temple was a matter of celebration for Trinidadian Hindus, as it was believed to be the home of their beloved god. While the politics of India were reflected here, they were not used to mobilize people. Hindu right-wing politics in Trinidad are pragmatic rather than dogmatic, in the knowledge that Hindus are not a majority in the country. Although people were aware of the history of Islamic invasion in South Asia, they did not seem concerned, as Hindu–Muslim relations in Trinidad are not the same as in India. What Ravi was advocating was a broader Hindu unity. It was unclear if this was directed against anyone, but its focus on India was clear. The vision of India was boundless, and was noticeable in people's appearance, self-presentation, and references in the Hindi language. They were still "nationalists", as Ravi observed.

He appeared to present his views on caste as a progressive who has a distaste for caste. Yet he has not made any efforts to counter caste. As an example he told me of an incident in Nagpur, at the RSS headquarters, when three brahmans preferred to eat separately as they would not share their food with others. A few days later, they realized they had isolated themselves from the rest and then decided to join the others. He said the Sangh did not enforce its views but allowed people to discover them for themselves. "Personal realization is a long-term solution." This seems like a Gandhian or passive mode of self-realization through the spiritual search for truth. In the Sangh, he said, they never asked about each other's caste because that would create divisions. I told him about the incident mentioned in Bhanwar Meghwanshi's memoir when he received mistreatment at the hands of the dominant caste, Sanghis. Ravi listened patiently and said the solution must have come from the top, for the Sangh discourages lateral discussion.

When I asked him about the brahmans who claim superiority based on birth, he said this was the result of arrogance and *abhimaani* (false pride). His belief in caste revolved around *guna* (virtue), karma (action) and *swabhav* (true self). All other interpretations of caste were unacceptable. He mentioned this twice during our discussion. It was almost as if he had memorized this answer in reply to the many questions he frequently faced about caste. It felt as if he was not responding to the caste question for the first time.

However, he believed that caste would become a global issue. He had a different take on the globalization of caste. This was due to the "Abrahamic intelligence forces that are working against Brahmic forces". I do not know what he meant by Brahmic, but it was distinct from the existing Western order. "The rise of Bharat [India]", according to Ravi, was seen as a "threat by the Western world". He specifically pointed to the United States and Britain: "Now that Bharat is achieving great heights, the enemies of progress will take on the country by destroying Bharat academically. They will look at the weak link. Their intentions are to find the fault lines inside Bharat. These weak spots are caste." He acknowledged that the Indian caste situation was volatile and that it could hamper the progress of the country. Like many others, Ravi thought caste issues had

1. Gangadhar Pantawane's African American reading list, at his residence in Aurangabad.

The Asian-African Nexus
Be Present for the Historic Commemoration of India's Martin Luther King, Jr.
Dr. B.R. Ambedkar's 107th B-day
Fulfill their unmet dream to join forces. Unite with Dalits to break casteism's 3,000 year grip.

Dr. Martin Luther King   Dr. B.R. Ambedkar
Crime: **Born Black**   Crime: **Untouchability**

Where: The Ralph Bunch Center
Time: 4/16/98 2218 6th St. N.W. 5-7 p.m.
Refreshments will be served.
Sponsors: GRADUATE STUDENT COUNCIL, Caribbean Student Assn. African Students Assn., International Student Assn., and Haitian Student Assn.
Isn't It Time We Stopped Pretending That American Racism is More exalted than IndianCasteism?

2. A poster for an Ambedkar Jayanti event at Howard University in 1998. This was the first such commemoration of Ambedkar's birthday at a historically Black US campus.

प्रधान मंत्री भवन
PRIME MINISTER'S HOUSE
NEW DELHI

June 22, 1982

Dear Mr. Berwa,

    I have your letter of the 14th June.

    My programme in the USA is already very rushed and it is not possible to add to it.

    Ours is one Government that has gone all out to help the weaker and poorest sections. There are many special facilities and programmes to help the Scheduled Castes and Tribes. Occasionally, incidents do take place but they are strongly dealt with. It does not help for those who are living in affluence abroad to comment on situations about which they have little knowledge.

                        Yours sincerely,

                        (Indira Gandhi)

Mr. Laxmi Berwa,
President, VISION
4804 Catherine Court.,
Clinton, Maryland,
U.S.A.

3. A letter from Prime Minister Indira Gandhi to Dr Laxmi Berwa, chaffing at the work of Dalits abroad.

4. Yogesh Varhade, founder of the Ambedkar Center for Justice and Peace, and Dr Berwa, one of the leaders of VISION, protesting outside the UN against Atal Bihari Vajpayee's government.

5. Milind Yengde, my father, protesting the Indian government's apathy towards the inclusion of caste in Durban. The banner reads: "DHARNA: To protest against the Indian government's objection to include the question of caste discrimination at the UN Conference Against Racial Discrimination held in Durban".

6. Milind Yengde with his old associate Raja Dhale, one of the co-founders of the Dalit Panthers and a leading literary figure in Marathi canon.

7. Ravi Maharaj donning his Trinidadian attire, which carries the symbols and colours of the flag.

8. Sadhuji, a Chamar performer and singer, at his residence in Debe.

9. Shiva Harijan Mandir in Debe.

10. The observance of Kathina, a Buddhist festival, at the Dr Ambedkar Memorial Committee of Great Britain, Wolverhampton.

11. Pandit Amar Sreeprasad at his Sunday congregation in Cunipia.

12. An informal meeting hosted at a labourers' camp in the UAE, September 2023. As with other photographs involving the working-class Dalit diaspora, the audience wanted me to be included too.

13. Author with the Dr Ambedkar Welfare Organization Malaysia in December 2024. Pictured are Datuk Panjamurthi, a leading figure of the Dalit movement in Malaysia and head of the organization, and office bearers Sambath Rao, Sasikumar M., K. Kalaiselvam and K. Krishnan.

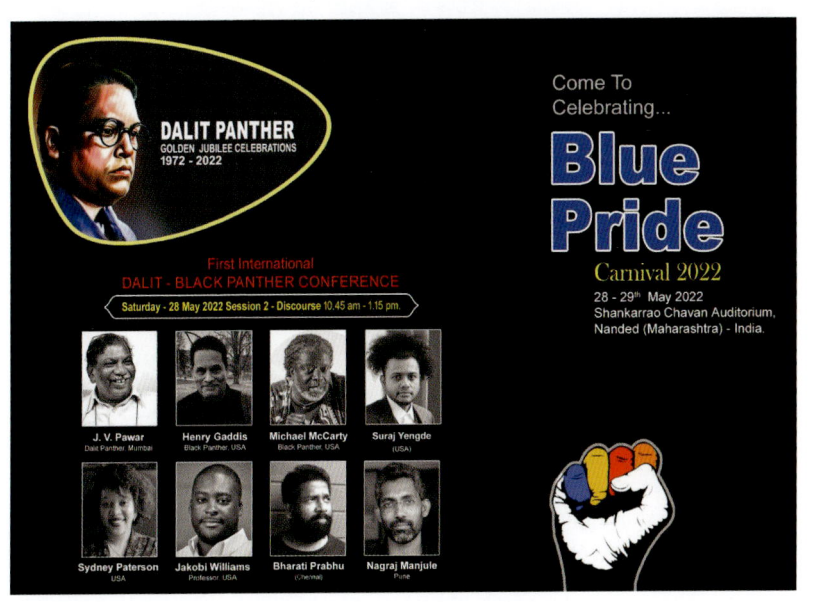

14. The Dalit Panthers' Golden Jubilee celebration, hosted by the Yuva Panthers in Nanded. It was the first formal meeting of Dalit Panthers and Black Panthers.

15. Dalit activists in India, July 2020, protesting the murder of George Floyd. Left to right: Ravi Keerthi, Bhimrao Kanshiram Keerthi, Mayuri Keerthi.

16. The Ambedkarite Student Group at the Indian High Commission in London. Such forms of visible student-led organizing and activism at overseas educational and government institutions have been noticeable since the late 2010s. The student groups organize through academic conferences and the observance of Ambedkar-related days.

to do with Indian and global politics, and not with his home country of Trinidad and Tobago.

Caste archives

To better grasp the state of contemporary castes in Trinidad, I conducted research in the National Archives of Trinidad and Tobago, looking at the arrival registers of Indian indentured labourers. These records provide detailed information about them, including people's personal particulars and caste affiliations. The register for the first ship that arrived in Trinidad carrying indentured labourers in May 1845 lacked comprehensive caste records, however—with the exception of the period between 1892 and 1896—those for ships arriving from October 1886 until 1916 consistently recorded caste details for indentured labourers arriving from Calcutta.

It is noteworthy that the spellings of names and castes were phonetic in the early registers. "Brahman" for instance was often spelt "bramon",[64] but the spelling improved over the years. When the list of castes was drawn up in India, the magistrates also recorded them based on their understanding of caste classifications. However, with the advent of modern registers and recording technologies in the twentieth century, caste information began to be documented more accurately in terms of format, phonetics and spelling. This standardization in Indian registry practices gradually extended to the distant colonies.

In the aftermath of the abolition of slavery, the system of indenture, as it evolved, was given a veneer of legality with provisions for an elaborate bureaucratic process of recruitment and supervision. Emigration agents were hired to recruit labourers. They often targeted rural areas of India where caste atrocity and feudal violence were prominent. They also looked for places where workers were docile and willing to work. With the help of the local administration, they then transported the workers to distant Calcutta for the onward journey, in the case of those headed for the Caribbean, of three months. Each labourer was given an emigration pass, which was an endorsement of their fitness to work. It carried the signature of the depot surgeon, who had examined the labourer and certified his or her capacity to undertake the journey and to labour in a tropical climate. The surgeon was tasked to ensure that the labourer was "free from all bodily and mental disease". The emigration agent working on behalf of the Government of Trinidad would make a declaration that he had engaged with the labourer, who was "willing to proceed to that country to work for hire; and that I have explained to him all matters concerning his engagement and duties". Thereafter the Protector of Emigrants would endorse the pass according to the protocols. This three-way verification was a way of demonstrating the formalized legal nature of indentureship, a contractual relationship freely entered into by all parties. It was a statement by the British colonial government that it was no longer in the business of slavery.

The references to caste in the lists are revealing. Notably, the brahmans are not the dominant or even a significant factor in registers for Trinidad. In fact, in one of the registers for a ship leaving Calcutta on 3 February 1891, there was no brahman caste mentioned, while the *Ganges* sailing on 24 November of 1910 included 36 brahmans among the 383 indentured labourers on board. For ships leaving from Calcutta, which served such areas as modern-day Bihar, Uttar Pradesh and West Bengal, the majority of castes recorded consisted of Chamar, Chamarin, Pasi, Gond, Kori, Thakur, Ahir, Lodh, Lohar, Musahar, Mussalman, Mochee, Sonar, Dusadh, Dhankar, Mallaah and so on. For those ships that left Madras, which served modern-day Andhra Pradesh, Tamil Nadu, Telangana and Karnataka, the castes included Kapu, Madiga, Paria, Mala, Dhoby, Reddy and so on.

THE DALIT REPUBLIC OF DIASPORA

The overwhelming representation of the untouchable castes as well as lower-caste shudras makes the case for Trinidad and Tobago being a Dalit–shudra haven. Over 90 per cent of the descendants of indentured labourers in Trinidad have a Dalit or shudra background. One can assume, in view of the caste character of the Central Provinces in India, that the Muslims who came were also from the lower castes.

Each ship that came from India also included women. Even the very first that arrived in Trinidad in 1845 had women on board, most in their twenties or thirties. The reference to Chamarin in the registers indicates the presence of Dalit women in the making of the economy of indenture. Their stories of endurance as well as the traumas they underwent have been well documented in the studies of Rhoda Reddock,[65] Brij Lal,[66] Goolam Vahed and Ashwin Desai, and, more recently, Gaiutra Bahadur.[67]

What happened to the Chamars, who appear frequently in the archives? Though "Chamar" continued to be used among the indentured labourers, the term carried negative connotations and even the Chamars started to disown both the term and the identity that went with it. In historical texts, one notices "Chamar" being used condescendingly. Even in the interviews that I conducted in the deep south of Trinidad it was clear that a generation earlier that term had been in popular use, but it now was much less used. Many of those to whom the term had been applied originally no longer used it in their self-declarations.

There are people, though, who continue to use the term. One is Sadhuji, a dancer and performer of Ramlilas, the folk re-enactments of the story of Ram. He took the art form and made it a statement of his spirituality and faith. Nonetheless, he was a Chamar, as his childhood memories indicate. Even when he started to gain attention for his art and develop an audience of his own, the Chamar identity followed him. But he appears unbothered by it. During my interview with him in Debe, in southern Trinidad, Sadhuji was ecstatic and jovial, refusing to play the caste role as part of the narrative of his life.

Shiva Harijan Mandir

During my research trip, I was informed that there was a temple, or *mandir*, that bore Harijan in its name.[68] My informant told me it had some caste-related history, but she was unsure. I immediately contacted the pandit there, who invited me to join them for the Sunday sermon. I thought it must be in a rundown area, as no one had mentioned to me where it was. However, when I arrived, I found a bright and colourful space where a few dozen devotees were offering their prayers. Teenagers and children occupied the stage, both male and female, who sang religious songs and played tabla, harmonium and other Indian musical instruments. The session went on for nearly two hours.

Two people appeared to be in charge of the activities. I went to one person who occupied a central seat and wore white clothes, to inform him that I had arrived. He told me that the pandit would attend to me. This was Siew Kumar Samlal, who was dressed in kurta and pyjama and was singing with the younger group of singers. The singing continued as the *havan* was being offered by a woman. The majority of the devotees were women. Their colour complexion was generally dark, with a few lighter-skinned people.

When the first session ended, the pandit invited me to join him on the the stage and announced to the congregation that they had a guest from India, and he would lead the reading of the Bhagavad Gita. I was alarmed and uncomfortable. I hadn't read the old Sanskrit in its original form since high school. So I requested the pandit to lead the chanting while I followed. The grammar of the Vedas is difficult on the tongue and requires practice. The pandit read it seamlessly while I attempted to catch up. The phonetics of the chanting and the pronunciation were certainly different from what I was used to hearing in India, but I managed. Following the *pooja*, the pandit invited me formally to the temple and introduced me to the congregation. He wanted to be interviewed publicly so that the congregation could participate in the discussion. Our discussion was conducted in the format of a structured group interview.

When I was referred to the Harijan Mandir, my informant told me about the caste nature of the temple. She indicated the "Harijan" dominance there. During my call, I asked the pandit about the temple's Harijan identity. He confirmed that the temple's name was Harijan, which refers to outcastes and untouchables. During the discussion at the temple, I learned that a Hindu saint from India, Keshav Das, had visited Trinidad in 1968. He wanted to teach dharma and sing the devotional songs of *bhakti*. Keshav Das was a well-known preacher who taught many Indians in the West and other diasporic societies about the Hindu religion. He was also a scholar who wrote books on the Bible and the Gita. It was his idea to give the name Harijan to the temple in Trinidad. The pandit and the congregation, however, were not aware of the reason behind the name, though the former knew that Gandhi had used it as the title of a weekly publication and had thereby helped popularize the term.

The pandit was also familiar with the Hindu scriptures' references to the caste system. Drawing on the references to Chaturvarnya (the *varna* system) in Krishna's discourse, the pandit described the characteristics and qualities of *guna* that were required for the caste system to fulfil its proper role in society. He formally introduced me to the congregation by saying, "We have a guest from Maharashtra, India, and he called me yesterday. He is searching for something or somebody in Trinidad. He asked if there are any of these in Trinidad context. At first, I said not, but in retrospect we are all what he is looking for." Instead of using the word "caste" or Dalit, he wanted me to initiate the conversation.

As the conversation began, he directed the focus of the congregation to caste. His interpretation was that the caste system had been forced upon society during colonial and postcolonial times.

> The colonial masters distorted the viewpoint of Shrimad Bhagavad Gita. The workers who were masses were meant to be kept down; that is where the word Harijan was given to untouchable people who are not fit for worship, but, yet still, without them the work could not have been done ... He was asking if there are any Harijans in Trinidad.[69]

A woman in her sixties who sat beside me and the pandit said, "We are all untouchables." She referred to the pioneering genealogist of Trinidad, Shamshu Deen, who has helped to connect Indo-Trinidadians with their roots in Bihar and Uttar Pradesh. The woman, citing Shamshu Deen, said there were no brahmans in Trinidad because there was no necessity for them to seek work in Trinidad: in India they were well-off and not deprived of food. Her great-grandfather came to Trinidad because he did not have enough to eat, she said.

When I asked why there exist brahman titles in Trinidad, everyone broke into laughter. The pandit then referred to the Trinidadian historian Brinslee Samaroo's work, which argued that by assuming different names, indentured labourers had arbitrarily acquired new caste identities. He then mentioned the line in Manusmriti, "Dharma must be taught to all." I then cited another verse that punished a shudra for reciting a religious text. He replied that the "fella who at that particular time is cleaning a toilet, it may not be the best time to chant, but you limit him from attaining the ultimate *moksha* ... Time, place and circumstance dictate how you make decisions." He meant to indicate the temporary nature of the shudra identity, that one is shudra while performing certain tasks. This could also mean that the Trinidadian experience of caste has evolved to make adjustments to caste identifiers and their immediate relationship with vocations.

I enquired of the congregation what they felt about the inauguration of the Ayodhya Temple and its celebration at the Hanuman Chalisa event. The pandit paused and cryptically said that anything that brings people together is a good thing. I probed further, saying that it was a controversial site, and asked if people knew about it. He said that people were aware that the Indian site had been invaded by Muslims, who damaged the original structures. But that did not translate into animosity towards other faiths. The reason for this is that in Trinidad Hindus and Muslims came together: survival didn't require religion but brotherhood, which continues today. However, contributions were sent individually for the temple's reconstruction, and the swamis, the leaders of the various Hindu sects, attended the inauguration.

Caste came up when talking about marriages in previous generations, but it was regarded as an irrelevant institution of those times. "The grey-haired people here had an arranged marriage, but now we don't have that in their grandchildren's generation. Now they just meet and marry each other."

I mentioned the Hathras gang rape incident of 2020, involving a Dalit girl, and how Dalits thereafter left Hinduism and embraced Buddhism. A woman in the congregation said that one couldn't blame Hinduism for that. The pandit then brought the Catholic faith into the discussion and mentioned how they wooed many in India towards the faith. "We have to thank god for our grandparents who took that trip here and did not live there." Everyone burst into laughter and said "correct". They were grateful to their ancestors who had left India and made them "lucky" as well as to the gurus who came to teach in Trinidad.

I asked the pandit if he had met anyone who identified as Harijan or Chamar. At the word Chamar, everyone burst into laughter. It was an object of ridicule, as discussed earlier in the chapter. The pandit explained how the word became associated with higher and lower, especially in terms of lightness of skin colour and hierarchy. But they hadn't yet come across anyone identifying as Harijan or Dalit.

My quest to find the Dalit in Trinidad continued.

Sadhuji, Chamar

I was informed by Pandita Indrani about a performer of Ramlila whom she had worked with for many years. She briefly mentioned that he had had to endure discrimination for being a Chamar. I called him, giving the pandita as a reference. He was anticipating the call and expressed his pleasure at being able to talk to me. He broke into the Bhojpuri dialect of Hindi, which he spoke fluently. I asked him about his story and introduced myself as a Chamar from the backward caste community to make the conversation easier. He said, in Bhojpuri, "Dhanya bhaag hain mere aapse baat karke" (It is my good fortune to speak with you). He narrated his experience of travelling in India, participating in various events and performing there.

His grandmother came from Ayodhya and his grandfather from Hariya in Uttar Pradesh. He was educated up to the fourth grade, and then, after his father passed away, he gave up school and started working in a lab. His grandmother, who brought him up until her death, initiated him into the spiritual life and supported him throughout. A group of seven *sadhus*—saints—lived near his house. He was interested in them, so he started to spend time with them. That is how he acquired the name Sadhu, which is what his grandmother started calling him. His original name was Buddhram Ramgulaam Matai, and he was born in 1941 in Hermitage village.

When I arrived at his place to conduct the interview, he came to touch my feet and said, in Hindi, "Dhanya bhaag hain hamaar jo aap aaye, kuch purveke bhaag hain" (It was my good fortune that you came to visit me; it must be good karma of the earlier life). He was an energetic and enthusiastic man in his eighties. His posture and speaking style indicated that he was ready to perform at any time.

His story was that of a young boy who was brought up under the influence of his religious grandmother, who would talk about religion and sing devotional verses. He became interested in religion and followed the path of hermits, learning with them and performing in their group. But life had different plans. He got a job that took him away from the full-time practice of the faith. But he persisted and would practise his religion after work till the late hours. Until about 50 years of age, he performed in the Ramlilas as Shiv. By the time he turned 50, he had taken an interest in "*naach*—dancing" and would take the parts of two characters—Shravan and a soldier of Ram's army.

How was it growing up? I had been informed that he had had to endure caste discrimination while performing in the Ramlilas. He brushed them aside and did not seem to care about them. But he stated that when he was growing up, there were many castes in existence. The ones who worked in the fields and with animals were Ahirs and Chamars. How did he know what his caste was? "My father informed me that we were Chamar."[70] Those who sold or ate pork were also called Chamar. This confirms what Niehoff and Clarke reported.

Sadhuji reiterated that the "Ramayana says don't ask caste". He kept on informing me how caste came to be misinterpreted in Trinidad. It was based on individual merit and actions—karma. Yet the brahmans kept on referring to him as a Chamar. Apart from them, no one had yet called him a Chamar. He seemed unbothered about this. When I asked him whether he had taught or knew about the mystic poet Ravidas, who came from an untouchable caste, he said one of his friends, Deo, who was also a Chamar, had a copy of a book by Ravidas that was brought by his father from India as an indentured labourer.

He reported that there were no castes today. However, he mentioned an event from a decade previously when he had gone to read the Ramayana in Golconda, Trinidad. The woman whose husband had died wanted a brahman for the function. Sadhuji informed her that he was one and was fit to do the job. She said he was neither a brahman, kshatriya nor vaishya but a shudra Chamar.

As a young man Sadhuji had seen casteism practised against his elders. He, too, experienced its effects. But he was not bitter. He was instead happy that it was in the past now. He confidently asserted that castes did not exist at present in Trinidad because they carried no weight in everyday life. Though he was a victim, he did not want that to define his identity, which was larger than that of a Chamar: he was someone who could perform the Ramlilas, who could teach the Ramayana, and sing various religious hymns. That enabled him to travel to India and brought honour on him. He was not willing to let names or terms bother him. His spirituality was so profound that these artificial divisions of the human order did not deter or trouble him.

Though he was unaware of the anti-caste movements and of Dr Ambedkar, Indo-Trinidadians like him bear the message of equality in their actions. In the absence of an Ambedkarite consciousness and any movement against discrimination based on caste, Indo-Trinidadians practise anti-caste principles in their daily lives, though without the support of any cultural organization. Those who might have protested against caste have been assimilated into the larger macro-identity of Hindus. One of the paradoxes of this is the noticeable absence of caste-based atrocities, which would have triggered anti-caste sentiments.

Conclusion: religion and society

Trinidad society is helpful in understanding the Indian–Hindu diaspora and its cultural forms. In the context of Caribbean nations, Trinidad has perhaps the most involved Indian diasporic nation. Here, politics and ethno-religious nationalism are larger concerns in the everyday interactions of Trinidadians, while religion is a hallmark of their memories and lived spirituality. This can be seen from the way they imitate and present as Indians. The Indian version that is practised is the product of the influences of popular media and YouTube videos. The Trinidadian Indian attraction to India has mainly to do with the Hindi language, the language of most prayers, and with Bollywood and Indian music. Indian politics are a topic of intense discussion.

The Indians of Trinidad have become nationalists because India represents for them a space of empowerment and assertion. The source of pride for the indentured labourers was their ancestral land. Hindu organizations which promote political Hinduism train youngsters to think about India as their ancestral country with pride. One of the lessons in Ravi's *shakhas* involves talking about India by way of stories of glory and honour. When someone looks down upon them in Trinidad or in other diasporic colonies, they assert their distant-nationalist identity even more strongly, despite living so far away from the ancestral land and not having ready access to it. Trinidadians still need a visa to enter India.

Even though caste exists in religious institutions and matters significantly for people trying to find worship and fellowship in the Hindu dharma, it doesn't impact on everyday practice in Trinidad. The near absence of caste in the everyday lives of people reveals Trinidad as a case of caste disengaging from the intense rigidities found in India. Several generations later, and far removed from their ancestral homeland, Indo-Trinidadians today ignore or overlook caste distinctions in their choices and actions. As the story goes, the majority of these Trinidadians are not brahmans and are therefore not concerned with the liturgy of the priest but rather with the sentiment of dharma. Travelling through Trinidadian villages and urban centres and interacting with Indo-Trinidadians made me realize that this was an a-caste society established by the subalterns who migrated there. Caste dominance only makes an appearance in the priesthood, which is also a functional role and which is confined to specific conservative brahmanical groups.

Trinidad helps us to understand what caste does to a community separated by thousands of miles and several generations from the motherland. My research found that though caste is not the first topic of discussion, it is a subtext in conversations in both private and religious matters. In public conversation, caste does not feature. But caste is a reality that is known to the younger generation as well, even though their distance from the temple may have loosened its grip. Temple sermons touch upon caste, not as a relic of the past but as a historical responsibility bestowed by the ancestors.

There isn't any noticeable anti-caste movement or anti-caste politics in Trinidad. Yet caste remains alive, though it is not challenged directly. It is a subtle presence and crops up most prominently in ritualism, religion, group affinities, marriages and positions of power. But these institutions and social relationships do not invite opposition or anti-caste politics to take root, as the majority of the Indian Hindu population still operate within the bounds of Hindu sanctity, which does not provide them with enough ammunition for cultural critique.

THE DALIT REPUBLIC OF DIASPORA

Another reason for this is the limited connection to or familiarity with anti-caste movements in India. The possibility of a Bahujan politics demanding social equality for disadvantaged or minority groups has not reached Trinidad. On the other hand, the Hindu right-wing has made significant inroads here. The future of the Trinidadian diaspora will serve as a case study to understand the process of realizing caste and nation. Trinidadians take notice of North American politics. Will this mean that anti-caste diasporic organizing will have any influence here? Some Caribbean Hindu scholars based in the United States have already come out in support of the Hindu right, while others stand apart from its politics. The dynamics of anti-caste politics have influenced some American Trinidadian Indians to call for the sanctity of Hindu dharma and push back against what they consider an affront to their politics.

Interaction with the state apparatus in North America falls under the purview of ethnicity and race. Will this type of politics and organizing influence the new wave of Trinidadian activism to claim equal rights devoid of caste? Young African Trinidadians have drawn attention to police brutality in their own country and its similarity to that witnessed in the United States. Though caste manifests differently, it is a concept that has to be brought into play with race, religion and nation. The question remains: What will happen to the racial dynamics in these countries? Will caste become another indicator of political divisions and conflicts? These are questions that researchers may be able to answer in a couple of decades.

5

COSMOPOLITAN DALIT UNIVERSALISM
DALIT ACTIVISM AND THE PROMISE OF A CASTELESS WORLD

A network of anti-caste activists who believe in Dr Ambedkar's mission of uprooting caste now exists worldwide. Believers in social justice and the "social transformation" of Indian society—a political slogan advocated by BAMCEF—are spreading across different parts of the world each year. The work done two generations ago, in the 1970s in India and the diaspora, is now reaching new heights.

There are movements centred around Ambedkar's name and organizations registered in major Western countries that carry Ambedkar's motto. Statues of Ambedkar are erected by his followers, and days and events commemorating Ambedkar and Dalit history are now observed as official occasions by universities, colleges, major states and city councils. People who adhere to Ambedkar's ideology have become leaders and public representatives in the UK. How it is that an Ambedkarite diasporic consciousness is reproduced with each new generation is a theoretical question that must be addressed in our study of transnationalism, ideology, and the reproduction of ethnic sociality.

In the diasporic world, religious practices have become part of national identity. India is associated with being a Hindu nation, but it encompasses multiple regional and caste identities. The stereotypical view of an Indian ethos is of a spiritual individual deeply rooted in traditional practices. However, some of these stereotypes are debunked and challenged by resurgent diasporic groups who confront this one-sided portrayal of their beliefs and practices.

Dalits in the diaspora have become prominent in recent times, making their presence known with statements about their condition and challenging their assumed inferiority in the caste system. They have done this by claiming power and contesting dominant caste views.

The experiences of migrant Dalits as indentured labourers differ from those of migrant workers and Dalit professionals. The first group has been discussed at length in an earlier chapter. The latter have more negotiating power than their predecessors a century ago. They are politically autonomous within class and caste formations. Early Dalit emigrants in the 1940s were supported by Ambedkar and the colonial government. Ambedkar devised scholarship programmes for students and scholars to pursue higher studies in the UK. Many became successful, with some remaining in the diaspora while others returned to find jobs in India.

In this chapter, we will examine the history of Dalit organizations worldwide. Drawing on field notes made in the Middle East, North America, the UK and Europe, I argue that there now exists a cosmopolitan Dalit universalism. Politically charged social groups advocating today for justice and lobbying against the state for their rights align with Ambedkar's brand of politics. Historically, Dalit groups who embraced Ambedkar's philosophy took it upon themselves to engage in socio-political work in the diaspora. With the advantage of being diasporic citizens with foreign passports, command of the English language and access to Western resources, these Dalits made their presence known to both the state and the public. By not aligning with Indian government propaganda or diplomacy, Dalit groups and individuals have bridged the gap between education, advocacy, cultural diplomacy and radical politics in their host and their home countries. Dalits have transcended the spatial and caste boundaries of local untouchability to become a global presence.

The antistatis of Dalits in the diaspora

Dalit mobility and transnational migration have been a feature of colonial modernity. During the time of British rule in India, Dalits moved along imperial networks to other colonial countries in Africa, the Indian Ocean islands and the Caribbean as well as to the UK and North America. This movement involved the transfer of migrant labour—as indentured labourers or "passengers"—during the nineteenth and twentieth centuries. Thereafter, the second half of the twentieth century saw the migration of a South Asian labour class to a wide range of receiving countries. The majority of this labouring class came from Dalit and lower-caste shudra groups. Given the nature of their work, which required hard physical and skilled labour in fields and factories, the lower-caste groups were well equipped and well suited for this. Additionally, the lower-caste population, as well as the outcastes, wanted to escape the highly degrading life they faced in India. Their migration provided them with the opportunity to seek a better life elsewhere. Despite the difficulties, many volunteered to make the long and arduous journey.

In the diaspora, caste identities could not be strictly reproduced in the indentured system, for two reasons. The first was the frequent reinvention of caste in the host society. Many indentured labourers who boarded the ships leaving India provided false names to the white colonial officials or recruiting agents who recorded their names. Many claimed dominant-caste names as their own.[1] During the long journey of approximately three to five months, many chose to reinvent themselves. So, when they arrived in a new land, they were ready with their new identities to start afresh. However, it was not an easy process as caste became a bureaucratic category attached to the labourer (See Chapter 4). Many stories of this kind have been recorded in research on indentured migration.

The second reason for the absence of a rigid caste-based religious order in the new society was the near absence of dominant twice-born castes among the indentured population. (There are, however, some records of a few brahman-caste workers who petitioned overseers to keep them separate from the lower castes, as their religious rules did not permit mixing.)[2] Moreover, maintaining preferential arrangements for higher castes would have been costly for the colonial government, which was unwilling to make special provisions in this regard. However, this does not mean that caste disappeared entirely. It was reproduced in new forms, adapting in this way to the host society. Many outcastes converted to Christianity and Islam to avoid the lower Hindu identity altogether. Additionally, there was a category of middle-caste, capital-owning "passenger" Indians who arrived to conduct commerce and establish businesses in the colonies. These distinctions are still present in different forms. Sometimes, they take the form of a regional identity; at other times, they continue as a lower-class status. This distinction is evident in spatial segregation and spiritual practices, such as temples or residential districts.

In the second half of the twentieth century, many working-class and professional-class Indian immigrants moved to Western countries in the context of post-war labour shortages. These highly educated Indians came to occupy premier positions in the job hierarchy. They came from specific caste groups, for access to higher education was strictly limited to the historically privileged metropolitan dominant castes. Devesh Kapur infers that about 90% of Indian Americans belong to the high/dominant caste heritage.[3] These dominant castes, who had benefited under the British Raj, continued to draw advantage after the ousting of the colonial regime. They replaced British personnel in the administration, the military and the service industry. Command of the English language significantly influenced their choice of migrating to the West.[4]

Thus, post-independence elites who were well versed in caste codes imported the same codes into their new worlds under the sacred guise of spiritual values. The practice of religious freedom allowed them to exercise caste-based rituals without interference from the host society. Often, any attempt by the host society to intervene was met with accusations of racism. As a result, the rigid practices of caste were eventually harmonized with cultural practices. Today, caste is practised without its being an offensive institution because it has gained cultural respect in the host society. However, these practices started to be challenged in the 1970s when some groups of Dalits in the United States and Britain organized in protest against caste (see Chapter 3).[5] This anti-caste legacy has continued with more assertive politics in the twenty-first century, led by a second batch of Indian immigrants since the 1990s.

The 1990s in India saw a growing sensitivity to caste issues. When the Mandal Commission recommended job reservations, this led to nationwide protests by the dominant castes, who had overwhelmingly cornered the top positions in government and society. At the same time, the 1990s saw the gradual liberalization of the economy, which opened the doors to the influx of foreign capital and made possible the exit of many professional Indians to the West. These two developments created opposing ideas and opposing reactions. Caste-based politics in India were both opposed and supported, and this conflict was carried by Indian migrants to the United States. Thus, many dominant-caste colleagues seized almost any opportunity to deride Dalits or lower caste colleagues by claiming they were incompetent, attributing their job positions to their status as beneficiaries of welfare. It was also claimed that these individuals did not have to work as hard as those who had obtained their position on merit alone. This argument is similar to the debate on affirmative action in America. In response, the newer generation of caste-assertive Dalits organized themselves to counter the hegemonic caste groups and assert their presence.

Theorizing the Dalit diaspora

The term "diaspora" is often applied to persecuted minorities who have escaped tragedies in their home country to settle in a host country. It is widely associated with Jewish immigrants and refugees, and it expresses loss, distance and longing. A diaspora refers to those displaced from their original homeland, with the emphasis on "original" to distinguish between settled migrants and those claiming indigenous belonging. The term gained political significance in the 1960s.

Paul Gilroy argues that "diaspora" is an old term with modern connotations, focusing more on memory than territory. The concept of diaspora has long been established, but in present-day times it is used for "nationalism and subaltern imperialisms".[6] The idea of a persecuted group establishing a new home elsewhere has acquired strong political meaning. Gilroy believes, however, that the value of the term lies in intercultural analysis and transnational formations.[7]

COSMOPOLITAN DALIT UNIVERSALISM

The term "Dalit diaspora" needs both historical and sociological exploration. Although Dalits in the diaspora did not and do not identify as such, their status as immigrants or citizens in a host country classifies them as a diaspora. It is a term distinguishing between those who belong and those striving to belong fully. However, it is not a straightforward concept. Dalits in the diaspora do not perceive their identity in the conventional diasporic sense because they do not view themselves as escaping war-like situations or claiming victimhood at the hands of state persecution, even though there are some aspects of both in their situation.

Another reason is that Dalits living abroad, mainly in Western countries, prefer to see themselves as an example of empowerment and assertion. Their identity is shaped by class-based self-perception. Their upward mobility gained through access to the job market and their potential for assimilation into the host society provide them with the confidence to claim citizenship on the basis of merit. The term "diaspora" is a category more suited to those who are refugees or are struggling to settle in the host country.

Other Dalit groups, who have been abroad for over 150 years and are not located in the West, also do not identify as a Dalit diaspora. The early immigrants transported within the colonial empire as indentured labourers were conscious of their caste. One of their motivations for travelling was to escape caste-based oppression. While some succeeded, others had to continue with the name registered on their pass for an initial phase. As a result, consciousness of their Dalit caste did not persist among the indentured labourers and succeeding generations in the diaspora. However, memories of their origins—the villages they came from and the marginalization they had experienced in India— were passed down through the generations.

The difference between Dalits in the diaspora and a Dalit diaspora lies in the difficulties of theorization. The two exist between the historical dimensions of caste and the potentialities of the future. The former assumes an agency-less subjectivity, fitting into roles established by dominant, hegemonic forces, in which the term "diaspora" aligns with dominant Hindu or Muslim representations. The latter conjures up the histories of a repressed past. The problem remains whether we can categorize people according to labels they have intentionally tried to avoid. Are categories created by people or are they constructed in the process of self-transformation over generations?

In her work on Indo-Trinidadians, Tejaswini Niranjana grapples with the question of diaspora versus Indians in Trinidad. She is uncertain how best to describe her subjects. They are not remittance-providing groups who live and work outside India, nor are they the high-status NRIs (non-resident Indians) living in the West, a group associated with recent Indian immigrants to whom an idealized notion of economic and political success is often attached. As the diasporic identity of Indians in Trinidad is unclear, Niranjana refers to them as a "subaltern diaspora".[8] She considers them a group occupying a disadvantaged position without access to elite networks in India. What, then, is the condition of the subordinated castes? Are they on a par with the rest of the Trinidadian Indians? What happened to the caste character of this diaspora? Dalits may or may not exist as identifiable groups, but their culture and origins do represent a specific story.

Thus, Dalits do not fit neatly into a diasporic profile. They are not easily categorized as simply racialized subjects, nor are they solely a nationalist diaspora focused on earning remittances and engaging in cultural activism abroad.[9] They are not outright nationalists nor are they of the revolutionary kind involved in "long-distance activism" that Benedict Anderson has discussed.[10] Dalits refuse to be grouped into either category because of their precarious and historically specific position. They are global visionaries who rely on cosmopolitan Dalit universalism, which draws upon the norms of humanity and the dignity of all. The international liberal rights-based order is one of the forums in which they contest the claims of their oppressors. They are committed to the ideals of India and are enriched by a constitutional morality, but they are not fanatical about the idea of India being ruled and governed by dominant-caste groups. Dalits are unlike the stereotypical version of the diaspora.

Dalits are not bound by the territoriality of their homeland, as is seen with other diaspora groups.[11] They are just as much Indian, but their attachment to their homeland does not change with their legal citizenship in the host country.[12] The problem with understanding the Dalit presence in a diasporic context is that they are not "political elites" often involved in bargaining for the "transnational nation-state". Dalits in the diaspora are human rights activists inadvertently involved in activism through their culture, religion and nationalism. This contrasts with the nationalism and festivities of dominant-caste Hindus, Muslims, Sikhs and Christians. The presence of Dalits and their claim to personhood makes them natural activists in the diaspora. Shrikant Borkar's work on Ambedkarites in the UK looks at the long-term activism produced over decades by Dalits. They exemplify a "defiant Indian diaspora" who "insist on creating a just and egalitarian society in their native countries".[13]

Dalits produce and reproduce the multiple meanings of space and race in the diaspora. In view of their caste location, their racial identity homogenizes their experience. By breaking the hegemonic imposition of their particular caste experiences, Dalit organization worldwide has created a pathway to channel democratic politics based on India's constitutional principles. These relate to social justice,[14] the economic redistribution of land and resources, legal justice, and equality before the law.

Early mobility

One of the earliest instances of anti-caste-conscious mobility in the twentieth century was the work of Dr Ambedkar. Ambedkar devised scholarship programmes and various initiatives to enable Dalits to travel overseas. Being a busy man with a hectic schedule, Ambedkar was not available for regular meetings abroad. Often he deputed his lieutenants to undertake these tasks. N. Sivaraj was asked to represent him at the Pacific Relations Committee conference in Montreal,[15] while P.N. Rajbhoj embarked on an East Asian Buddhist tour with stops in Europe.[16] However, Ambedkar had several plans to put the Dalit rights movement on the international agenda. This is why he reached out to W.E.B. Du Bois who had also approached the UN in 1945. In the 1920s and 1930s, he had wanted the League of Nations to include caste in its agenda, along with race.

Around the same time, Ambedkar set out to create a broad network of Dalits worldwide. He envisioned global politics working as a pressure group on the Indian government, run as it was by caste Hindus. Realizing early on that local struggles would not provide an easy solution to their grievances, and after experiencing British intervention in the cause of Dalits, Ambedkar recognized the importance of engaging non-Indian actors. To create cultural soft power, he devised government-aided schemes such as scholarships and state support for Dalits to establish themselves in India and abroad.

Those who remained faithful to the Ambedkarite cause were given the chance to go abroad to study further or find employment as working-class labourers, blue-collar workers or professionals in India. Their children, the second generation, were educated in good schools, mostly convents, and provided with a head start to secure good jobs and pursue a particular lifestyle. Some of these second-generation children took jobs in the civil service, while others followed professional careers inside and outside India. The following generation—the third—went abroad for higher education and settled outside India, becoming citizens of foreign countries.

What about those who did not come from the same background, yet went on to develop careers in a foreign country? This chapter will look at new entrants who emigrated at the beginning of the twenty-first century and analyse how they pursued their project of fostering Ambedkarite consciousness and building community in the country where they settled. Some of the organizations discussed here were started by people in vulnerable positions in the host country, with job insecurity and facing hostile conditions back home. Despite all these difficulties, anti-caste Ambedkarite networks were established to counter the Indian government's propaganda and expose its failure to protect Dalit rights and halt the atrocities committed upon constitutionally protected categories of people.

One feature of anti-caste organization around the world has been its ability to unite anti-caste Dalit believers under the banner of Ambedkar, Ravidas, Valmiki, Dalit Christian or Buddhist congregations. Not all conform to the same identity, but the aim to raise their community's issues and seek justice through global pressure connects disparate groups into a unified bloc. An urgency to provide support and render justice characterizes such activism. Often, the modus operandi of anti-caste Ambedkarite organizing has been to protest on the streets, outside Indian missions abroad, and at UN offices. Although they have not yet achieved the status of a movement, through extensive networking within and outside India, and through professional settings, Dalits have forged ties around social justice and cultural exchange.

Global Ambedkarite organizing

There are various forms of Ambedkarite organization. These can be divided into two categories: street fighting and cultural celebrations. Ambedkarite groups engage in both forms with equal enthusiasm. Often, the cultural celebrations invite more participation than the street-fighting mode of activism. Leaders trained in social movements do not encourage street fights; instead, they prefer inter-group dialogue through cultural events such as observing anniversaries. The anniversary of Ambedkar's birth, known as Bhim Jayanti or Ambedkar Jayanti, is a prime occasion for annual gatherings. Additionally, Ravidas Jayanti is also an occasion for personal gatherings, social interactions, and organizational decision-making.

Street-fighters usually have developed an understanding of society through their lived experiences and education about their history by participating in social movements back home. Their class backgrounds and educational qualifications vary, and this influences their strategy and attitude towards protests. Some groups advocate a tit-for-tat response against caste atrocities like arson, rape and assault. But most middle-class Dalits with middle-class backgrounds, homes and professional status prefer to follow more conventional protocols. These two approaches often contradict each other. However, the zeal to counter casteism in India and abroad remains common.

By challenging the casteist attitudes of the dominant castes who have neutralized caste oppression through religious and cultural practices, organizing against caste manages to cross caste boundaries and incorporate broader anti-brahmanical groups who are not Dalits. The South Asian progressive groups who oppose casteism and caste atrocities have found their way into Ambedkarite organizing in the West. Dalit groups that continue to fight against caste have devised strategies to identify perpetrators of caste who have hidden their true intentions by promoting a narrow interpretation of religious freedom that undermines intra-religious caste critique. Some right-wing-supporting religious and social groups in the diaspora run by dominant castes are seen as hidden casteist groups who have advanced the agenda of caste supremacy covertly rather than in the open. Thus, by arguing for more representation and respect for minority religious communities, the dominant castes have mastered the art of promoting their supremacist values by advocating a particular version of their spirituality and religious organizing.

Most often, Dalit protests target institutionalized right-wing religious and educational groups that promote pro-caste politics or caste blindness. Many forms of educational training, part-time language teaching, and cultural and religious practice favour a dominant-caste narrative. As a result, Dalits are cautious about such institutional bodies, fearing they are being used to undermine their cause and history. One prominent incident that arose was the California textbook issue, where the representation of caste was not well received by Hindu students and their parents, who lobbied for curriculum changes. However, Dalit and progressive anti-caste groups united to push back against the Hindu right-wing groups seeking to neutralize caste.[17]

One striking feature of Dalit organizing abroad is that it is not sponsored or supported by India-based institutions. The migration of many dominant-caste groups across religions was facilitated by an extended chain of supporting networks.[18] But unlike Hindu, Muslim or Sikh-based social and religious groups with networks of capital and institutions, Dalits in host countries established their own networks by seeking out like-minded people wherever they settled.

As an example of this, I receive calls about once a month from people who have arrived in different parts of the world, enquiring about Ambedkarite groups or Dalits in the area. Wherever I found myself in the world during my travels, I would send out a message to WhatsApp groups, enquiring about the existence of Dalit networks.

Take another example in Europe. A Dalit professional from India who worked in the medical industry took a job in Norway. As soon as he arrived there, he started seeking out people from his community. After failing to find anyone, he reached out to an Ambedkarite organization in America. Though the organization was based on another continent, he was confident he would obtain leads or contacts. In the end, by means of the vast network of digitally connected Dalits, like-minded people were found in his vicinity. This possibility of establishing contact with someone in a foreign country who belongs to a particular caste group was previously unforeseen, but, due to the growth in technology and increasing Dalit emigration, it is now common.

What began as an attempt to establish their equality has now become an international pressure group against caste atrocities and indignities. Usually, a convinced Ambedkarite with a sense of his or her historical position and the struggle for equality would establish an organization to connect with others and air the community's grievances about what was happening in India. The organizing, as we shall see below, is not limited to social and cultural activities. It has evolved into a strong diasporic political force that acts as a kind of para-nation to support Dalit political initiatives back home.

Vivek Kumar, in his research conducted about a decade ago in America, discovered the prevalence of caste dynamics through the existence of caste-based bodies of Dalits, brahmans and lower dominant-caste groups from different linguistic states in India.[19] Kumar studied matrimonial websites that facilitated unions strictly between similar castes.[20] He also came across the brahman Samaj of North America, a platform for brahman youth to connect with one another globally and help find potential partners within the brahman community.

Kumar profiles the categories of Dalits that can be regarded as making up the Dalit diaspora. Student professionals—mostly engineers and doctors—were among the new arrivals who came on various visas, sometimes green cards, to settle in the United States. In addition, Kumar found "clinical psychologists, businessmen, taxi drivers, mechanics, motel owners, gas station owners, car garage owners, deli owners".[21] This diversity adds to the complexity of the Dalit presence in America, which is not tied to one profession or network. It is an evolving group of heterogeneous professionals and organizations of Dalit individuals.

The influx of IT professionals from the 1990s marked a new phase in the story of Dalits in India and abroad.[22] The agitation around the recommendations of the Mandal Commission to reserve jobs for Backward castes brought about a new level of consciousness in the country. In response, right-wing Hindu fundamentalists demolished the Babri Mosque to divert public attention. This phase highlighted the divide between dominant castes and lower castes known as Other Backward Classes (OBCs). However, the main target of right-wing Hindu attention was Dalits, who not only supported the OBCs in protecting their rights but also counter-protested against those demanding the elimination of job reservations.

A widespread narrative suggests that many dominant castes left India for better opportunities elsewhere owing to the perceived lowering of standards in India. However, what is not discussed or theorized as much is the impact of this caste consciousness among lower castes and Dalits during that decade. Many Dalits looked to explore opportunities across the world that had been opened up by the liberalization of the economy.

The post-1990s Indian emigration changed the demographics of Indian castes in the West. They now included lower- and Dalit-caste groups who came with a heightened sense of caste consciousness. A generation earlier, these communities were generally less educated and typically involved in fieldwork or industrial labour. There were notable exceptions, such as P.P. Lakshman, who pursued a master's degree at Cornell University on a Fulbright fellowship;[23] Dr Shoba Singh, who in 1953 earned a PhD from Johns Hopkins University; Namdeo Nimgade, who went to Wisconsin to write his doctorate in soil sciences;[24] and M.N. Wankhede, who submitted his thesis in English literature to the University of Florida in 1966. The 1960s saw the involvement of pioneering Dalit professionals in diverse fields in the United States. However, this did not continue, and the trend was only resumed in the 1990s.

The 1990s saw engineers and management professionals educated at Indian Institutes of Management and Technology taking up prestigious positions in the finance and IT sectors in America, the UK and some European countries. Many went on to become leaders in their workplaces, while a notable few achieved successful business careers.

The growth of Dalit assertion through the spread of Ambedkar's ideas worldwide by his followers has underscored the importance of anti-caste activism. Shielding caste and its atrocities is no longer a private, domestic affair; it is now receiving robust international engagement. This has brought a challenge to both the state and defenders of caste theism, who previously faced little protest, certainly not on the scale seen today. Almost every egregious move by caste-believing groups globally is met with protest from local Ambedkarite chapters, supported by the extensive network of Ambedkarite groups worldwide. In addition to writing and co-signing letters of support, there is also a sharing of knowledge and other resources to create better advocacy. The cause of one Ambedkarite organization in one country becomes the cause of many Ambedkarite organizations elsewhere in the world. A unique aspect of anti-caste organizing is thus the ability to become part of the anti-caste struggle without being a member of the national community.

Not only intellectual resources but also funds are channelled for a united effort against the forces supporting caste. To expand solidarity work, joint conferences are organized to advance the Dalit cause and its future vision. Academic deliberations form the core of Ambedkarite cultural diplomacy. There is a strong interest in advancing democratic dialogue and establishing an institutional base for spreading the message at international conferences and seminars. Dr Ambedkar's ideas are discussed and debated at foreign universities with the support and sponsorship of Dalit diaspora organizations.

Region, religion and castes in Dalit organizing

The organizations surveyed in this book are limited to India. However, the anti-caste efforts of Nepalese youth remain one of the highlights of anti-caste activism. The student campaign to add caste to the California State University's discrimination policy was led by a Dalit student of Nepalese origin, Prem Pariyar. Similarly, cross-border anti-caste initiatives are directed by Dalit leaders from Nepal, such as Pradip Pariyar, Amar Bishwakarma and Sarita Pariyar, among a host of well-known artists, writers and poets. Among the prominent bodies advocating for Dalit justice in Nepal are Dalit Women's Advancement of Nepal, Nepalese American Social Organization, and the International Commission for Dalit Rights.

Ambedkarites form a congregation of people containing a diversity of interests and origins. Given their linguistic, regional and religious diversity, Dalits do not share a single identity, as with any other group. However, what binds them together is their common experience shared across region, religion and language. The broader scope of casteism exists by rejecting equality and respect as standards of caste society. The Dalit groups from Punjab form perhaps the largest Ambedkarite diaspora worldwide. Following them, the Maharashtra Dalits help communicate Ambedkar's message to various professional networks and beyond. The Hindi-speaking Dalits are another significant presence in largely North Indian organizations. Though heavily invested in Periyar's Self-Respect Movement, the Tamil diaspora has not demonstrated the same Ambedkarite zeal found among other state diasporas. The same applies to people from Kerala, Karnataka and the Telugu-speaking states.

In view of India's federalism, Dalit organizing is located within the power structures of state-defined identities. However, in their refusal to be co-opted into the state-defined Hindu structure, Dalits have produced a novel critique of the state and religion. The various Dalit congregations serve differing purposes. Some are only meant to offer spiritual brotherhood in a foreign country, though at the back of their minds they are fully aware of their past of humiliation. In worshipping ancestors and deities, the devotees perform a forceful critique of ritualized casteism as observed in practice. They displace the tyranny of the oppressor which has been instrumental in their departure from the established faith. In establishing Ravidas *gurudwaras*, an alternative *sangat* (place of worship) has been created by Dalits who are proud of their caste (see Appendix). They push back against the bullying of feudal-dominant castes.

The same applies to the worshippers of Bhagwan Valmiki, who have established separate Hindu temples, distancing themselves from the brahman-Baniya-dominated Hindu temples. The Valmiki temples regard the sage Valmiki as their central deity—their accepted ancestor. By displacing brahmans from the nexus of religion and ritual, Dalits articulate an anti-caste ethos not only to challenge but also to replace the "cunning and cruel" brahmans responsible for removing them from a position of equality in worship in their temples. There is a strong feeling of the need to rebut any attempts by the oppressors to co-opt them into their forms of worship for self-serving ends. When the report by the Equality and Human Rights Commission (EHRC) in the UK was published, establishing the existence of castes, the Hindu temples got the Valmiki temple leadership to sign a letter against the report. When this was discovered by the Valmiki temple authorities, they protested and withdrew the letter.[25] The president of the temple told me that they were misled by the Hindu temple leaders about the content of the letter.

Christian Dalits in the diaspora continue to face discriminatory treatment in the diasporic Christian world. Some Dalit-centric non-profit organizations in the United States are run by Christian Dalits connected to charitable bodies and influential churches. These reflect the existence of casteism in both the public and private spheres. There are also separate congregations and churches catering to Dalit community members who feel excluded and disrespected. I have witnessed such congregations in Massachusetts, Pennsylvania and Illinois.

The rise of Dalit Christians with their accompanying Ambedkarite consciousness has brought many Dalit Christian narratives into the mainstream. Pastors and preachers of various denominations from the Dalit community hold anti-caste gatherings and offer their churches' support to Ambedkarite organizing. Given their connections with Christian institutions in the US, Dalit Christians have a degree of access to government authorities, which is then used to influence political decision-making regarding caste atrocities in India. In the United States, Dr Laxmi Berwa established contacts with the US Senate Committee on Foreign Relations and urged them to hold the

Indian prime minister Indira Gandhi accountable for caste atrocities in India (see Chapter 3).

Similar observations can be made about Buddhists who claim an intellectual lineage with Ambedkar's legacy, as they followed in his footsteps and took his guidance as their own. Buddhist Ambedkarites exercise a certain moral superiority, proudly flaunting their Buddhist identity in diverse caste meetings. It is a way for Buddhists to show non-Buddhists that Ambedkar's path to Buddha was free of blind belief, a rational choice demanding action against injustice. Buddhist Ambedkarites have consciously chosen to follow the Buddhist path despite difficulties and the refusal of the majority of Dalits, who have not changed their faith but remained tied to it. They have embraced Ambedkar but not other creeds. The creed of Ambedkarism changes its shape and form depending on context and content.

Buddhist Ambedkarites have established *viharas*—places of worship and fellowship—in the UK, specifically in Wolverhampton and in Southall, London. In Canada, there are Ambedkarite Buddhist *viharas* in Toronto and Edmonton. Apart from these formal bodies, there are also a few informal congregations in private homes or gatherings celebrating important days in the life of the Buddha. One notable occasion is Ambedkar's conversion to Buddhism on 14 October, observed as Dhamma Deeksha Day. Vesak Day, the celebration of the Buddha's birthday, is another event that connects Ambedkarite Buddhists with the larger Buddhist community from South Asia, Southeast Asia and Western Buddhists. In Oman and Bahrain, the Buddhist Ambedkarite community is closely involved with the Sri Lankan embassy, which regularly hosts Buddhist prayer meetings and *dhamma* talks (homilies or discourses) for devotees.

All these diverse expressions do not always coexist harmoniously. There are contestations and debates among the various branches of Dalits, each finding different ways to tackle their issues by means of their own chosen methods. Often, these separate and diverse methodologies of countering caste are challenged by other Dalits who have found a different formula to oppose Brahmanism and caste. Given the nature of belief, the Dalit calls for justice and preferred methods of action are informed by people's individual experiences with caste. Caste solidarity for Dalits involves acknowledging castes while protesting against the vile nature of casteism. For dominant castes, it is the other way round. They deal with caste so as to preserve and authenticate it for present times by devising theories and making a case for its relevance.

The Dalit diaspora can thus be seen as rebellious, challenging not only the nature of caste but also the raison d'être of caste practitioners. They prioritize reason and their experience of oppression rather than the written word of spiritual texts that do not guarantee freedom and dignity in real life. Therefore, studying Dalit organizing means examining their outreach in different parts of the world and assessing how Dalits challenge the existence of caste and those groups who uphold it. Anti-caste values are central to the Ambedkarite identity, thus involving a new identity for the South Asian or, more specifically, Indian diaspora. The ability of caste to transcend time and space must be analysed through its multiple locations—the diasporic nations—which draw from one site of origin—India.

Below, we will examine Dalit organizations in significant regions of the world and the way in which they represent a distinct cause, shaped by their lived experiences and their vision for the future. In many ways, they have become the decision-makers who, in the diaspora, have acquired authority to remove themselves from the atrocity-prone clutches of casteist groups in India. Empowered by the spirit of human rights and assuming a new identity as equal and respected individuals, Dalits in the diaspora have found new ways to channel their rage against the injustices of dominant-caste groups. They use civil rights conventions to their advantage in the non-caste public sphere. This wouldn't have been possible in India given the immanent nature of the caste system, which regulates caste paradigms to the disadvantage of oppressed castes—Dalits in particular.

The individual stories we explore are remarkable in that they tell of the everyday experiences of ordinary individuals. What elevates their persona? It is the fundamental anchoring of their lives with a larger purpose, aligning them with a community that has a longer memory and draws on an original body of foundational thought. These individuals have chosen to participate in my inquiry and share what they have experienced and discovered in their own localities.

Dalits in the UK

In this section we will examine the leading Dalit organizations in the UK and other countries whose presence as an anti-caste force has highlighted the cause of the Ambedkarite and the religious Buddhist movement. A profile of these organizations helps to understand the nature of Dalit Ambedkarite organizing abroad and allows us an opportunity to enter the activist world of these bodies. The many stories concerning caste globally illustrate how complex but unified the collective can be. In matters of common concern such as atrocities in India or the Indian government's anti-Dalit programmes, anti-caste organizing organically connects participants via the internet and private networks on WhatsApp or email groups. I have observed this online organizing since 2011.

Various community-centred initiatives are implemented by means of email campaigns and lobbying. After a project is proposed by a member of one organization, it is then considered by leaders of other organizations. Once it is accepted, depending on the project's merit and appeal, funds are then raised. These funds are typically modest. More extensive projects, such as building new institutions or organizations, are facilitated by a collective of organizations. This is a common strategy in organizing among Dalits abroad. In countries where it is not possible to register the organization, such as in the Middle East, Indian-based organizations or sister organizations elsewhere are called upon to help with fundraising and transferring resources to the relevant individuals or bodies. Below, we shall examine the profiles of organizations from different countries. Some are discussed in detail because of their importance or their history in the particular region. The ethnographic work to assemble this information was conducted from 2012 onwards.

Dr Ambedkar Memorial Committee of Great Britain

One rarely sees a large portrait of Dr Ambedkar on the walls of the giant complex that is home to the Dr Ambedkar Memorial Committee of Great Britain (DAMC), in Wolverhampton in the English Midlands. You might circle around the building, trying to find the entrance as the complex is spread over a large area, intersecting two streets. Once you find the gate decorated with elephant art, you are greeted by a life-size statue of a man holding a constitution. Instead of pointing his signature finger, the statue invites people to experience *dhamma*. A founding member of DAMC, Jagdish Rai, commented on the statue's unique position, saying it appeals to *ehipassiko*—a word used frequently by Buddha, which means "come and see for yourself".

As I entered the gate, I noticed white-clothed men, women and children bustling within the premises of the *vihara*, the Wat Phramaha Somboon Buddha Vihara. This name hints at the influence of the Thai monk who played an important role during the early days of the organization and served the community for thirty-three years. Men were dressed in white suits, while women wore white Punjabi dresses or sarees. Cars of various makes were parked outside. The festive atmosphere was due to the observance of Kathina—a Buddhist event at which monks are served after the *varsha* (rainy season retreat).

I had been invited to attend a Kathina programme by a Buddhist monk from Nepal, Venerable Sujano. He phoned and asked if I would attend the event hosted by Ambedkarite Buddhists. Although in 2011 I lived in Birmingham, about half an hour's distance from Wolverhampton, and had heard of this remarkable organization, I hadn't been able to visit. It was now time for me to witness this organization and its much-talked-about leadership that shies away from self-advertisement. The leaders of the organization are rarely seen in the limelight. They are senior community members who are devoted to the cause while continuing their work as full-time business professionals.

On this rainy October day, a white *pandal* (marquee) had been erected on the premises of the Buddha *vihara* where meals and chai would be served to the guests. A determined group of volunteers was ready to attend to each guest entering the *pandal*. Amid Covid regulations, seating distance was observed, and the community members behaved in a disciplined and respectful way. Unlike other diaspora events I had witnessed, this wasn't a loud gathering with people passing the time with chit-chat. The guests, who were all known to each other, formed into groups and shared pleasantries. Most of the devotees were Punjabi-speaking. The environment was vibrant but pious.

The gathering was awaiting the arrival of a phalanx of monks who would be offered new robes and other items. It was a whole-day affair. The *vihara* included a big guest hall with a raised stage that could easily accommodate around 300 people. Called the Dr Ambedkar Memorial Community Centre or Ambedkar Buddhist Community Centre, it had been inaugurated on 14 October 2000. On one side of the hall, members of the organization sang songs in Punjabi and Hindi, expressing their gratitude to the Buddha and the monks. The songs and the music were composed by members of the congregation. As soon as the contingent of monks arrived, there was a rally on the street led by the *sangha* (monastic community), followed by children playing on the *dhol* and *tasha* (drums). The rally was led by a woman holding a *panchsheel* (Buddhist) flag. The devotees filed behind one another in a column of four, making a long line. After it arrived in the *vihara*, the event commenced in the hall, at which the *sangha* offered blessings under the senior monk's direction and chanted the prayers. The monks were of diverse ethnic backgrounds, from Thai and Nepalese to various British nationalities, all chanting in Pali. The vibration of their chanting charged the atmosphere. Following this, the head monk offered a discourse in English. Ven. Sujano concluded by offering a discourse in Hindi.

It was exhilarating for me to witness this scene played out in a hall owned by Ambedkarite Buddhists whose walls recorded the name of Dr Ambedkar. This is not to be found commonly elsewhere, apart from a few notable exceptions in the UK and Canada. The Dr Ambedkar Memorial Committee of Great Britain, Wolverhampton, is an outstanding institution. The DAMC's staunch dedication and commitment to Ambedkar and his counsel is clear to see. Secondly, it was remarkable to see a Punjabi community of Dalits in the diaspora—they are mostly affiliated with Sikh, Hindu or the newly formed Ravidasia religion elsewhere in the world—proudly carrying out Buddhist ceremonies and observing important dates in the Ambedkarite Buddhist calendar. Thirdly, the organization lived by the legend it had created for itself. I have rarely encountered organizations whose members include second-generation Buddhists cleaving to the discipline.

The DAMC lives by the advice and counsel of Dr Ambedkar, who wanted his people to embrace a Buddhist past rooted in spiritualism and social justice. He at one stage envisioned making the entire Republic of India an enlightened Buddhist India, Prabuddha Bharat. He also saw the need to internationalize the Buddhist cause by aligning with other Buddhist countries. The Wolverhampton Ambedkarite Buddhists offer testimony to the potential of Ambedkar's envisioned world. They are a community of Dalits who subscribe to a Buddhist identity and hold on to it by passing it on to the next generation through the celebration of important days in the Buddhist calendar. A brief study was conducted by Mark Juergensmeyer in the 1970s on the diversity of Dalits in Wolverhampton, including the followers of Ravidas and Buddha who took the path of Ambedkar.[26] They have paved the way for the establishment of an Ambedkarite Buddhist culture in the UK. Not only this, but the organization has also created the world's first Dr Ambedkar Museum hosting rare artefacts belonging to Ambedkar, including clothes, pens and other items preserved and donated by Nanak Chand Rattu, Ambedkar's private secretary. The committee has also sponsored the publication of books penned by Rattu.

By examining the DAMC, we can better understand how Ambedkarite Buddhist politics have shaped overseas cultural relations among the diaspora. This case study is also helpful in revealing the potential of Dalit universalism. For by developing an autonomous anti-caste culture through the deployment of a critical Ambedkarite lens, this Ambedkarite Buddhist organization has influenced other Dalit organizations in the diaspora. Their focus, though, is their home country, India. The UK and Canada are the only countries outside India that have functional Ambedkarite Buddhist *viharas* maintaining a firm commitment to the ideology and praxis of Dr Ambedkar.[27] It is an intergenerational model that is both visible and not so visible in the political and social agendas of the Ambedkarite cause.

The radicalism of Buddhism

At a Sunday service at the DAMC complex in Wolverhampton, a senior monk in his seventies, Bhante Abhipassano, delivered a talk in Hindi. He paid respects to the Buddha and Ambedkar, and explained Ambedkar's ideals and politics for an anti-caste society. He talked about the inequality and discrimination embedded in the Hindu religion. He denounced those Dalits who found comfort in the Hindu religion and its torturous existence in Indian society. The Dalit community, he said, had to come out of its Dalitness and assert itself. Even though it has a large following, the community has not been able to create its own mass movement. In his closing remarks, the monk offered a prayer that ended with: "May this gathering and the Dalit community at large receive the guidance of Buddha and Ambedkar. This is the blessing of the Buddha Dhamma Sangh."[28] This was then translated into English by a member of the *vihara*, Dev Suman, one of the leading organizers of the DAMC, along with a discourse on Dhammapada (a collection of sayings by the Buddha).

The story of Bhante Abhipassano is emblematic of the commitment of the Ambedkarite Buddhists. Before his ordination he was known as Darshan Ram Jassal.[29] Born in 1942 in Pakistan, he arrived in England in 1961. After the formation of the DAMC, Jassal was its president until 1974. Under his leadership, the organization grew and undertook several landmark initiatives.

In 2000 the monk Chandra Bodhi wrote an essay in a souvenir brochure commemorating the 109th anniversary of the birth of Dr Ambedkar. In it, he did not hold back in lambasting the Hindu religion's shortcomings. He narrated the story of the archer Eklavya and his teacher, Dronacharya, from the Mahabharata. Eklavya was a pupil extraordinaire, whose skills were unmatched.

Seeing that this outcaste had a talent that Dronacharya had never seen before, the feared brahman teacher demanded Eklavya's thumb as a *guru dakshina* or "teacher's gift"—an accepted ritual. Eklavya readily offered his thumb, thereby ending the career of one of India's greatest archers.

Chandra Bodhi contrasted this story with that of Dr Ambedkar. At school, a brahman teacher had intimidated the young Bhimrao because of his caste. However, unlike Eklavya, Bhimrao gave an appropriate response to his teacher. "Sir, this is none of your business. If you refer to my caste again, the consequences will be no good." This boy, Chandra Bodhi continued, was to become the "hero of the revolution in India". The story as the monk told it adds fictional elements to what is known of young Ambedkar's life. However, by contrasting the experiences of Eklavya and Ambedkar—both outcastes of Hindu society—the monk explained to his readers that the contradiction lay within Hinduism. Had Eklavya replied to his teacher in the same way Ambedkar did, perhaps history would be different. The monk juxtaposes two epochs. In the first the talented Eklavya disappears into oblivion. In the case of Ambedkar, who refused to follow the standards set by the brahmanical Hindu society, a revolution was started. Eklavya could also have led a revolution. But his opportunity was taken away by his teacher. That is why the Hindu religion is "a home of inequality", proclaimed the monk. The "Hindu system arouses class war". Thus, the only way to obtain equality was to convert to a "non-Hindu religion".[30] Citing Dr Ambedkar's speech of 1935 in which he declared that though he was born a Hindu, he would not die as one, Chandra Bodhi told his readers of how Ambedkar was tempted by offers from both Muslims and Christians, but he turned them down and followed the path of the Buddha. That is why Ambedkar is regarded with such reverence in the Buddhist community in India.

COSMOPOLITAN DALIT UNIVERSALISM

The history of the DAMC is full of episodes of political and religious activism on the part of Ambedkarites abroad. What stands out is their unbounded faith in Ambedkar and his movement. This is also characteristic of many Ambedkarite Buddhist organizations worldwide. Their followers have refused to give up on the radical measures proposed by Ambedkar, which involve reverence towards the Buddha and to Ambedkar's anti-caste politics.

Images of Ambedkar accompany the Buddha throughout the Wolverhampton campus. I enquired about this from Dev Suman. Why does his organization feel strongly about positioning Ambedkar in relation to the Buddha? Dev Suman referred to Japanese Buddhism, in which Buddhist temples carry a photo of their teacher who brought Buddhism to Japan. Similarly, he said, Ambedkar had to be set alongside Buddha as he had brought the *dhamma* to his community. This form of symbolism can be understood on many levels. The first is the establishment of equality in human terms. Secondly, it is a tribute and act of reverence to their leader who showed them the path of the Buddha. Thirdly, it is a denunciation of the forces that belittle or undermine their efforts to seek justice. Fourthly, it helps create a global fellowship of Buddhists by spreading their views through the ambassador of their community—Ambedkar. And, finally, it is meant to inspire other Dalits and non-Dalits to emulate their spiritual and social path.

The narratives of the DAMC

> "Ambedkar is an energy, it cannot be created nor be destroyed. He can be only transferred from one generation to another."
> — From *Golden Jubilee Souvenir*, DAMC, 21 July 2019

Bishan Dass Bains is a member of the DAMC and was an organizer of the Ambedkarite movement in the UK in the

1960s. His active political work and university qualifications enabled him to make a foray into British politics. He was first a member of the Republican Party of Great Britain, an offshoot of the Republican Party of India. Eventually, he joined the Labour Party, which was open to immigrants and fought against racism. As a member of Labour, he contested the local council elections and became councillor for the metropolitan borough of Wolverhampton in 1979. In 1986 he was elected mayor of the City of Wolverhampton, becoming the first South Asian mayor to hold that position anywhere in the UK,[31] and the first member of the Dalit community outside India to be elected to public office. The second was M.G. Pandithan of Malaysia (more on him in the next section).

Bains had an illustrious career in public life. He took on two struggles: that against racism and against casteism. His memoir, *Pride vs. Prejudice One Man's Fight against Racism and Inequality*, describes the story of his life and the various caste-based and colour-based prejudices he had to face. Interestingly, the book's subtitle focused on race, as he saw himself as a victim of racism in the UK. He acknowledged that he had wanted to draw the attention of Western society, especially the British, towards his experiences as a brown South Asian and a Dalit.[32] His memoir, published in India by an Ambedkarite press, gives an account of his mayoralty from 1986 to 1987. It also describes the internal Labour Party politics leading to his mayoral nomination, highlighting the racist sentiments within the party and the country as a whole that led to his defeat.[33]

As a front-rank leader in a white society, Bain's experiences were largely colour-based. He also joined various Indian organizations, only to be disheartened. His experience of the Indian Workers' Association, one of the oldest and most active groups of Indian immigrants in the UK, left him bruised. The organization was run by Jat men, who opposed his political ascension. They worked together to defeat Bains in elections to the leadership despite his being a fellow Punjabi and a trade unionist.

Bains remained a committed Ambedkarite, which he acknowledged publicly when he was inaugurated as mayor, crediting Dr Ambedkar as his "guru". In addition, he kept abreast of the Buddhist movement. It was natural for him to gravitate towards the DAMC, which he came to serve and of which he remained a friend, offering his help whenever required. He wrote an essay in the DAMC souvenir booklet in which he offered an overview of the organization and related it to the politics of the anti-caste movement from the time after Ambedkar's death till the present. He did not hold back in expressing his opinions. The piece was educative in providing historical anecdotes and analysis of the past, but it was also a forthright, hard-hitting piece of radical writing. As an expert observer of the situation, Bains provided useful perspectives from various angles.[34]

The DAMC is widely known as it has hosted prominent Dalit leaders from India. One of them was Kanshi Ram, who featured the DAMC in his monthly journal *The Oppressed Indian* after his visit to the UK. In his piece he said he had not found UK Dalits open to new understandings, and he seemed upset by their suspicions and interrogations about him and his mission.

Although the DAMC is an important organization of the Dalit diaspora and has been noticed by several scholars working in the field of Dalit activism in the diaspora,[35] there is still a need for an in-depth profile that can shed light on the organization as a movement and as a mission. For the DAMC identifies itself as being in the service of both Ambedkar and Buddha. Dev Suman told me in an interview that "being able to serve in the mission of Babasaheb [Ambedkar] and Buddha has been the highlight of the organization".[36]

Organized Ambedkarite activism against caste started in the UK. The work here gave inspiration to those activists organizing in other parts of the world, who adopted a similar modus operandi to put across their viewpoints. In the early years, organizations in the UK developed solidarities with Ambedkarites elsewhere through their common support of BAMCEF and Kanshi Ram's Bahujan Samaj Party (BSP). What united Dalits everywhere was Ambedkarism, and the political movement that supported this sounded a clarion call for anti-caste activism. That is how the seeds of Ambedkarite Dalit cosmopolitanism were sown by the working-class, immigrant Dalit populations overseas. They paved the way for professionals in America, the Middle East, Canada and Australia to build Ambedkarite solidarities through cultural and social organizations. These organizations are testimony to the rise of the Dalit presence and their discourse in the diasporic world.

Dalits in the United States

The Ambedkar International Mission

One of the leading and most vocal Dalit groups in the United States is the Ambedkar International Mission (AIM), which, while autonomous, is connected to a body of AIMs worldwide. AIM in fact started in Malaysia. According to one of its founding members, D. Karunakaran,[37] he and Raju Kamble, whom he met as a colleague in the government engineering services in Delhi, began working for BAMCEF with Kanshi Ram, the founder of that organization. As part of their work, they would visit various slums in the Delhi region and spend time knocking on people's doors to make them aware of their rights.[38] After resigning from the government service, they went to Malaysia to work in the private sector. Here they would come together and celebrate the birthdays of both Ambedkar and Buddha. During one such celebration on 14 April 1992 at Karunakaran's house, they spent the evening with their wives and children discussing how to initiate projects such as "paying back to society". After long deliberations, they resolved to start an organization with an international mission at its heart. In this way the Ambedkar International Mission began on 15 April 1992. Today, there are nearly 15 AIM offshoots worldwide. We will look at a few of them.

AIM in Malaysia

One of the leading figures of the Dalit movement in Malaysia, Dato Panjamurthi, who was a child of Indian labourers, became an ardent Ambedkarite as the result of Raju Kamble's influence. Panjamurthi began working at the University of Putra Malaysia as a lab assistant in 1971. He was an active member of the Malaysian Indian Congress (MIC). Founded in 1946, the party engaged in alliance politics with the Malay and Chinese parties. Panjamurthi's friend and associate M.G. Pandithan, a parliamentary secretary to the Trade and Industry Ministry, was elected to the central working committee of the MIC in 1986. Pandithan soon rose to become vice-president of the party. The then president, Samy Vellu, grew insecure and tried to clip his wings. Pandithan was fired from the party in 1988. When he was unsuccessful in petitioning for his reinstatement, he founded his own party, the Indian Progressive Front (IPF), in 1990 with Panjamurthi as general secretary. Pandithan and Panjamurthi were Dalits and, like the majority of their supporters, were identified by their caste. Their struggle against caste injustices in Malaysia was reported widely.[39]

After the launch of the IPF, the two, along with their cadres, toured the country, and witnessed large masses of people from "30–40 thousand" gathering at their rallies. It was then that they realised that the Dalits constituted the majority of the Indian Malay population. However, they did not succeed electorally. Nevertheless, the IPF remained a lasting symbol of resistance and opposition in Malaysian politics. Its leader, Pandithan, was elected to the Senate in 1995 and became a recognized figure in Malaysian politics.

The IPF was the first Dalit national political party outside India. The reports of its rallies were read with interest by a young engineer from India: Raju Kamble. Along with his associates Vijay H. and Vilas Gaikwad and a few others, he sought to meet Panjamurthi and Pandithan. At the meeting, they were introduced to the work of Dr Ambedkar and were recruited into the Dalit movement.

In 1998 they decided to hold the First World Dalit Convention. Pandithan, now a senator, was the host of the convention and R.K. Narayan, the first Dalit president of India, the patron. The convention brought together 600 delegates, including Dalit leaders from various political parties. Panjamurthi reports that at the convention, they saw how Dr Ambedkar's name was misused by the party politicians. Thus, they sought to reclaim his reputation and start an organization in his name. Raju Kamble was the mover of these ideas. Panjamurthi credits him with bringing Ambedkar's work to light. His emphasis on education and organizing attracted the attention of Dalits in Malaysia. Following the Dalit convention, Dr Ambedkar International Mission, comprising Dalit Malaysians and Dalit expatriates, received an added boost.

Malaysia is a unique case in that it was not recent arrivals but the old generation of the colonial diaspora that embraced their caste identity. However, this did not come about without problems. According to Panjamurthi, there is still a sense of inferiority among Dalits concerning caste in Malaysia, which hinders unity among them.

AIM in the United States

The American chapter of AIM was initiated after Raju Kamble arrived in the United States and began making connections with other Ambedkarites in that country. After AIM was founded, those who headed it started by organizing annual meetings and celebrations of anniversaries in the lives of Ambedkar and Buddha at which families could gather together and talk to each other, share moments and mobilize politically. The family gatherings continue to be a feature of the organization today. One of the purposes was to ensure the younger generation became closely affiliated with the community and sensitized to the cause. This tradition has been continued in particular by one offshoot, the Ambedkar Association of North America, which holds annual picnics for Dalits where families and children meet and socialize around community issues. Another forum that includes children and the younger generation is the regular weekly online *viharas* where education and *dhamma* discourse are provided. These events are primarily facilitated by people from the Vidarbha region of Maharashtra.

Along with AIM, other prominent and well-organized bodies in the United States are the Ambedkar Buddhist Association of Texas; Guru Ravidas Sabha of New York; Guru Ravidas temples in Fresno and Union City (California), Selma and Pittsburgh; Gurdwara Shri Guru Ravid Temple of Sacramento; Shri Guru Ravidass Sat Sangat, Yuba City (California); Shri Guru Ravidas Sabha of Bay Area, San Francisco; the Ambedkar Association of North America; the Ambedkar King Study Circle; the Boston Study Group; and many other loosely formed state-wide Ambedkarite groups. While they cooperate closely, they conduct themselves as independent entities with their own objectives and missions. What differentiates them from one another are politics and religion, each having their own affiliations in this regard. However, none adhere to the brahmanical Hindu religion.

AIM's base is in New York. This gives them the advantage of proximity and easy access to the United Nations and the Indian consulate along with being an axis to New York, Pennsylvania and New Jersey. They mount protest actions against atrocities in India and take the Government of India to task for its inability to curb violence against Dalits in India. They also regularly interact with the United Nations and its organizations, to brief them on issues relating to Dalits. Many functions hosted by civil society groups at the UN include representatives of AIM. They co-sponsor such events or offer logistical support to Dalit organizations from India who need local representatives for their activities in New York.

The aim of the AIM leadership is to bring immediate relief to injustices wrought upon their community in India. Like many Ambedkarite organizations in America, AIM is less adept at strategy and long-term planning. They exercise caution in their activism. Many fear repercussions from the American as well as Indian governments. Since members have family, jobs and investments in both countries, they prefer not to upset the status quo.

Run by second-generation, middle-class Dalits, AIM is well organized and well run. They lobby with the administration and conform to the standards of both their host country and country of origin. Any issue that would go against the predominant views of the current dispensation is not taken on board. They are an inward-looking body with a limited grasp of international and domestic politics. That is why they are absent from cross-cultural protests in America, limiting themselves to matters concerning Dalits. Occasionally, they take part in political alliances against the Rashtriya Swayamsevak Sangh (RSS) and the Bharatiya Janata Party (BJP). But they do not take up positions against any religion. The profile of AIM in the States has evolved since the death of its founder, Raju Kamble. It has yet to take creative steps to advance the work of the anti-caste movement in the

United States. But it has been an inspiration for many other organizations that were formed in later years.

AIM has been instrumental in organizing academic conversations on campuses. Their annual gatherings are often held at university campuses in the form of conferences. Speakers from India and abroad are invited to discuss the ideals of Ambedkar and the state of Dalits in India. Until recently, the majority of the conversations were focused on India. But US and diasporic concerns are now actively debated in these formal gatherings. AIM is primarily a cultural organization with agitational impulses and is involved in hosting cultural activities. This is why the leadership has supported the Dalit Film and Cultural Festival in New York which I hosted in 2019.[40] Since the leaders come from a non-working-class background, their approach to the issue of Dalit rights is based on their life experiences, which inclines them to cultural and social activism. Many Ambedkarite groups have taken a cue from their strategy and evolved into stand-alone, autonomous AIMs worldwide. If not AIM, they carry the word Ambedkar, Buddha or Dalit in their names.

The story of the American anti-caste movement is the most well-known because of the freedom it has in conducting its activities and its access to the media. The prominence of the US movement helps ensure recognition of the Ambedkarite movement worldwide. Recently, organizations in the United States have looked to state and local governments to legislate anti-caste provisions. One success was achieved with the city council of Seattle. While the State of California senate voted in favour of anti-caste legislation in 2023, it was vetoed by Governor Gavin Newsom.[41] With supporters and opponents at loggerheads outside the assembly hall, the issue became one of the most discussed in the summer of 2023. On one side stood brahmanical Hindu and allied groups while on the other were Dalits, Sikhs, Muslims, Hindu progressives and other civil society bodies.

After the veto, the activists and organizers withdrew from the public fray.

Governor Newsom's statement when issuing the veto was telling. He said that Californian laws prohibited discrimination based on "sex, race, colour, religion, ancestry, national origin, disability, gender identity, sexual orientation, and other characteristics". These protections were "liberally construe[d]" by law. He argued that caste was covered "under these existing categories", which made the bill "unnecessary".[42] Many activists concluded, rightly or wrongly, that Newsom had come under pressure from South Asian elite-caste people who were big donors to his election campaign. Some suspected he made the decision so as not to upset the majority consensus in the state. In all this, the influence of the Hindu right was exaggerated as the number of caste-holding Hindus form by far the majority in California, but the strategy worked in favour of opponents of the caste bill.

Global Ambedkarites of the Middle East

Ambedkarites, who proudly own their identity and reject the imposition of the Hindu category, claim a unique position in society. Foreign countries usually identify the immigrant with his or her national or religious society. While belonging to both yet refusing the imposition of these identities, Dalit immigrants aspire to create a new self. This new self is an old formation, yet by rejecting an identity as lower caste, it continually reinvents itself. Thus, a wide network of global Ambedkarites has arisen who exhibit a spirit of community pride and a commitment to giving back to society.

The general profile of the professional class of Dalits is similar in various countries. But in the United Arab Emirates (UAE), I met a class of workers living in camps in Dubai, Abu Dhabi and Muscat, Oman whom I had not encountered elsewhere.

Organizing a meeting or a programme with them was impossible in their residential premises, for the camps are strictly surveilled. At the entrance to the camps are security guards, who form the primary point of contact between the camp and the outside world. Any gathering of people involving visitors from outside is strictly recorded. They were prohibited so often that I had to conduct interviews outside the camp's fence. I was advised not to exit the car and to talk to the men from inside the vehicle while they stood outside in the dim light.

I managed to get access to one camp on a Thursday night. The meeting was facilitated by a young Dalit supervisor from Mumbai who organized the gathering discreetly. It was done quietly without alerting anyone. Holding a meeting of any kind is usually not allowed. If one is caught, the repercussions are more severe than just losing one's job. The police are feared on account of their strict application of the rules, especially concerning labourers, who are frequently the subject of human rights violations and abuses by both their employers and the state.

When I came to the camp, the labourers were spending some quiet time on their own. After a day's hard work, they were bathing or cooking their dinner. As I entered with a colleague and local Ambedkarites, they smiled with curiosity and were happy that outsiders had come to visit them. Their hospitality was noteworthy. Despite the meagre facilities, they offered us tea as we sat on the floor. The room had two bunk beds. As we chatted, the labourers asked about life in America and shared their experiences of work. The informal hierarchy among labourers depended on the amount of time each had spent in the camp. One person had worked there for nearly fifteen years. He gave counsel and advice to all the newcomers. People leaned on him for matters concerning their work and their families.

The workers were literate but not highly educated. The younger lot were day labourers back home who had undertaken the journey to earn better money. In order to get to the Middle East, they had had to sell things or loan money to pay the agent who prepared their documents and arranged their jobs. Those in their forties and fifties were working to support their adult children's education or to pay for their marriages. Once the children have been taken care of, building a house or owning some property is their priority. Since they do not have a future in the Middle East, they look forward to returning to their homes and starting a business. Whenever I spoke to the labourers, some wanted to explore the possibility of moving elsewhere.

In the scorching heat, I met young Punjabi Dalits who work in the construction industry. They had come to greet me. They followed their community's news on social media and were aware of political events back home. Despite being youngsters, their attitude towards their community and their awareness of coming from a Dalit community were strikingly mature. They had seen my videos on YouTube and other social media platforms. They asked me about community issues and what could be done to improve the life of "our people back home". They were willing to donate to the cause of the community. In fact they had been approached by some youngsters from the state of Telangana who were collecting funds to support various parties or causes. Besides being aware of the political issues concerning their community, they were socially aware because most had come from rural areas and had witnessed caste in practice and its exactions. As they had limited access to the kinds of resources and opportunities available to dominant castes, they were forced to accept difficult working conditions in the Middle East.

Kuwait Ambedkarites

There are four prominent Dalit organizations in the Islamic nation of Kuwait: Sant Ravidass Organization, Punjabi Ambedkarites, Dhamma Group, and Tamil Ambedkarites.

Each of these organizations has a specific purpose. The Punjabi workers have organized to give political support to Dalit parties back home. The Dhamma group is an organization of Marathi Ambedkarites, many of whom have arrived in the last five or six years and came together through mutual contacts. This group consists of professional workers employed in diverse industries. The Tamil Ambedkarites comprise workers and professionals. Together with the Punjabi Ambedkarites, they are the most organized Dalits in the country.

Most of the work carried out in Kuwait is directed at providing educational, political and social support in India. Funds are raised for specific projects, and people donate accordingly. Once the donations are made, the money is transferred to the organizations, schools, hostels or even media companies back in India. Given the restrictions placed by the Kuwait government on social organizing, the Kuwait Ambedkarites have chosen to work under the radar and not advertise their work. They do not have a website nor have they registered the organization. They work on an ad hoc and need-to-know basis. There are regular monthly meetings to update members on their activities. Two prominent days are celebrated by the small but well-organized Dhamma Group. They now plan to start new initiatives with the purpose of "paying back to society", a slogan popular among Ambedkarites worldwide. Each member contributes depending upon their social and economic condition.

Dr Ambedkar Mission Sabha, Kuwait

One of the most impressive Ambedkarite diaspora groups is led by labourers from Punjab in Kuwait. It is known as the Dr Ambedkar Mission Sabha. One of its leaders, J.S. Dihana, a plumber from Punjab, arrived in Kuwait in 2012. After one year of his arrival, he got together with a few people who identified as Ambedkarites and started the Dr Ambedkar Mission Sabha.

Its purpose is to organize labourers across Kuwait and encourage them to work to promote Ambedkarism. Their organization supports the Bahujan Samaj Party (BSP) and follows the ideology of Ambedkar and Kanshi Ram.

No other group I interviewed and observed over the previous ten years had declared their political affiliation except a group of workers in the UK, who were also incidentally BSP supporters. Upon asking why they affiliated so openly, Dihana said, "Our aim is clear. We are convinced about our objectives. We don't live a two-faced life who will adjust according to their convenience. If we are BSP supporters, then so be it. We believe in the ideology of Sahab Kanshi Ram and Babasaheb [Ambedkar], thus we've resolved to support."[43] During online interviews, a number of professional-class Dalits were astonished to hear such a bold statement.

Dihana has managed to recruit 300 labourers for his mission who work in plumbing, bricklaying and carpentry. Whenever a new labourer arrives, if they are from a Dalit background, they are often already aware of the Sabha or else are advised by colleagues to get in touch with Dihana and the Sabha activists. Regular meetings are convened, and literature is distributed among the labourers. Each member is encouraged to read and then discuss a text at the next meeting. At the meetings, the younger ones are trained to engage critically with the text and are invited to speak from the platform. "We want to inject confidence and prepare our next gen[eration] leaders how to organize," Dihana said.

One of the ways the Sabha has managed to make its way in the challenging arena of labourers, many of whom would usually avoid being part of such organizing, was by being at the forefront of social work. They try to combat alcoholism among the youth. Eight years of persistent work has started to produce results. Now, instead of getting drunk, young workers attend meetings and share the passion for social transformation. In addition, the Sabha also gives job-related advice and offers basic help for struggling labourers.

One of the striking features of the Sabha is that their organizer, Dihana, has rented a room which is not only his residence but also the office of the Sabha and a centre for meetings. The room is decorated with a larger poster of Ambedkar and his message pasted on the wall. On the other walls are portraits of Kanshi Ram, Ambedkar and Buddha. In one corner of the small room is a bed bunk and in the other a bookcase filled with Ambedkar's books in Punjabi. Next to it is a refrigerator and a wooden podium with four chairs.

Another Punjabi Dalit organization is Sat Guru Ravidas Sabha, the only Dalit body to be officially registered. Owing to the severe restrictions on organizing events, Dalits in Kuwait, Oman, Bahrain, Qatar and Saudi Arabia work without any formal structure. The Guru Ravidas Sabha has been active since 2009, and it is also led by a labourer, who is a poet, writer and *ghazal* writer. He is Lashkari Ram Jakhu. He has both a bachelor's and a master's degree. He had worked across the world doing odd jobs. This experience as well as his degrees qualifies him for the position of providing leadership to the Dalit labourers.

As a rule, Ravidasias cannot have a *gurudwara*, so they have a virtual *sangat*. But their three annual events are held on a grand scale, when they celebrate the birthdays of Guru Ravidas, Guru Nanak and Dr Ambedkar. These have been happening regularly over the years. Their organization has 300 members from the labouring class who are trying to find spiritual salvation. With their mix of social and cultural activities, Dalits have a means of supporting each other and contributing to the mission of Ambedkarism. This form of organization provides moral support and a basis for the political socialization of fellow Dalits, as a way of taking them out of their isolation and alleviating their homesickness.

VCK cadres of Kuwait

Another organization working in the same spirit is the Thaiman Cultural Association, an associate of the Viduthalai Chiruthaigal Katchi (VCK) party of Tamil Nadu, whose main aim is the abolition of the Hindu caste system and the introduction of equality among Tamil people. The name Thaiman derives from the magazine that Thirumavalavan, leader of the VCK Party, edits. In the 1980s, Anbarasan, a tenth-grade dropout, left Tamil Nadu to search for a job in Mumbai. He took odd jobs just to get by before working on repairing cars. Anbarasan lived in the Worli slums in a thatched-roof house with other labourers. In the area an Ambedkar statue had been set up and Anbarasan came to realize what respect Ambedkar had in Tamil Nadu.

There were often police raids in the area. Once, when the police arrived, they noticed Ambedkar's statue and two of the policemen immediately saluted it. Anbarasan observed this with great surprise. When the police came back later and enquired about the statue, Anbarasan, who had started to learn Hindi, replied that local people looked up to Ambedkar as their messiah. The policemen relaxed and became affable towards him. Anbarasan was pleasantly surprised to see that his hero was also respected by the policemen. He then toured other parts of Mumbai to see how Ambedkar was recognized and celebrated. This emboldened him.

During the mid-1990s, after a gruesome caste atrocity in Tamil Nadu, Thirumavalavan (Thiruma), politician as well as firebrand writer and scholar, gained prominence. His speech was a turning point for the Dalit movement of the time, and he became a celebrity whose popularity has not diminished in three decades. Thiruma has remained single, devoting his life to the protection of caste-oppressed people. With a PhD in religious studies, Thirumavalavan is a major contributor to anti-caste thought in Tamil Nadu.[44]

COSMOPOLITAN DALIT UNIVERSALISM

Inspired by Thiruma's work, Anbarasan became a follower of his. Wherever he went, he sought to promote and support the VCK and the Dalit Panthers of Tamil Nadu. When he left for Kuwait to explore job opportunities there in 1993, he carried the mission of Ambedkar with him. He started organizing labourers in an effort to meet their needs and demands. His work of ensuring that the bodies of labourers who have died reach their homes has received wide recognition. In addition, he has also managed to establish good relations with Indian and Kuwaiti authorities. People usually rely on him to sustain themselves in the midst of unemployment or resolve workplace conflict. Given the strong labour networks and dense connections among workers, Anbarasan has created a public presence.

When he arrived to work in Kuwait, he met up with a fellow Dalit activist and labourer, Radhakrishnan, now renamed Ilaiah Gautam after conversion to Buddhism, who was then organizing Dalit labourers. They celebrated the first Ambedkar Jayanti in 1994 at a labour camp by cutting a small cake. Ever since, they have not looked back. They observe five anniversaries per year: Ambedkar's and Periyar's births and deaths and the Tamil harvest festival Pongal.

The Thaiman Cultural Association is a membership-based organization in which members pay annual fees that, in turn, are used to help labourers. In addition, Anbarasan raises funds during the visits of dignitaries from India. He publishes souvenir booklets that details the activities of VCK and his organization in Kuwait. Advertisements are invited from business people and individuals, and in this way funds are built up. His initiatives receive wide publicity. The year 2019 saw Kuwait's largest Ambedkar Jayanti celebration, with many Ambedkarite organizations celebrating together.

Anbarasan has said, "Kuwait is the only country with so many organizations that each group is attached to some cause and different political parties back home."⁴⁵ He is not wrong. Another Periyarist organization in Kuwait is run by an engineer, Muthu Kumar, who has organized a literary movement. Muthu believes in the important role to be played by Periyar's social justice movement Dravidar Kazhagam (DK) and its global network. Muthu has managed to host Tamil-centred events in Kuwait with speakers and scholars from Tamil Nadu and involving people from across all caste and class groups. "We do not have any class barriers among Tamilians in Kuwait," Muthu said proudly.⁴⁶

Ambedkar International Mission, UAE

Unlike other Dalit organizations in the Middle East, the Ambedkar International Mission (AIM) in the UAE was formed some time ago, in 1994 in fact, by a handful of Ambedkarites from Maharashtra. It is now a robust and mature organization with influence and heft.

In the early 1990s Raju Kamble, the doyen of the Ambedkar International Missions, which are now active across the world, arrived from Malaysia to take up a new position in the UAE. Being interested in connecting with fellow Ambedkarites, he met up with Dr Mhaske, a physician who practised in the UAE; Ramesh Dahas, a businessman; Yashpal; and Sandeep Kardak, who worked in the airline industry.

At the weekend, along with others, Kamble would visit labour camps to present books to the labourers, and persuade them to attend social awareness programmes. As is the general model now, family-based meetings would be convened at someone's house. A breakthrough in the work among the labourers was made when Maruti Kharve, a plumber who had come to the UAE from India, started spending time among the labourers, trying to encourage them to join the movement. He would visit various labour camps at the weekend at his own expense. His work bore fruit among drivers, plumbers, electricians and accountants, who started to meet regularly. They became more active members of the organization and donated monthly to assist the "pay back to society" initiatives.

One of the early organizers, Sandeep Kardak, said that "labourers were the most honest people", who worked hard for the movement.[47] Raju Kamble had advised his colleagues in the movement to spend at least five to seven days in their villages in India and identify young students whom they could support educationally.[48] Accordingly, members of AIM in the UAE started to identify students whom the organization would collectively help in their studies and guide in their careers.

This type of organizing continues today. Recently, AIM in the UAE helped to revive a Dalit student boarding facility in Nashik in Maharashtra. Similarly, AIM team members visit labour camps to meet workers and learn about their problems. Social media have now become a valuable source of connecting with other Ambedkarites. AIM has also created an introductory video for newcomers joining the organization. Each year in January, an agenda for the year is distributed listing the dates of monthly meetings. The most important dates have to do with the celebration of Ambedkar's birthday in April, his conversion to Buddhism in October, and the anniversary of his death in December. Aside from this, regular fundraising and project-based initiatives continue throughout the year. The team comprises people from Backward classes who participate in cultural events.

AIM in the UAE is an interesting mix of constituencies. It largely has professionals as core members. However, their presence is also felt in the labour campsites. Owing to company surveillance, many labourers do not take part openly in the day-to-day activities of AIM beyond the labour camp. Nevertheless, there is a network of labourers and professionals on WhatsApp. Labourers can easily contact fellow Dalits in the city by this means. The AIM activists make monthly visits to the sites and update each other on their work. I was informed that the annual gathering to celebrate Ambedkar Jayanti (Ambedkar's birthday) draws over a thousand people from across the UAE. The professional class organizes transport and food for the workers to come to town and attend the celebrations. One of the organizers told me that they see every Indian state represented in the gathering. He was drawing attention to the cosmopolitan character of Dubai, which boasts of having all nationalities represented in the country.

Dalit migrant workers of the UAE

The majority group that forms the base of the Ambedkarite organizations consists of people employed in the lower echelons. These are labourers, construction workers, supermarket employees, hotel workers and cleaning staff. There are no precise numbers of Dalit migrant workers. But this has not discouraged them from seeking out their kind. In the migrant labour regime of the UAE, almost all workers experience the same harsh conditions. However, the Dalit workers' situation is peculiar. This is because, by earning more than 20,000 rupees in the UAE, which is the average salary of a graduate clerk in India, Dalit workers feel a sense of privilege and relative responsibility towards their community.

The story of migrant labourers from the South Asian region differs from that of cohorts from other regions. The first reason is the nature of their treatment back home. The second is that their social background defines them as a separate community. Additionally, their position in the predestined class structure of their home country easily translates into a "lower" status within the Emirati political economy. Finally, their forced segregation and the Dalitification of their resources make their lives in the UAE unendingly difficult.

COSMOPOLITAN DALIT UNIVERSALISM

Among the diverse demographics to be found in the UAE there are various castes, particularly among migrant labourers from South Asia and India. Religion and linguistic differences tie migrant labourers together. Their food choices and the need to share their lives in cramped spaces create an inescapable intimacy and familiarity. In some camps, the choice of a roommate is not up to the labourers but to their company. Therefore, some have to wait, sometimes for years, for a bed to become vacant so that a preferred person can join them. At the campsites where construction workers work, the informal hierarchy of the labourers is based on how much time one has spent outside India. If a labourer has worked in the West or in Southeast Asia for some years, he is regarded as knowledgeable and resourceful. The labourer's education level and working style become attractive qualities for others. Age also adds another dimension of recognition.

Meghwal is a Hindi-speaking Rajasthani Dalit migrant labourer in his fifties. He is also a vocal Ambedkarite. He observed the anti-caste activism of BAMCEF in his village in his youth. Ever since, he has closely followed their activities. Meghwal has a particular stature in the closed camp. His mostly young followers are people from his background who look up to him for advice and guidance. The relationships are formed on the basis of their identity as migrant labourers from India, but caste provides these bonds with a sense of familiarity. Their stories are unique, but their hopes are similar. They want to support their families and raise their kids with better life opportunities. Meghwal recently contacted me asking if I knew of any opportunities for his son, who is a graduate. He believes that there is not enough work on offer in the Indian government job sector, and so his son has to move away to find work in the Western world.

What connects these labourers are their common fate in a familiar space, their hard work, the pain of separation from their families, and their hopes and aspirations. These aspirations are tied to trying to earn money for family, while for some it involves paying attention to the needs of the community. As Ambedkar Jayanti approached, the construction workers from Rajasthan and Uttar Pradesh, who came together as a group in one of the camps, sent me a WhatsApp message. They wanted to keep in touch with a scholar friend I had introduced them to and ask her to be a chief guest at the Ambedkar Jayanti programme in the camp. They knew only her first name, and, since she came with me, they had appreciated her presence. But when I told them her last name, which was a brahman name, they replied with a voice note saying that though they wouldn't have a problem hosting her, other organizations whom they partnered with might object. The tone of the message was negative. They would rather avoid having a brahman preach to them on one of the most important days of the year. This was emblematic of their determination not to allow people with an oppressor-caste background to interfere with or impose on their work and philosophy.

In my research I have not yet encountered inter-caste-related rifts or disputes at the campsites. Sensitivity to caste was noticed and observed by various caste members. Given the strict surveillance of the campsites, the possibility of creating a caste issue was perhaps pre-empted. The imposed intimacy of the camps offers various opportunities for social and personal interactions. Has this resulted in caste-based tensions? If so, how are these tensions avoided? If not, what is it that makes this tension a marginal issue? These questions need to be explored in detail. Such an inquiry has the potential to tackle the question of caste in transit and migration. Labour and caste intertwine to produce interesting outcomes outside their place of origin. Does migration really alter the reality of caste over generations, as it seems to do in indentured societies? Or does the twenty-first-century memory of caste offer liberation from caste by rejecting and contesting its existence?

Overseas supporters of BSP

The topic of overseas supporters of the Bahujan Samaj Party (BSP) deserves book-length treatment. Over the past decade of my research on Dalit activism abroad, I have noticed that the activists involved in political work were solely dedicated to the BSP. And, always, these supporters were workers and labourers. My first encounter took place in London in 2011. During my fieldwork there, I was introduced to Punjabi workers who lived in cramped quarters. They were construction workers. However, after a hard day's work they would organize migrant Indian workers into BSP cadres.

Over the past ten years, I have seen this consistency among BSP workers who came from rural or semi-urban areas of North India. They had been trained back home. Many of the lead organizers had engaged in the party's activities at the local level or had been impressed by the party workers. Often they came from a BAMCEF background. Although BSP has no official overseas wing, nor do they have any particular party interest in foreign workers, nevertheless people have lined up behind the party. BSP's lack of interest in foreign workers was explained to me by the party's former national general secretary, Suresh Mane. He said that owing to frequent suspicions from the Indian government and opponents about "foreign funding" that the party might receive, the party stopped any direct engagement with foreign workers. But that does not mean that the party leadership is unaware of their activities.

Mayawati, the BSP's national leader, was invited to the UK to inaugurate Ambedkar Hall in Wolverhampton in the mid-2000s. Many Dalits in the diaspora have unequivocally supported the activities of the BSP. Most often, Punjabi Dalits found immediate relevance in the party's activities. In addition, vocal BSP supporters came from Maharashtra, Telangana, Uttar Pradesh, Karnataka, Kerala and Madhya Pradesh, among other states. Apart from BSP, there were also supporters of the Republican Party of India in Maharashtra, VCK in Tamil Nadu, and Congress among Dalit diaspora groups.

The BSP supporters I met during my fieldwork in Dubai were from Telangana and Punjab. All were working-class labourers involved in organizing under strict supervision. I was struck by two groups in different campsites in the Dubai region who consisted of disciplined, active citizens of their home state. The Telangana group was led by Vijesh, an activist from Karimnagar in Telangana. Vijesh was a graduate who had joined the BSP party in his youth. After hearing speeches on caste issues and learning about Kanshi Ram, he was attracted to the movement. He swiftly became a party cadre. Over the years, he engaged in party activities. Lately, after the bureaucrat-turned-politician R.S. Praveen Kumar joined BSP, Vijesh lent his support to Kumar. He has worked with Telugu-speaking labourers in various campsites. They have a formal membership programme where each worker pays 10 dirhams for life membership. Receipts are given, and the money is sent back to India. Even though they were paid under 1,200 dirhams as a salary, these workers were inspired to donate towards the party's mission.

Vijesh dreams of portraying Dr Ambedkar's image on the famous Burj Khalifa tower in Dubai. He wants to show the world that they are no longer to be ignored. He also wants to put Praveen Kumar on Burj Khalifa. Along with other workers, Vijesh donates money to the movement regularly. When asked why they do this, his response was that they foresee their return to power. It was a hopeful wish for their future, and they needed to work towards it. These Dalit workers outside India did not

COSMOPOLITAN DALIT UNIVERSALISM

see any other party as a viable option in their state. Through trial and testing, they found BSP to be the viable instrument for entrusting their faith. Vijesh works in a supermarket. He uses WhatsApp to extend his contacts with workers in other industries.

There was another group of Punjabi workers who were committed followers of BSP. They were truck drivers, machine operators and construction workers who had been working in Dubai for over fifteen years. Some of these members were graduates. They had read Ambedkar and drew inspiration from his life and mission. Many of them still regularly read Ambedkarite literature. Their primary source of knowledge was YouTube and Facebook videos of Punjabi scholars analysing the Bahujan vision for them. They diligently follow updates in Punjab and connect with other Ambedkarites in the diaspora via Zoom and other forms of online meeting.

Although there is a Ravidasia community, the radical Ambedkarites were not entirely in sympathy with their activities. The Ravidasia community was planning to build a *gurudwara* in the UAE. One of the BSP workers, who was erudite and clear in his programme and speech, told me there are so many broken *gurudwaras* in Punjab. "If you build one, it will break. We need to think beyond them."[49] The Punjabi workers organize within the campsites to discuss and debate their beliefs together. They offer support and guidance to new arrivals from India. They have formed a closed network which operates intimately as a group and also as part of larger organizing efforts. They also contribute to party activities. Recently, in the Punjab state election in 2022, when other BSP supporters from across the world went to campaign for the party, some of the UAE members also participated, while others who couldn't go gave contributions to the party.

What makes the BSP party workers unique was that they were not officially appointed, nor did they have a direct connection with the party leadership. They were trained in anticipation of becoming the ruling class, and for that to become a reality, they were convinced that a collective effort was needed. In contrast, the professional class and blue-collar workers did not assertively align with BSP. The working class, on the other hand, believed it essential to demonstrate their loyalty to the cause. Upon learning about my presence in Paris, Parminder, a Parisian Dalit worker, visited me at a conference there in 2018. He was elated to see other Dalits in the audience. He decided to pay for all the participants' lunch at a nearby bar. When he left, he told me that he was pleased to see the children of Babasaheb (referring to Ambedkar) at such an illustrious conference.

Parminder is also among the few thousand party supporters from abroad who return to India to campaign for assembly elections in Punjab. In the 2022 election, he spent ten days carrying out a door-to-door campaign in his hometown. When I called to catch up with him, he said he was in India and had done his bit. He was pleased with the work of BSP. The alliance with the Jat-dominated Shiromani Akal Dal (SAD) party was not looked upon kindly by other Dalits in the diaspora; however, being a sincere party supporter, Parminder defended his party's position. He was also happy that Mayawati, the leader of BSP, waved at a group he was part of in acknowledgement of them.

Unlike Parminder, Balwinder in Vienna thought the prospects of BSP slim. He instead preferred to support the militant Azad Samaj Party (ASP). Balwinder was an active ASP supporter after being, until recently, a die-hard supporter of BSP. With the change in political movements in India, the self-made radical cadre has found itself in new political alignments.

Parminder and Balwinder are Dalit workers who are always focused on the nation's cause. Both left Punjab in their twenties; they made France and Austria their homes, respectively. Their children speak the language of their country of birth. In their fifties, Parminder and Balwinder hope for a Dalit future. They are connected across the world through Ravidas Sabhas and, more so, through the overseas BSP supporters' group. This is a space of contestation, sharing, arguments and debates. Friendships are made and also broken over intense political discussions. There is, however, agreement on one thing: no future can be decided without an Ambedkarite party.

AIM, Bahrain

With fifteen to sixteen families acting as regular members and with some single men from the labour camps, AIM in Bahrain mobilizes support in the Middle East for educational projects in India. Shailesh Pillewar, an energetic Ambedkarite Buddhist from Kamptee, Nagpur, supervises the activities of AIM in Bahrain. Shailesh was my point of contact with various Gulf Ambedkarite groups. He became attached to the Ambedkarites at an early age in India and has carried this Ambedkarite consciousness wherever he has gone. He couldn't be as involved when he was employed by the government in Hyderabad as he would have liked, but he decided to give himself over fully when he came to Bahrain.

His strategy for creating a movement was to search for his community's people. He did what most of the activists in the diaspora did during the 2000s. In those years, a popular social networking site, Orkut, was created which allowed one to filter subscribers according to religion. It then became easy for people to join groups and connect with others. That is how he started to find people and connect with them. He first met Ilaiah Gautam, an Ambedkarite, in Bahrain. In 2006 he invited Bhante Chandra Bodhi, the Buddhist monk we have met before, to visit Bahrain. There was a programme in his honour. Bhante Chandra Bodhi informed them about the existence of other Ambedkar International Missions worldwide.

Then, a meeting with Sanjay Samant, an engineer, resulted in the formation of an Ambedkarite group. They called Raju Kamble, who granted them permission to run AIM in Bahrain. Whenever the Bahrain team wanted to organize an event or celebration, they requested a letter from AIM in the United States and submitted it to the embassy, claiming to be a subsidiary of that group. In 2008, Bhante Chandra Bodhi paid a visit again, and this time Raju Kamble was present.

In the presence of Bhante Chandra Bodhi, AIM was formally established in Bahrain in April 2008 with two objectives: paying back to society and promoting the culture bequeathed them by Ambedkar, i.e. Buddhism. Most of their activities took place in Shailesh's plush bungalow, which has the space and amenities to conduct events. Since it was not a registered organization, there wasn't a strict structure, but rather it was decentralized. Like many Gulf Ambedkarite groups, there is no organizational leader. However, there are project leaders who work on a project basis. They observe four special days in the year: Ambedkar's birth and death anniversaries, his conversion day, and Buddha Jayanti. In view of their strong Buddhist ties, they also started to make contact with the Sri Lankan embassy.

Education became their primary focus. They reached out to rural students, especially at the primary level in India. They started organizing education fairs. Given the lack of information and awareness of scholarships and various government schemes for students, Shailesh Pillewar and Sanjay Samant put together a booklet entitled *Tayari Bhavishya Ki* (Preparing for the Future), which was circulated among various Yahoo groups.

The Jawahar Navodaya school scheme offers free boarding and education across India. As many dominant castes put their children into the Navodayas, depriving Dalit students of places, AIM in Bahrain started to offer coaching and training for entrance exams to Navodaya schools. This then was extended into helping other students beyond primary school. They also invested in law school students. The Common Law Admission Test (CLAT), a qualifying exam for law schools, became their next focus. As a result, they were able to recruit a few students who successfully passed the CLAT exams and are now placed in national law schools in India. Their education projects are active in Orissa, Bihar and other North Indian states. Usually, someone in the AIM team proposes a project to the body. Collectively, a decision is taken by assessing the merits and demerits of the proposal. Once approved, the project is funded and its execution is meticulously followed by the body. AIM Bahrain's focus remains education. However, for all the guidance and help students receive, one rule is required of them: to maintain *sheel* (morality), one of the cardinal principles in Buddhism, as Shailesh said in an interview with me.

The majority of the AIM Bahrain members are Buddhist and the organization prefers to keep it a Buddhist organization. Owing to their religious affiliation, many joined, just as equally some left. This experience is not unique to the Bahrain organization. It has been observed across the board that wherever strong Buddhist ties are practised, membership has decreased. Pillewar remarked that Buddha has, in fact, become an attraction for many non-Maharashtrians. "The North Indian members think of Buddha as a Hindu, so they also end up joining." The Bahrain Ambedkarite group is diverse in age and regional representation. They have members from Gujarat, Jharkhand and some southern states. However, the Maharashtrian Buddhists form the majority.

As their activities began to be recognized, they gained confidence. That's why AIM in Bahrain decided to go public. To celebrate festivals like Ambedkar's birthday, they distributed leaflets, created Facebook pages for a wider audience, and requested the local radio station to run stories on the event.

In addition to AIM, there is another group led by labourers from Kerala called Ambedkar Innovative Mission. In view of the language barriers, neither of the groups can understand the other, which is why membership of each is confined to people from a particular state.

In all of the Ambedkarite organizations, there is a prominent women's presence. Many of the women are educated, and most of them have jobs. Dr Pradnya, for example, is a radiologist in Bahrain who is an active Ambedkarite. Likewise, wherever I spoke, the presence of professional women was promoted and equally appreciated by community members and the organizational leadership. Equality in the relations between men and women came to them naturally. In the Middle East, the presence of women is not often seen. Yet these Ambedkarite gatherings had women in responsible positions regularly leading the meetings.

Conclusion

This chapter has aimed to explore Dalit and Ambedkarite presence in different countries, using ethnographic data to analyse cosmopolitan Dalit universalism. This chapter has limited its focus to a few organizations in specific localities. It has not covered Canada, Australia or European countries. In Canada, there are the Ravidas Sabhas, Buddhist Ambedkarite groups on the east and west coasts, and civil society groups such as the Chetna Association. The Chetna Association is more widespread and connected with diverse groups and university bodies. They facilitate annual Ambedkar lectures and have organized lobbying efforts with the state government of British Columbia, city councils on the west coast, and the parliament of Canada.

The Chetna Association was instrumental in organizing the International Dalit Conference in Vancouver in 2003. They repeated the conference twenty years later in 2023. Owing to problems with visas, many speakers from India could not attend. I was one of the advisors to the conference. Aside from academic discussions, the Chetna Association is a liaison body that works on behalf of Dalits with the Canadian government, other faiths, civil society partners, educational institutes and diverse organizations to take positive steps in recognizing Dalit rights. Their lobbying resulted in British Columbia declaring 14 April as an International Day of Equality. They also donated copies of Dr Ambedkar's writings to the city council libraries, initiating a phase of book diplomacy in Canada.

Global organizations working against caste are primarily led by Indians and by those who identify with the politics of Dr Ambedkar. The politics of the diasporic anti-caste activism that began in the 1960s culminated in several lobbying efforts to secure anti-caste legislation and in several legal cases in Western societies. Caste in the diaspora is witnessing a new life of its own. Its future will depend on how the current situation is handled. One thing is certain: caste will eventually become a primary concern for host societies. As I write this, cases of caste discrimination have been filed in the courts in the United States, Canada, UK, Austria and Australia. In Australia a comprehensive study of caste discrimination has been undertaken.[50]

This awareness doesn't necessarily evoke a passionate response to host societies' historical problems, such as racism. However, Dalits in India and the diaspora have kept abreast of the anti-racist movements in the West. There is a conscious strategy to deal with the white superstructure while Dalit immigrants also try to establish themselves and navigate their way in the new host society. Many Dalits, like other Indians in the finance and technology sectors, occupy an upper-middle-class status in the West. Their lifestyle is surrounded by white power structures, and in view of the lack of community activism in coordination with movements of locally oppressed people, active solidarities, with some exceptions, are barely existent.[51]

However, the movement against caste is being shepherded by working-class labourers in the Middle East. They are more focused and aware of the immediate political necessities that concern people of their backgrounds. The difference in Dalit activism abroad has to do with strategy and approach. Strategies are decided according to one's location, immigration status, job security, and career progress. American Dalits often practise measured caution in their activism. They are overly concerned about the response they may receive from their employers should they participate in any events or protests. In contrast, workers in the Middle East, who are subject to extreme surveillance, boldly and smartly continue the work of recruiting more members and applying their energy to political change in India.

6

CONCLUSION

BIOGRAPHY OF DALIT AGONISM—FIELD NOTES FROM THE DIARY OF AN ARCHIVIST

As this book has shown, there are many parallels between the experiences of race and caste oppression, parallels which make it natural for the caste-oppressed to turn to Black struggles and keep abreast of their politics and movement. But what of the dominant castes, in India and the United States, who have sided with the Black movement? Black Lives Matter-like organizations have more to teach the dominant castes than the caste-oppressed. The Dalit struggle does not need to be reminded of the principle of universal human dignity that has always been at its foundation. It does not need to be reminded of the core methods of Black Lives Matter, which match Ambedkar's call for the oppressed to educate, organize and agitate. It is rather the dominant castes who need to recognize that they are carriers of a social and religious creed that cannot tolerate human equality. It is they who need to do more to educate themselves about their privilege and violent prejudices, to organize and agitate against the caste system rather than for it. The dominant-caste Indians' opposition to the racism of white people merely consolidates their own elite position. Calls will continue to be made for them to acknowledge their accountability for caste injustice, supplemented by calls for equality and social justice, until they confront their own casteism, racism and religious hatred.

The oppressed know that Indian institutions need drastic overhaul to root out casteism. It is the dominant castes, as they watch the institutional reforms in the United States in response to Black Lives Matter, that need to come to the same realization. India's oppressed know their suffering is tied to the caste system and its place in religious belief, just as Black people know that racism is tied to slavery and its place in the story of the United States.

Black people have always known where white hatred comes from. It comes from white fear of supposedly savage and unruly Black bodies, which they need the police to shoot down; from the fear of Black knowledge and success, to which they shut the door at every point. White fear is cowardly and denies everyone else a fair chance. White fear demands Black death because, without the torture and mutilation of Black bodies, the white public does not feel powerful and secure. The United States has raised a society based on this fear.

A century ago, the grand intellectual of America W.E.B. Du Bois diagnosed the condition in an essay he called "The Souls of White Folk". "I see in and through them," he wrote, "for I am native, not foreign, bone of their thought and flesh of their language ... I know their thoughts and they know that I know." What Du Bois knew was this:

> So long, then, as humble black folk, voluble with thanks, receive barrels of old clothes from lordly and generous whites, there is much mental peace and moral satisfaction. But when the black man begins to dispute the white man's title to certain alleged bequests of the Fathers

CONCLUSION

in wage and position, authority and training; and when his attitude towards charity is sullen anger rather than humble jollity; when he insists on his human right to swagger and swear and waste—then the spell is suddenly broken and the philanthropist is ready to believe that Negroes are impudent ...

After this the descent to hell is easy. I can see on the pale, white faces ... a writing of human hatred, a deep and passionate hatred, vast by the very vagueness of its expressions.[1]

To claims of the superiority of white culture, Du Bois answered by pointing to the carnage of the First World War. "This is not Europe gone mad; this is not aberration nor insanity; this *is* Europe; this seeming Terrible is the real soul of white culture ... This is where the world has arrived—these dark and awful depths and not the shining and ineffable heights of which it boasted."

This was Du Bois's gift to white people—the gift of self-knowledge. Perhaps the reason Ambedkar admired him so greatly was that so much of what Du Bois said about white fear also describes dominant-caste fear, and the murderous heart Du Bois found at the centre of white culture has its equivalent at the centre of brahmanical dominant-caste culture. The gift of Black justice movements is to give white people another chance to know and abandon the monstrosity they have created. Its gift to the dominant castes is the chance to recognize their own reflection in this monstrosity. They need to take it.

Caste, race and identity

The radical discourse surrounding caste and race struggles addresses an audience that preserves the memory of historical actors. Over time, this discourse has adapted its strategies. The hyper-ideological base has now been assumed by individuals whose group identity aligns with that of previous generations while differing in class and upbringing. Consequently, political responses to injustice have become more assertive and demanding. Within the power structures, there exist both uncompromising individuals and those willing to employ force to suppress protests.

The two supporting features of Dalit politics were literature and social movement. Literature and social movements worked interchangeably. Oftentimes, the power of social organizing and what could be learned from it informed the creativity of writers, poets and artists. Many emerged from the social movements to become authors of note. Literature also played a prominent role in the Dalit community, as it formed part of Dalit life. As we have seen in Chapter 2, literature was an exercise in affirming the arrival of the assertive, educated and articulate Dalit. This was the initial concern that literature as a whole engaged with. However, as the Dalit canon became established by the work of a wide variety of writers and poets in Maharashtra, it took a more focused position directed towards political goals. It was, after all, the intention of literature, as M.N. Wankhede defined it, to open space for Dalits in literary culture, which had previously obscured and overlooked the Dalit enterprise.

Wankhede pointed out that society and literature are intimately connected,[2] because any literature cannot exist apart from society. Society, he argued, reflected some kind of influence on literature. This was because the writer "does not live in silos. He is a product of the environment that he inhabits, and he, in turn, has the power to change the environment." Wankhede illuminated the power a writer holds to make changes in society. But, he warned, if "the writers waste the power then it will be a crime". This exemplifies what writing and literature meant for the Dalit community. Not only was literature a theoretical guide for the Dalit movement, it was also an assertion of dignity demanded by the newly educated class. It reflected the equality

CONCLUSION

and standards of life that education brought to Dalits. Thus, the literature of the Dalit canon was always driven by social change. The reason for this, Janardhan Waghmare and other writers have claimed, was the decisive influence of Dr Ambedkar,[3] whose politics and social views were predicated on social change. His towering presence animated the minds of Dalit writers.

As I researched the prospects of caste worldwide, one issue that remained with me was the role of caste in the system of transoceanic labour indenture. While the Atlantic represented a passage to slavery, the Indian Ocean was the route of indenture and slavery. Both labour systems were hostile to the dignity and rights of labourers, while the condition of their women and children was equally pitiable. Some of their stories still move me when I read them again. While the system of American slavery carried with it the national identity of an inferior serf class from West Africa, the Indian indentured system was heavily dependent on brahmanical caste. In India, the feudal caste system was allowed by the British to continue because it contributed to their revenues. The untouchables and shudras who were peasants working their own land—casteized labour in India—were easy sources of labour to exploit. In addition, dominant castes were also recruited as indentured labourers and were placed alongside the lower castes to work on the plantations in the British colonies.

Although overseas the divisions that were apparent in India's agrarian caste landscape were difficult to reproduce, caste as a system of identity continued. People often assumed higher identities on their arrival in the colonies. Subsequently, over the generations and especially after the former colonies became independent, an originally rigid system had turned into a fluid source of identity and recognition. Moreover, in the common conditions of the diaspora, diverse castes came together united by a common Indianness. However, the Hindu identity that was prevalent among nineteenth-century indentured labourers was vastly different from that created in the post-independent Republic of India.

The story of Trinidad island provides a good example of what happened to caste when it was transported to a distant colonized land. Caste was observed not only as a system of ritual but also under the intense labour regime. This meant serving on the plantation and yet having to recognize and abide by notions and practices of caste. This happened organically. The earlier arrivals brought with them the regional cultures and languages of Hinduism—Bhojpuri, Awadhi and Hindustani. Much later, they were confronted by missionaries of conservative brahmanical Hinduism who came to the colonies across Africa and the Caribbean bringing with them a hardened version of Hindu identity in which Muslims were othered and Hindus presented as superior. Many local Hindus who had never visited India but only heard about it from preachers came to look to their motherland as guardian of a powerful historical faith, which needed to be defended. However, not everyone joined up.

This caused a division among the faithful in the Hindu Trinidadian community, which continues till now. The brahmanical Hindu organizations in Trinidad operate like a corporate body, with their own set of schools, professional communications and media enterprises, and temples. This model was taken from the Christian missionaries in Trinidad. Despite the respected position the Hindu faith held among Indians on the island, many converted out of it. At the same time, some progressive Hindu practitioners who identified with the spiritual rather than political aspects of Hinduism initiated a reform programme. Worried by the rise of the right-wing Hindu nationalists in the BJP and RSS in India, these educated Hindu Trinidadians took issue with the former's interpretation of Hinduism which gave rise to the ideology of Hindutva.

CONCLUSION

The debate between progressives and the Hindu right takes place at temples, at public functions and Hindu festivals. The division is sharp but it does not carry over into an acrimonious public spat. However, organizations of the two parties do not intermix and their followers are advised not to socialize with each other. Public events hosted by one body only attract the presence of its own congregation. Small, local congregations are a feature of Hindu practice in Trinidad. One of the distinctive aspects of Hinduism in Trinidadian life is the dominance of Brahmanism and brahmanical rituals. But who is a pandit and what their traits consist of is hotly debated. This is what makes the story of caste in present-day Trinidad so interesting in a global study.

The descendants of Dalits and shudras now occupy important positions in Trinidadian society. They identify as Hindus and Indo-Trinidadians, while the caste badge their ancestors had to carry with their emigration pass is no longer mentioned in conversation or everyday discussions. Their religious identity became a means of engaging with non-Indians on the island, eventually becoming central to their heritage. It was further reinforced by social and religious movements that made the Ramayana and the Hindu religion an article of faith and memory for descendants. The Hindu identity mobilized on the island informs the spirited cause of Indian political representation in Trinidad. Instances of anti-Muslim rhetoric as seen in Hindu nationalism in India were not evident during my research on the island. Although the uncomfortable historical issue of Muslim invasion triggers some emotions, they do not spill over into the public sphere. "Trinidad is a trinity of Brahma, Vishnu and Mahesh [Shiva]," said a Sathya Sai devotee who is also a chartered accountant. For him, the different names of the Hindu gods represented the same essence.

I could not find anyone who identified as a Dalit, but there was a man named Sadhuji, a devout Hindu, who sang ballads and performed the Ramayana for the people. The Hindus acknowledged him and his work as more important than theirs. Sadhuji had visited India and found solace in the Ayodhya Temple. This demonstrates how integral religiosity has been to the lives of outcastes, whose only salvation was to submit to the authority of the gods they had been taught to revere. Those who indoctrinated this feeling aided the cause of religion sans caste, as they found the dominant category of religion worked better in their favour than caste did. Caste also functioned to further legitimize the sanctity of the *shastras*, complemented by the lore of the Ramayana, which is the national text of Trinidadian Hindus.

The emphasis on caste reiterated by the brahmanical groups of Trinidad is challenged by non-brahmans such as Pandit Amar, who says he likes to question everything that does not convince him. He did not accept the episode in the Ramayana of Rama chopping off the head of Shambuka, the shudra meditator, in a bid to achieve spiritual wisdom. According to him, he had been told by brahman pandits that this was a later insertion by Muslim invaders. When questioned about this, he asked me to send him the texts and materials that would reveal the co-optation and "betrayal" of those brahmans who had sided with the invaders.

Though the registers of Trinidadian identity account for ethnic, racial, national and religious forms, there also exist caste sensibilities among Indian Hindu Trinidadians. The national and religious framework allows caste-based recognition to operate in society. Although ordinary Trinidadian people claim not to believe in caste, this does not take account of the existence of caste names, rituals and identities that still operate at religious and administrative levels. The Dalit caste has integrated into what it means to be Hindu in the Caribbean. Although one does not find Dalits claiming their caste identity outright, caste-based identities do exist in multiple forms. Caste is not a singular idiom of Hindu Trinidadian society, nor is it a secular approval of the uniqueness of caste society. The example of Trinidad may indeed support the view that caste society does not need an outcaste body as an active agent for it to exist. Without Dalits, the caste system can imagine its preferred nature by placing flexible hierarchies in vertical chambers operating in the background as a reference point without recreating the models of the *varna* order.

Caste evolves through new ideas that maintain its existence as the heritage of a superior past for those dislocated by the everyday brutalities of the caste system. The diasporic affirmation of caste is not intended to rank people in daily life but to justify its existence as a planned social order, which was eventually corrupted by Muslim and British invasions of the land of Hindustan. Episodes of caste atrocity and caste violence are abhorred by Trinidadian Hindus, who do not identify with that aspect of Indian culture. Even those who advocate for a unified pan-Hindu identity distance themselves from such explicit practices of caste order. The version of the caste system that exists in Trinidad involves compulsive adherence to shastric norms and a localised struggle between conservative brahmanical orthodoxy and educated subaltern resistance. All the while, the Ati-shudra body is not mentioned in the debate on caste. The reason for this is that untouchable groups have overcome the disadvantage of their caste location, and the general Hindu society is also aware of the imperative of not reproducing Indian standards of untouchability.

New archives of caste

The sporadic activism against caste in the West and the counter-lobbying by the brahmanical right in America—comprising Hindu, Sikh, Muslim, Jain and Christian conservative lobbies—invite us to think critically about minority groups in the United

States as well as the West more generally. What does this new social class of minorities tell us, considering that Indians are usually regarded as one and the same thing? The assertion of Dalits in challenging the caste system at the university level and carrying a united fight to the UN and other places of power has disturbed people's understanding of Indian identity. It has also presented us with an emerging archive. One such archive preserved by the activist Laxmi Berwa, comprising his records and writings, is now in my possession. I have collected other resources since 2015, such as oral interviews in British Columbia from an ongoing project, and over time I intend to create an archive of Dalit diaspora history.

Additionally, several other official reports concerning caste have been commissioned and published.[4] More recently, Rutgers University's Task Force on Caste Discrimination came out with a comprehensive report on caste, providing guidelines and recommendations on how to define caste, on the interventions that educational institutions need to take, and what caste-based discrimination entails.[5] Similarly, in Australia, the Human Rights Commission undertook a macro-survey of the caste situation in Australia. Their findings incorporate the experiences of many caste-oppressed students.

This raises the question: does the United States foster community revolutions? In the larger diasporic struggle for justice, the United States represents the leading centre of empire. US hegemony is likely to continue as the second and third generation of Dalits assimilate into the American order, thereby confirming its legitimacy. However, I have recently noticed a sense of reservation and distance from leading Dalit activists and political leaders towards America or the Indian diaspora. About a decade ago, there was a surge of activists and scholars heading West. But lately, it seems to me, there has

CONCLUSION

been a decline in enthusiasm for America among Indian-based political and social actors.

This may be due partly to the absence of any credible social movements that openly align with Dalit political parties back home. Also, the Dalit diaspora has not openly declared its association and solidarity with similar groups. A political party leader from Maharashtra once told me on the phone in a scolding tone that diaspora Dalits think they are the smartest and that they know what is best for the community in India. He said he lives in India and is aware of the political situation more keenly than those abroad who are trying to effect change. Earlier the same leader had told me about the sorry state of the UK Ambedkarites, which he had experienced a couple of decades previously when he went to Britain with the president of India on an official visit. There is an apathy in India towards the diaspora, as their needs and demands are not always agreeable to leaders back home. Though this is not always the case, I have seen a similar instance involving another political leader from India.

The professional-class Dalits are mostly hesitant to declare an anti-state position in America. There is also a lack of political education among the diasporic population who, barring rare exceptions, have not involved themselves in political organizing. Leaders of major Dalit diaspora groups are rooted in middle-class Indian activism back home. Their work revolves around cultural activities, organizing festivals and get-togethers. At times of atrocities and social upheaval, they try to fundraise. Their working style is one that favours passive change and slow intervention.

Occasionally, some Dalit diaspora groups align with Indian political parties, yet there is no consensus among its members. The Dalit diaspora Ambedkarite organizations have distanced themselves from political leaders in India and have not made significant contributions to the movements back home. An exception to this is the Malaysian Ambedkarites, who started off as a political group before embracing their caste as a form of self-assertion in the face of injustices in Malaysia. They discovered Ambedkar as an outcome of their activism and did not begin their foray into politics as a result of Ambedkar. Their belief in radical change through political intervention thus predates their embrace of Ambedkar's philosophy. For them, Ambedkar was one of their proud ancestors, who led the Dalit population towards freedom, fought the British, and wrote the Indian Constitution.

The Malaysian Dalits are largely Tamilians with several generations of history in the country. Their reference point in respect of heritage and politics is Tamil Nadu. Their socialization, enculturation, self-assertion and feeling of belonging to Malaysia are all drawn from a strong sense of being Tamilian. The history of caste resistance as well as the sense of a non-Aryan base, funnelled through Tamil literature and Tamil newspapers in the past, still animates the Malaysian Dalits and inclines them towards India. Religion is another anchor for the Tamilians in Malaysia. Annual pilgrimages and visits to native villages are common activities among both Dalits and non-Dalits. Frequent flights to Chennai from Kuala Lumpur demonstrate the interconnectivity of the Peninsular regions.

For their part, the Dalits who are politically active in Malaysia have also found refuge in a politics of cooption and assimilation. Given the emphasis on Tamilian heritage, the relations that govern the Malaysian Dalits are also shaped by the localized nature of exported caste relations. This means that one can trace one's heritage to the pre-indenture period and on this basis formalize one's relations in both private and public affairs. In marriages and social gatherings, caste is still an overarching factor. One informant told me that when they—referring to dominant castes—attend public events or gatherings, they try to escape as soon as they can. They do not want to associate with others, beyond public exchanges. The existence of the Gounder association in Malaysia, for example, is a reflection of how such caste associations become normalized among the diaspora.

Perhaps because of this, the Dalits have taken to Ambedkar's ideals to assert their position. It is also advantageous because of the pacifist, stateist methods he used to achieve his goals. This does not hurt anyone and invites friendship from non-Dalit groups. While some non-Dalits support their cause, the Dalit leaders whom I interviewed were extraordinarily grateful to receive support. It appeared almost a patron–client relationship without any emphasis on Dalit agency. Receiving such support from the dominant castes was a matter of contention among Dalit groups.

In other diasporic Dalit organizations, politics and social activism are not on the agenda. Rehabilitation of victims of atrocity and education are priorities of the organizations that bear Ambedkar's name in America, Canada and Australia. Since the Middle Eastern Ambedkarites could not contribute with political lobbying or social organizing, they focused on funding small-scale activities such as coaching centres or individual students pursuing higher education. Since they themselves were first- or second-generation educated people, they valued education. Besides, this was the most honourable and easiest way to contribute to society.

In the United States there is now rarely research-based advocacy or lobbying with senatorial representatives, as seen in the earlier phase of Dalit organizing in America. I was an active member of many Ambedkarite organizations from 2015 to 2020 in America. During this period, I observed that the issue of social justice remained a priority. However, this had to do not with the United States but with the activities of social justice organizations in India. Political and pedagogical interventions were not on their agenda. They were reluctant to declare their allegiances to any cause that appeared controversial. One of the aims of these organizations was to become a familiar face for newcomers to America, to assist them with their networks and act as a social group of professionals who mostly interacted on the phone and met once or twice a year.

America's multi-award winning senior investigative reporter Phillip Martin at WGBH radio persuaded the Pulitzer Center to fund a project to investigate caste in America. This was the first full-length media attempt to examine caste in America.[6] Although the relationship between caste and its American origin story is well known, as I have demonstrated elsewhere,[7] there had not yet been a contemporary investigation into the South Asian immigrant population in America. This multi-part series covered these experiences not only in colleges but also in workplaces in America. The project established the extent of discrimination against Dalit people of South Asian heritage.

There are many other countries and groups outside South Asia that also have caste-like systems in their respective societies. These include West and East Africa, the Horn of Africa, Latin America, and parts of East Asia. But there has not been dedicated research that covers caste experiences among various peoples outside South Asia. This is something that I hope to do in the near future. Hierarchical social groupings and the heritage of birth-based rank are not a unique feature of South Asian castes only. There exist similar forms operating on a societal level within intra-group relations. Once a study is undertaken, it may provide us with new dimensions for examining caste in the twenty-first century.

In time to come, there will be many studies that analyse caste in various countries and among diverse ethnic groups. More research projects will be sponsored, which will create a good resource for further research. The Dalit diasporic question needs to be studied as not just a story of caste but also as a story about the anthropological enculturation of a new

CONCLUSION

identity, which becomes part of social and national policy and demography.

The aim of this book has been to show that caste and its lived reality were not solely an enterprise of Indian demography and geography. From the work of outsiders, as I showed in the Introduction, we can understand how castes were formed in the Indian context and how they adapted to the tradition of a brahmanical cult. Castes were not an original invention by foreign observers even though the heavy hand of Mediterranean travellers, early Iberian scholars and British administrators found in caste an easily explainable justification for the vast *jatis* that were incomprehensible to both outsiders and insiders. A violent and unbreakable system of occupational hierarchies fixing the brahmans on the top and Chandals—the outcastes—at the bottom, with multiple caste groups in between, posed challenges to all who sought to understand the situation. To justify this evolving system, the brahmans also authored various treatises over time and called them spiritual documents, making them part of the brahmanical canon.

Caste was shaped not just by the dominant groups but also by the victims of caste discrimination. Research has demonstrated how subaltern caste groups asserted their agency and presented their cause as an important refutation of the caste views held by the dominant-caste actors. Caste was profoundly shaped during the colonial encounters. It not only gave subtle agency to the caste actors but also provided space for radical assertions. The British colonial administration used caste to edge out the Dalit toilers from the land and grant title deeds to the dominant castes. Through the enactments of law, the British administration made Dalits vulnerable and open to exploitation. One glaring example was the Punjab Land Alienation Act of 1900. Similar instances occurred in South India involving the lands of untouchables and Tribals.[8]

As caste was being shaped by the Dalits in India, it also underwent an overhaul in the diasporic spaces, led by Dalit indentured labourers in the Caribbean. One can argue that a similar pattern could be found in other colonial indentured societies. Caste was not an imported dogma but a new quality of life that was refashioned by those who couldn't resist its incursion into the daily life of spiritual practice. Thus the story of caste cannot be understood by focusing on the South Asian landscape: one has to extend the study to other places where caste was interpreted, embraced and rejected. Caste reveals how localized institutions provided a basis for the imaginative impulses of caste to survive amidst amorphous forms. Caste, therefore, is a journey, an itinerary of global identities and demographics. Caste is a global story.

ACKNOWLEDGEMENTS

In my earlier book, I had a slim list of acknowledgements. This one is different.

This book was the collective effort of many people who have directly and indirectly helped in conducting the fieldwork, writing the thesis that led to this book, or who have simply been there to support me. The order of the names is in no way a representation of their status in the project but a humble token of appreciation.

I started to work on this book without a concrete plan. I have been part of the international Ambedkarite movement since I left India in 2011 to pursue higher studies in the UK. There, I was introduced to various email groups and local organizations. I started to spend time with them as a student activist and volunteer. I became proactive in 2012 when the project of buying a property for Ambedkar Centre near Washington DC picked up steam. I, too, contributed to the project as it felt like we were all part of one community—so far from one another, yet intimately connected.

However, it was not until I went to the US in the fall of 2015 that I started to take a research interest in the Dalit community there. There was so much happening. The activities were conducted in real time, and it felt surreal; it was impossible not to

ACKNOWLEDGEMENTS

notice this momentum. Thus, I started to write and think about the Ambedkarites of the US. Being a participant-observant to the movement, I gained a front-seat view of the mission, activities, ideas and philosophies that govern the movement.

But it was not limited to the US. Canada and the UK became other anchors for observing the complex Dalit movement abroad. With many castes, religions, languages, regions and ideologies playing their roles, having a cojoined effort is a disciplinary task. It is a very sensitive space to operate in. Alliances can break just as easily as they are formed. With no clear political agenda at hand, Ambedkarite activism operates in the domain of cultural politics and social activities, such as education.

In addition to the West, the Middle East, Australia, Southeast Asia and East Asia proved to be important points of analysis. I had planned to visit more countries, but this was not possible due to the inability to secure visas.

I also had no funding to visit those sites and do the fieldwork. Thus, I had to rely on the generosity of friends and their time to welcome me into their abode and provide local logistical support. Without the friends spread afar and new ones made on the way, this research would not have been completed to satisfaction. I have greatly benefited from their belief in the potential of the book project and in my activism. I am in debt to many friends who stepped up and sheltered me in their private spaces, generously giving and never asking for anything in return. The people acknowledged below have directly contributed to my fieldwork and research, while some were around as I was writing the book in various countries.

My gratitude to the Ford Foundation for their consistent support, particularly President Darren Walker, who is a mentor, a friend and a warm hug on a cold night. His commitment to me and his belief in my ideas have given me confidence that I would otherwise need years to gain.

ACKNOWLEDGEMENTS

Henry Louis Gates Jr., my mentor and professor, has been by my side since 2017. His investment in me makes me align with my goals and encourages me to walk on this path gainfully.

Cornel West has been a brother and a lover of solidarity that I seek from him. He has been by my side continuously. Our work and commitment to the cause continues.

Ava DuVernay has been a caring friend. Her encouragement and energy are transcendental.

Khalil Gibran Muhammad for his brotherhood, mentorship and affectionate support to me.

Faisal Devji, who was my supervisor for my second doctorate at the University of Oxford, engaged with my doctoral thesis. All while I was also working on this book in stolen moments. Inadvertently, the book and PhD thesis were submitted at the same time. Faisal provided encouragement and also helped explore resources within Oxford—though scant, they were a token of the belief Faisal had in me.

My supervisor for my first doctorate, Dilip Menon, introduced me to diasporic literature. During the formative stages of my PhD, when he wasn't my supervisor yet, he provided me with books and articles. Those fruitful years of learning about a new area have stayed with me. The references were handy in writing this book.

Jim Cashel is a rock—in belief and in my work. Jim and Anne Ching generously supported me through the turbulent times of my doctorate that coincided with Covid. Incidentally, it was also the time when I was in the thick of researching and writing this book.

At the University of Pennsylvania, I am grateful to have received mentorship and comradeship in John L. Jackson Jr., Tukufu Zuberi for his handholding and care, and Davesh Soneji for all things Philly.

I have presented aspects of this book to the public in various forms, predominantly at public lectures and keynotes that I have been invited to deliver over the years. In Berlin, at the Institute for Cultural Inquiry, I am grateful to Sarath Jakka for inviting me to debate the topic in 2021. At the University of Edinburgh, I was invited to deliver the Annual Ambedkar Memorial Lecture, 2022. I am grateful to Hugo Gorringe for his invitation and support to many Dalit students in his ambit. The School of Oriental and African Studies in London invited me to deliver the opening keynote lecture on caste and Blackness at the 'Worldmaking Beyond SOAS' conference in 2022. I am grateful to Awino Okech and Adam Habib. At Stanford University, Thomas Blom Hansen and Sharika Thiranagama, and at Columbia University, Anupama Rao, facilitated discussions on various chapters that were presented at the respective institutes. In Trinidad, at the Oliver Cromwell Cox Conference in 2024 at the University of the West Indies, St. Augustine, I was asked to present the research findings from Trinidad, and at Jawaharlal Nehru University, New Delhi, Harish Wankhede responded to another chapter at a talk hosted by JNU Academic. The comments and critiques from them and other members of the public have enriched the findings presented here. I remain grateful to them. Thanks to Dr Laxmi Berwa who shipped me neatly arranged boxes of his life's work in 2017. He wanted me to do something with them.

The Caravan, the venerable enterprise out of India, gave my piece on the Dalit–Black movement's comparison a cover story. Roman Gautam pushed many buttons to excavate the findings. The chapter in this book is different but has the influence of Roman's insight.

TRINIDAD

When the research was drawn up, Devan Maharaj was excited when I spoke to him about featuring Trinidad, his home country. He introduced me to the legend Sam Maharaj, a humorous and tall union leader of Trinidad. Uncle Sam took me in like his

ACKNOWLEDGEMENTS

son and provided all the contacts and local logistical support during my first phase of fieldwork. His support during the first field trip in Trinidad was immensely helpful. He was more than excited to plan meetings and site visits. It is for sharing his plate and providing a roof over my head and, beyond that, being a charming elder that made my research pursuits even bolder. I dedicate Chapter 4 to him.

Arvind Singh in Trinidad was introduced to me by our mutual friend, Anantanand. Arvind facilitated the meetings with diverse actors and connected me to the Hindu community of Trinidad. Pandita Indrani opened doors to conversations about caste within the temple community of Trinidad. Raviji, the patron of the Hindu movement in Trinidad.

Pandit Amar Sreeprasad, who is one of the protagonists, helped me navigate the Hindu question of Trinidad and exposed me to the caste subtleties. He spent days traveling with me on both visits.

Che Applewhait directed me towards the nooks and corners of Trinidad during the first phase of my travel and introduced me to his aunt, Rhona, and Anthony during my second trip. Both were so gracious and accommodated me for nearly a month in their house.

BAHRAIN

Shailesh Pillewar was an anchor to the Middle East Ambedkarite community. He introduced me to almost everyone who is reported on in the book. Like most of the informants, Shailesh and Shubhangi Pillewar also hosted me and helped me make connections.

UAE

Vijay Dhutale, Mogallan Bhagat, Ngozi Erondu, Linesh Khobragade, Ratnakar Dandavate, Sanjay Kumar.

ACKNOWLEDGEMENTS

QATAR
Harshal Tirpude, Safa Karman.

OMAN
Chetan Dhore, Sandeep Mohite.

CANADA
Greater Toronto Area:

Amarjit Badhan, Matt and Mitra Varhade, Vaishali and Nitin Duphare, and Anand Balley.

British Columbia:

Jai Birdi, Param Kainth, Surjit and Manjeet Bains, Anita Lal, Major Mal, Yuwaraj Narnaware, Mo, Anne Murphy.

UK
Scotland:

Bhante Sujano in Aberdeen, who sheltered me during the tumultuous times.
Pallavi Navasagare, Prashant Khandekar, Nitin Kadam, Hugo Gorringe.

Greater London:

Shrikant Borkar, the chronicler of the Dalit diaspora movement in the UK, introduced me to diverse actors in the field. Dev Suman, Meena Dhanda, Pritam Singh in Wolverhampton. Arun Gautam, the archivist of the Dalit community of the UK. Madhuri Hirekar, Gautam Chakravarty, Harbans Lal Virdee, Santosh Dass, Ken Hunt, Nathaniel Adam Tobias, Satpal Muman, Nitin Thulkar and other leaders of the movement. Jesus Chairez Garcia, Salil Shetty, Sushant Singh, Mulkait Singh Bahal, C L Virdee, Ranjith Baudh.

ACKNOWLEDGEMENTS

Oxford:

Asang Wankhede, Joel Littler, Mike Collins, Surajkumar Thube.

SAUDI ARABIA

Sanjay Samant, Shrish Sonawane, Panthak Bhalchakra.

USA

California:

Prasanna and Shalaka Gajbhiye, Rohit Meshram, Nalan, Cheran, Karthik Shanmugam, Thomas Blom Hansen, Sharika Thiranagama, Takshak Chahande, Prajwal Thool in the Bay Area. Nicole Ranganathan, Prem Chumber, Dr Brar and Minnie in Yuba City. Harshal Dofe, Jaya Dofe, Ben Kaila, Naresh Barsagade, Anjali Arondekar, Paul and Tammy Garnes in Southern California, Akash Gaikwad, Anam Akhter, Alisha Gaikwad, Abikal Borah in San Diego.

New York, New Jersey and Pennsylvania:

Vinaya and Milind Thamke, Milind Awasarmol, Nandita and Nivedita Pantawane, Nitin Suryatale, Laxmikant Rode, Anupama Rao, Manan Ahmed, Vyjayanthi Rao, Satyajit Somvanshi, Monali Mahedia, Nilay Shah, Vineet Mahedia, Sushil Raj, Akash Yengde, Bobby Guiliani, Vikas Tatad, Paul Divakar, Juliet Mureriwa, Carly Machado, Sajin.

Biju Matthew and Sangeeta Kamat were among the first people who heard about this book project when it was in its nascent stage.

Amherst:

Shabazz, Dee, Carlie and Gary Tartakov, Christopher Queen, Alyson, Augustine, Bharat Rathod.

ACKNOWLEDGEMENTS

Cambridge:

Phillip Martin and Bianca Baggio, who are my caretakers in Cambridge, Massachusetts. Magda Matache for being a friend and comrade in our common struggles. Jaspal Singh, Hardeep Kaur, Arif Hussaini, Swaroop Thool, Pradeep Mahale, Mahesh Admankar, Amol Ragade, Sanjay Bhagat, Paul Malachi, Velma DuPont, Krishnakali Lewis, Shawn Lee, Abby Wolf, Gbemisola Abiola, Boston Study Group members.

Seattle:

Prashant Nema, Lalit Khandare, Lokesh Kamble, Tanmay Waghmare.

Midwest region:

Kevin Brown, Anand Venkatkrishnan, Shireen Hamza, Nageswari and Raj Cherukonda, Laura Brueck, Ivy Wilson, Jakobi Williams, Maulik Shrimali, Mahesh Wasnik, Vivek Chavhan, Vikas Gawai, Shailaja Paik, Gaurav Pathania.

Atlanta:

Sandeep Chavan, Pratik Khobragade.

Texas:

Jagdish and Kunda Bankar, Yogesh and Shilpa Khankal, Kamlesh and Yasha Nandagawali, Bharat and Amrapali More, Anup and Monali Meshram, Scott Stroud, Vishal Thakare, Meenakshi Yadav, Anmol Mehra, Kalyani Khobragade, Ashish Patil, Manoj and Sunita Shambharkar.

NEPAL

Kathmandu:

Pradip Pariyar, Sarita Pariyar, Raj Rajak, Kunda Dixit, Shiva Gyawali, Sailee Choudhary, Aahuti.

ACKNOWLEDGEMENTS

PORTUGAL

Lisbon:

Rosa Maria Pérez, Inês Lourenço, Douglas Santos, João Mendonça.

Coimbra:

Luis Octavio Santos, Raoni, Rafael Francisco dos Santos Fernandes, Petro Safronov, Alcides Marques.

AUSTRIA

Vienna:

Marlene Rutzendorfer, Balwinder Singh.

FRANCE

Paris:

Parminder Singh, Neils Planel.

INDIA

Mangesh Dahiwale, Prashant Ingole, Sumedh Paradhe, Bharathi Prabu, Kaki Madhavarao, Dilip Chavan, Sachin Sarode, Rahul Pradhan, Keshav Waghmare, Achal Prabhala, Sunaina Pamudurthy, Akar Patel, Subhash Yengde, Rajendra and Sujata Dhoke, Prashant Rokade, Harish Kumar, Jayapal Dethe, Anand Teltumbde, J V Pawar, Raosaheb Kasabe, Sukhadeo Thorat, Gopal Guru, Kancha Illaiah, Milind Awad, Harish Wankhede, Anurag, Kavita Verma, Sanjay Verma, Vinay Bambole, Kunal Kamra, Y S Alone, Vivek Kumar. Hari Narke initiated a preliminary dialogue on the topic of research in Pune, Vinod Shirsath, Abhijit Vaidya, Girish Kuber, Abhijieet Tamhane, Sumesh Sharma, Prabhakar Kamble, Gautamiputra Kamble, Kapil Patil.

ACKNOWLEDGEMENTS

AUSTRALIA
Parag Moon, Vaibhav Gaikwad, Ajay Niranjane.

SPAIN
Chetan Suryawanshi, Nikhil Verma.

GERMANY
Gajendran Ayyathurai, Gajanan Talwar, Kama Maclean, Sajan Mani, Arjun Appadurai, Mahmoud Al-Zayed, Nate, Rupa Viswanath, Deepali Wighe, Vesna.

SWITZERLAND
Vibha Kamble, Jean Claude, Debjani Bhattacharyya.

KENYA
Attiya Warris, Sara and David Muthami, Watetu Kamugi, Zahid Patel, Kathleen Anangwe.

SLOVENIA
Mirjana and Marco Kravcar, Sonja Jerak-Zuiderent, Teun Zuiderent-Jerak, Darko Kastigar, Oskar Savarin, Jelena Medic, Gašper, Nic, Dilip Kaneria, Vlado Radic, Alek Stošić, Edita Nemec, Katja Fidler.

Sangha

Bhante Chanderbodhi, London and Toronto;
Bhante Sujano, Aberdeen;
Bhante Vinaya Rakkhita, Bangalore;
Bhante Arrayawagnso, Chiang Mai, Thailand.

I would like to thank Publisher Michael Dwyer for choosing to publish the book, Assistant Editor Mei Jayne Yew, copy-editor

ACKNOWLEDGEMENTS

Russell Martin, and proofreader Rebecca Hirst. I thank David Godwin for working with my ideas. Two anonymous reviewers generously provided much-needed critical feedback.

The Yengdes—they remain the source of strength to me. In memoriam: Papa (Milind (Metta) Yengde), Aai (Chandrabhagabai Vishwanath Yengde).

Mummy (Rohini), Sunanda, Mohan, Amrapali, Deepak, Pavan, Samyak, Pranali, Akash, Harsh, Prerana, Charwika, Bala. Nitin helped procure sources from India. Tjaša has been by my side for the past few years and was the first in many instances to receive my ideas and respond with her honeyed candour. May she accept to be my Kalyāṇamitta.

I have not mentioned the names of many due to privacy and security concerns.

ARCHIVES

The National Archives of Trinidad & Tobago;
Dr Laxmi Berwa Archives;
Dalit–Ambedkarite Diaspora Archives

Suraj Milind Yengde
April 2025

APPENDIX

LIST OF DALIT ORGANIZATIONS

Name	Location	Year of formation	Contact
	CANADA		
AISRO Canada	Vancouver	2016	
Ambedkar Center for Justice and Peace	Toronto	1991	https://acjpglobalnetwork.org/
Ambedkar International Social Reform Organization Canada	Surrey		http://www.aisrocanada.com/
Ambedkarite International Coordination Society of Canada	Vancouver		https://www.facebook.com/groups/1320702834936761/
Bhagwan Valmik Sabha	Ontario		
Chetna Association of Canada	Vancouver	1999	www.chetna.ca
Dhamma Waves	Toronto	2020	https://www.facebook.com/share/v/HRtWxxNWuBbW7BGj/?mibextid=WC7FNe
Dr Ambedkar International Mission Inc. Canada	Calgary	1994	https://aimscanada.org/
Dr Ambedkar Mission Toronto	Toronto	1978	https://www.ambedkarmission.com/
Gurdwara Ravidass Sikh Temple	Toronto		
Guru Ravidass Community Centre	Calgary		
Shri 108 Sant Sarwan Dasa Charitable Trust	Vancouver		

Shri Guru Ravidass Sabha	Vancouver		https://www.shrigururavidasssabha.ca/
Shri Guru Ravidass Sabha	Burnaby		https://www.facebook.com/sgrsvbcc/
Shri Guru Ravidass Sabha	Ontario		https://www.facebook.com/Shri.Guru.Ravidass.Sabha.Ontario/
Shri Guru Ravidass Temple	Toronto		
Shri Guru Ravidass Temple Gurbani Sagar	Montreal		https://www.facebook.com/p/Shri-Guru-Ravidass-Temple-Gurbani-Sagar-Montreal-100064682499898/
South Asian Dalit and Adivasi Network	Toronto	2020	https://www.facebook.com/p/Sadan-South-Asian-Dalit-Adivasi-Network-Canada-100067345244312/
Sri Guru Ravidass Sabha	Brampton		
	UNITED STATES		
Ad Dharma Brotherhood USA	California		
Ambedkar Association of North America	Novi	2008	www.aanausa.org
Ambedkar Du Bois Society	Northwestern University	2022	
Ambedkar International Center	Washington D.C.		https://ambedkarinternationalcenter.org
Ambedkar International Mission	London	1975	
Ambedkar International Mission at Virginia Tech	Blacksburg	2023	https://gobblerconnect.vt.edu/organization/aim-vt
Ambedkar King Study Circle	California	2016	akscusa.org
Ambedkar Legal Services	New York		
Ambedkar Periyar Study Circle at ASU	Arizona State University, Tempe, AZ		https://asu.campuslabs.com/engage/organization/acs
Ambedkarite Buddhist Association of Texas	Dallas, TX	2004	https://abatusa.org/

Organization	Location	Year	URL
Ambedkarite Students of Columbia University	New York	2022	https://www.facebook.com/share/67ud2FSP1315WkaM/?mibextid=WC7FNe
Bahujan Scholars	Amherst	2021	bahujanscholars.org
Begumpura Cultural Society of New York	New York		https://www.facebook.com/begumpurany/
Bhim International Foundation USA	California		
Boston Study Group	Boston	2017	https://www.bostonstudygroup.com/
California for Justice	San Francisco		
Caste Equity Legal Task Force	California		https://sites.google.com/view/casteequitylegaltaskforce/home
Dalit Solidarity	San Diego		https://dalitsolidarity.org/
Dalit Solidarity Forum USA	New York/New Jersey	1999	https://dalitsolidarityforumusa.com
Desh Doaba	California		https://www.deshdoaba.com/
DFW Shri Guru Ravidass Organization	Mesquite		https://dfwravidassia.blogspot.com/
Dr B R Ambedkar International Mission Center	Dallas, Texas		https://www.aimcenterhouston.org/
Dr Ambedkar International Mission	New York		https://www.ambedkarmission.org
Equality Labs	California		
Guru Ravidas Temple	Selma, CA		
Indigo Student Collective	University of Texas, Austin		
Jai Bhim Atlanta	Atlanta		https://www.instagram.com/jaibhimatlanta/
Maharishi Valmiki Temple	Yuba City, CA		https://maharishivalmiktemple.com/
Midwest Ambedkarites, USA	Chicago	2020	
Oregon Caste Abolition Collective	Oregon	2023	https://sites.google.com/view/oregoncasteabolition/home?authuser=0
Paine Phulé Foundation	California	2024	

Name	Location	Year	URL
Periyar Ambedkar Study Circle	New Jersey	2017	https://pascamerica.org/
Periyar International USA	Illinois	1994	https://periyarinternational.com/
Shri Guru Ravidass Sabha	Sacramento		https://www.facebook.com/@shrigururavidasstemplesacramento/
Shri Guru Ravidass Sat Sangat	Yuba City, CA		https://shri-guru-ravidass-sat-sangat.hub.biz/
Shri Guru Ravidass Temple	Fresno, CA		https://www.facebook.com/ShriGuruRavidassSabhaFresno/
Shri Guru Ravidass Temple	Yuba City, CA		https://ravidastemple.com/
Shri Guru Ravidass Temple	Seattle, WA		https://www.facebook.com/people/Shri-Guru-Ravidass-Sabha-Seattle/100091648955377/
Shri Guru Ravidass Temple	New York		https://www.instagram.com/explore/locations/30780371/shri-guru-ravidas-sabha-of-new-york-inc/
Shri Guru Ravidass Temple	Pittsburg, CA	1985	https://srigururavidasstemple.com/home-page
Shri Guru Ravidass Temple	Bay Area, CA		https://www.sgrdsabhabayarea.com/
Shrui Guru Ravidas Sabha Bay Area	Union City, CA		https://www.facebook.com/p/Shri-Guru-Ravidas-Sabha-Bay-Area-California-100064300767327/
UC Collective for Caste Abolition	California		https://www.coalitionforcasteabolition.org/
UT Student Coalition Caste Abolition	University of Texas, Austin	2023	
UNITED KINGDOM			
Ambedkar International Mission	London	1975	
Ambedkar Mission Society, Bedford	Bedford	1972	https://www.facebook.com/p/ambedkarmissionsociety-bedford-61567125695630/
Ambedkar Society	SOAS		https://soasunion.org/organisation/13241/
Anti-caste Discrimination Alliance	Hertfordshire	2008	https://www.acdauk.org.uk/

Bhagwan Valmik Ashram, Birmingham	Birmingham		
Bhagwan Valmik Sabha	Oxford		
Bhagwan Valmik Sabha	London		
Bhagwan Valmik Sabha	Bedford		https://www.facebook.com/p/Bhagwan-Valmiki-Sabha-Bedford-100064390073928/
Bhagwan Valmik Sabha, Birmingham	Birmingham		https://bvsbirmingham.org.uk/
British Ravidassia Heritage Foundation	Bedfordshire	2022	https://www.brhfoundation.com/
Buddha Dhamma Association	Southall		
Buddhist Ambedkarite Maitry Sangha	London		https://ukbams.wordpress.com/about/
Caste as Practice	Cambridge		
CasteWatch, UK	Plaistow	2003	https://www.castewatchuk.org/
Central Valmiki Sabha International	Coventry		https://www.facebook.com/p/Central-Valmiki-Sabha-International-UK-100081351022906/
Dalit Solidarity Network	London		https://dsnuk.org/
Dera 108 Sant Baba Gobind Dass Memorial Temple UK	Wolverhampton		
Dera Baba Gobind Dass Ji Memorial Temple	Wolverhmapton		
Dr Ambedkar Community Centre	Derby		https://ambedkarcommunitycentre.co.uk/
Dr Ambedkar Community Centre	Wolverhampton		https://www.ambedkartimes.com/Dr%20Ambedkar%20Societies.htm
Dr Ambedkar Memorial Committee of Great Britain	Wolverhampton	1969	https://drambedkar.org.uk/
Dr Ambedkar Mission Society Scotland	Scotland		https://www.facebook.com/AmritBaniShriGuruRavidassSabhaPortugal

Organisation	City	Year	URL
Dr B R Ambedkar Memorial Trust	London		
Federation of Ambedkarite and Buddhist Organisations UK	London	1984	https://www.facebook.com/FABO.uk/?locale=en_GB
Global Ambedkar	London	2017	https://www.facebook.com/share/1HMtsr6bsG/?mibextid=wwXlfr
Guru Ravidass Bhawan	Birmingham		https://www.gururavidassbhawan.org/
Kanshi TV (Shri Guru Ravidass Mission International)	Birmingham	2011	https://www.kanshitv.co.uk
Maharishi Valmiki Sabha	Coventry		https://mvscoventry.org.uk/
Oxford Ambedkar Initiative	Oxford		
Punjab Buddhist Society	Wolverhampton	2004	https://www.dhamma.ru/sadhu/1145-punjab-buddhist-society
Ravidassia Community Center	Hitchin		
Shri Guru Ravidass Bhawan Strood	Kent		https://www.facebook.com/groups/953016805103175/
Shri Guru Ravidass Community Glasgow	Glasgow		https://find-and-update.company-information.service.gov.uk/company/SC626462
Shri Guru Ravidass Community Scotland	Glasgow		https://find-and-update.company-information.service.gov.uk/company/SC598097
Shri Guru Ravidass Cultural Association of Erith and Belvedere	Erith		
Shri Guru Ravidass Dharmik Sabha	Willenhall		
Shri Guru Ravidass Dharmik Sabha	Wolverhampton	1963	
Shri Guru Ravidass Gurdwara, Kent	Gravesend		https://www.facebook.com/GRGGK/?locale=en_GB
Shri Guru Ravidass Sabha	Bradford		
Shri Guru Ravidass Sabha	Southampton		https://www.facebook.com/Gururavidasssouthampton/
Shri Guru Ravidass Sabha	Southall		http://sgrds.org/

Name	Location	Year	URL
Shri Guru Ravidass Sabha (Sikh Temple)	Derby		
Shri Guru Ravidass Sabha and Welfare Cultural Association	Southampton		
Shri Guru Ravidass Sabha CIC	Erskine		
Shri Guru Ravidass Sangat	Luton		https://www.facebook.com/ShriGuruRavidassSangatLuton/?locale=en_GB
Shri Guru Ravidass Temple	Coventry		
Shri Guru Ravidass Temple	Darlaston		https://www.facebook.com/p/Shri-Guru-Ravidass-Temple-Darlaston-6154900022926/
Shri Guru Ravidass Temple	Berkshire		
Shri Guru Ravidass Temple and Community Center	Leicester		
Shri Guru Ravidass Temple Foleshill	Coventry		https://www.facebook.com/bhagwanvalmikashrambirmingham/
Shri Guru Ravidass Temple Newham	London		https://www.facebook.com/p/Shri-Guru-Ravidass-Sabha-Newham-London-100066017235147/
Shri Guru Valmiki Sabha	Southall		https://valmiksabhasouthall.co.uk/
Sri Guru Ravidass Ji Sabha	Rochester		
Sri Guru Ravidass Ji Temple	Walsall		https://www.worldgurudwaras.com/gurudwaras/shri-guru-ravidass-temple-walsall/
Sri Guru Ravidass Sabha	Bedford		https://www.gururavidasssabhabedford.com/
The Christian Network Against Caste Discrimination	London		https://www.cnacd.co.uk/
Voice of Dalit International	Greenford	1999	https://www.vodintl.org.uk/
Wat Phramaha Somboon Buddha Vihara	Wolverhampton		https://www.facebook.com/drambezdkar.org.uk/

	MALAYSIA	
Dewan Pendidikan India	Selangor	
Dr Ambedkar Welfare Organization Malaysia	Selangor	
United Indian Progressive Front	Kuala Lumpur	
	IRELAND	
Ambedkarite Buddhist Society of Ireland	Dublin	2025	https://www.facebook.com/share/16AsPudWe9/
Babasaheb Ambedkar Mission Society of Ireland	Dublin		
	FINLAND	
10K Buddhist Millionaire	Finland	2024	https://www.facebook.com/share/g/1GrpL7uKgr/
	UNITED ARAB EMIRATES	
Ambedkar International Mission–AIM	Dubai	1997
Indian Maitri Sangha, UAE	Dubai	2022
Global BAMCEF Diaspora	UAE	2018
Satyashodhak group UAE	Dubai	
	HUNGARY	
Dr Ambedkar School	Miskolc		http://www.ambedkar.hu
WBR News	Hungary	2000	WorldBuddhistRadio.com

	NEPAL		
Dalit Lives Matter Nepal	Kathmandu	2021	https://dalitlivesmatter.org/
Dalit Welfare Organization	Kathmandu		https://dwo.org.np/
Feminist Dalit Organisation	Kathmandu	1994	https://fedonepal.org/
Rastriya Dalit Network	Kathmandu	2004	https://www.rdnnepal.org.np/
Samari Urthan Sewa	Nepal	2008	Samariutthan.org.np
Samata Foundation	Kathmandu	2009	https://samatafoundation.org/about-us/
	PAKISTAN		
Dalit Sujaag Yejreek	Sindh	2014	https://en.m.wikipedia.org/wiki/Dalit_Sujag_Tehreek
Pakistan Dalit Solidarity Network	Karachi	2008	
Scheduled Caste Federation of Pakistan	Islamabad		
	DENMARK		
Ambedkar International Mission, Nordic	Copenhagen	2023	None
International Dalit Solidarity Network	Copenhagen	2000	https://idsn.org/about-us/
	NORWAY		
Ambedkar International Mission, Norway	Oslo	2024	https://www.facebook.com/groups/540282432401727/?ref=sharehttps%3A%2F%2Fm.facebook.
Oslo Anti-Caste Book Circle	Oslo	2020	
	BAHRAIN		
Dr Ambedkar International Mission Bahrain	Bahrain	2008	www.aimbah.com

	QATAR		
IQ group	Doha		
We The People	Doha		
	OMAN		
Dr Ambedkar International Mission, Oman (AIM Oman)	Muscat	2006	http://aimoman.org/about-2/
Phule Shahu Ambedkar Organization Oman	Muscat		
	KUWAIT		
Dhamma Group	Kuwait City		
Dr Ambedkar Mission Sabha Kuwait	Kuwait City		https://www.facebook.com/groups/648601218663451/?_rdr
Dharma Group Kuwait	Kuwait City	2015	
Sant Guru Ravidass Sabha	Kuwait City		
Thaiman Cultural Association	Kuwait City		
	SAUDI ARABIA		
SAAVIKA	Al Khobar		
	SPAIN		
Ambedkar International Mission, Spain	Madrid	2025	https://www.facebook.com/groups/958334639732871
Shri Guru Ravidass Bhawan Society Barcelona	Barcelona		https://www.facebook.com/p/shri-guru-ravidass-bhawan-society-barcelona-spain-100064492667740/?profile_tab_item_selected=mentions&_rdr

	PORTUGAL	
Amrit Bani Shri Guru Ravidass Sabha Portugal	Lisbon	https://www.nzgururavidassabha.co.nz/about
	NEW ZEALAND	
NZ Guru Ravidass Sabha Inc.	Auckland	https://www.facebook.com/p/Guru-Ravidass-Temple-Bombay-Hill-Auckland-100069643784615/
Shri Guru Ravidass Temple	Hastings	https://www.facebook.com/GuruRavidassTempleHastingsNz/?ref=py_c
	ITALY	
Bhagwan Valmik Sabha	Marche	https://www.facebook.com/bhagwanvalmikisabhamarcheitaly/
Shri Guru Ravidass Darbar	Bergamo	https://www.facebook.com/p/Shri-Guru-Ravidass-Darbaar-Bergamo-Italy-100069403808730/
Shri Guru Ravidass Temple	Vicenza	https://www.facebook.com/profile.php?id=100064725334602
Shri Guru Ravidass Temple	Verona	https://www.facebook.com/profile.php?id=100064414940947
	THE NETHERLANDS	
AIM Netherlands Facebook Group	Amsterdam	https://facebook.com/groups/aim.netherlands/
Ambedkar International Mission Netherland	Amsterdam	https://www.facebook.com/profile.php?id=61572604212578
Ambedkar Periyar Study Circle	Amsterdam	https://www.facebook.com/groups/241116943114671/
Dr Babasaheb Ambedkar International Mission, Europe	Leidschendam	

Guru Ravidass Temple Den Haag	The Hague		https://www.facebook.com/p/Guru-Ravidass-Temple-Den-Haag-100067798991019/
Shri Guru Ravidass Temple	Amsterdam		https://www.facebook.com/ShriGuruRavidassTempleAmsterdamHolland/
GREECE			
Shri Guru Ravidass Sabha	Koropi		https://www.facebook.com/shrigururavidasssabha/
GERMANY			
Ambedkarite in Europe	Frankfurt	2019	
AIM Europe	Frankfurt		https://ambedkarineurope.org
Dr Ambedkar Mission Society Europe	Offenbach am Main		
Gurughar Shri Guru Ravidass Ji	Oberursel		
Shri Guru Ravidass Ji e. V.	Frankfurt am Main		
FRANCE			
Begumpura Aid International	Villiers-le-Bel		https://www.begampuraaidinternational.com/
Gurudwara Shri Guru Ravidass	Paris		
FIJI			
Gurdwara Sahib	Nasinu		

	AUSTRIA		
Ambedkar Aid International Pay Back To Society Vienna	Vienna		
Indische Kultur & Sozialer Verein Wien	Vienna		https://www.facebook.com/AMBEDKAR91/
Shri Guru Ravidass Temple	Vienna		
	AUSTRALIA		
Ambedkarite Buddhist Community Australia	Maddington		https://abcaustralia.org/
Dr Ambedkar International Mission Australia	Australia		https://www.ambedkarmission.net/contact-us/
Indian Buddhist Community	Melbourne	2022	https://www.indianbuddhistcommunity.org/
Periyar Ambedkar Thoughts Circle	Queensland		https://www.facebook.com/PeriyarAmbedkarThoughtsCircleAustralia
Shri Guru Ravidass Sabha	Brisbane		
Shri Guru Ravidass Sabha	Melbourne		https://www.facebook.com/p/Shri-Guru-ravidass-sabha-Melbourne-100064682170175/
Shri Guru Ravidass Sabha Sydney Inc.	Sydney		https://sgrssydney.com.au/our-organization/
	JAPAN		
Dr Ambedkar International Mission	Japan		https://www.facebook.com/AIMJapan/
Dr Babasaheb Ambedkar International Association for Education	Sagamihara		https://www.baiae.org/about-us/

***an updated list can be found on www.surajyengde.com

LIST OF ILLUSTRATIONS

1. Gangadhar Pantawane's African American reading list. (Author's photo, 2022)
2. A poster for an Ambedkar Jayanti event at Howard University in 1998. (Courtesy of Laxmi Berwa)
3. A letter from Prime Minister Indira Gandhi to Dr Laxmi Berwa. (Courtesy of Laxmi Berwa)
4. Yogesh Varhade and Dr Berwa protesting outside the UN against Atal Bihari Vajpayee's government. (Courtesy of Laxmi Berwa)
5. Milind Yengde, my father, protesting the Indian government's apathy towards the inclusion of caste in Durban at the Nanded's district headquaters. The banner reads: On behalf of Maitri Mission 2-7 September 2001 DHARNA: To protest against the Indian government's objection to include the question of caste discrimination at the UN Conference Against Racial Discrimination held in Durban".
6. Milind Yengde with his old associate Raja Dhale, one of the co-founders of the Dalit Panthers.

LIST OF ILLUSTRATIONS

7. Ravi Maharaj donning his Trinidadian attire. (Author's photograph, April 2024)
8. Sadhuji at his residence in Debe. (Author's photograph, May 2024)
9. Shiva Harijan Mandir in Debe. (Author's photograph, April 2024)
10. The observance of Kathina, a Buddhist festival, at the Dr Ambedkar Memorial Committee of Great Britain. (Author's photograph, March 2022)
11. Pandit Amar Sreeprasad at his Sunday congregation in Cunipia. (Author's photograph, May 2022)
12. An informal meeting hosted at a labourers' camp in the Middle East, September 2023. (Author's photograph, September 2023)
13. Author with the Dr Ambedkar Welfare Organization Malaysia. (Author's photograph, December 2024)
14. The Dalit Panthers' Golden Jubilee celebration, hosted by the Yuva Panthers in Nanded. (Courtesy of Yuva Panthers)
15. Dalit activists in India, July 2020, protesting the murder of George Floyd.
16. The Ambedkarite Student Group at the Indian High Commission in London. (Author's photograph, December 2021)

NOTES

INTRODUCTION: THE OCCIDENTAL AND ORIENTAL TREATMENT OF CASTE

1. S.V. Ketkar, *History of Caste in India: Evidence of the Laws of Manu on the Social Conditions in India during the Third Century A.D. Interpreted and Examined: with an Appendix on Radical Defects of Ethnology* (Ithaca, NY: Taylor and Carpenter, 1916).
2. G.S. Ghurye, *Caste and Race in India* (Bombay: Popular Prakashan, [1932] 1969).
3. S. Thorat, *Dalits in India: Search for a Common Destiny* (New Delhi: Sage, 2009).
4. L. Dumont, *Homo Hierarchicus: The Caste System and Its Implication* (Chicago: University of Chicago Press, 1970).
5. B.G. Tilak, *The Arctic Home in the Vedas: Being Also a New Key to the Interpretation of Many Vedic Texts and Legends* (Poona: Messrs. Tilak Bros., [1903] 1925).
6. B.R. Ambedkar, "The Annihilation of Caste", in Vasant Moon (ed.), *Dr Babasaheb Ambedkar: Writings and Speeches*, vol. 14, part 2 (Mumbai: Govt of Maharashtra, 1995), pp. 23–96.
7. N. Dirks, *Castes of Mind: Colonialism and the Making of Modern India* (Princeton: Princeton University Press, 2001).
8. B.R. Ambedkar, *The Untouchables: Who Were They and Why They Became Untouchables* (New Delhi: Amrit Book Co., 1948) in *Dr Babasaheb: Writings and Speeches*, vol. 7 (Mumbai, Govt of Maharashtra, 2013), p. 241.

9. Ibid., p. 244.
10. Ibid., pp. 275–7.
11. Ibid., p. 265.
12. Ibid.
13. Ibid., pp. 266, 267.
14. Ambedkar uses this premise of extreme physical segregation and intense isolation to explain the condition of the untouchables in Hindu India.
15. Ibid., p. 273.
16. D.D. Kosambi, *An Introduction to the Study of Indian History* (Bombay: Popular Book Depot, 1956).
17. V.M. Narasimhan et al., "The Formation of Human Populations in South and Central Asia", *Science* 365, no. 6457 (2019).
18. Fa-Hien, *A Record of Buddhistic Kingdoms: Being an Account by the Chinese Monk Fa-Hien of His Travels in India and Ceylon (A.D. 399–414) in Search of the Buddhist Books of Discipline*, trans. James Legge (Delhi: Oriental Publishers, 1971), p. 43.
19. Ibid.
20. P. Banerjee (ed.), *Textual Lives of Caste Across the Ages: Hierarchy, Humanity and Equality in Indian History* (London: Bloomsbury, 2024).
21. For this section I draw inspiration from Ambedkar's historical methodology. Ambedkar used Megasthenes's and al-Bīrūnī's texts as a reference to make his case in "Untouchables or the Children of India's Ghetto", in V. Moon (ed.), *Dr Babasaheb Ambedkar: Writings and Speeches*, vol. 5 (Mumbai: Govt of Maharashtra, 1989).
22. J.W. McCrindle, *Ancient India as Described by Megasthenês and Arrian: Being a Translation of the Fragments of the Indika of Megasthenês Collected by Dr Schwanbeck, and of the First Part of the Indika of Arrian* (Calcutta and Bombay: Thacker & Co.; London: Trübner & Co., 1877), pp. 40–1.
23. Ibid., p. 44n.
24. H.G. Rawlinson, *Intercourse between India and the Western World from the Earliest Times to the Fall of Rome* (Cambridge: Cambridge University Press, 1916).
25. On Arrian's quote, see McCrindle, *Ancient India*.

26. Ambedkar's observation on the Mahars explains the fluid nature of kshatriya titles. Up until the seventeenth century kshatriya had not hardened into a theological caste. It was available for new rulers. One example of this is Shivaji Bhonsale, who counted himself as a kshatriya, even though he belonged to the peasant caste of Maharashtra.
27. Rawlinson, *Intercourse between India and the Western World*, p. 58.
28. Ibid.
29. Ibid., pp. 28–9.
30. Strabo, *The Geography of Strabo*, vol. 1, trans. H.C. Hamilton and W. Falconer (London: Henry G. Bohn, 1858), p. 109.
31. I am grateful to Mahmoud al-Zayed for sharing with me al-Bīrūnī's text and for encouraging me to explore it while commenting on an early version of this chapter presented at the Berlin Institute of Cultural Inquiry in 2021.
32. Muḥammad ibn Aḥmad Bīrūnī, *Alberuni's India: An Account of the Religion, Philosophy, Literature, Geography, Chronology, Astronomy, Customs, Laws and Astrology of India*, vol. 1, ed. E. Sachau (London: Kegan Paul, Trench, Trübner & Co., 1888).
33. Ibid., p. xix.
34. See ibid., Chapter IX, p. 100.
35. Ibid., p. xxi.
36. Chapters 12, 23, 24, and 27 exclusively deal with the Puranas.
37. Ibid., p. 101.
38. The same genealogical references are also found in Ambedkar's writings on untouchables and their conditions. In the chapter "The House the Hindus Have Built", Ambedkar brings into focus these markers. See V. Moon (ed.), *Dr Babasaheb Ambedkar: Writings and Speeches*, vol. 5 (Mumbai: Govt of Maharasthra, 1989), pp. 145–69.
39. *Alberuni's India*, p. 136.
40. Ibid., p. 137.
41. Ibid.
42. R.A. Schermerhorn, "When Did Indian Materialism Get Its Distinctive Titles?", *Journal of the American Oriental Society* 50 (1930), pp. 132–8.
43. Their origin is debated. Some identify them in the first millennium BCE while others into antiquity—which meant that the disbelief in

God and karma always existed among humans. God and other creations came at a later stage. R. Bhattacharya, "Development of Materialism in India: The Pre-Cārvākas and the Cārvākas", *Esercizi Filosofici* 8, no. 1 (2013), pp. 1–12, http://hdl.handle.net/10077/12943.

44. Schermerhorn, "When Did Indian Materialism Get Its Distinctive Titles?", pp. 133, 134.
45. P. Gokhale, *Lokāyata/Cārvāka: A Philosophical Inquiry* (New Delhi: OUP, 2015).
46. L.Y. Avacharmal, *Ambedkarit Chalwal āni Hyderabad Sansthanatil Dalit Mukti Sangram* (Pune: Sugawa Prakashan, 1987), pp. 20–1.
47. I thank Keshav Waghmare, a chronicler of Marathwada's Dalit history for directing me to this part of the history. On the Marathwada and Nizam history, see P.R. Venkatswamy's autobiography, *Our Struggle for Emancipation* (Hyderabad: Hyderabad Book Trust, 2020).

1. COLONIAL DALITALITY: CENSUS CASTES

1. Sir Daniel Ibbetson, who was a superintendent of Punjab province, developed a theory of caste as an occupation category on the basis of the division of labourers. See C.J. Fuller, "Ethnographic Inquiry in Colonial India: Herbert Risley, William Crooke and the Study of Tribes and Castes", *Journal of the Royal Anthropological Institute* 23, no. 3 (2017), pp. 603–21; D.C.J. Ibbetson, *Report of the Census of the Panjab 1881*, vol. 1: *Text* (Lahore: Central Gaol Press, 1883); J.A. Baines, *Census 1881: Operations and Results in the Presidency of Bombay, Including Sind*, vol. 1: *Text* (Bombay: Government Press, 1882).
2. B.R. Ambedkar, *Riddles in Hinduism: The Annotated Critical Selection* (New Delhi: Navayana, 2016).
3. An excellent history of this is provided by Joel L. Lee in *Deceptive Majority Dalits, Hinduism, and Underground Religion* (Cambridge: Cambridge University Press, 2021).
4. On a similar but twentieth-century discourse between Gandhi, Ambedkar and Arya Samaj, see N. Kolge, *Gandhi against Caste* (Gurgaon: PRH, 2018).
5. V. Prashad, *Untouchable Freedom: A Social History of a Dalit Community* (Delhi: OUP, 2000), pp. 68–78.

6. Ibid., p. 69. On the Muslim Dalits, see Lee, *Deceptive Majority*.
7. D. Ibbetson, *Memorandum on Ethnological Inquiry in the Punjab* (Lahore: Government of India, 1882); C.E. Luard, *Ethnographical Survey of the Central India Agency: Monograph no. III, Bundelkhand Castes* (Lucknow: Newal Kishore Press, 1909); H. Risley, *The Tribes and Castes of Bengal: Ethnographic Commentary*, 2 vols. (Calcutta: Bengal Secretariat Press, 1892).
8. *Census of India*, 1911, vol. 1, part 1, Report, p. 129, in V. Prashad, *Untouchable Freedom: A Social History of an Untouchable Community* (New Delhi: Oxford University Press, 2000), pp. 71–2.
9. C.S. Adcock, *The Limits of Tolerance: Indian Secularism and the Politics of Religious Freedom* (New York: Oxford University Press, 2014), p. 37.
10. Ibid.
11. Prashad, *Untouchable Freedom*, p. 81.
12. E.A.H. Blunt, "United Provinces of Agra and Oudh," in *Census of India*, 1911, vol. XV, part I, Report (Allahabad: Govt. Press, 1912); also see E.A.H. Blunt, *The Caste System of Northern India: With Special Reference to the United Provinces of Agra and Oudh* (London: Oxford University Press, 1931); L. Dumont, *Homo Hierarchicus: The Caste System and Its Implication* (Chicago: University of Chicago Press, 1970), p. 136.
13. S. Padmanabh, "Census in Colonial India and the Birth of Caste", *Economic and Political Weekly* 46, no. 33 (2011), pp. 51–8.
14. R.B. Bhagat, "Census Enumeration, Religious Identity and Communal Polarization in India", *Asian Ethnicity* 14, no. 4 (2013), pp. 434–48.
15. S. Chakravorty, *The Truth about Us: The Politics of Information from Manu to Modi* (Delhi: Hachette India, 2019), p. 120.
16. C. Jangam, *Dalits and the Making of Modern India* (New Delhi: Oxford University Press, 2017).
17. K. Bharati, "Swami Achhootanand 'Harihar': A Profile," *Forward Press*, 8 Feb. 2019, https://www.forwardpress.in/2019/02/swami-achhootanand-harihar-a-profile/
18. M. Juergensmeyer, *Religious Rebels in the Punjab: The Ad Dharm Challenge to Caste* (Delhi: Navayana Publishing, 2009).

19. Risley, *The Tribes and Castes of Bengal*.
20. The book largely argued for the Indo-Aryan and Dravidian miscegenation and imposition of endogamy in the Aryan stock.
21. B.R. Ambedkar, "Castes in India: Their Mechanism, Genesis, and Development", in Vasant Moon (ed.), *Dr Babasaheb Ambedkar: Writings and Speeches*, vol. 1 (Bombay: Govt of Maharashtra, 1979), p. 21.
22. Ibid., p. 17.
23. B.G. Tilak, *The Arctic Home in the Vedas: Being Also a New Key to the Interpretation of Many Vedic Texts and Legends* (Poona: Messrs. Tilak Bros., [1903] 1925).
24. S. Bayly, *Caste, Society and Politics in India from the Eighteenth Century to the Modern Age* (Cambridge: Cambridge University Press, 1999), see Intro and ch. 1.
25. Ibid., p. 3.
26. N. Dirks, "The Invention of Caste: Civil Society in Colonial India", *Social Analysis* 25 (1989), pp. 42–52; N. Dirks, *Castes of Mind* (Princeton: Princeton University Press, 2001).
27. Dirks, *Castes of Mind*, p. 202.
28. Max Weber, the pioneering sociologist, was somewhat similar in his observation of caste as a religious doctrine of status.
29. J.C. Heesterman, *The Inner Conflict of Tradition: Essays in Indian Ritual, Kingship, and Society* (Chicago: University of Chicago, 1985).
30. S.V. Ketkar, *History of Caste in India: Evidence of the Laws of Manu on the Social Conditions in India during the Third Century A.D. Interpreted and Examined: With an Appendix on Radical Defects of Ethnology* (Ithaca, NY: Taylor and Carpenter, 1916), ch. 1.
31. Ibid., p. 28.
32. Ambedkar, "Castes in India", pp. 3–22.
33. Ibid.
34. Bayly, *Caste, Society and Politics*, p. 30.
35. One can also explore the speculative re-reading of history by Sharad Patil who observed the evolution of jati society from varna gradations as a testament of change in Indian society. S. Patil, *Caste-Feudal Servitude: The Studies in Jati-based Feudalism, Its Philosophies and Aesthetics* (Shirur: Mavlai Prakashan, 2006).

36. Ibid., pp. 30, 31.
37. Ibid, p. 37.
38. For a brief survey of Jats, see S. Yengde, "Dalitality: Jats in the Modern World", *Indian Express*, 24 Dec. 2023, https://indianexpress.com/article/opinion/columns/jats-in-india-history-lifestyle-statewise-jats-numbers-in-india-9080587/.
39. Bayly, *Caste, Society and Politics*, pp. 50–1.
40. Ibid., p. 54.
41. Ibid., p. 52–64. On Marathas, see S. Gordon, *The Marathas, 1600–1818* (Cambridge: Cambridge University Press, 1993), doi:10.1017/CHOL9780521268837.
42. On the nineteenth-century reconfiguration of western Indian caste, see R. O'Hanlon, "In the Presence of Witnesses: Petitioning and Judicial 'Publics' in Western India, circa 1600–1820", *Modern Asian Studies* 53, no. 1 (2019), pp. 52–88, doi: 10.1017/S0026749X17000968.
43. Bayly, *Caste, Society and Politics*, p. 38.
44. Also see, P.K. Yasser Arafath, "From Battuta to Makhdum II: Savarna Habitus, Corporeal Shields, and Caste Acoustics on the Malabar Coast", in P. Banerjee (ed.), *Textual Lives of Caste across the Ages: Hierarchy, Humanity and Equality in Indian History* (London: Bloomsbury, 2024).
45. Ibid. pp. 37, 39, 40.
46. Ibid., p. 40.
47. Ibid., p. 41.
48. Ibid., p. 4.
49. For a theological argument see Dumont, *Homo Hierarchicus*; Das Veena, "The Uses of Liminality: Society and Cosmos in Hinduism", *Contributions to Indian Sociology* 10, no. 2 (1976), pp. 245–63.
50. See Dirks, *Castes of Minds*.
51. Bayly, *Caste, Society and Politics*, p. 27; J.P. Parry, *Caste and Kinship in Kangra* (London: Routledge, [1979] 2015).
52. S. Yengde, *Caste Matters* (Gurgaon: Penguin Random House, 2019).
53. I have met many Dalits who have disclosed to me their Dalit identity in secrecy. This has happened in Indian metro cities, overseas, and even at Harvard University.

54. Bayly, *Caste, Society and Politics*, p. 53. On rituals and caste, see Heesterman, *The Inner Conflict of Tradition*, chs. 1, 2 and 7.
55. S. Madara, "Congress 'saampanaath', United Front 'naaganaath' aur BJP 'phan taana hua Cobra", YouTube, 17 September 2015, https://www.youtube.com/watch?v=JsCm5elQLB4. Thanks to Satvendar Madara and Sumedh Paradhe for preserving and directing me to this resource.

2. AFFAIRS OF LETTERS: DALIT RESPONSES TO BLACK LITERATURE

1. J. Balasubramaniam, "A Case for Dalit Journalism", *Telegraph India*, 28 Jan. 2021, https://www.telegraphindia.com/opinion/a-case-for-Dalit-journalism/cid/1804909.
2. Ravikumar, "Iyothee Thass and the Politics of Naming", *Sunday Pioneer*, 28 Sept. 2005, https://www.countercurrents.org/Dalit-ravikumar280905.htm.
3. Balasubramaniam, "A Case for Dalit Journalism". Goolam Vahed, South Africa's leading scholar on the South African Indian diaspora community, told me that he had come across many Tamil language periodicals in the archives.
4. Gangadhar Pantawane, *Journalist Dr Babasaheb Ambedkar* (Nagpur: Abhijit Prakashan, 1987).
5. Owing to the lack of documentary evidence, it is difficult to link these to Bansode. But references to him are found in existing newspapers of the times, Pantawane suggests. *Maharancha Sudharak* may be the first Dalit-centric journal.
6. R.B. Chincolkar, "Bahujan vrutapatra: stithi – gati", ch. 5 in "Swatryantrapurv kalatil bahujanachi vrutapatre", PhD thesis, Department of Journalism and Mass Communication, Dr Babasaheb Ambedkar Marathwada University, Aurangabad, 2007, http://hdl.handle.net/10603/92035.
7. I partly draw this assertion from Gayatri Spivak's "Debate on Postmodernism (1984)", YouTube, 14 May 2023, https://www.youtube.com/watch?v=cVfTgiE4FAY.
8. J.V. Pawar, *Ambedkarottar Ambedkari Chalwal*, vol. 1 (Mumbai: Asmita Communications, 2018).

9. U. Bhoite and A. Bhoite, "The Dalit Sahitya Movement in Maharashtra: A Sociological Analysis", *Sociological Bulletin* 26, no. 1 (March 1977), pp. 63, 64.
10. G. Pantawane, "Evolving a New Identity: The Development of a Dalit Culture", in Barbara Joshi (ed.), *Untouchable! Voices of the Dalit Liberation Movement* (London: Zed Books, 1986), p. 84.
11. Ibid.
12. B.S. More, "Marathwada Dalit Federation cha zamin satyagraha", Pamphlet no. 1, in A. Teltumbde, *Iconoclast: A Reflective Biography of Dr Babasaheb Ambedkar* (Gurgaon: Penguin, 2024).
13. A. Kumar, "B.R. Ambedkar on Caste and Land Relations in India", *Review of Agrarian Studies* 10, no. 1 (2000), http://ras.org.in/9537f8b9e25675f8de579ef0e1db6beb.
14. A.D. Fulzele, *Ambedkari Chalavalitil Dadasaheb Gaikwad Yanche Yogdan* (Mumbai: Lokvangmay Gruh, 2012).
15. S. Limbale, *Shatakatil Dalit Vichar* (2nd edn, Pune: Dilipraj Publications, 2007), p. 33.
16. Pawar, *Ambedkarottar Ambedkari Chalwal*; A. Teltumbde, *Dalits, Past, Present and Future* (New Delhi: Routledge, 2017).
17. J. Shaikh, *Outcaste Bombay: City Making and the Politics of the Poor* (Seattle: University of Washington Press, 2021), pp. 123–4.
18. Sathe was among the foremost literary figures of India. See M. Awad, *The Life and Work of Annabhau Sathe: A Marxist–Ambedkarite Mosaic* (New Delhi: Gaur Publishers, 2010); A.B. Sathe, Presidential Address, Mumbai, 2 March 1958, in Arjun Dangle (ed.), *Dalit Sahitya: Dalit Ek Abhyas* (Mumbai: Maharashtra State Literature-Culture Society, 1978), pp. 191–5.
19. I attended one in New Delhi in 2023 and delivered the closing address. Dalit conferences are held in regional languages across India. Aravind Malagatti, "Dalit Sahitya Parishad" (1998), https://www.youtube.com/watch?v=X7VeChk2P8E&ab_channel=AravindMalagatti.
20. Bhoite and Bhoite, "The Dalit Sahitya Movement in Maharashtra", pp. 63, 64.
21. S. Yengde, "The Nation Maker", in R. Kaur and N. Mathur (eds.), *The People of India: New Indian Politics in the 21st Century* (Gurgaon: Penguin Viking, 2022), pp. 1–16.

22. J.V. Pawar, *Dalit Panthers: An Authoritative History* (New Delhi: Forward Press, 2017).
23. J. Contursi, "Political Theology: Text and Practice in a Dalit Panther Community", *Journal of Asian Studies* 52, no. 2 (May 1993), pp. 320–39.
24. P. Sirsat, "A Milestone Movement: Hope and Disillusionment", *Outlook*, Dalit Panthers Special Issue, 15 Aug. 2023, pp. 66–70.
25. R. Athawale, interview with the author, Mumbai, 27 Jan. 2023.
26. H.L. Gates, Jr. (ed.), *The Classic Slave Narratives* (New York: Signet, [1987] 2012).
27. Ibid.
28. F. Douglass, *My Bondage and My Freedom* (New York: Miller, Orton and Mulligan, 1855).
29. Ibid., Intro, p. 15, https://www.gutenberg.org/files/202/202-h/202-h.htm#link2H_4_0032.
30. B.R. Ambedkar, "Slaves and Untouchables", in Vasant Moon (ed.), *Dr Babasaheb Ambedkar: Writings and Speeches*, vol. 5 (Mumbai: Govt of Maharashtra, 2008), pp. 9–18.
31. Ambedkar drew upon the work of Charles Johnson, *The Negro in American Civilization*, to build his argument about American slavery.
32. M. Desai, "Caste in Black and White: Dalit Identity and the Translation of African American Literature", *Comparative Literature* 67, no. 1 (2015), p. 95.
33. Shaikh, *Outcaste Bombay*, p. 130.
34. M.N. Wankhede, "Friends! Times Is Up for the Irresponsible Writers", Presidential Address, Dalit Sahitya Sammelan, 17 Jan. 1976, in Dangle, *Dalit Sahitya*, p. 235.
35. Author's translation.
36. Wankhede, "Friends!", p. 241.
37. A. Dangle (ed.), *Poisoned Bread: Translations from Modern Marathi Literature* (Hyderabad: Orient BlackSwan, 2011), Intro.
38. Senior Dalit writer Arjun Dangle talks about the influence of Wankhede in *Dalit Panther*.
39. Janardhan Waghmare, interview, Zoom, 21 April 2021.
40. Wankhede, "Friends!", p. 232.
41. M.N. Wankhede, V.L. Kulkarni, R.G. Jadhav, M.P. Rege and M.B.

Chitnis, "Maharashtratil aaj udayache samskrutik sangharsh āni vangmayin samasya", *Asmita*, issue 1, Discussion dates 16 Nov. 1967 to 21 Nov. 1967, reproduced in Dangle, *Dalit Sahitya*, pp. 1–20.

42. See A. Dangle, "Nivedan," in Dangle, *Dalit Sahitya*; J.M. Waghmare, "Negro Vangmay va Dalit Vangmay", in Dangle, *Dalit Sahitya*.
43. Wankhede, "Friends!"
44. Shaikh, *Outcaste Bombay*.
45. Gratitude to Gangadhar Pantawane's Nandita and Nivedita Pantawane for providing me with this information.
46. J. Waghmare, *Negro Vangmay va Dalit Vangmay* (American Negro: Literature and Culture) (Pune: Padmagandha Prakashan, 1978), p. 389.
47. Dangle, "Nivedan", p. 14.
48. Ibid., p. 24.
49. Testimonials, Narendra Shelar, Second Padmashree Dr Gangadhar Pantawane Lecture Series, 27 March 2022 (online).
50. E. Zelliot, "Dalit: New Cultural Context for an Old Marathi World", in *From Untouchable to Dalit: Essays on the Ambedkar Movement* (New Delhi: Manohar, 1992), p. 268.
51. G. Guru, "The Politics of Naming", *Seminar*, 471, "Dalit", November 1998, p. 15.
52. B. Bagul, "Dalit Literature Is but Human Literature", in Dangle, *Poisoned Bread*.
53. Waghmare was the fifth president of Asmitadarsh Sahitya Sammelan, Kolhapur, 1989. Vijaykumar Rana Khandare, "Dr Janardhan Waghmare yanchya sahityacha abhyas", PhD thesis, Department of Marathi, University of Pune, 2009, p. 344.
54. Waghmare, interview, Zoom, 21 April 2021.
55. Ibid.
56. N. Kurundkar, *Aakalan* (Pune: Deshmukh and Company, 1985).
57. J. Waghmare, "American Negro Vangmay: Prerana āni Pravrutti" (American Negro Literature: Motivation and Tendency), in *American Negro: Sahitya āni Sankruti* (Pune: Padmagandha Prakashan; 2008), p. 356.
58. Ibid.
59. Ibid., p. 358.

60. J. Waghmare, *The Quest for Black Identity: A Critical Study of Postwar American Black Novel* (Pune: Sugava Prakashan, 2001), p. 3.
61. Waghmare, *Negro Vangmay āni Dalit Chalwal*, p. 388.
62. Waghmare, *The Quest for Black Identity*, p. 2.
63. Ibid., p. 5.
64. Ibid., p. 8.
65. Ibid., p. 8.
66. J.O. Horton and L.E. Horton, *Slavery and the Making of America* (New York: Oxford University Press, 2004). The authors demonstrate how the import of slaves changed the cultural, political and economic landscape of America. The arrival of slaves brought with it their own skills, culture, religion and languages, which helped America to form its identity as a nation; while the demand of slaves for liberty brought with it embedded ideas of American freedom and democracy.
67. Waghmare, *Negro Vangmay āni Dalit Chalwal*, p. 381. My translation.
68. Waghmare, "Negro Vangmay va Dalit Vangmay".
69. B.R. Ambedkar, *Who Were the Shudras? How They Came to Be the Fourth Varna in the Indo-Aryan Society* (Bombay: Thacker and Co., 1947).
70. Waghmare, *Negro Vangmay āni Dalit Chalwal*, p. 382.
71. Ibid., p. 390.
72. Ibid., p. 389.
73. C. Sumner, *The Question of Caste: Lecture by Hon. Charles Sumner* (Boston: Wright and Potter, 1869), https://www.loc.gov/item/43049574/.
74. M.J. Phule, *Slavery, in the Civilised British Government under the Cloak of Brahmanism*, trans. P.G. Patil (Mumbai: Govt of Maharashtra, [1873] 1991).
75. Scholars such as S.D. Kapoor argue that Ambedkar's earlier experiences in New York, especially Harlem, gave him a nuanced understanding of African American life; that episode needs further treatment. See S.D. Kapoor, "B.R. Ambedkar, W.E.B. Du Bois and the Process of Liberation", *Economic and Political Weekly* 38, no. 51/52 (2003), p. 5345.
76. G. Pantawane, "Presidential Address, Pahile Vishwa Marathi Sahiya Sammelan San Jose, 14, 15, 16 February 2009", p. 17. I am grateful to

Nandita Pantawane in New Jersey for unearthing a copy of the speech for me.
77. Ibid., p. 17.
78. Ibid., p. 16.
79. Ibid., p. 26.
80. Ibid.
81. L. Hughes, "The Negro and the Racial Mountain", in R. Walser (ed.) *Keeping Time: Readings in Jazz History* (New York: Oxford University Press, 1999), p. 57.
82. Ibid., p. 55.
83. Ibid., p. 56.
84. Pantawane, "Presidential Address", p. 7.
85. Ibid., pp. 5–6.
86. S. Yengde, "Supreme Subalterns", in M. Banerjee and J.J.P. Wouters (eds.), *Subaltern Studies 2.0 Being against the Capitalocene* (Chicago: Prickly Paradigm Press, 2022), pp. 191–206.
87. I am grateful to Harish Wankhede for this critique given as a response to an earlier version of this chapter presented at JNU Academic forum on 10 October 2023.
88. For more on this, see D. Immerwahr, "On B.R. Ambedkar and Black–Dalit Connections", https://faculty.wcas.northwestern.edu/daniel-immerwahr/Ambedkar.pdf.
89. *Black Panther*, 11 May 1974, p. 17. I am grateful to J.V. Pawar for sharing the news clipping with me.

3. RACE AND CASTE: IN THE AGE OF DALIT–BLACK LIVES MATTER

1. An earlier version of this chapter was published as a cover story for the magazine *The Caravan* under the title "The Harvest of Casteism".
2. M. McLaughlin, *The Long, Hot Summer of 1967: Urban Rebellion in America* (New York: Palgrave Macmillan, 2014).
3. Louis Goldberg, one of the authors and researchers of the report, wrote its conclusion. In it, he proposed a way out of the impasse and that was to transfer real power for decisions to the young militants in the ghettoes. It acknowledged the political relevancy of marginalized and oppressed American citizens. S.M. Gillon, *Separate and Unequal:*

The Kerner Commission and the Unraveling of American Liberalism (New York: Basic Books, 2018), see ch. 7 and Introduction; also see Jelani Cobb with Matthew Guariglia (eds.), *The Essential Kerner Commission Report* (New York: Liverlight, 2021), Intro by Cobb.

4. McLaughlin, *The Long, Hot Summer of 1967*, p. 43.
5. Gillon, Separate and Unequal, p. 137.
6. Ibid., p. 44.
7. R. Shellow with D. Boesel, L. Goldberg, G. Marx and D. Sear, *The Harvest of American Racism: The Political Meaning of Violence in the Summer of 1967* (Ann Arbor: University of Michigan Press, 2018).
8. J.E. Zelizer, "Introduction to the 2016 Edition of the Kerner Report", in *The Kerner Report: National Advisory Commission on Civil Disorders* (Princeton: Princeton University Press, 2016).
9. Ibid., pp. xxvii–xxviii.
10. Ibid., p. xxxii.
11. S. Patton, "White People Are Speaking Up at Protests", *Washington Post*, 2 June 2020, https://www.washingtonpost.com/outlook/2020/06/02/white-people-black-protests/.
12. S. Verma, "India Enters 'Amrit Kaal' with Growing Atrocities against Dalits", NewsClick, 2 October 2022, https://www.newsclick.in.
13. For a timeline of the Civil Rights Act and the background story, see C. Risen, *The Bill of the Century: The Epic Battle for the Civil Rights Act* (London: Bloomsbury Press, 2014).
14. On the historical work of incarceration and policy, see K.G. Muhammad, *The Condemnation of Blackness: Race, Crime, and the Making of Modern Urban America* (new edition, Cambridge, MA: Harvard University Press, [2010] 2019). The new preface sets the tone of the contemporary moment of Black uprising and the state of historical injustice.
15. A. Teltumbde, *Dalits: Past, Present and Future* (New Delhi: Routledge, 2017); K.M. Ashok and S.J. Boopalan, "Indian Christians in Conflict: Dalit Christian Movement in Contemporary India", in S.J. Hunt (ed.), *Handbook of Global Contemporary Christianity: Themes and Developments in Culture, Politics, and Society* (Leiden: Brill, 2015), pp. 308–24.
16. On the social history and contemporary politics vis-à-vis a Hindu

nation and a Muslim minority with African roots, see, G. Reddy, "Our Blood Is Becoming White: Race, Religion and Siddi Becoming in Hyderabad, India", *American Anthropologist* 126, no. 2 (2024), pp. 1–10, DOI:10.1111/aman.13945.

17. B.R. Ambedkar, "Annihilation of Caste", in Vasant Moon (ed.), *Dr Babasaheb Ambedkar: Writings and Speeches*, vol. 14, part 2 (Mumbai: Govt of Maharashtra, 1995), pp. 23–96.
18. V. Prashad, "Afro-Dalits of the Earth, Unite!", *African Studies Review* 43, no. 1 (2000), pp. 189–201, https://doi.org/10.2307/524727; V. Prashad, "Badges of Color: An Afro-Dalit Story", *Z Magazine*, http://www.hartford-hwp.com/archives/52a/073.html.
19. Guru, "The politics of naming", p.18.
20. Teltumbde, *Dalits: Past, Present and Future*.
21. "IV. Nomenclatures", Submissions to the Round Table Conference, 1930–1931, IOR/Q/RTC/2, IOR/Q/RTC/24, British Library, London.
22. "Dalit Panthers Manifesto", Internet Archive, https://archive.org/details/idoc_pub_Dalit-panthers-manifesto.
23. The Dalit Panther & Rebel Poet Who Shook the World—Namdeo Dhasal Interview with Nikhil Wagle", IBNLokmat, YouTube, https://www.youtube.com/watch?v=2Hxiq4IEaFo
24. V. S. Naipaul, *India: A Million Mutinies Now* (New York: Viking, 1990).
25. S. Biko, *I Write What I Like* (Oxford: Heinemann, 1978), S. Yengde, *Dalit-Black Thought: An Intellectual History of Caste & Race*, University of Oxford D.Phil Thesis, 2024.
26. Arjun Dangle's recent biography of the Dalit Panthers gives another, methodical take on the situation: *Dalit Panther Aadhorekhit Satya* (Mumbai: Lokvangmay Gruha, 2021).
27. R. Dhale, "Dalit Panther First Conference, Nagpur, 1974", in J.V. Pawar, *Ambedkarottar Ambedkari Chalwal*, vol. 4: *1972–1977* (Mumbai: Asmita Communications, [2010] 2022), pp. 419–28.
28. Interview with J.V. Pawar by telephone, 5 March 2024.
29. Pawar, *Ambedkarottar Ambedkari Chalwal*, vol. 4, pp. 432–5.
30. R.D. Mogle, "Dalit Panther: Tatwa āni Vyvahar, ek Rajkiya Abhyass",

PhD thesis, Swami Ramanand Teerth Marathwada University, Nov. 2021, p. 80.

31. See the essays by M.S.A. Rizvi, P.K. Yasser Arafath and R. Sarwate in P. Banerjee (ed.), *Textual Lives of Caste across the Ages: Hierarchy, Humanity and Equality in Indian History* (London: Bloomsbury, 2024).

32. B.P. Mandal, *The Mandal Commission Report: National Commission for Backward Classes*, 2 vols., 1980, https://www.ncbc.nic.in/Writereaddata/Mandal%20Commission%20Report%20of%20the%201st%20Part%20English635228715105764974.pdf.

33. V. Kumar, *Dalit Assertion and Bahujan Samaj Party* (New Delhi: Samyak Prakashan, [2001] 2013); K. Chandra, *Why Ethnic Parties Succeed: Patronage and Ethnic Head Counts in India* (New York: Cambridge University Press, 2004).

34. M.J. Phule, *Slavery, in the Civilised British Government under the Cloak of Brahmanism*, trans. P.G. Patil (Mumbai: Govt of Maharashtra, [1873] 1991), p. 3.

35. D. Immerwahr, "Caste or Colony? Indianizing Race in the United States", *Modern Intellectual History* 4, no. 2 (2007), pp. 275–301.

36. Letter from B.R. Ambedkar to W.E.B. Du Bois, c. July 1946, W.E.B. Du Bois Papers, Series 1, Correspondence, University of Massachusetts Library, https://credo.library.umass.edu/view/full/mums312-b109-i132.

37. Letter from W.E.B. Du Bois to B.R. Ambedkar, 31 July 1946, W.E.B. Du Bois Papers, Series 1, Correspondence, University of Massachusetts Library, https://credo.library.umass.edu/view/full/mums312-b109-i133.

38. J.V. Pawar, *Ambedkarottar Ambedkari Chalwal*, vol. 1 (Mumbai: Asmita Communications, 2018).

39. J.V. Pawar, *Dalit Panthers: An Authoritative History* (New Delhi: Forward Press, 2018).

40. Interview with J.V. Pawar, Ambedkar Bhavan, Mumbai, 27 December 2024.

41. Dalit Panthers' Position (*Bhoomika*) (original Marathi version), "Who Are Our Enemies?" (translation by the author), p. 6.

42. Ibid., p. 5.

43. Dhale's archive is yet to be formalized and digitized, but his papers have been published as a collection edited by Indira Athawale, *Raja Dhale: Samagra Lekhan*. Dhale edited few magazines and periodicals. *Chakravarty* was an ambitious project; a unique blend of calligraphy, design, typography, text arrangement, artworks and literature.
44. The pictorial archive for this is preserved on the Dalit Panthers Archive Instagram page (courtesy of Ramesh Shinde), https://www.instagram.com/p/CBAx0geJROj/?utm_source=ig_web_copy_link&igsh=MzRlODBiNWFlZA==.
45. See S. Yengde, "The Nation Maker", in R. Kaur and N. Mathur (eds.), *The People of India: New Indian Politics in the 21st Century* (Gurgaon: Penguin Viking, 2022), pp. 1–16.
46. Some of the state units were gathered in the 1980s especially in Gujarat, Punjab, Delhi and Uttar Pradesh. S. Yengde, "Chronicling the Dalit Panthers", *Outlook*, 15 Aug. 2023; also see Pawar, *Ambedkarottar Ambedkari Chalwal*, vol. 1.
47. I am grateful to J.V. Pawar for sharing this article with me, which is now in my possession too. "BPP Greets Dalit Panthers of India's Untouchables", *Black Panther*, 11 May 1974, p. 17.
48. For a detailed biography of Vijaya Lakshmi Pandit, see M. Bhagavan's authoritative work, *Vijaya Lakshmi Pandit* (New York: Penguin, 2023).
49. M.E. Latham, *The Right Kind of Revolution: Modernization, Development, and U.S. Foreign Policy from the Cold War to the Present* (Ithaca: Cornell University Press, 2011), p. 66.
50. M. Bhagavan (ed.), *India and the Cold War* (Chapel Hill, NC: University of North Carolina Press, 2019).
51. S. Yengde, "Ambedkar's Foreign Policy and the Ellipsis of 'Dalit' from the International Activism", in S. Yengde and A. Teltumbde (eds.), *The Radical in Ambedkar: Critical Reflections* (New Delhi: Allen Lane, 2018), pp. 86–106.
52. B.R. Ambedkar, "Statement by Dr B.R. Ambedkar in Parliament in Explanation of his Resignation from the Cabinet, 10 October 1951", in Vasant Moon (ed.), *Dr Babasaheb Ambedkar: Writings and Speeches*, vol. 14, part 2 (Mumbai: Govt of Maharashtra, 1995), pp. 1321–3.
53. B.R. Ambedkar, "Scheduled Castes' Case to be Presented before

U.N.O., Bombay, Jan. 17, 1947", in H. Narke (ed.), *Dr Babasaheb Ambedkar: Writings and Speeches*, vol. 17, part 1 (Mumbai: Education Department, Govt of Maharashtra, 2003), p. 358.
54. V. Thakur, "When India Proposed a Casteist Solution to South Africa's Racist Problem", *The Wire*, 4 April 2017, https://thewire.in/diplomacy/exploring-casteism-in-indias-foreign-policy/amp/.
55. G.P. Jooste to D.D. Forsyth, SAB, BVV, vol. 5, 10/2, part 1, Department of Foreign Affairs, National Archives of South Africa. See S. Sundaram and V. Thakur, "A Pragmatic Methodology for Studying International Practices", *Journal of International Political Theory* 17, no. 3 (2021), pp. 337–55, https://doi.org/10.1177/1755088219879177.
56. Ibid.
57. Dalit Panther *Bhoomika* (translation).
58. This quote is not to be found in the final speech published on the Government of India's website. CNN reported these words of Omar Abdullah at a news conference: "We believe that the caste issue is not linked to the main subject of this conference, which is racism ... You cannot equate casteism with racism." Instead, the statement on the official website showed Abdullah's condemnation as well as his distancing of himself from the mandate of the conference: "We are firmly of the view that the issue of caste is not an appropriate subject for discussion at this Conference." He went on to argue that the UN was not a place to discuss caste. "It is neither *legitimate* nor feasible nor practical for this World Conference or, for that matter, even the UN to legislate, let alone *police individual behaviour* in our societies. The battle has to be fought within our respective societies to change thoughts, processes and attitudes; indeed, the hearts and souls of our peoples. This is the task that we pledge ourselves to remain engaged in" (emphasis mine). CNN World News, "India Shuns Calls to Talk Caste with U.N.", 17 Aug. 2001, https://edition.cnn.com/2001/WORLD/asiapcf/south/08/17/india.caste/; Ministry of External Affairs, "Statement by Shri Omar Abdullah, Minister of State for External Affairs, India, at The World Conference Against Racism, Racial Discrimination, Xenophobia and Related Intolerance", Media Center, 2 Sept 2001, https://www.mea.gov.in/articles-in-indian-media.htm?dtl/16937/Statement+by+Shri+Omar+Abdullah+Minister+of+State+for+

External+Affairs+India+at+The+World+Conference+Against+Racism+Racial+Discrimination+Xenophobia+and+Related+Intolerance.

59. A commemorative volume was published in the wake of the Durban conference: B. Natarajan and P. Greenough (eds.), *Against Stigma: Studies in Caste, Race and Justice since Durban* (Hyderabad: Orient BlackSwan, 2008).

60. United Nations, *Report of the Committee on the Elimination of Racial Discrimination*, The Committee on the Elimination of Racial Discrimination (CERD), 61st Session, 5–23 August 2002 (New York: United Nations, 2002), pp. 112–13.

61. "Report by Mr Glele-Ahanhanzo, Special Rapporteur on Contemporary Forms of Racism, Racial Discrimination, Xenophobia and Related Intolerance, submitted pursuant to Commission on Human Rights resolution 1998/26", in D. Keane, *Caste-Based Discrimination in International Human Rights Law* (London: Routledge, 2016), p. 270.

62. B. Natarajan, "Misrepresenting Caste and Race", *Seminar* 572 (April 2007), p. 65.

63. Ibid., p. 67.

64. D. Pyper, *The Equality Act 2010: Caste Discrimination*, Briefing Paper no. 06862, 3 Aug. 2018, House of Commons Library, https://researchbriefings.files.parliament.uk/documents/SN06862/SN06862.pdf.

65. For a legal application of the "but-for" legal maxim making a case for caste's validity to be protected under the framework of race-based protections, see, K. Brown, L. Khandare, A. Waughray, K. G. Dau-Schmidt, and T. Shaw, "Does U.S. Federal Employment Law Now Cover Caste Discrimination Based on Untouchability?: If All Else Fails There Is the Possible Application of Bostock v. Clayton County", N.Y.U. *Review of Law and Social Change* 46, no.2 (2022), pp. 117-174.

66. "Addressing Indian Council of World Affairs, Secretary-General Urges India to Be 'Driver' in Transformative Push towards Peace, Human Rights, Clean Development", United Nations Press SG/

SM/16459, 12 Jan. 2015, https://press.un.org/en/2015/sgsm16459.doc.htm.
67. A. Chakraborty, "'Racism Is Real', Sammy Urges Cricket to Do Better", Reuters, 10 Sept. 2020, Reuters, https://www.reuters.com/article/idUSKBN2611L0/.
68. Statement in possession of the author. The statement was one of its kind. The Chinese American group of Boston took exception to its language and framing. The leaders of the Asian American Commission were in discussion with the author on several issues concerning Dalits. What seemingly irritated the Chinese American group was the reference to the Panthers. P. Marcelo, "Asian Commission Criticized for Black Lives Matter Statement", AP News, 8 June 2020, https://apnews.com/article/0b36a78f87eeb942001f26de2966c279.
69. B. Angelo, "Toni Morrison: The Pain of Being Black", *Time*, 22 May 1989, https://content.time.com/time/subscriber/article/0,33009,957724,00.html.
70. For a Sikh diasporic feminist perspective, see A.K. Hundle, "Sikh Diasporic Feminisms: Provocation 1", *Sikh Formations* 13, no. 4 (2017), pp. 237–40, doi:10.1080/17448727.2017.1419679.
71. P. Ranjan (ed.), *Mahishahur: A People's Hero* (New Delhi: The Marginalised/Forward Press, 2017).
72. A. Subramanian, "Indians in North Carolina: Race, Class, and Culture in the Making of Immigrant Identity", *Comparative Studies of South Asia, Africa and the Middle East* 20, no. 1 (2000), p. 105. Ibid., pp. 112–13.
73. Ibid., p. 105.
74. Ibid.
75. Ibid., pp. 112–13.
76. Subramanian calls this a "capitalist success".
77. B.R. Ambedkar, *What Congress and Gandhi Have Done to the Untouchables* (Bombay: Thacker and Co., 1945).
78. BBC, "Bhimrao Ambedkar's Iconic Interview from 1955", YouTube, 17 March 2023: https://www.youtube.com/watch?v=Wf3VJCpNMqI&ab_channel=BBCNewsIndia.
79. B.R. Ambedkar, Address to Constituent Assembly, 25 Nov. 1949.

80. A. Desai and G. Vahed, *The South African Gandhi: Stretcher-Bearer of Empire* (Palo Alto: Stanford University Press, 2015).
81. BBC, "'Racist' Gandhi Statue Removed from University of Ghana", 13 Dec. 2018, https://www.bbc.com/news/world-africa-46552614; on the context of Gandhi's public iconography and Africa, see S. Shankar, *An Uneasy Embrace: Africa, India and the Spectre of Race* (London: Hurst and Co., 2021); S.S. Vittorini, "Modi and the Mahatma: The Politics of Statues and the Saffronisation of India–Africa Relations", in K. King and M. Venkatachalam (eds.), *India's Development Diplomacy and Soft Power in Africa* (Woodbridge: Boydell and Brewer, 2021), pp. 79–98.
82. K. Donlevy and C. Campanile, "NYC Gandhi Statue Obliterated by Vandals, Second Attack in Two Weeks", *New York Post*, 18 Aug. 2022, https://nypost.com/2022/08/18/queens-gandhi-statue-vandalized-for-second-time-in-two-weeks/.
83. "Speech by Angela Davis", YouTube, 18 Dec. 2016, https://www.youtube.com/watch?v=6hHYnrM-NOc&t=1385s.
84. Purvi Mehta's interviews with Laxmi Berwa records the year of formation of VISION as 1978.
85. A profile of Berwa's work and overseas activism is provided by P. Mehta, "Diaspora as Spokesperson and Watchdog: Laxmi Berwa, VISION, and Anti-caste Activism by Dalits in the United States", *Diaspora: A Journal of Transnational Studies* 21, no. 1 (Spring 2021), pp. 64–86.
86. Interview with Ram Gautam by telephone, 24 June 2020.
87. Ibid., with additional inputs from Berwa and Varhade. The information on the organizational history is diverse as many of the living participants are elderly and their versions of the story are told from the vantage point of their view of the movement.
88. United States Committee on Foreign Relations, "Senator Charles McC. Mathias Jr. to Dr Laxmi Berwa, August 17, 1982, July 23, 1982"; "Senator Paul S. Sarbanes to Dr Laxmi Berwa, August 17, 1982", Archives of Laxmi Berwa, courtesy of Suraj Yengde.
89. Carlyle Murphy, "Indian Caste Aims Protest at Gandhi", *The Washington Post*, 29 July 1982, https://www.washingtonpost.

com/archive/politics/1982/07/30/indian-caste-aims-protest-at-gandhi/4737537c-109a-4c8f-866f-202b52f1913e/
90. "Prime Minister's House, New Delhi, letter to Mr Berwa, June 22, 1982", Archives of Laxmi Berwa, courtesy of Suraj Yengde.
91. VISION, "Letter from Laxmi Berwa, President of VISION to Indira Gandhi, July 7, 1982", Archives of Laxmi Berwa, courtesy of Suraj Yengde.
92. Interview with Yogesh Varhade by telephone, 25 June 2020.
93. Ibid. Interview with Varhade, Mumbai, June 2019.
94. S. Yengde, "Dalit in Black America: Race, Caste and the Making of Dalit–Black Archive", *Public Culture* 35, no. 1 (2023), p. 32, DOI 10.1215/08992363-10202374.
95. We will learn more of Raju Kamble in ch. 5.
96. I helped facilitate a symposium on the black and Dalit struggles in partnership with the Boston chapter of the Black Lives Matter movement in 2017. After the killing of George Floyd, numerous Ambedkarite groups issued statements in support of the Black Lives Matter protests that I helped coordinate.
97. V. Prashad, *The Karma of Brown Folk* (Minneapolis: University of Minnesota Press, 2001).
98. M. Alexander, *The New Jim Crow: Mass Incarceration in the Age of Colorblindness* (New York: The New Press, 2012).
99. https://www.indiatoday.in/india/story/over-2150-cases-of-deaths-in-judicial-custody-govt-1928310-2022-03-22.
100. During the communal riots in Delhi in February and March, multiple reports accused the police of aiding anti-Muslim mobs, and of attacking Muslims themselves. One viral video showed policemen surrounding five badly injured Muslim men, beating and swearing at them as they were forced to sing the national anthem. One of the men, Faizan, later died.
101. Interview with J.V. Pawar by telephone, Mumbai, 5 March 2024.
102. B.V. Jondhale, "Panthermadhil Vaad Vivaadankade Pahatana", *Maharashtra Times*, 10 April 2022, https://marathi.indiatimes.com/editorial/samwad/the-discussion-on-the-role-of-dangles-the-work-of-panthers-and-the-ambedkar-movement-in-the-book-Dalit-panther-/articleshow/90754961.cms.

103. P. Sirsat, "A Milestone Movement: Hope and Disillusionment", *Outlook*, Dalit Panthers Special Issue, 15 Aug. 2023, pp. 66–70.
104. IBN Lokmat, "The Dalit Panther & Rebel Poet Who Shook the World".
105. Pawar, *Ambedkarottar Ambedkari Chalwal*, vol. 4, p. 316.
106. Ibid., p. 311.
107. R. Athawale, "Need for Ideological Ambedkarism", *Outlook*, Dalit Panthers Special, 15 Aug. 2023, p. 74.
108. S. Mondal, "The Panthers Growl Again: A Short Memoir of a Historic Dalit–Black Conference", *News Minute*, 2 June 2020, https://www.thenewsminute.com/news/panthers-growl-again-short-memoir-historic-Dalit-black-conference-164604.
109. H. Gaddis, "Black Panther and Dalit Panther Unity in 21st Century", *Outlook*, 15 Aug 2023, https://www.outlookindia.com/national/black-panther-and-dalit-panther-unity-in-21st-century-news-311564.
110. M. King, "Black Lives Matter Power Grab Sets Off Internal Revolt", *Politico*, 10 Dec. 2020, https://www.politico.com/news/2020/12/10/black-lives-matter-organization-biden-444097.

4. THE DALIT REPUBLIC OF DIASPORA: A CASE STUDY OF TRINIDAD

1. This chapter is dedicated to Sam Maharaj, the legendary trade unionist and feisty activist who had a high level of intolerance to injustice. His story remains to be written. Mr Maharaj accompanied me on almost all the interviews in Trinidad. He was more than a friend. He was also in many ways the interlocutor with his world about which I write. However, the findings reported in this chapter are solely mine and do not in any way make Mr Maharaj responsible for their shortcomings. Grateful acknowledgments to Arvind Singh, Pandit Amar Sreeprasad, Indira Rampersad and Jaidath Maharaj. On my second trip, Rhona and Anthony Chin were my guardians who took immense pains to make my fieldwork and stay comfortable.
2. P. van der Veer and S. Vertovec, "Brahmanism Abroad: On Caribbean Hinduism as an Ethnic Religion", *Ethnology* 30, no. 2 (1991), pp. 149–66.

3. Ibid., pp. 157–9.
4. B.R. Ambedkar, "Annihilation of Caste", in Vasant Moon (ed.), *Dr Babasaheb Ambedkar: Writings and Speeches*, vol. 14, part 2 (Mumbai: Govt of Maharashtra, 1995), pp. 23–96.
5. B.R. Ambedkar, "What Path to Salvation (Mukti Kon Pathe?): Dr Ambedkar's Address to the Bombay Presidency Mahar Conference, 31st May 1936, Bombay", trans. Vasant Moon, https://franpritchett.com/00ambedkar/txt_ambedkar_salvation.html.
6. This is evident in the works on South Africa and other diasporic regions.
7. Schwartz studies a village, Boodram, that largely comprised Hindus. Here he found 99 per cent of marriages were endogamous. However, among the Hindus 45 per cent were endogamous, and 47 intra-*varna*, i.e, among the *varnas* of the social order. B.M. Schwartz, "Caste and Endogamy in Trinidad", *Southwestern Journal of Anthropology* 20, no. 1 (1964), pp. 58–66.
8. L. Braithwaite, "Social Stratification in Trinidad: A Preliminary Analysis", *Social and Economic Studies* 2, nos. 2/3 (1953), pp. 5–175.
9. M. Klass, "East and West Indian: Cultural Complexity in Trinidad", *Annals of the New York Academy of Sciences* 83, no. 5 (1960), pp. 855–61.
10. The studies that inspired me were B.M. Schwartz (ed.), *Caste in Overseas Indian Communities* (California: Chandler Publishing House, 1967); T. Niranjana, *Mobilizing India: Women, Migration and Music between India and Trinidad* (Durham: Duke University Press, 2006); R.K. Jain, "Race Relations, Ethnicity, Class and Culture: A Comparison of Indians in Trinidad and Malaysia", *Sociological Bulletin* 38, no. 1 (March 1989). I thank Dilip Menon, who suggested I read them during my early years of doctoral studies. These extraordinary studies of science and investigation remain with me.
11. S. Vertovec, *Hindu Trinidad: Religion, Ethnicity and Socio-economic Change* (Basingstoke: Palgrave Macmillan, 1992); N. Jayaram, "The Metamorphosis of Caste among Trinidad Hindus", *Contributions to Indian Sociology* 40, no. 2 (2006), pp. 143–73.
12. B.V. Lal, *Chalo Jahaji: On a Journey through Indenture in Fiji* (Canberra: ANU Press, 2012).

13. S.A. Singh, "Hinduism and the State in Trinidad", *Inter-Asia Cultural Studies* 6, no. 3 (2005), pp. 353–65, DOI: 10.1080/14649370500169987
14. See National Archives of Trinidad and Tobago, Indian Indentureship Collection, List of the General Registers of Indian Indentured Laborers, 1845–1917, https://www.natt.gov.tt/sites/default/files/images/General-Registers-of-Indian-Indentured-Labourers.pdf.
15. A. Niehoff, "The Function of Caste among the Indian of Oropuche Lagoon, Trinidad", in Barton M. Schwartz (ed.), *Caste in Overseas Indian Communities* (California: Chandler Publishing House, 1967), p. 152.
16. Interview with Karran Nancu, president of GOPIO, Trinidad chapter, 13 May 2022, Chaguanas, Trinidad.
17. C. Clarke, "Caste among Hindus in a Town in Trinidad: San Fernando", in Schwartz, *Caste in Overseas Indian Communities*, p. 177.
18. Ibid., p. 175.
19. Ibid., p. 177.
20. T. Niranjana, *Mobilizing India: Women, Music and Migration between India and Trinidad* (Durham, NC: Duke University Press, 2005), p. 27.
21. Ibid., ch. 1.
22. Clarke, "Caste among Hindus in a Town in Trinidad", pp. 173–4.
23. Ibid.
24. Ibid., p. 179.
25. Caste in some cases is seen as a ritualized conception only. For a critical assumption of caste and its relation to rituality, see D. Gupta, "Introduction: The Certitudes of Caste; When Identity Trumps Hierarchy", *Contributions to Indian Sociology* 38, nos. 1/2 (2004), pp. 5–15. Also see G.G. Raheja, *The Poison in the Gift: Ritual, Prestation, and the Dominant Caste in a North Indian Village* (Chicago: University of Chicago Press, 1988).
26. Clarke, "Caste among Hindus in a Town in Trinidad", p. 191.
27. Ibid., p. 194.
28. Ibid., p. 193.
29. I thank Tamil scholar and writer Ravikumar for pointing to this evidence. Ravikumar reports that Srinivasan had written about the reach of Parayan to indentured societies in his autobiography.

NOTES

30. D. Alagirisamy, "The Self Respect Movement and Tamil Politics of Belonging in Interwar British Malaya, 1929–1939," *Modern Asian Studies* 50, no. 5 (Sept. 2016), p. 1549. I am grateful to Karthick Manoharan for helping me with this resource.
31. V. Kumar, "Understanding Dalit Diaspora", *Economic and Political Weekly* 39, no. 1 (2004), p. 115.
32. Taken from Clarke's study, "Caste among Hindus in a Town in Trinidad", pp. 193–4.
33. B. Samaroo, *Adrian Cola Rienzi: The Life and Times of an Indo-Caribbean Progressive* (Macoya, Trinidad: Royards Publishing Company, 2022), p. 146.
34. L. Roopnarine, *Indo-Caribbean Indenture: Resistance and Accommodation, 1838–1920* (Kingston, Jamaica: University of West Indies Press, 2007), ch. 3.
35. Sam Maharaj, interview, Trinidad, 13 May 2022.
36. Roopnarine, *Indo-Caribbean Indenture*.
37. Ibid., p. 74.
38. Ibid.
39. Department of Philosophy and Religion, "Historical Background of the Department of Philosophy and Religion, Faculty of Arts, BHU", https://www.bhu.ac.in/Site/UnitHomeTemplate/1_110_652.
40. SWAHA International, "About Us", https://www.swahainternational.org/about/.
41. Ibid.
42. Ibid.
43. Interview with Jaidath Maharaj, north Trinidad, 22 May 2022.
44. Hindu society developed into "elastic and antinomic" forms incorporating various caste cultures. That is how the concept of animal sacrifice and meat eating was retained among the people. See Roopnarine, *Indo-Caribbean Indenture*, p. 75.
45. Niehoff, "The Function of Caste", p. 159.
46. Interview with the *dharmacharya*, 21 May 2022.
47. Roopnarine, *Indo-Caribbean Indenture*, p. 76.
48. Interview, San Fernando, 18 May 2022.
49. Niehoff, "The Function of Caste", p. 156.
50. An Act to amend the Kabir Association of Trinidad (Incorporation)

Ordinance, 1932, Fourth Session Eleventh Parliament, Republic of Trinidad and Tobago, *Legal Supplement Part C to the "Trinidad and Tobago Gazette"* 58, no. 76 (6 June 2019), https://www.ttparliament.org/wp-content/uploads/2022/01/b2019h15g.pdf.

51. J. de Souza, "Parasram, Man of the People", *Trinidad and Tobago Newsday*, 27 Oct. 2019, https://newsday.co.tt/2019/10/27/parasram-man-of-the-people.

52. I take the phrase from Suryakant Waghmore, who argues politeness coexists alongside vulgarity and violence. "From Hierarchy to Hindu Politeness: Caste Atrocities and Dalit Protest in Rural Marathwada", in S. Jodhka and J. Manor (eds.), *Contested Hierarchies, Persisting Influence: Caste and Power in Twenty-First Century India* (Hyderabad: Orient BlackSwan, 2017), pp. 111–39.

53. The interview was conducted again on 24 April 2024. Most of the direct quotations cited here refer to this specific interview.

54. V. Menon, R. Bikhchandani and H. Laeeq, "Somnath and Gyanvapi Temples Were Rebuilt – Long Ago by Maratha Queen Ahilyabai Holkar", *The Print*, 25 June 2022, https://theprint.in/past-forward/somnath-and-gyanvapi-temples-were-rebuilt-long-ago-by-maratha-queen-ahilyabai-holkar/1009037/.

55. A. Pawariya, "The Modi Legacy No One Is Talking About: He Is Following in Footsteps of Ahilyabai Holkar by Revamping Hindu Holy Sites", *Swarajya*, 9 Oct. 2020, https://swarajyamag.com/politics/the-modi-legacy-no-one-is-talking-about-he-is-following-in-footsteps-of-ahilyabai-holkar-by-revamping-hindu-holy-sites.

56. "Trinidad's Ravji Targets Youth", *Hinduism Today*, Jan. 1990, https://www.hinduismtoday.com/magazine/january-1990/1990-01-trinidad-s-ravji-targets-youth/.

57. Ibid.

58. Chinmaya Mission, Trinidad and Tobago, Facebook, 6 July 2020, https://www.facebook.com/chinmayamissionTT/photos/a.169592369761006/3021851697868378/?type=3.

59. Interview with Ravindranath Maharaj, Diwali Nagar, 24 April 2024.

60. S. Shankar, *An Uneasy Embrace: Africa, India and the Spectre of Race* (London: Hurst and Co., 2022).

61. Interview with Ravindranath Maharaj, Diwali Nagar, 24 April 2024.

62. "Epic Hanuman Chalisa ChanTTing at the Divali Nagar", *Trinidad and Tobago Newsday*, 25 April 2024, https://newsday.co.tt/2024/04/26/epic-hanuman-chalisa-chantting-at-the-divali-nagar/.
63. A video recording of the same can be found on my YouTube channel. "Orisha Leader Baba Somoren Offering Prayers at the Epic Hanuman Chalisa ChanTTing 03", YouTube, 28 April 2024: https://www.youtube.com/watch?v=yn9xOZ-Z8v0.
64. This is evident in the earlier caste records of 1886. The records of the *Brenda* leaving Calcutta port carry the earlier caste signifiers.
65. R. Reddock, "Freedom Denied: Indian Women and Indentureship in Trinidad and Tobago, 1845–1917", *Economic and Political Weekly* 20, no. 43 (1985), WS79–87; R. Reddock, "Indian Women and Indentureship in Trinidad and Tobago 1845–1917: Freedom Denied", *Caribbean Quarterly* 54, no. 4 (2008), pp. 41–68, https://doi.org/10.1080/00086495.2008.11829735.
66. Lal, *Chalo Jahaji*.
67. G. Vahed and A. Desai, *Inside Indian Indenture A South African Story 1860-1914* (Pretoria: HSRC Press, 2010); G. Bahadur, *Coolie Woman: The Odyssey of Indenture* (Chicago: University of Chicago Press, 2013).
68. I am grateful to Pandita Indrani, a scholar of Hinduism from Trinidad, for making the connections and introducing me to the pandit at the Shiva Harijan Mandir and to Sadhuji. Indrani is a Hindu feminist who studied Indian philosophy at the University of Pune, now Savitribai Phule University, Pune. She now advises many Hindu groups and serves on boards while disseminating the Hindu faith across North America. When she was put up for the position of first woman Pandit in Trinidad and Tobago, people like Ravi, Vijay Narayansingh and her grandfather backed her.
69. Interview, Shiva Harijan Mandir, April 2024. All the subsequent quotes are taken from this interview except the ones where the Pandit spoke on the phone.
70. Interview with Sadhuji, Debe, 24 April 2025.

5. COSMOPOLITAN DALIT UNIVERSALISM: DALIT ACTIVISM AND THE PROMISE OF A CASTELESS WORLD

1. The historian of the Middle Ages Michael Harney calls this phenomenon "falsifying pedigree" by those in the caste system who are not privileged. By doing this, the impact and influence of caste are sealed by those very people whose agency is at stake in the caste system. Michael Harney, *Race, Caste, and Indigeneity in Medieval Spanish Travel Literature* (New York: Palgrave Macmillan, 2015), pp. 9–10.
2. Vahed and Desai, *Inside Indian Indenture*.
3. D. Kapur, *Diaspora, Development, and Democracy: The Domestic Impact of International Migration from India* (Princeton: Princeton University Press, 2010).
4. For more on South Asian migration to the West, especially America, see, M.S. Khandelwal, *Becoming American, Being Indian, An Immigrant Community in New York City* (Ithaca: Cornell University Press, 2002); Padma Rangaswamy, *Namaste America: Indian Immigrants in an American Metropolis* (University Park: Pennsylvania State University Press, 2000); A. Sahay, *Indian Diaspora in the United States: Brain Drain or Gain* (Lanham MD: Lexington Books, 2009); S. Chakravotry, D. Kapur and N. Singh, *The Other One Percent: Indians in America* (New York: OUP, 2016); V. Bald, *Bengali Harlem and the Lost Histories of South Asian America* (Cambridge, MA: Harvard University Press, 2013); Prashad, *The Karma of Brown Folk*.
5. For more on South Asian migration to the West, especially America, see, M.S. Khandelwal, *Becoming American, Being Indian, An Immigrant Community in New York City* (Ithaca: Cornell University Press, 2002); Padma Rangaswamy, *Namaste America: Indian Immigrants in an American Metropolis* (University Park: Pennsylvania State University Press, 2000); A. Sahay, *Indian Diaspora in the United States: Brain Drain or Gain* (Lanham MD: Lexington Books, 2009); S. Chakravotry, D. Kapur and N. Singh, *The Other One Percent: Indians in America* (New York: OUP, 2016); V. Bald, *Bengali Harlem*

and the Lost Histories of South Asian America (Cambridge, MA: Harvard University Press, 2013); Prashad, The Karma of Brown Folk.
6. P. Gilroy, "Diaspora", *Paragraph* 17, no. 3 (1994), p. 207.
7. Ibid.
8. T. Niranjana, *Mobilizing India: Women, Music and Migration between India and Trinidad* (Durham, NC: Duke University Press, 2005), Intro.
9. D. Ratha, "Resilient Remittances", *Back to Basics*, International Monetary Fund, Sept. 2023, pp. 8–9.
10. B. Anderson, *The Spectre of Comparisons: Nationalism, Southeast Asia, and the World* (London: Verso, 1998).
11. S. Vertovec, *Transnationalism* (London: Routledge, 2009).
12. N. Glick-Schiller and G.E. Fouron, "The Generation of Identity: Redefining the Second Generation within a Transnational Social Field", in P. Levitt and N.C. Walters (eds.), *The Changing Face of Home: The Transnational Lives of the Second Generation* (New York: Russell Sage Foundation, 2002), pp. 168–208.
13. S. Borkar, "Who Are the Defiant Indian Diasporas", *Outlook Weekly*, 17 April 2021, https://www.outlookindia.com/national/web-exclusive-who-are-the-defiant-indian-diasporas-news-380490.
14. P. Kurien, "The Racial Paradigm and Dalit Anti-Caste Activism in the United States", *Social Problems* 70, no. 3 (2023), pp. 717–734.
15. S. Yengde, "Ambedkar's Foreign Policy and the Ellipsis of 'Dalit' from the International Activism", in S. Yengde and A. Teltumbde (eds.), *The Radical in Ambedkar: Critical Reflections* (New Delhi: Allen Lane, 2018).
16. S. Yengde, "At Japan Convention, Dalit and Burakumin People Forge Solidarity", *The Wire*, 11 Oct. 2018, https://thewire.in/caste/at-japan-convention-Dalit-and-burakumin-people-forge-solidarity.
17. S. Yengde, "Why Hinduism and the Violence of Caste Are Two Sides of a Coin", *Huffington Post*, 20 May 2016, http://www.huffingtonpost.in/suraj-yengde/why-hinduism-and-the-viol_b_10059872.html.
18. I studied the patterns in southern Africa. See S. Yengde, "South–South Migration: An Ethnographic Study of an Indian Business District in Johannesburg", PhD thesis, Interdisciplinary Social Sciences, University of the Witwatersrand, Johannesburg, 2015.

19. V. Kumar, "Different Shades of Caste among the Indian Diaspora in the US", *Transcience* 12, no. 1 (2021), pp. 1–13.
20. During my visit to one of the suburbs of Chicago, a Telugu Dalit couple took me out for breakfast at an Indian restaurant. They pointed me to the local Indian newspaper's caste-based matrimonial classified ads.
21. Ibid., p. 5.
22. Vivek Kumar calls this the "new diaspora" as opposed to the older one choreographed during the indentured era. V. Kumar, "The New Dalit Diaspora: A Sociological Analysis", in K.L. Sharma and R. Singh (eds.), *Dual Identity: Indian Diaspora and Other Essays* (New Delhi: Orient BlackSwan), pp. 227–62.
23. Kumar, "Different Shades of Caste", p. 4.
24. N. Nimgade, *In The Tiger's Shadow: The Autobiography of an Ambedkarite* (Delhi: Navayana, 2011). Also see the foreword to the book by Christopher Queen.
25. Interview with the president, Bhagwan Valmik Mandir, Southall, 10 March 2012.
26. *Religion Rebels in the Punjab*, chapter 22.
27. Recently the Washington DC-based Ambedkar International Center began to house monks at its site, but it is not a *vihara* yet.
28. Ethnographic notes, Wolverhampton, 24 Oct. 2021.
29. R. Paul, "A Brief Biography of Bhante Abhipassano, Formerly Mr Darshan Ram Jassal", *Golden Jubilee Souvenir* (Wolverhampton: Dr Ambedkar Memorial Committee of Great Britain, 21 July 2019), pp. 31–5.
30. Bhante Chandra Bodhi, "Buddhism and Dr Ambedkar", *Dr Ambedkar Souvenir, 2000* (Wolverhampton: Dr Ambedkar Memorial Committee of Great Britain, 2000), p. 65.
31. This claim is taken from Bains's memoir, *Pride vs. Prejudice: One Man's Fight against Racism and Inequality* (Jalandhar: Malind Prakashan, 2015).
32. Comment section, R. Chander, "Pride vs. Prejudice", *Diplomatic Titbits Blog*, 15 Nov. 2016, https://diplomatictitbits.blogspot.com/2016/11/pride-vs-prejudice.html.
33. One of the first autobiographies of Dalits in the diaspora was by

Kartar Chand, who left India in his early twenties and moved to Scotland. After living there for a few years he took the journey to the US. He settled in Wisconsin with his family. K. Chand, *An Onward Journey: A Story of Love, Perseverance and Faith* (Madison: Heavenly Enterprise Midwest, 2020).

34. Bishan Dass Bains, "Dr B.R. Ambedkar Memorial Committee", *Golden Jubilee Souvenir, 2019* (Wolverhampton: Dr Ambedkar Memorial Committee of Great Britain, 2019), pp. 54–7.
35. E. Hardtmann, *The Dalit Movement in India: Local Practices, Global Connections* (New Delhi: Oxford University Press, 2009). See also Nicolas Jaoul, "Beyond Diaspora: Ambedkarism, Multiculturalism and Caste in the UK", *South Asia Multidisciplinary Academic Journal* [online] 27 (2021), http://journals.openedition.org/samaj/7489.
36. Interview with Dev Suman by telephone, 5 Nov. 2021.
37. D. Karunakaran, "AIM: Dr Ambedkar International Conference, Malaysia", 14, 15 April 2024, https://www.youtube.com/watch?v=mDM5yTMQ1Ew.
38. Raju Kamble also narrated this part of the story to me in 2016.
39. Interview with Dato Panjamurthi, by Zoom, 12 Dec. 2004.
40. A. Ramchandran, "Dalit Film and Cultural Festival: Celebrating Dalit Cinema in New York", *New Indian Express*, 23 Feb. 2019, https://www.newindianexpress.com/entertainment/tamil/2019/Feb/23/celebrating-Dalit-cinema-1942692.html; also https://web.archive.org/web/20191210192136/; https://www.Dalitfilmfest.com/abou
41. A. Qin, "Newsom Vetoes Bill Banning Caste Discrimination", *New York Times*, 7 Oct. 2023, https://www.nytimes.com/2023/10/07/us/california-caste-discrimination.html.
42. Office of the Governor, State of California, 7 Oct. 2023, https://www.gov.ca.gov/wp-content/uploads/2023/10/SB-403-Veto-1.pdf.
43. Zoom interview with Jagvir Singh Dihana, 15 May 2021.
44. I spent two days with Thirumavalavan documenting his journey and activism. A video diary is available on my YouTube channel: Suraj Yengde, "Two days with Thol Thirumavalavan, MP", https://youtu.be/QBsVgFDWvuE
45. Zoom interview with Anbarasan, 16 May 2021.
46. Zoom interview with Muthu Kumar, 16 May 2021.

47. Interview with Kardak, Dubai, 12 March 2022.
48. On Raju Kamble, see S. Yengde, "How a chemical engineer became the ambassador of the Dalit movement", The Print, 26 August 2018: https://theprint.in/opinion/how-a-chemical-engineer-became-the-ambassador-of-international-Dalit-movement/105638/.
49. Interview, Sonepat campsite, Dubai, 12 March. Names of the informants and their locations have been anonymized for the protection of their identities.
50. A. Wankhede, "Even in Australia alarming levels of caste discrimination exist. We must fight it with evidence", *The Guardian*, 29 October 2024, https://www.theguardian.com/australia-news/commentisfree/2024/oct/30/even-in-australia-alarming-levels-of-caste-discrimination-exists-we-must-fight-it-with-evidence
51. S. Yengde, "Iterations of Shared Dalit–Black Solidarity", *The Seminar* 737, no. 1 (2021), pp. 83–96.

6. CONCLUSION: BIOGRAPHY OF DALIT AGONISM— FIELD NOTES FROM THE DIARY OF AN ARCHIVIST

1. W.E.B. Du Bois, "The Souls of White Folk", in E. Foner, N. Huggins and H.L. Gates Jr. (eds.), *W.E.B. Du Bois: Writings* (New York: Library of America, 1987), p. 925.
2. M.N. Wankhede, "Bandachaya yashasvitesaathi atmashodh aavshyak", in A. Dangle (ed.), *Dalit Sahitya: Ek Abhyas* (Mumbai: Maharashtra State Literature-Culture Society, 1978), p. 29.
3. J. Waghmare, "Negro Vangmay va Dalit Vangmay", in Dangle, *Dalit Sahitya: Ek Abhyas* (Dalit Literature A Study), pp. 179–88.
4. My effort to archive the Dalit diaspora is an attempt to build material sources and account for the economy of nostalgia, which is driven by the desire to create and curate one's own memory as a responsibility—or what Anjali Arondekar calls a "historical desire" as future knowledge coded in an archival mindscape. On the state of the archive, Anjali Arondekar tests the paucity of curation and what constitutes an archive amidst exaggeration and vastness of resources. A. Arondekar, *Abundance. Sexuality's History* (Durham, N.C.: Duke University Press, 2023), Introduction and Chapter 2.
5. Rutgers University Task Force on Caste Discrimination, *Caste-Based*

Discrimination in U.S. Higher Education and at Rutgers, August 2024, https://rutgersaaup.org/wp-content/uploads/2024/08/Rutgers-Caste-Report-August-2024.pdf

6. "Caste Discrimination in the USA: A Public Radio and Online Series", Pulitzer Center, 25 Feb. 2019, https://pulitzercenter.org/projects/caste-discrimination-usa-public-radio-and-online-series.
7. S. Yengde, "American Caste: A Secret History", *Michigan Quarterly Review* 61, Special Issue: Fractured Union; American Democracy on the Brink (Sept. 2022), pp. 700–8. See also I. Wilkerson, *Caste: The Origins of Our Discontents* (New York: PRH, 2020).
8. D. Kumar, "Landownership and Inequality in Madras Presidency: 1853–54 to 1946–47", *Indian Economic and Social History Review* 12, no. 3 (1975), pp. 229–61, https://doi.org/10.1177/001946467501200302.

BIBLIOGRAPHY

Primary Sources

Personal Archives of Dr. Laxmi Berwa
National Archives of Trinidad and Tobago

Secondary Sources

Adcock, C.S., *The Limits of Tolerance: Indian Secularism and the Politics of Religious Freedom* (New York: Oxford University Press, 2014).

Alagirisamy, D., "The Self Respect Movement and Tamil Politics of Belonging in Interwar British Malaya, 1929–1939", *Modern Asian Studies* 50, no. 5 (2016), pp. 1547–75.

Alexander, M., *The New Jim Crow: Mass Incarceration in the Age of Colorblindness* (New York: New Press, 2012).

Ambedkar, B.R., "Annihilation of Caste", in V. Moon (ed.), *Dr Babasaheb Ambedkar: Writings and Speeches*, vol. 14, part 2 (Mumbai: Education Department, Govt of Maharashtra, 1995; reprint, Dr Ambedkar Foundation, 2014), pp. 23–96.

——, "Castes in India: Their Mechanism, Genesis, and Development", in V. Moon (ed.), *Dr Babasaheb Ambedkar: Writings and Speeches*, vol. 1 (Mumbai: Education Department, Govt of Maharashtra), [1979] 2014), pp. 3–22.

——, "The House the Hindus Have Built", in V. Moon et al. (eds.) *Dr Babasaheb Ambedkar: Writings and Speeches*, vol. 5 (Mumbai: Education Department, Govt of Maharashtra, 1989), pp. 145–69.

——, Letters from B.R. Ambedkar to W.E.B. Du Bois, W.E.B. Du Bois Papers, Series 1, Correspondence, University of Massachusetts Library, https://credo.library.umass.edu/.

——, *The Mahars: Who Were They and How They Became the Untouchables?*, in H. Narke et al. (eds.), *Dr Babasaheb Ambedkar: Writings and Speeches*, vol. 17, part 2 (Mumbai: Education Department, Govt of Maharashtra, 2003), pp. 137–50.

——, *Riddles in Hinduism: The Annotated Critical Selection* (New Delhi: Navayana, 2016).

——, "Scheduled Castes' Case to be Presented before U.N.O., Bombay, Jan. 17, 1947", in H. Narke (ed.), *Dr Babasaheb Ambedkar: Writings and Speeches*, vol.17, part 1 (Mumbai: Education Department, Govt of Maharashtra, 2003)

——, "Slaves and Untouchables", in V. Moon (ed.), *Dr Babasaheb Ambedkar: Writings and Speeches*, vol. 5 (Mumbai: Education Department, Govt of Maharashtra, 2008), pp. 9–18.

——, "Statement by Dr B.R. Ambedkar in Parliament in Explanation of His Resignation from the Cabinet, 10 October 1951", in Vasant Moon (ed.), *Dr Babasaheb Ambedkar: Writings and Speeches*, vol. 14, part 2 (Mumbai: Education Department, Govt of Maharashtra, 1995; reprint, Dr Ambedkar Foundation, 2014), pp. 1321–3.

——, Submissions to the Round Table Conference, 1930–1931, British Library, London, IOR/Q/RTC/2, IOR/Q/RTC/24.

——, "Untouchables or the Children of India's Ghetto", in V. Moon (ed.), *Dr Babasaheb Ambedkar: Writings and Speeches*, vol. 5 (Mumbai: Education Department, Govt of Maharashtra, 1989), pp. 1–111.

——, *The Untouchables: Who Were They and Why They Became Untouchables* (New Delhi: Amrit Book Co., 1948), in *Dr Babasaheb Ambedkar: Writings and Speeches*, vol. 7 (Mumbai: Govt of Maharashtra, 2013).

——, "We Will Carry on All India Land Satyagraha Even against Central Government", in H. Narke (ed.), *Dr Babasaheb Ambedkar: Writings and Speeches*, vol.17, part 3 (Mumbai: Education Department, Govt of Maharashtra, 2019), pp. 498–9.

——, *What Congress and Gandhi Have Done to the Untouchables* (Bombay: Thacker and Co., 1945).

——, "What Path to Salvation (Mukti Kon Pathe?): Dr Ambedkar's Address to the Bombay Presidency Mahar Conference, 31 May

1936, Bombay", translated by V. Moon, https://franpritchett.com/00ambedkar/txt_ambedkar_salvation.html.

———, *Who Were the Shudras? How They Came to Be the Fourth Varna in the Indo-Aryan Society* (Bombay: Thacker and Co., 1947).

Anderson, B., *The Spectre of Comparisons: Nationalism, Southeast Asia, and the World* (London: Verso, 1998).

Anderson, J.D., "Sir Herbert Risley, K.C.I.E., C.S.I.", Royal Anthropological Institute, https://www.therai.org.uk/archives-and-manuscripts/obituaries/herbert-risley.

Andrew, B. and J.B. Leslie (ed.), *Inside African Anthropology: Monica Wilson and Her Interpreters* (Cambridge: Cambridge University Press, 2013).

Angelo, B., "Toni Morrison: The Pain of Being Black", *Time*, 22 May 1989, https://content.time.com/time/subscriber/article/0,33009,957724,00.html.

Arafath, P.K.Y., "From Battuta to Makhdum II: Savarna Habitus, Corporeal Shields, and Caste Acoustics on the Malabar Coast", in P. Banerjee (ed.), *Textual Lives of Caste across the Ages: Hierarchy, Humanity and Equality in Indian History* (London: Bloomsbury, 2024).

Arondekar, A., *Abundance. Sexuality's History* (Durham, N.C.: Duke University Press, 2023).

Ashok, K.M. and S.J. Boopalan, "Indian Christians in Conflict: Dalit Christian Movement in Contemporary India", in S.J. Hunt (ed.), *Handbook of Global Contemporary Christianity: Themes and Developments in Culture, Politics, and Society* (Leiden: Brill, 2015), pp. 308–24.

Athawale, R., "Need for Ideological Ambedkarism", *Outlook*, 15 August 2023, Dalit Panthers Independence Day Special Issue, pp. 70–4.

Avacharmal, L.Y., *Ambedkarit Chalwal āni Hyderabad Sansthanatil Dalit Mukti Sangram* (Pune: Sugawa Prakashan, 1987).

Awad, M., *The Life and Work of Annabhau Sathe: A Marxist-Ambedkarite Mosaic* (New Delhi: Gaur Publishers, 2010).

Ayyathurai, G., "Emigration against Caste, Transformation of the Self, and Realization of the Casteless Society in Indian Diaspora", *Essays in Philosophy* 22, no. 1/2 (2021), pp. 45–65.

Bagul, B., "Dalit Literature Is but Human Literature (Dalit Sahitya He Tar Maansache Sahitya)", translated by M. Malshe, in A. Dangle (ed.),

Poisoned Bread: Translations from Modern Marathi Dalit Literature (Hyderabad: Orient BlackSwan, 1994), pp. 271–89.

———, "Dalit Sahitya He Tar Maansache Sahitya", Sinhagarjana, Diwali Ank, 1975, in A. Dangle (ed.), *Dalit Sahitya: Ek Abhyas* (Mumbai: Maharashtra State Literature-Culture Society, 1978), pp. 135–52.

Bahadur, G., *Coolie Woman: The Odyssey of Indenture* (Chicago: University of Chicago Press, 2013).

Baines, J.A., *Census 1881: Operations and Results in the Presidency of Bombay, including Sind*, vol. 1: *Text* (Bombay: Government Press, 1882).

Bains, B.D., "Dr B.R. Ambedkar Memorial Committee", *Golden Jubilee Souvenir, 2019* (Wolverhampton: Dr Ambedkar Memorial Committee of Great Britain, 2019), pp. 54–7.

———, *Pride vs. Prejudice: One Man's Fight against Racism and Inequality* (Jalandhar: Malind Prakashan, 2015).

Balasubramaniam, J., "A Case for Dalit Journalism", *Telegraph India*, 28 January 2021, https://www.telegraphindia.com/opinion/a-case-for-dalit-journalism/cid/1804909.

Bald, V., *Bengali Harlem and the Lost Histories of South Asian America* (Cambridge, MA: Harvard University Press, 2013).

Banerjee, P. (ed.), *Textual Lives of Caste across the Ages: Hierarchy, Humanity and Equality in Indian History* (London: Bloomsbury, 2024).

Bayly, S., *Caste, Society and Politics in India from the Eighteenth Century to the Modern Age* (Cambridge: Cambridge University Press, 1999).

BBC, "Bhimrao Ambedkar's Iconic Interview from 1955", YouTube, https://www.youtube.com/watch?v=Wf3VJCpNMqI&ab_channel=BBCNewsIndia.

———, "'Racist' Gandhi Statue Removed from University of Ghana", 13 December 2018, https://www.bbc.com/news/world-africa-46552614.

Bhagat, R.B., "Census Enumeration, Religious Identity and Communal Polarization in India", *Asian Ethnicity* 14, no. 4 (2013), pp. 434–48.

Bhagavan, M. (ed.), *India and the Cold War* (Chapel Hill, NC: University of North Carolina Press, 2019).

———, *Vijaya Lakshmi Pandit* (New York: Penguin, 2023).

Bhandarkar, D.R., "Foreign Elements in the Hindu Population", *Indian Antiquary* XL (1911), pp. 7–37.

Bhante Chander Bodhi, "Buddhism and Dr Ambedkar", *Dr Ambedkar*

BIBLIOGRAPHY

Souvenir, 2000 (Wolverhampton: Dr Ambedkar Memorial Committee of Great Britain, 2000), pp. 65–7.

Bharati, A., *The Asians in East Africa: Jayhind and Uhuru* (Chicago: Nelson-Hall Co., 1972).

Bharati, K. "Swami Achhootanand 'Harihar': A Profile", *Forward Press*, 8 February 2019, https://www.forwardpress.in/2019/02/swami-achhootanand-harihar-a-profile/.

Bhattacharya, R., "Development of Materialism in India: The Pre-Cārvākas and the Cārvākas", *Eercizi Filosofici* 8, no. 1 (2013), pp. 1–12, http://hdl.handle.net/10077/12943.

Bhoite, U. and A. Bhoite, "The Dalit Sahitya Movement in Maharashtra: A Sociological Analysis", *Sociological Bulletin* 26, no. 1 (1977), pp. 60–75.

Birdi, M.L., "BJP's Attempt to Saffronise the Indian Constitution", *Dr Ambedkar Souvenir, 2000* (Wolverhampton: Dr Ambedkar Memorial Committee of Great Britain, 2000), pp. 53–5.

Bīrūnī, Muḥammad ibn Aḥmad, *Alberuni's India: An Account of the Religion, Philosophy, Literature, Geography, Chronology, Astronomy, Customs, Laws and Astrology of India*, 2 vols., translated by Edward C. Sachau (London: Kegan Paul, Trench, Trübner and Co., 1888 and 1910).

Blight, D., "What Frederick Douglass Revealed – and Omitted – in His Famous Autobiographies", History.com, 12 March 2019.

Blunt, E.A.H., *The Caste System of Northern India: With Special Reference to the United Provinces of Agra and Oudh* (London: Oxford University Press, 1931).

——, "United Provinces of Agra and Oudh", in *Census of India*, 1911, vol. XV, part I, Report (Allahabad: Govt. Press, 1912).

Borkar, S. "Who Are the Defiant Indian Diasporas", *Outlook Weekly*, 17 April 2021, https://www.outlookindia.com.

Braithwaite, L., "Social Stratification in Trinidad: A Preliminary Analysis", *Social and Economic Studies* 2, no. 2/3 (1953), pp. 5–175.

Bronkhorst, J., *Greater Magadha: Studies in the Culture of Early India* (Leiden: Brill, 2007), parts I and II.

Chakraborty, A., "'Racism Is Real', Sammy Urges Cricket to Do Better", Reuters, 10 September 2020, https://www.reuters.com/article/idUSKBN2611L0/.

Chakravorty, S. *The Truth about Us: The Politics of Information from Manu to Modi* (Delhi: Hachette India, 2019).

Chakravotry, S., D. Kapur and N. Singh, *The Other One Percent: Indians in America* (New York: OUP, 2016).

Chand, K., *An Onward Journey: A Story of Love, Perseverance and Faith* (Madison: Heavenly Enterprise Midwest, 2020).

Chander, R., "Pride vs. Prejudice", *Diplomatic Titbits Blog*, 15 November 2016, https://diplomatictitbits.blogspot.com/2016/11/pride-vs-prejudice.html.

Chandra, K., *Why Ethnic Parties Succeed: Patronage and Ethnic Head Counts in India* (New York: Cambridge University Press, 2004).

Chincolkar, R.B., "Bahujan vrutapatra: stithi – gati", ch. 5 in "Swatryantrapurv kalatil Bahujanachi vrutapatre", PhD thesis, Department of Journalism and Mass Communication, Dr Babasaheb Ambedkar Marathwada University, Aurangabad, 2007, http://hdl.handle.net/10603/92035.

Clarke, C., "Caste among Hindus in a Town in Trinidad: San Fernando", in B.M. Schwartz (ed.), *Caste in Overseas Indian Communities* (California: Chandler Publishing House, 1967), pp. 165–99.

Clarke, C. and G. Clarke, *Post-colonial Trinidad: An Ethnographic Journal* (New York: Palgrave Macmillan, 2010).

CNN World News, "India Shuns Calls to Talk Caste with U.N.", CNN, 17 August 2001, https://edition.cnn.com/2001/WORLD/asiapcf/south/08/17/india.caste/.

Cobb, J. and M. Guariglia (eds.), *The Essential Kerner Commission Report* (New York: Liverlight, 2021).

Cohn, B.S., "Notes on the Study of Indian Society and Culture", in M. Singer and B. Cohn (eds.), *Structure and Change in Indian Society* (Chicago: AldineTransaction, 1968), pp. 3–28.

Contursi, J., "Political Theology: Text and Practice in a Dalit Panther Community", *Journal of Asian Studies* 52, no. 2 (1993), pp. 320–39.

Dalit Panthers, "Dalit Panthers Manifesto", Internet Archive, https://archive.org/details/idoc_pub_dalit-panthers-manifesto.

Dangle, A., *Dalit Panther Ek Adhorekhit Satya* (Dalit Panthers: An Emphasized Truth) (Mumbai: Loksvangmay Gruh, 2021).

———, *Dalit Saahitya Ek Abhyas* (Dalit Literature: A Study) (Mumbai: Maharashtra State Literature-Culture Society, 1978).

———, "Introduction", in *Poisoned Bread: Translations from Modern Marathi Literature* (Hyderabad: Orient BlackSwan, 2011).

BIBLIOGRAPHY

——, "Nivedan", in A. Dangle (ed.), *Dalit Sahitya Ek Abhyas* (Dalit Literature: A Study) (Mumbai: Maharashtra State Literature-Culture Society, 1978), pp. 1–43.

Davis, A., "Speech by Angela Davis", YouTube, 18 December 2016, https://www.youtube.com/watch?v=6hHYnrM-NOc&t=1385s.

Desai, A. and G. Vahed, *Inside Indian Indenture: A South African Story, 1860–1914* (Pretoria: HSRC Press, 2010).

——, *The South African Gandhi: Stretcher-Bearer of Empire* (Palo Alto: Stanford University Press, 2015).

Desai, M., "Caste in Black and White: Dalit Identity and the Translation of African American Literature", *Comparative Literature* 67, no. 1 (2015), pp. 94–113.

Dhale, R., "Dalit Panther First Conference, Nagpur, 1974", in J.V. Pawar, *Ambedkarottar Ambedkari Chalwal*, vol. 4, *1972–1977* (3rd edn, Mumbai: Asmita Communications, [2010] 2022), pp. 419–28.

Dirks, N., *Castes of Mind: Colonialism and the Making of Modern India* (Princeton: Princeton University Press, 2001).

——, "The Invention of Caste: Civil Society in Colonial India", *Social Analysis* 25 (1989), pp. 42–52.

Donlevy, K. and C. Campanile, "NYC Gandhi Statue Obliterated by Vandals, Second Attack in Two Weeks", *New York Post*, 18 August 2022, https://nypost.com/2022/08/18/queens-gandhi-statue-vandalized-for-second-time-in-two-weeks/.

Douglass, F., *My Bondage and My Freedom* (New York: Miller, Orton and Mulligan, 1855).

Du Bois, W.E.B., "The Souls of White Folk", in E. Foner, N. Huggins and H.L. Gates, Jr. (eds.), *W.E.B. Du Bois: Writings* (New York: Library of America, 1987), pp. 923–38.

Dumont, L., *Homo Hierarchicus: The Caste System and Its Implications*, translated by Mark Sainsbury (Chicago: University of Chicago Press, 1974).

Eastley, A., "Area of Enigma: V.S. Naipaul and the East Indian Revival in Trinidad", *ARIEL: A Review of International English Literature* 41, no. 2 (2010), pp. 23–45.

Fa-Hein, *A Record of Buddhistic Kingdoms: Being an Account by the Chinese Monk Fâ-Hien of His Travels in India and Ceylon (AD 399–414)* in

Search of the Buddhist Books of Discipline, translated by J. Legge (Delhi: Oriental Publishers, 1971).

Fitzhugh, E., J.P. Julien, N. Noel and S. Stewart, "It's Time for a New Approach to Racial Equity", McKinsey Institute for Black Economic Mobility, 2 December 2020, updated 25 May 2021, https://www.mckinsey.com/bem/our-insights/its-time-for-a-new-approach-to-racial-equity.

Fuller, C.J., "Ethnographic Inquiry in Colonial India: Herbert Risley, William Crooke and the Study of Tribes and Castes", *Journal of the Royal Anthropological Institute* 23, no. 3 (2017), pp. 603–21.

Fulzele, A.D., *Ambedkari Chalavalitil Dadasaheb Gaikwad Yanche Yogdan* (Mumbai: Lokvangmay Gruh, 2012).

Gaddis, H., "Black Panther and Dalit Panther Unity in 21st Century", *Outlook*, 15 August 2023, Dalit Panthers Independence Day Special Issue, https://www.outlookindia.com/national/black-panther-and-dalit-panther-unity-in-21st-century-news-311564.

Gandhi, I., "Prime Minister's House, New Delhi, Letter to Mr. Berwa, June 22, 1982", Archives of Laxmi Berwa.

Gates, H.L., Jr. (ed.), *The Classic Slave Narratives* (New York: Signet [1987] 2012).

Ghurye, G.S., *Caste and Race in India* (Bombay: Popular Prakashan, [1932] 1969).

Gillon, S.M., *Separate and Unequal: The Kerner Commission and the Unravelling of American Liberalism* (New York: Basic Books, 2018).

Gilroy, P., "Diaspora", *Paragraph* 17, no. 3 (1994), pp. 207–12.

Gokhale, P., *Lokāyata/Cārvāka: A Philosophical Inquiry* (New Delhi: Oxford University Press, 2015).

Gordon, S., *The Marathas, 1600–1818* (Cambridge: Cambridge University Press, 1993).

Gorringe, H., *Panthers in Parliament: Dalits, Caste, and Political Power in South India* (New Delhi: Oxford University Press, 2017).

Gupta, D., "Introduction: The Certitudes of Caste; When Identity Trumps Hierarchy", *Contributions to Indian Sociology* 38, nos. 1/2 (2004), pp. 5–15.

Guru, G., "The politics of naming", *Seminar*, 471, 'Dalit', November 1998, pp. 14-18.

BIBLIOGRAPHY

Hardtmann, E.M., *The Dalit Movement in India: Local Practices, Global Connections* (New Delhi: Oxford University Press, 2009).

Harney, M., *Race, Caste, and Indigeneity in Medieval Spanish Travel Literature* (New York: Palgrave Macmillan, 2015).

Heesterman, J.C., *The Inner Conflict of Tradition: Essays in Indian Ritual, Kingship, and Society* (Chicago: University of Chicago Press, 1985).

Hinduism Today, "Trinidad's Ravji Targets Youth", January 1990, https://www.hinduismtoday.com/magazine/january-1990/1990-01-trinidads-ravji-targets-youth/.

Horton, J.O. and L.E. Horton, *Slavery and the Making of America* (New York: Oxford University Press, 2004).

Hughes, L., "The Negro and the Racial Mountain", in Robert Walser (ed.), *Keeping Time: Readings in Jazz History* (New York: Oxford University Press, 1999).

Hundle, A.K., "Sikh Diasporic Feminisms: Provocation 1", *Sikh Formations* 13, no. 4 (2017), pp. 237–40.

Ibbetson, D.C.J., *Memorandum on Ethnological Inquiry in the Punjab* (Lahore: Government of India, 1882).

——, *Report of the Census of the Panjab 1881*, vol. 1: *Text* (Lahore: Central Gaol Press, 1883).

IBN Lokmat, "The Dalit Panther & Rebel Poet Who Shook the World—Namdeo Dhasal Interview with Nikhil Wagle", YouTube, 12 Feb 2025: https://www.youtube.com/watch?v=2Hxiq4IEaFo

Immerwahr, D., "Caste or Colony? Indianizing Race in the United States", *Modern Intellectual History* 4, no. 2 (2007), pp. 275–301.

——, "On B.R. Ambedkar and Black–Dalit Connections", https://faculty.wcas.northwestern.edu/daniel-immerwahr/Ambedkar.pdf.

Indian High Commission of Trinidad & Tobago, "Diaspora in Trinidad and Tobago", Indian High Commission of Trinidad and Tobago, https://www.hcipos.gov.in/page/diaspora-in-trinidad-and-tobago/.

Jain, R.K., "Race Relations, Ethnicity, Class and Culture: A Comparison of Indians in Trinidad and Malaysia", *Sociological Bulletin* 38, no. 1 (1989), pp. 57–69.

Jan, T., J. McGregor and M. Hoyer, "Corporate America's $50 billion promise", *Washington Post*, 23 August 2021, https://www.washingtonpost.com/business/interactive/2021/george-floyd-corporate-america-racial-justice/.

BIBLIOGRAPHY

Jangam, C., *Dalits and the Making of Modern India* (New Delhi: Oxford University Press, 2017).

Jaoul, N., "Beyond Diaspora: Ambedkarism, Multiculturalism and Caste in the UK", *South Asia Multidisciplinary Academic Journal* [online], 2021, accessed 4 February 2022, http://journals.openedition.org/samaj/7489.

Jayaram, N., "The Metamorphosis of Caste among Trinidad Hindus", *Contributions to Indian Sociology* 40, no. 2 (2006), pp. 143–73.

Jigyasu, C.P., *Adihindu Andolan ke Pravartak Shree 108 Swami Achhootanand Ji 'Harihar': Jeevani, Siddhant aur Bhashan* (1960).

Johnson, C. S., *The Negro in American Civilization: A Study of Negro Life and Race Relations in the Light of Social Research* (New York: Henry Holt and Co., 1930).

Jondhale, B. V., "Panthermadhil vaad vivadaankade pahataannaa", *Maharashtra Times*, 10 April 2022, https://marathi.indiatimes.com/editorial/samwad/the-discussion-on-the-role-of-dangles-the-work-of-panthers-and-the-ambedkar-movement-in-the-book-dalit-panther-/articleshow/90754961.cms.

Juergensmeyer, M., *Religious Rebels in the Punjab: The Ad Dharm Challenge to Caste* (Delhi: Navayana Publishing, 2009).

Kapoor, S.D., "B.R. Ambedkar, W.E.B. Du Bois and the Process of Liberation", *Economic and Political Weekly* 38, no. 51/52 (2003), pp. 5344–9.

Kapur, D., *Diaspora, Development, and Democracy: The Domestic Impact of International Migration from India* (Princeton: Princeton University Press, 2010).

Karunakaran, D., "AIM: Dr Ambedkar International Conference, Malaysia", 14 and 15 April 2024, https://www.youtube.com/watch?v=mDM5yTMQ1Ew.

Keane, D., *Caste-Based Discrimination in International Human Rights Law* (London: Routledge, 2016).

Ketkar, S.V., *History of Caste in India: Evidence of the Laws of Manu on the Social Conditions in India during the Third Century AD Interpreted and Examined* (Ithaca, NY: Taylor and Carpenter, 1909).

Khandare, V.R., "Dr Janardan Waghmare Yaanchya Saahityacha Abhyas", PhD thesis, University of Pune, 2009.

BIBLIOGRAPHY

Khandelwal M.S., *Becoming American, Being Indian: An Immigrant Community in New York City* (Ithaca: Cornell University Press, 2002).

King, M., "Black Lives Matter Power Grab Sets Off Internal Revolt", *Politico Magazine*, 10 December 2020, https://www.politico.com/news/2020/12/10/black-lives-matter-organization-biden-444097.

Klass, M., "East and West Indian: Cultural Complexity in Trinidad", *Annals of the New York Academy of Sciences* 83, no. 5 (1960), pp. 855–61.

Kolge, N., *Gandhi against Caste* (Gurgaon: PRH, 2018).

Kosambi, D.D., *An Introduction to the Study of Indian History* (Bombay: Popular Book Depot, 1956).

Kumar, A., "B.R. Ambedkar on Caste and Land Relations in India", *Review of Agrarian Studies* 10, no. 1 (2000), http://ras.org.in/9537f8b9e25675f8de579ef0e1db6beb.

Kumar, D., "Landownership and Inequality in Madras Presidency: 1853–54 to 1946–47", *Indian Economic and Social History Review* 12, no. 3 (1975), pp. 229–61.

Kumar, V., *Dalit Assertion and Bahujan Samaj Party* (New Delhi: Samyak Prakashan, [2001] 2013).

——, "Different Shades of Caste among the Indian Diaspora in the US", *Transcience* 12, no. 1 (2021), pp. 1–13.

——, "The New Dalit Diaspora: A Sociological Analysis", in K.L. Sharma and R. Singh (eds.), *Dual Identity: Indian Diaspora and Other Essays* (New Delhi: Orient BlackSwan), pp. 227–62.

——, "Understanding Dalit Diaspora", *Economic and Political Weekly* 39, no. 1, (2004), pp. 114–16.

Kurien, P., "The Racial Paradigm and Dalit Anti-Caste Activism in the United States", *Social Problems* 70, no. 3 (2023), pp. 717–34.

Kurundkar, N., *Aakalan* (Pune: Deshmukh and Company, 1985).

Lal, B.V., *Chalo Jahaji: On a Journey through Indenture in Fiji* (Canberra: ANU Press, 2012).

Latham, M.E., *The Right Kind of Revolution: Modernization, Development, and U.S. Foreign Policy from the Cold War to the Present* (Ithaca: Cornell University Press, 2011).

Lee, J., *Deceptive Majority: Dalits, Hinduism, and Underground Religion* (Cambridge: Cambridge University Press, 2021).

Limbale, S., "Introduction", to *Shatakatil Dalit Vichar* (2nd edn, Pune: Dilipraj Publications, 2007).

BIBLIOGRAPHY

Luard, C.E., *Ethnographical Survey of the Central India Agency*, Monograph no. III: *Bundelkhand Castes* (Lucknow: Newul Kishore Press, 1909).

Maharaj, S., "SDMS, the Fruit of a Divided History", *Trinidad and Tobago Newsday*, 5 January 2020, https://newsday.co.tt/2020/01/05/sdms-the-fruit-of-a-divided-history/.

Mandal, B.P., "The Mandal Commission Report", *National Commission for Backward Classes*, vols. 1 and 2, 1980, https://www.ncbc.nic.in/Writereaddata/Mandal%20Commission%20Report%20of%20the%201st%20Part%20English635228715105764974.pdf.

Marcelo, P., "Asian Commission Criticized for Black Lives Matter Statement", AP News, 8 June 2020, https://apnews.com/article/0b36a78f87eeb942001f26de2966c279.

Martin, P., "Caste Discrimination in the USA: A Public Radio and Online Series", Pulitzer Centre, 25 February 2019, https://pulitzercenter.org/projects/caste-discrimination-usa-public-radio-and-online-series.

McCrindle J.W., *Ancient India as Described by Megasthenês and Arrian: Being a Translation of the Fragments of the Indika of Megasthenês Collected by Dr Schwanbeck, and of the First Part of the Indika of Arrian* (Calcutta and Bombay: Thacker and Co.; London: Trübner and Co., 1877).

McLaughlin, M., *The Long, Hot Summer of 1967: Urban Rebellion in America* (New York: Palgrave Macmillan, 2014).

Mehta, P., "Diaspora as Spokesperson and Watchdog: Laxmi Berwa, VISION, and Anti-Caste Activism by Dalits in the United States", *Diaspora: A Journal of Transnational Studies* 21, no. 1 (Spring 2021), pp. 64–86.

Menon, V., R. Bikhchandani and H. Laeeq, "Somnath and Gyanvapi Temples Were Rebuilt – Long Ago by Maratha Queen Ahilyabai Holkar", *The Print*, 25 June 2022, https://theprint.in/past-forward/somnath-and-gyanvapi-temples-were-rebuilt-long-ago-by-maratha-queen-ahilyabai-holkar/1009037/.

Meshram, K., "Wankhede, Manohar Namdev", *Marathi Vishwakosh*, https://vishwakosh.marathi.gov.in/32434/.

Ministry of External Affairs, "Statement by Shri Omar Abdullah, Minister of State for External Affairs, India, at the World Conference Against Racism, Racial Discrimination, Xenophobia and Related Intolerance", Media Center, 2 September 2001.

Mogle, R.B., "Dalit Panther: Tatwa āni Vyvahar, ek Rajkiya Abhyas", PhD thesis, Swami Ramanand Teerth Marathwada University, Nanded, 2021.

Mondal, S., "The Panthers Growl Again: A Short Memoir of a Historic Dalit–Black Conference", *News Minute*, 2 June 2020, https://www.thenewsminute.com/news/panthers-growl-again-short-memoir-historic-dalit-black-conference-164604.

More, B.S., "Marathwada Dalit Federation cha zamin satyagraha", Pamphlet no. 1, in A. Teltumbde, *Iconoclast: A Reflective Biography of Dr Babasaheb Ambedkar* (Gurgaon: Penguin, 2024).

Morton, S. (ed.), *John Morton of Trinidad* (Toronto: Westminster Co., 1916).

Muhammad, K.G., *The Condemnation of Blackness: Race, Crime, and the Making of Modern Urban America* (Cambridge, MA: Harvard University Press, [2010] 2019).

Naipaul, V. S., *India: A Million Mutinies Now* (New York: Viking, 1990).

Natarajan, B., "Misrepresenting Caste and Race", *Seminar* 572 (April 2007), pp. 65–6.

Natarajan, B. and P. Greenough (eds.), *Against Stigma: Studies in Caste, Race and Justice Since Durban* (Hyderabad: Orient BlackSwan, 2008).

Newsday, "Epic Hanuman Chalisa ChanTTing at the Divali Nagar", *Trinidad and Tobago Newsday*, 25 April 2024, https://newsday.co.tt/2024/04/26/epic-hanuman-chalisa-chantting-at-the-divali-nagar/.

Niehoff, A., "The Function of Caste among the Indian of Oropuche Lagoon, Trinidad", in Barton M. Schwartz (ed.), *Caste in Overseas Indian Communities* (California: Chandler Publishing House, 1967), pp. 149–66.

Nimgade, N., *In the Tiger's Shadow: The Autobiography of an Ambedkarite* (Delhi: Navayana, 2011).

Niranjana, T., *Mobilizing India: Women, Migration and Music between India and Trinidad* (Durham: Duke University Press, 2006).

O'Hanlon, R., "In the Presence of Witnesses: Petitioning and Judicial 'Publics' in Western India, circa 1600–1820", *Modern Asian Studies* 53, no. 1 (2019), pp. 52–88, 10.1017/S0026749X17000968.

Oonk, G., *Settled Strangers: Asian Business Elites in East Africa (1800–2000)* (New Delhi: Sage Publications, 2013).

BIBLIOGRAPHY

Padmanabh, S., "Census in Colonial India and the Birth of Caste", *Economic and Political Weekly* 46, no. 33 (2011), pp. 51–8.

Pantawane, G., "Evolving a New Identity: The Development of a Dalit Culture", in B. Joshi (ed.), *Untouchable! Voices of the Dalit Liberation Movement* (London: Zed Books, 1986), pp. 79–86.

——, "Presidential Address", Pahile Vishwa Marathi Sahiya Sammelan San Jose (US), 14, 15, 16 February 2009.

——, *Patrakaar Dr. Babasaheb Ambedkar (Journalist Dr Ambedkar)* (Nagpur: Abhijit Prakashan, 1987).

Parry, J.P., *Caste and Kinship in Kangra* (London: Routledge, [1979] 2015).

Patil, S. *Caste-Feudal Servitude: the Studies in Jati-based Feudalism, Its Philosophies and Aesthetics* (Shirur: Mavlai Prakashan, 2006).

Patton, S., "White People Are Speaking Up at Protests: How Do We Know They Mean What They Say?", *Washington Post*, 2 June 2020, https://www.washingtonpost.com/outlook/2020/06/02/white-people-black-protests/.

Paul, R., "A Brief Biography of Bhante Abhipassano, Formerly Mr. Darshan Ram Jassal", *Golden Jubilee Souvenir* (Wolverhampton: Dr Ambedkar Memorial Committee of Great Britain, 21 July 2019), pp. 31–5.

Pawar, J.V., *Ambedkarottar Ambedkari Chalwal*, vol. 1 (Mumbai: Asmita Communications, 2018).

——, *Ambedkarottar Ambedkari Chalwal*, vol. 4 (3rd edn, Mumbai: Asmita Communications, [2010] 2022).

——, *Dalit Panthers: An Authoritative History* (New Delhi: Forward Press, 2017).

Pawariya, A., "The Modi Legacy No One Is Talking About: He Is Following in Footsteps of Ahilyabai Holkar by Revamping Hindu Holy Sites", *Swarajya*, 9 October 2020, https://swarajyamag.com/politics/the-modi-legacy-no-one-is-talking-about-he-is-following-in-footsteps-of-ahilyabai-holkar-by-revamping-hindu-holy-sites.

Porter, J., "Caste in India", *American Anthropologist* VIII (January 1895), pp. 23–30.

Prashad, V., "Afro-Dalits of the Earth, Unite!", *African Studies Review* 43, no. 1 (2000), pp. 189–201.

——, "Badges of Color: An Afro-Dalit Story", *Z Magazine*, March 2000, http://www.hartford-hwp.com/archives/52a/073.html.

———, *The Karma of Brown Folk* (Minneapolis: University of Minnesota Press, 2001).

———, *Untouchable Freedom: A Social History of a Dalit Community* (Delhi: Oxford University Press, 2000).

Pyper, D., "The Equality Act 2010: Caste Discrimination", Briefing Paper no. 06862, 3 August 2018, House of Commons Library, https://researchbriefings.files.parliament.uk/documents/SN06862/SN06862.pdf.

Qin, A., "Newsom Vetoes Bill Banning Caste Discrimination", *New York Times*, 7 October 2023, https://www.nytimes.com/2023/10/07/us/california-caste-discrimination.html.

Raheja, G.G., *The Poison in the Gift: Ritual, Prestation, and the Dominant Caste in a North Indian Village* (Chicago: University of Chicago Press, 1988).

Ramchandran, A., "Dalit Film and Cultural Festival: Celebrating Dalit Cinema in New York", *New Indian Express*, 23 February 2019, https://www.newindianexpress.com/entertainment/tamil/2019/Feb/23/celebrating-dalit-cinema-1942692.html.

Rangaswamy, P., *Namasté America: Indian Immigrants in an American Metropolis* (University Park: Pennsylvania State University Press, 2000).

Ranjan, P. (ed.), *Mahishahur: A People's Hero* (New Delhi: The Marginalised and Forward Press, 2017).

Ratha, D., "Resilient Remittances", *Back to Basics*, International Monetary Fund, September 2023.

Ravikumar, "Iyothee Thass and the Politics of Naming", *Sunday Pioneer*, 28 September 2005, https://www.countercurrents.org/dalit-ravikumar280905.htm.

Rawlinson, H.G., *Intercourse between India and the Western World from the Earliest Times to the Fall of Rome* (Cambridge: Cambridge University Press, 1916).

Reddock, R., "Freedom Denied: Indian Women and Indentureship in Trinidad and Tobago, 1845–1917", *Economic and Political Weekly* 20, no. 43 (1985), pp. WS79–87.

———, "Indian Women and Indentureship in Trinidad and Tobago, 1845–1917: Freedom Denied", *Caribbean Quarterly* 54, no. 4 (2008), pp. 41–68.

Reddy, G., "'Our Blood Is Becoming White': Race, Religion and Siddi Becoming in Hyderabad, India", *American Anthropologist* 126, no. 2 (2024), pp. 1–10.

Risen, C., *The Bill of the Century: The Epic Battle for the Civil Rights Act* (London: Bloomsbury Press, 2014).

Risley, H.H., *The Tribes and Castes of Bengal: Ethnographic Glossary*, vols. 1 and 2 (Calcutta: Bengal Secretariat Press, 1892), https://archive.org/details/TheTribesAndCastesOfBengal/page/n9/mode/2up.

——, *The Tribes and Castes of India*, 2 vols. (Calcutta: Bengal Secretariat Press, 1891).

Roopnarine, L., *Indo-Caribbean Indenture Resistance and Accommodation, 1838–1920* (Kingston, Jamaica: University of West Indies Press, 2007).

Rutgers University Task Force on Caste Discrimination, *Caste-Based Discrimination in U.S. Higher Education and at Rutgers*, August 2024, https://rutgersaaup.org/wp-content/uploads/2024/08/Rutgers-Caste-Report-August-2024.pdf

Ryan, S. and T. Stewart, *The Black Power Revolution of 1970: A Retrospective* (St Augustine, Trinidad and Tobago: I.S.E.R., University of the West Indies, 1995).

Sahay, A., *Indian Diaspora in the United States: Brain Drain or Gain* (Lanham MD: Lexington Books, 2009).

Samaroo, S., *Adrian Cola Rienzi: The Life and Times of an Indo-Caribbean Progressive* (Macoya, Trinidad: Royards Publishing Company Limited, 2022).

Sarbanes, P., "Senator Paul S. Sarbanes to Dr Laxmi Berwa, August 17, 1982", Archives of Laxmi Berwa.

Sathe, A.B., "Presidential Address, Mumbai, 2 March 1958", in Arjun Dangle (ed.), *Dalit Sahitya: Ek Abhyas* (Mumbai: Maharashtra State Literature-Culture Society, 1978), pp. 191–5.

Schermerhorn, R.A., "When Did Indian Materialism Get Its Distinctive Titles?", *Journal of the American Oriental Society* 50 (1930), pp. 132–8.

Schiller, N.G. and G.E. Fouron, "The Generation of Identity: Redefining the Second Generation within a Transnational Social Field", in P. Levitt and N.C. Walters (eds.), *The Changing Face of Home: The Transnational Lives of the Second Generation* (New York: Russell Sage Foundation, 2002), pp. 168–208.

Schwartz, B.M., "Caste and Endogamy in Trinidad", *Southwestern Journal of Anthropology* 20, no. 1 (1964), pp. 58–66.

—— (ed.), *Caste in Overseas Indian Communities* (California: Chandler Publishing House, 1967).

Senart, E., *Caste in India*, translated by E. Denison Ross (London: Methuen, 1930).

Shaikh, J., *Outcaste Bombay: City Making and the Politics of the Poor* (Seattle: University of Washington Press, 2021).

Shankar, S., *An Uneasy Embrace: Africa, India and the Spectre of Race* (London: Hurst and Co., 2021).

Shellow, R. (ed.), *The Harvest of American Racism: The Political Meaning of Violence in the Summer of 1967* (Ann Arbor: University of Michigan Press, 2018).

Singh, H., *Recasting Caste: From the Sacred to the Profane* (New Delhi: Sage, 2014).

Singh, S.A., "Hinduism and the State in Trinidad", *Inter-Asia Cultural Studies* 6, no. 3 (2005), pp. 353–65.

Sirsat, P., "A Milestone Movement: Hope and Disillusionment", *Outlook*, 15 August 2023, Dalit Panthers Independence Day Special Issue, pp. 66–70.

Smith, J.M., "Introduction", to Frederick Douglass, *My Bondage and My Freedom*, https://www.gutenberg.org/files/202/202-h/202-h.htm#link2H_4_0032.

Souza, J.D., "Parasram, Man of the People", *Trinidad and Tobago Newsday*, 27 October 2019, https://newsday.co.tt/2019/10/27/parasram-man-of-the-people/.

Spivak, G., "Debate on Postmodernism (1984)", YouTube, 14 May 2023, https://www.youtube.com/watch?v=cVfTgiE4FAY.

Strabo, *The Geography of Strabo*, vol. 1, translated by H.C. Hamilton and W. Falconer (London: Henry G. Bohn, 1858).

Subramanian, A., "Indians in North Carolina: Race, Class, and Culture in the Making of Immigrant Identity", *Comparative Studies of South Asia, Africa and the Middle East* 20, no. 1, (2000), pp. 105–14.

Sumner, C., *The Question of Caste: Lecture by Hon. Charles Sumner* (Boston: Wright and Potter, 1869), https://www.loc.gov/item/43049574/.

Sundaram, S. and V. Thakur, "A Pragmatic Methodology for Studying

International Practices", *Journal of International Political Theory* 17, no. 3 (2021), pp. 337–55.

Tamhane, A., "Dalit Panther la pannashit tarun karnaare don divas!", *Loksatta*, 30 May 2022, https://www.loksatta.com/maharashtra/dalit-panther-meeting-50-years-of-dalit-panther-50th-anniversary-of-dalit-panther-party-70-2949304/.

Teltumbde, A., *Dalits, Past, Present and Future* (New Delhi: Routledge, 2017).

Thakur, V., "When India Proposed a Casteist Solution to South Africa's Racist Problem", *The Wire*, 4 April 2017, https://thewire.in/diplomacy/exploring-casteism-in-indias-foreign-policy/amp/.

Thorat, S., *Dalits in India: Search for a Common Destiny* (New Delhi: Sage, 2009).

Tilak, B.G., *The Arctic Home in the Vedas: Being Also a New Key to the Interpretation of Many Vedic Texts and Legends* (Poona: Kesari; Bombay: Messrs. Ramchandra Govind and Son, 1903).

United Nations, "Addressing Indian Council of World Affairs, Secretary-General Urges India to Be 'Driver' in Transformative Push towards Peace, Human Rights, Clean Development", United Nations Press SG/SM/16459, 12 January 2015, https://press.un.org/en/2015/sgsm16459.doc.htm.

———, *Report of the Committee on the Elimination of Racial Discrimination*, Committee on the Elimination of Racial Discrimination (CERD), 61st Session, 5–23 August 2002 (New York: United Nations, 2002).

Veena, D., "The Uses of Liminality: Society and Cosmos in Hinduism", *Contributions to Indian Sociology* 10, no. 2 (1976), pp. 245–63.

Veer, P.V. and S. Vertovec, "Brahmanism Abroad: On Caribbean Hinduism as an Ethnic Religion", *Ethnology* 30, no. 2 (1991), pp. 149–66.

Venkatswamy, P.R., *Our Struggle for Emancipation* (Hyderabad: Hyderabad Book Trust, 2020).

Verma, S., "India Enters 'Amrit Kaal' with Growing Atrocities against Dalits", NewsClick, 2 October 2022, https://www.newsclick.in.

Vertovec, S., *Hindu Trinidad: Religion, Ethnicity and Socio-economic Change* (Basingstoke: Palgrave Macmillan, 1992).

———, *Transnationalism* (London: Routledge, 2009).

VISION, "Letter from Laxmi Berwa, President of VISION to Indira Gandhi, July 7, 1982", Archives of Laxmi Berwa.

BIBLIOGRAPHY

Vittorini, S.S., "Modi and the Mahatma: The Politics of Statues and the Saffronisation of India–Africa Relations", in K. King and M. Venkatachalam (eds.), *India's Development Diplomacy and Soft Power in Africa*. (Woodbridge, UK: Boydell and Brewer, 2021), pp. 79–98.

Waghmare, J.M., "American Negro Vangmay: Prerana āni Pravrutti" (American Negro Literature: Motivation and Tendency).

———, "Negro Vangmay va Dalit Vangmay", *Maay Marathi*, Dalit Sahitya Visheshank, August 1975, in A. Dangle (ed.), *Dalit Sahitya: Ek Abhyas* (Mumbai: Maharashtra State Literature-Culture Society, 1978), pp. 179–88.

———, *Negro Vangmay Ani Dalit Chalwal* (American Negro: Literature and Culture) (Pune: Padmagandha Prakashan, 1978).

———, "The Problem of Identity in the Postwar American Negro Novel with Special Reference to Ralph Ellison and James Baldwin", PhD thesis, Marathwada University, Aurangabad, November 1979, https://shodhganga.inflibnet.ac.in/handle/10603/104797.

———, *The Quest for Black Identity: A Critical Study of Postwar American Black Novel* (Pune: Sugava Prakashan, 2001).

Waghmore, S., *Civility against Caste: Dalits Politics and Citizenship in Western India* (London and Delhi: Sage, 2013).

———, "From Hierarchy to Hindu Politeness: Caste Atrocities and Dalit Protest in Rural Marathwada", in S. Jodhka and J. Manor (eds.), *Contested Hierarchies, Persisting Influence: Caste and Power in Twenty-First Century India* (Hyderabad: Orient BlackSwan, 2017), pp. 111–39.

Wankhede, M. N., "Bandachaya yashasvitesaathi atmashodh aavshyak", in Arjun Dangle (ed.), *Dalit Sahitya: Ek Abhyas* (Mumbai: Maharashtra State Literature-Culture Society, 1978), pp. 24–30.

———, "Bejabaabdaar Lekhakanchi Saddi Sampleli Aahe (Friends! Time Is Up for the Irresponsible Writers)", Presidential Address, Dalit Sahitya Sammelan, 17 January 1976, in A. Dangle (ed.), *Dalit Sahitya: Ek Abhyas* (Mumbai: Maharashtra State Literature-Culture Society, 1978), pp. 231–43.

Wankhede, M.N., V.L. Kulkarni, R.G. Jadhav, M.P. Rege and M.B. Chitnis, "Maharashtratil Aaj Udayache Samskrutik Sangharsh āni Vangmayin Samasya", *Asmita*, issue 1, Discussion dates: 16 November 1967 to 21 November 1967, reproduced in A. Dangle (ed.), *Dalit*

Sahitya: Ek Abhyas (Mumbai: Maharashtra State Literature-Culture Society, 1978), pp. 1–20.

Wilkerson, I., *Caste: The Origins of Our Discontents* (New York: PRH, 2020).

Yengde, S., "Ambedkar's Foreign Policy and the Ellipsis of 'Dalit' from the International Activism", in S. Yengde and A. Teltumbde (eds.), *The Radical in Ambedkar: Critical Reflections* (Gurgaon: Allen Lane, 2018), pp. 86–106.

——, "American Caste: A Secret History", *Michigan Quarterly Review*, Special Issue: Fractured Union: American Democracy on the Brink, 61 (September 2022), pp. 700–8.

——, "At Japan Convention, Dalit and Burakumin People Forge Solidarity", 11 Oct 2018, *The Wire*, 11 October 2018, https://thewire.in/caste/at-japan-convention-dalit-and-burakumin-people-forge-solidarity.

——, *Caste Matters* (Gurgaon: Penguin Random House, 2019).

——, "Chronicling the Dalit Panthers", *Dalit Panthers*, Independence Day Special Issue, 15 August 2023, pp. 58–61.

——, "Dalitality: Jats in the Modern World", *Indian Express*, 24 December 2023, https://indianexpress.com/article/opinion/columns/jats-in-india-history-lifestyle-statewise-jats-numbers-in-india-9080587/.

——, "Dalit in Black America: Race, Caste and the Making of Dalit–Black Archive", *Public Culture* 35, no. 1 (2023), pp. 21–41.

——, "Do. Baabaasaaheb Aanbedkr yaanchyaa muknaaykchi aajhi garj kaa aahe?", BBC Marathi, 31 January 2020, https://www.bbc.com/marathi/india-51311062.

——, "How a Chemical Engineer Became the Ambassador of International Dalit Movement", *The Print*, 26 August 2018, https://theprint.in/opinion/how-a-chemical-engineer-became-the-ambassador-of-international-dalit-movement/105638/.

——, "Iterations of Shared Dalit–Black Solidarity", *The Seminar* 737, no. 1 (2021), pp. 83–96.

——, "The Nation Maker", in R. Kaur and N. Mathur (eds.), *The People of India: New Indian Politics in the 21st Century* (Gurgaon: Penguin Viking, 2022), pp. 1–16.

——, "South–South Migration: An Ethnographic Study of an Indian

Business District in Johannesburg", PhD thesis, Interdisciplinary Social Sciences, University of the Witwatersrand, 2016.

——, "Supreme Subalterns", in M. Banerjee and J.J.P. Wouters (eds.), *Subaltern Studies 2.0 Being against the Capitalocene* (Chicago: Prickly Paradigm Press, 2022), pp. 191–206.

——, "Why Hinduism and the Violence of Caste Are Two Sides of a Coin", *Huffington Post*, 20 May 2016, http://www.huffingtonpost.in/suraj-yengde/why-hinduism-and-the-viol_b_10059872.html.

Zelizer, J.E., "Introduction to the 2016 Edition of The Kerner Report", *The Kerner Report: National Advisory Commission on Civil Disorders* (Princeton: Princeton University Press, 2016).

Zelliot, E., "Dalit: New Cultural Context for an Old Marathi World", in *From Untouchable to Dalit: Essays on the Ambedkar Movement* (New Delhi: Manohar, 1992), pp. 261–92.

INDEX

Abdullah, Omar, 115
Abhipassano, Bhante, 222–3
Abu Dhabi, 234
ABVP. *See* Akhil Bharatiya Vidyarthi Parishad (ABVP)
Achutanand, Swami, 28
Adi Dravida, 48
Adi-Dravidan (monthly journal), 49
Aditya Purana, 9
Adivasi Mahasabha, 56
Adivasis, 39, 41, 95, 97–9, 101, 102, 103, 104, 114, 121, 132
Africa
    migration of labouring class, 199
Ahir, 33, 184, 191
Akhil Bharatiya Vidyarthi Parishad (ABVP), 175
Alexander, 6
Amar, Pandit, 264
Ambedkar Association of North America, 231

Ambedkar Center for Justice and Peace (ACJP), 128
Ambedkar Innovative Mission, 254
Ambedkar International Mission (AIM), 228–34
    in Bahrain, 251–4
    in Malaysia, 228, 229–30
    UAE, 242–4 in
    in the United States, 230–4
Ambedkar International Mission, 130
Ambedkar Jayanti, 208, 241, 244, 246
Ambedkar Nagar, 17
Ambedkar, Dr B.R., 2–3, 16, 18, 28–9, 41–2, 44, 50, 87, 192
    caste, readings of, 30–5
    conversion to Buddhism, 216
    Dalit modern writings, 48–52
    Dalit Panthers, 100–7
    Dalit separatism, 38–9
    on Dalit term, 100–2

INDEX

Dalit literature and its politics, 53–9
Dalit-land, 107–11
diplomacy, casteism in, 111–18
Eklavya's story, 223–4
Gandhian intervention, 123–6
network of Dalits, 206–7
109th anniversary of the birth, 223
scholarship programmes, 198, 206
speech of 1935, 224
See also Buddhism; "Poona Pact"; Round Table Conference
Ambedkar, Yashwant, 55
Ambedkarism, 79, 108–10
Ambedkarite diasporic consciousness, 197–8
Ambedkarite organizations, 208–13
categories, 208–9
cultural diplomacy, 208, 213
enquiring about, 209–10
Middle East, 234–47, 251–4
struggle for equality, 210
UK, 218–28
US, 228–34
Ambedkarwadi Sahitya Sammelan, 57
America. See United States (US)
American Civil War, 60, 96
American Negro: Sahitya *āni* Sankruti (American Negro: Literature and Culture), 69–70
Amsterdam, 125
Anderson, Benedict, 204

Andhra Pradesh, 184
Annamalai, Velu, 130–1
Annan, Kofi, 17
anti-caste activism Nepalese youth efforts, 213
anti-caste Ambedkarite networks, 207
anti-caste-conscious mobility, 206–7
anti-Muslim rhetoric, 263
Antyaja, 9–10
Apte, S.S., 171–2
Aranguez, 157
Arrian, 7
Arya Samaj, 16, 24, 26, 156–7
The Asian American Commission of the Commonwealth of Massachusetts, 119
Asmita (Sense of Identity) (periodical), 65
Asmitadarsh Sahitya Melava, 56
Asmitadarsh, 65–9, 79, 82
ASP, 44
AT&T Bell, 127
Athawale, Ramdas, 58, 59, 135
Aurangabad, 20, 54, 56, 59, 63–5
Australia, 93, 255, 266
Austria, 255
Ayodhya Temple, 180–1, 189
Azad Samaj Party (ASP), 250

Babri Mosque, demolition of, 211
Backward Castes, 40, 41, 43, 69, 190, 211
See also Mandal Commission
Badhatua, 10

INDEX

Bagul, 68
Bahadur, Gaiutra, 185
Bahishkrit Bharat (Outcaste India) (periodical), 50
Bahrain, 239
AIM in, 251–4
Buddhist Ambedkarites, 216a
Bahujan Samaj Party (BSP), 42, 44, 103, 228, 238
overseas supporters of, 247–51
Bahujans (subaltern majority), 44
Bains, Bishan Dass, 225–7
Baldwin, James, 71, 82
BAMCEF (Backward and Minorities Central Employees Federation), 41–2, 44, 130, 197, 228, 245
Banaras Hindu University, 157
Bangalore, 172
Bangladesh War (1971), 127
Baniyas, 84, 87, 149
Bansode, Fagoji, 50
Barve, Anil, 102
Barwe, V.N., 50
Bayly, Susan, 30, 32, 34, 40
BDP. *See* Bhartiya Dalit Panthers (BDP)
Belgium, 93
Benares (Varanasi), 172–3
Bengal, 5
Bengali, 88
Berwa, Dr Laxmi Narain, 18, 114, 127–8, 129, 136, 215, 266
Bhagavad Gita, 10, 163, 186–7
Bhandare, R.D., 55
Bharat Sevashram Sangh, 167
Bharat Varsha, 177

Bharat, Chief Ricardo, 178
Bhartiya Dalit Panthers (BDP), 58–9, 126, 135
Bharatiya Janata Party (BJP), 42, 181, 232, 262
Bhoite, A., 57
Bhoite, U., 57
Bhojpuri, 190
Bhoomika (position document), 64, 101, 102, 113
Bhumihar, 34
Bible, 187
Bihar, 5, 34, 162, 184, 188, 253
al-Bīrūnī, 8–11
Bisram, 148
Black American literature, 51, 52–3, 59–63
Black Consciousness movement, 102
Black History Month, 131
Black Lives Matter, 75, 93, 95, 96–7, 119, 125, 130, 137, 257, 258
Black Panther (newsletter), 88, 110
Black Panther Party, 58, 88, 101, 128–9
 See also Dalit Panther movement
Black people, 47, 61–2, 70, 72, 80, 81, 83, 90–1, 93, 95–8, 103, 111, 118–23, 131–2, 150
Black population
Waghmare and literature, 69–73
#BlackLivesMatter, 94
blue-collar workers, 206, 250
Blunt, E.A.H., 27
Bodhi, Bhante Chandra, 223–4, 251, 252

359

INDEX

Bombay
Dalit Panthers, 100–7
Borkar, B.D., 44
Borkar, Shrikant, 205
Boston, 130
Boudh Sahitya Parishad, 56
Brahman Samaj of North
    America, 210–11
Brahmanism, 8, 12, 25–6, 76, 141, 148
    Caribbean, sanatanists of, 157–61
    diplomacy, casteism in, 111–18
    Hindu identity, 161–2
    Non-brahman pandit, 165–71
    Trinidadian Hindus, 152–7
    Trinidadian, identity in, 164–5
    See also Bharatiya Janata Party (BJP)
    See also Economically Backward Castes
Brahmanization, 25
brahmans, 4–5, 9–11, 31, 34, 84, 87, 97
Britain, 93, 117, 182
    Dalits protest against caste, 201
    EHRC Report, Caste, 215
British Columbia, 254, 255, 266
"Broken Men" (Dalits), 3
Bruce, Dickson D., 60
BSP. *See* Bahujan Samaj Party (BSP)
Buddhism, 2, 12, 102, 137, 138, 189
Buddhism, radicalism of, 222–5
Buddhist Ambedkarites, 216

See also DAMC (Dr Ambedkar Memorial Committee of Great Britain)
Buddhist Society of India, 44
Burj Khalifa, 248
Burma, 49, 151

Calcutta, 183, 184
California State University, 213
California textbook issue, 209
California, 78, 117
Campu Temple, 167
Canada, 127, 158
    Buddhist Ambedkarites, 216, 222
    International Dalit Conference (Vancouver, 2003), 254–5
    International Day of Equality, 255
Caribbean, 142, 151–2, 193
    sanatanists of, 157–61, 199, 262, 264
caste-based politics, 202, 210
caste-based religious order, 200
caste-based rituals, 201
casteism, 99
"Castes in India", 32
Census Commissioner, 25
Ceylon (Sri Lanka), 49, 151
Chaguanas, 180
Chamar, 149, 155, 163–4, 184, 185–6, 190–1
Chamarin, 184
Chandals, 5, 7, 10, 12, 271
Charvakas, 12
Chennai, 131
Chetna Association, 254–5

INDEX

Chicago, 90
China, 5, 110
Chinmayananda Ashram, 169
Chinnaiah, E.V., 114
Chitnis, M.B., 65
Chitpavan, 34
Chokamela, 15
Christian Dalits, 215
Christianity, 59, 150, 153, 161, 200
Christians, 24, 60, 97, 98, 121, 153, 161
Chuhras, 24
Cisco, 117
Civil Rights Act (1964) (America), 96, 106–7
Clarke, Colin, 146, 148
Cleaver, Eldridge, 82
Cleaver, Kathleen, 108
Columbus, Christopher, 178
Committee on the Elimination of Racial Discrimination (CERD), 114–17
Common Law Admission Test (CLAT), 253
Cuba, 110
Cullen, Countee, 62, 71
Cunupia, 167

Dadar, 56
Dalit, 16–21, 23–8
  African American literature, 59–63
  caste scholarship, subjectivity of, 14–16
  Dalit Panthers, 100–7
  dalit politics and organizing, 40–1
  dalit separatism, 38–9
  on Dalit term, Ambedkar, 100–2
  Dalit–Black Lives Matter, 130–2
  Dalit-land, 107–11
  literature and its politics, 53–9
  modern writing. 48–52
  pre-modern Dalit modernity, 12–14
  subjectivity of, caste in, 36–8
  Waghmare and literature, 69–73
  World Marathi Literary Conference, 78–82
  See also Buddhism; Christianity; Islam
Dalit Bandhu, 50
Dalit Convention (1998), 152
Dalit diaspora, theorization, 202–5
Dalit Federation, 101
Dalit Film and Cultural Festival, 233
Dalit History Month, 131
Dalit mobility, 199–200
Dalit Natya Parishad, 56
Dalit Natya Sammelan, 56–7
Dalit Ninad (1947), 50
Dalit organizations
  Ambedkar's philosophy, 198–9
  Ambedkarite organization, 208–13
  region, religion and castes in, 213–18
Dalit Panther movement, 58–9, 78–9, 86, 100–7, 135
  diplomacy, casteism in, 111–18

INDEX

Dalit Panthers of India, 135
Dalit Panthers: An Authoritative History (Pawar), 132–3
Dalit Sahitya Parishad, 56
Dalit Sahitya Sansad, 56
Dalit Sevak, 50
Dalit Shoshit Samaj Sangharsh Samiti, 103
Dalit Women's Advancement of Nepal, 213
"Dalitsthan", 108
DAMC (Dr Ambedkar Memorial Committee of Great Britain), 219–22
    Buddhism, radicalism of, 222–5
    narratives of, 225–8
Dangle, Arjun, 64
Darshan Ram Jassal, 223
Darwin's theory, 29
Darwinism, 29
Das, Bhagwan, 18, 114
Das, Keshav, 187
Davis, Angela, 108, 126
Debe, 185
Deccan, 28, 34
Deen, Shamshu, 188
Delhi, 94, 172
Department of English, 63
Desai, Ashwin, 185
Detroit, 90
Dhale, Raja, 19–20, 51, 106, 132
Dhamma Deeksha Day, 216
Dhamma Group, 236, 237
Dhankar, 184
Dharma, 9
Dhasal, Namdeo, 19, 101–2, 106, 132

Dhoby, 184
"diaspora", term, 202–5
Dihana, J.S., 237–8, 239
Dinmitra (newspaper), 49
Dirks, Nicolas, 31, 32
Diwakar, Chhote Lal, 94
Dom, 10
dominant castes nationwide protests (1990s), 201
Dostoevsky, 71
Douglass, Frederick, 60
Dr Ambedkar Mission Sabha, 237–9
Dr Ambedkar Museum, 222
Dr Babasaheb Ambedkar Marathwada University, 64, 71
Dravida Pandian (journals), 48
Dravidar Kazhagam (DK), 242
DS-4 (Dalit Shoshit Samaj Sangharsh Samiti), 42
Du Bois, W.E.B., 61–2, 79–80, 88, 105–6, 112, 206, 258–9
Dubai, 234
Dumont, Louis, 31
Durban conference, 115
Durban, 18, 114–15
Durga (goddess), 121
durust group, 55
Dusadh, 184

Economically Backward Class, 40
economy, liberalization of, 201–2, 211
Egypt, 6, 111
Elayaperumal Committee, 106
Ellison, Ralph, 62, 71
England, 60

INDEX

Equality and Human Rights Commission (EHRC), 214
Equiano, Olaudah, 60
European Caucasian race, 29

Facebook, 249, 253
Fa-Hein (Faxian), 5
Fiji, 49
First Indians ("Out of Africa" migrants in India), 4
Floyd, George, 85, 92, 94, 99, 130
Fox News, 136
Fulbright Fellowship, 63

Gaikwad, Bhaurao (Dadasaheb), 54–5
Gainesville, 63
Gait, Edward A., 25
Gamre, Krishna, 135
Gandhi Service League, 152
Gandhi statue, 125
Gandhi, Indira, 127, 215
Gandhi, Mohandas, 38, 124
    See also "Poona Pact"; Round Table Conference
Ganpati festivals, 163
Garud (1926) (newspaper), 50
Gayatri Mantra, 167
General Register of Indian Immigrants, 144
Geneva, 18
Germany, 93
Ghana, 111
Ghazni, Mahmud, 8
Gillon, 91
Gilroy, Paul, 202
Ginsburg, David, 91

Gita, 160
Golconda, 192
Gond, 184
Gosain brahmans, 146
Government of India Act (1935), 27–8
Government of India, 69
Greene, Petey, 129
Griha, Lokvangmay (Waghmare), 70
Gujar, 33
Gujarati, 88
Gulamgiri (Slavery) (Phule), 104
Gupta, Dipankar, 116–17
Guru, Gopal, 100
Guyana, 180
Gyaan Deepak Kirtan Mandali (GDKM), 157–8

Hadi, 10
Hamas, 136
Hammon, Jupiter, 60
Hanuman Chalisa, 162–3, 179, 189
Hanuman Jayanti, 163
Hanuman, 162–4, 179–81
Haraksingh, Kusha, 153, 157
Harappan lands, 4
Hardas, L.N., 50
Harijan Mandir, 186–90
Harijan, 186–90
Harlem Renaissance, 62, 70–1
Harlem, 62, 90
Harvard University, 122
Harvest of Racism, The (document), 91
Haryana, 33

363

INDEX

Hathras gang rape incident (2020), 189
Hayden, Robert, 108
Hayley, Alex, 82
Hermitage village, 192
Herodotus, 6
Hindi, 88, 148, 159, 168, 181, 190, 191, 193
Hindi-speaking Dalits, 214
Hindu Maha Sabha, 165
Hindu Prachar Kendra, 172–3
Hinduism Today (magazine), 174
Hinduism, 2, 11, 26, 99, 155, 160
    Caribbean, sanatanists of, 157-61
    caste scholarship, subjectivity of, 14–16
    cultural differences, 118–23
    Dalit Panthers, 100–7
    dalit politics and organizing, 40–1
    dalit separatism, 38–9
    dalit subjectivity, caste in, 36–8
    on Dalit term, Ambedkar, 100–2
    Dalit–Black Lives Matter, 130–2
    Dalit-land, 107–11
    diplomacy, casteism in, 111–18
    Hindu identity, 161-2
    Hindu right-wing, 171-83
    identity in, 164-5
    modern writing. 48–52
    pre-modern Dalit modernity, 12–14
    racism, 89–93
    literature and its politics, 53–9
    Trinidadian Hindus, 152-7
    Waghmare and literature, 69–73
    World Marathi Literary Conference, 78–82
Hindus, 9, 13, 24, 74, 140
    Caribbean, sanatanists of, 157-61
    dalit separatism, 38–9
    Hindu identity, 161-2
    Hindu right-wing, 171-83
    identity in, 164-5
    Trinidadian Hindus, 152-7
Hindutva, 262
History of Caste in India (Ketkar), 32
Hiwrale, Sukhram, 65
Holkar, Ahilyabai, 173
Hough, 90
Houston, 66
Howard University, 129
Hughes, Langston, 62, 71, 80–2, 108
human rights activists, 205
Human Rights Commission, 266
Hurston, Zora Neale, 62, 71

Ibrahim, Dato' Seri Anwar, 152
indentured migration/indentured labourers, 199–200, 203, 272
India, 1, 47, 73, 158
    African American literature, 59–63
    caste scholarship, subjectivity of, 14–16
    cultural differences, 118–23
    Dalit Panthers, 100–7

INDEX

dalit politics and organizing, 40–1
dalit separatism, 38–9
dalit subjectivity, caste in, 36–8
on Dalit term, Ambedkar, 100–2
Dalit–Black Lives Matter, 130–2
Dalit-land, 107–11
diplomacy, casteism in, 111–18
literature and its politics, 53–9
modern writing, 48–52
pre-modern Dalit modernity, 12–14
racism, 89–93
Waghmare and literature, 69–73
World Marathi Literary Conference, 78–82
Indian American Forum for Political Education, 122
Indian Americans, 201
Indian Christians, 24
Indian Constitution, 125
Indian emigration, post-1990s, 212
Indian Institutes of Management and Technology, 212
Indian National Congress, 42, 54–7, 106, 124, 127
Indian Ocean, 199
Indian Premier League, 118
Indian Progressive Front (IPF), 229–30
Indian Workers' Association, 226
Indica (Megasthenes), 5, 7–8
Indonesia, 111
Indo-Trinidadians, 204
Indrani, Pandita, 190
Interesting Narrative of the Life of Olaudah Equiano, or Gustavus Vassa, the African, The (Equiano), 60
International Commission for Dalit Rights, 213
International Convention on the Elimination of All Forms of Racial Discrimination, 114
International Dalit Conference (Vancouver, 2003), 254–5
Internationalism, 59
Islam, 8, 10, 150, 153, 200
Islamism, 59
Israel, 85
Israel–Palestine war, 136
IT professionals, 211

Jadhav, R.G., 65
Jaidath, 160–1
Jakhu, Lashkari Ram, 239
Janata (The People) (weekly), 50, 56
Janata Dal, 55–6
Janta Colony, 17
Japanese Buddhism, 225
Jatav, Vikas Kumar, 94
Jawahar Navodaya school, 252–3
Jewish immigrants, 202
Jim Crow and Civil Rights Movement, 64–5
Johannesburg, 125
Johns Hopkins University, 127
Johnson, Lyndon B., 90, 91–2

INDEX

Joshi, Barbara, 68

Kabir Panth Association (KPA), 165
Kabir, 15, 165
Kamathipura, 106
Kamble, Arun, 58
Kamble, B.C., 55
Kamble, Raju, 130, 228–9, 230, 232, 242, 243, 252
Kannada, 88
Kapila, 9
Kapu, 184
Kapur, Devesh, 201
Kardak, Sandeep, 243
Karnataka, 184
Karunakaran, D., 228–9
Kashi Vishwanath Dham, 173–4
Kashi Vishwanath Temple, 173
Kathina programme, 220
Kavtha, 69
Kerala, 94, 254
Kerner Commission, 90–1
Kerner Jr., Gov. Otto, 90–1
Kerner report, 92
Ketkar, S.V., 32
Khaparde, D.K., 41
Kitab-ul-Hind (History of India) (al-Bīrūnī), 8, 11
Kolhapur, 20
Koli, 33
Kori, 184
KPA. *See* Kabir Panth Association (KPA)
Krishna, 10, 160, 187
Kshatriyas, 35, 154
Kulkarni, V.L., 65

Kumar, Muthu, 242
Kumar, R.S. Praveen, 248
Kumar, Vivek, 152, 210–11
Kurmi (a non-elite agrarian caste), 33, 165, 171
Kurundkar, Narahar, 70, 74–5
Kuwait Ambedkarites, 236–42
    Dr Ambedkar Mission Sabha, 237–9
    Viduthalai Chiruthaigal Katchi (VCK) cadres, 240–2

LA Times (newspaper), 110
Labour Party, 226
Lakshman, 180
Lal, Brij, 185
Latur, 69
Laws of Manu. *See* Manusmriti (Laws of Manu)
League of Nations, 206
LeRoi Jones (Amiri Baraka), 82
LGBTIQ+ communities, 160
Linlithgow, Lord, 39
Lodh, 184
Lohar, 184
Lokayats, 12
London, 125
"long-distance activism", 204–5
long-term activism, 205
Luther King Jr., Martin, 88, 92, 124
Luther King, Martin, 126

Madiga, 184
Mahabharata, 177, 223–4
Mahad, 74
Maharaj brahmans, 146

INDEX

Maharaj, Ravindranath (Ravi), 171–83, 193
Maharaj, Sam, 155
Maharashtra Bouddha Sahitya Sammelan, 74
Maharashtra Dalits, 214
Maharashtra Public Service Commission, 64
Maharashtra State Award, 70
Maharashtra, 55–7, 106, 136
Maharattha (periodical), 50
Maithili, 34
Majoor Patrika (1918–22) (newsletter), 50
Mala, 184
Malaya, 49, 151
Malayalam, 88
Malaysia, 152, 268–9
   AIM in, 228, 229–30
Malaysian Ambedkarites, 267–8
Malaysian Indian Congress (MIC), 229
Malcolm X, 72
Mallaah, 184
Mandal Commission, 103, 201, 211
Manusmriti (Laws of Manu), 3, 5, 11, 74, 188
Maoist, 102
Maratha Malwa kingdom, 173
Maratha, 33
Marathi language, 20, 56, 75, 79, 100
Marathwada, 16, 20, 54, 69
Marava, 33
Martin, Phillip, 270
Marxism, 59
Marxist, 66
Mass Movement, 132
Matai, Buddhram Ramgulaam, 191
Mathias Jr., Charles McC., 127–8
Mathura, 5
Matsya Purana, 9
Mauritius, 49
Maurya, Chandragupta, 5, 6
Mayawati, 42, 247, 250
Mayo, Katherine, 63
Mazhabis, 24
McKay, Claude, 71
McKissick, Floyd, 92
Meghwanshi, Bhanwar, 182
Megasthenes, 5, 6–8, 13
Meshram, Waman, 44
Mhaske, Dayanand, 58
Middle East
   AIM in Bahrain, 251–4
   Ambedkar International Mission (AIM), UAE, 242–4
   Global Ambedkarites of, 234–47
   Kuwait Ambedkarites, 236–42
   VCK cadres, 240–2
Milind College, 56, 63–5
Milind Sahitya Sabha (periodical), 65
minorities, 41, 94, 97, 98, 102, 103, 120, 121
Mochee, 184
Modi, Narendra, 94, 174–5
Mohammed, 180
Mooknayak (Leader of the Voiceless), 50

INDEX

Moolnivasis, 13
Morrison, Toni, 119
Most Backward Class, 40
See also Mandal Commission
Mother India (Mayo), 63
Moynihan Report, 92
Mugowalia, Mangoo Ram, 28
Muhammad, Khalil Gibran, 97
Müller, F. Max, 30
Mulnivasi Sangh (Indigenous Group), 44
Mumbai, 56, 90, 134, 172
Musahar, 184
Muscat, 234
Muslims, 9, 13, 14, 16, 24–5, 26, 69, 98, 99, 121, 122, 132, 140, 150, 153, 180, 185, 189
Mussalis, 24
Mussalman, 184
My Bondage and My Freedom (Douglass), 61

nadurust group, 55
Nagpur, 181
Naipaul, V.S., 102, 134
Namasudra, 5
Nanan, 152
Nanded, 16–17, 136
Narayan Dev, Keshav (Patitpaavandas), 50
Narayan, R.K., 230
Narrative of the Life of Frederick Douglass, an American Slave, Written by Himself (Douglass), 60–1
Natarajan, Balmurli, 116–17

National Archives of Trinidad and Tobago, 183
National Campaign for Dalit Human Rights, 115
National Crime Records Bureau, 94, 136
National Human Rights Commission, 132
Native Son (Wright), 71
Naxalites, 102
Nearchos, 7–8
"The, Negro Artist and the Racial Mountain", 80–1
"Negro Sahitya", 79
"Negro–Dalit sahitya", 69
Nehru, Jawaharlal, 111–12
Nepalese American Social Organization, 213
New Jersey, 90
New York City, 105
New York Post (newspaper), 128
New York Times (newspaper), 90
New York, 62
Newark, 90
Newsom, Gavin, 233–4
Newsweek (newspaper), 90
Niagara Falls, 127
Nicator, Seleucus I, 5
Nidān (journal), 157–8
Nigeria, 60
Nimbalkar, Waman, 65
Niranjana, Tejaswini, 204
Nixon, Richard, 92
Nomadic Tribes, 66
North America, 128
North Carolina, 122
North India, 25, 27, 168

INDEX

North Korea, 110
NRIs (non-resident Indians), 204
Nyang, Sulayman S., 129

Oman, 216, 234, 239
Onesikritos, 7–8
Oppressed Indian, The (journal), 227
Orisha, 180
Orissa, 253
Orkut, 251
Oru Paisa Tamizhan (Tamilan), 49
Other Backward Classes (OBCs), 40, 102–3, 211
  See also Mandal Commission

Pacific Relations Committee conference (Montreal), 206
Palestine, 85
Panday, Basdeo, 164
Pandit, Vijaya Lakshmi, 111
Pandithan, M.G., 226, 229–30
Panjamurthi, Dato, 229, 230
Pantawane, Gangadhar, 53, 65–8, 69, 78–82
Parasaram, Pandit Rampersad, 168–9
Parayan (weekly), 49, 151
Paria, 184
Parivartan Sahitya Mandal, 56
Pasi, 184
Patanjali, 9
Patitpaavan, 50
Patton, Stacey, 93
Pawar, J.V., 102, 106, 108, 132
People of India, The (Risley), 29
Persad-Bissessar, Kamla, 179

Petey Greene's Washington (TV Show), 129
Phule, Jyotirao, 41, 69–70, 78, 104–5, 110
Phule-Ambedkar Panchayat, Dalit, 56
Phule–Shahu–Ambedkar, 67–8
Pillewar, Shailesh, 251, 252
"Poona Pact", 124
post-independence elites, 201
post-war labour shortages, 201
Prabhu, Dr Bharathi, 131
Prabuddha Bharat (Enlightened India) (periodical), 50, 56, 63–4
Pradhan, S.M., 58
Pragatik Vichar Manch Trust, 66
Prasad, Pandit Hari, 157
Prashad, Vijay, 99
Pride vs. Prejudice One Man's Fight against Racism and Inequality (Bains), 226
"Problem of Identity in the Postwar American Negro Novel with Special Reference to Ralph Ellison and James Baldwin" (1980), The, 64
professional-class Dalits, 206, 267
  migration, 200–1
Punjab, 21, 24, 44
Punjab Dalits, 214
Punjab Land Alienation Act (1900.), 271
Punjabi Ambedkarites, 236, 237
  Dr Ambedkar Mission Sabha, 237–9
  Sat Guru Ravidas Sabha, 239

INDEX

Puranas, 9
Purogami Vichar Manch, 56

Qatar, 239

race theory, 1
racism, 18, 91, 92, 94, 95, 105, 111, 112, 120, 132
    anti-racism, 114–18
Rai, Jagdish, 219
Rai, Lala Lajpat, 63
Raidas, 15
Rajasthan, 33
Rajbhoj, P.N., 18, 50, 206
Rajputs, 33
Ralph Ellison, 82
Ram Navami festival, 163
Ram, Kanshi, 41–3, 44, 103, 131, 227, 228, 248
Rama, King, 11, 162–4, 180–1, 185
Ramayana, 141, 163, 162, 167, 177, 180, 191, 264
Ramcharitamanas (Tulsidas), 162, 180
Ramlilas, 192
Randhir, Umakant, 58
Rao, B.S. Venkat, 17
Rashidi, Runoko, 130
Rashtriya Swayamsevak Sangh (RSS), 138, 172, 174–5, 181, 232, 262
    See also Bharatiya Janata Party (BJP)
Rathinam, Rev. John, 48
Rattu, Nanak Chand, 222
Rau, B.N., 112–13

Ravidas *gurudwaras*, 214
Ravidas Jayanti, 208
Ravidas, 192
Ravidasia community, 249
Ravikumar, D., 131
Rawlinson, H.G., 6, 7
Raymane, Professor, 65
realism, 59
Reddock, Rhoda, 185
Reddy, 184
Rege, M.P., 65
religious freedom, 201, 209
religious practices, as part of national identity, 198
Republican Party of India, 42, 54–6, 59, 106
Rienzi, Adrian Cola, 153
Rig Veda, 4, 12, 30
right-wing Hindu fundamentalists, 211
Risley, Herbert Hope, 29
Roopchand, Sreeprasad, 167
Roopnarine, Lamarsh, 157
Rostenkowski, Senator Dan, 127
Round Table Conference, 38, 101
Rupwate, D.D., 55
Rutgers University's Task Force on Caste Discrimination, 266

Sadhu, 190–1
Sadhuji, 185–6
Samant, Sanjay, 252
Samaroo, Brinslee, 153, 188
Samata (Equality), 50
Samata Sainik Dal, 44
Samlal, Siew Kumar, 186
Sammy, Darren, 118

INDEX

Sampurnanand Sanskrit Vishwavidyalaya, 172
San Fernando, 146
San Jose, 78
Sanatan Dharma Maha Sabha (Maha Sabha), 156–7, 168, 170, 178
Sangare, Bhai, 58
sangha (monastic community), 221
Sankhya philosophy, 9
Sanskrit, 155–7, 168, 171
Sant Ravidass Organization, 236
Saraswat, 34
Sarbanes, Paul S., 127–8
Sat Guru Ravidas Sabha, 239, 254
Sathe, Anna Bhau, 56
Satyashodhak Samaj, 69
Saudi Arabia, 239
All India Scheduled Caste Federation (SCF), 17, 57, 101
Scheduled Castes, 40, 100, 106, 114, 128
Scheduled Tribes, 40, 101, 114, 128
Schuyler, George, 88
Seale, Bobby, 126
Seminar (magazine), 116
Senart, Emelié, 31
Shaikh, Juned, 65
Shaikh, Malika Ambar, 134
shakti (divine energy or power), 163
Shambuka, 11
Shankar, Shobana, 178
Sharma, L.N., 157
Shirke, Dadasaheb, 50
Shiromani Akal Dal (SAD), 250
Shiv, Sena, 132
Shiva, 163
Short, Randy, 129
shudras, 7, 9, 11, 66, 102–3, 148, 185
Siddharth College, 56
Siddharth Sahitya Sangh, 56
Sikhs, 16, 24, 121
Singapore, 49
Singh, Dr Shobha, 127
Singh, Jaswant, 114–15
Singh, Ranveer, 127
Sita, 162, 180
Sitaram, 162–4
Sivaraj, N., 28, 54, 206
Slavery, in the Civilised British Government under the Cloak of Brahmanism (Phule), 104–5
Smith, James McCune, 61
Smith, John William, 90
Sonar, 184
Sonule, Harihar Rao, 17
Sooryodhayam (newspaper), 48
Sorabjee, Soli, 115
Souls of Black Folk, The (Du Bois), 61, 80
"The Souls of White Folk" (Du Bois), 258–9
South Africa, 19, 49, 85, 102, 112–13, 125
South Asia, 150, 181
Soviet Union, 113
Sreeprasad, Pandit Amar, 159, 165–6, 169–71
Srinivasan, Rettamalai, 28, 49, 101, 151

INDEX

State of California anti-caste legislation, 233–4
Steppe people, 4–5
Strabo, 7, 8
"subaltern diaspora", 204
Subramanian, Ajantha, 122–3
Sudharak (newspaper), 49
Sujano, Venerable, 220, 221
Suman, Dev, 223, 225, 227
Sumner, Charles, 78
Sundar, B. Shyam, 17, 28
Surudhay, 19
Surve, Narayan, 70
SWAHA, 157–61
swayamsevak, 173

Taliban, 17
Tamil Ambedkarites, 236, 237, 240–2
Tamil diaspora, 214
Tamil Nadu, 131, 184, 268
Tamil, 88
Tamilian, 268
Tanganyika, 49
Tarde, Gabriel, 29
Tayari Bhavishya Ki, 252
Taylor, Breonna, 92
Taylor, Keeanga-Yamahtta, 131
Telangana, 184, 248
Teltumbde, Anand, 100
Telugu, 88
Texas, 66, 130
Thaiman Cultural Association, 240, 241
Thakurs, 87, 113, 184
Thass, Pandit Iyothee, 48–9, 131
Thirumavalavan (Thiruma), 240
Thiruvenkatasamy, Pandit, 48
Tilak, B.G., 30
Time (magazine), 90
TIME100 Next list (2021), 44
Tobago, 158, 181, 183
transnational migration, 199–200
Trinidad, 140–2
    Caribbean, sanatanists of, 157–61
    Hindu identity, 161–2
    Hindu right-wing, 171–83
    identity in, 164–5
    racialism and dalithood, 150–2
    Trinidadian Hindus, 152–7
    See also India
Trinidadian community
    Hinduism in, 262–5
Trinidadian Hinduism, 144
Trump, Donald, 138

UAE
    AIM in, 242–4
    Dalit migrant workers of, 244–7
UK (United Kingdom)
    Ambedkar Hall, Wolverhampton, 247
    Buddhist Ambedkarites, 216
    Dalits in, 218–28
    Valmiki temple leadership, 215
    See also DAMC (Dr Ambedkar Memorial Committee of Great Britain)
UN convened the World Conference Against Racism, Racial Discrimination,

INDEX

Xenophobia and Related Intolerance, 114
UN Convention (1965), 116–17
UN Special Rapporteur on Contemporary Forms of Racism, 116
UN World Conference, 18
Union of India, 69
United National Congress party, 168
United Nations General Assembly, 69, 112
United Nations Organization (UN), 17–18, 111–12
United Nations, 231, 232, 266
United States (US), 18, 29, 47, 58, 59–60, 62, 80, 82, 95, 129, 174, 195, 265–6, 269–70
   California textbook issue, 209
   caste-based politics, 202
   Christian Dalits, 215–16
   cultural differences, 118–23
   Dalit professionals in diverse fields, 212
   Dalit-land, 107–11
   Dalits in, 211, 228–34
   Dalits protest against caste, 201
   Gandhian intervention, 123–6
   racism, 89–93
   uprisings, 89
   See also Black Lives Matter
University of Durban-Westville, 157
University of Ghana, 125
Untouchable! Voices of the Dalit Liberation Movement (Joshi), 68

Untouchables: Who Were They and Why They Became Untouchables, The (Ambedkar), 2
Up from Slavery (Washington), 61
US Foreign Relations Committee, 127
US law, 109
Uttar Pradesh, 33, 44, 94, 104, 162, 184, 188

Vahed, Goolam, 185
Valmiki Ramayana, 11
Valmiki, Bhagwan, 214
van der Veer, Peter, 141–2
Varhade, Yogesh, 18, 127, 128
Varma, Bhagya Reddy, 17, 28
Vedas, 2, 10, 74, 159, 186
Vedic culture, 12
Vellu, Samy, 229
Vertovec, Steven, 141
Vesak Day, 216
Viduthalai Chiruthaigal Katchi (VCK), 240–2, 248
Vietnam, 90
viharas, 216, 219, 220
Vikhroli, 19
Virginia, 137
Vishnu Purana, 9
Vishnu, 9
Vishwa Hindu Parishad (VHP), 171–2, 176
VISION (Volunteers in Service to India's Oppressed and Neglected), 126–8

Waghmare, Janardhan, 64, 73–4, 261

INDEX

Walangkar, Gopal Baba, 49
Wankhede, M.N., 63–4, 65–6, 72, 260
Washington DC, 125, 129
Washington Examiner (magazine), 136
Washington Post (Newspaper), 128, 129
Washington, Booker T., 61–2
Watts, 90
West Africa, 178
West Bengal, 184
West Indies, 60
West, Cornel, 131
What Congress and Gandhi Have Done to the Untouchables (1946) (Ambedkar), 39
WhatsApp, 218, 243, 246, 249
Wolverhampton Ambedkarite Buddhists, 219–22
working-class, 206
migration, 200–1
World Dalit Convention, First (1998), 230
World Hindu Conference (2000), 176
World Marathi Literary Conference I, 78
World War I, 259
Wright, Richard, 71, 82

Xuanzang, 7

Yogasutra (Patanjali), 9
YouTube, 193, 249
Yuva Panthers, 136

Zelizer, Julian E., 91
Zoom, 249